GREEN REVOLUTION?

CAMBRIDGE COMMONWEALTH SERIES

Published in association with the Managers of the Cambridge
University Smuts Memorial Fund for the Advancement of
Commonwealth Studies

General Editor: E. T. STOKES, *Smuts Professor of the History
of the British Commonwealth, University of Cambridge*

TITLES PUBLISHED BY
THE CAMBRIDGE UNIVERSITY PRESS

John S. Galbraith: Mackinnon and East Africa, 1878–1895
G. Andrew Maguire: Toward 'Uhuru' in Tanzania
Ged Martin: The Durham Report and British Policy
Ronald Robinson (editor): Developing the Third World

TITLES PUBLISHED BY MACMILLAN

Roger Anstey: The Atlantic Slave Trade and British Abolition, 1760–1810
T. R. H. Davenport: South Africa: A Modern History
B. H. Farmer (editor): Green Revolution? Technology and Change in
                        Rice-Growing Areas of Tamil Nadu
                        and Sri Lanka
Partha Sarathi Gupta: Imperialism and the British Labour Movement,
                        1914–1964
Ronald Hyam and Ged Martin: Reappraisals in British Imperial History
W. David McIntyre: The Rise and Fall of the Singapore Naval Base
B. R. Tomlinson: The Indian National Congress and the *Raj*, 1929–1942
                   The Political Economy of the *Raj*, 1914–1947:
                   The Economics of Decolonization in India
John Manning Ward: Colonial Self-Government: The British Experience,
                     1759–1856

GREEN REVOLUTION?

Technology and Change in Rice-growing Areas of Tamil Nadu and Sri Lanka

Edited by

B. H. Farmer
Director, Centre of South Asian Studies
University of Cambridge

Foreword by Sir Joseph Hutchinson, FRS

First edition 1977
Reprinted 1979

ELBS edition first
published 1980

Published by
THE MACMILLAN PRESS LTD
London and Basingstoke
Associated companies in Delhi Dublin
Hong Kong Johannesburg Lagos
Melbourne New York Singapore
Tokyo

ISBN 0 333 19679 1 (hardcover)
ISBN 0 333 27339 7 (paperback)

Printed in Hong Kong

Contents

	List of Figures	vii
	Foreword by Sir Joseph Hutchinson	ix
	Editor's Preface	xi
	Glossary	xiv
1	Technology and Change in Rice-growing Areas *B. H. Farmer*	1
2	Setting the Stage *B. H. Farmer, C. M. Madduma Bandara, V. Shanmuga Sundaram and W. P. T. Silva*	7
3	Paddy and Rice Statistics in Sri Lanka *Barbara Harriss*	20
4	Bias in Perception of Agrarian Change in India *John Harriss*	30
5	Research Methodology *Robert Chambers, B. Nanjamma Chinnappa, Barbara Harriss and B. W. E. Wickremanayake*	37
6	Selective Adoption as a Strategy for Agricultural Development: Lessons from Adoption in S.E. Sri Lanka *H. D. Dias*	54
7	Chena–Paddy Interrelationships *W. P. T. Silva*	85
8	Adoption of the New Technology in North Arcot District *B. Nanjamma Chinnappa*	92
9	The Limitations of HYV Technology in North Arcot District: the View from a Village *John Harriss*	124
10	Pahalagama: a Case Study of Agricultural Change in a Frontier Environment *John Harriss*	143
11	Agricultural Extension: Myth, Reality and Challenge *Robert Chambers and B. W. E. Wickremanayake*	155
12	Tractors, Profit and Debt in Hambantota District, Sri Lanka *Barbara Harriss*	168
13	Rural Electrification and the Diffusion of Electric Water-lifting Technology in North Arcot District, India *Barbara Harriss*	182
14	Impact of the Cultivation of High-Yielding Varieties of Paddy on Employment and Income *B. Nanjamma Chinnappa and W. P. T. Silva*	204

15 Implications of Changes in Agriculture for Social Re-
    lationships at the Village Level: the Case of
    Randam   *John Harriss*   225
16 Social Implications of Changes in Agriculture in Hamban-
    tota District   *John Harriss*   246
17 Marketing Scarce Chemical Inputs: an International
    Comparison   *Barbara Harriss*   256
18 Besieging the Free Market: the Effects of the Paddy-Rice
    Levy   *Barbara Harriss*   268
19 Paddy-Milling: Problems in Policy and the Choice of
    Technology   *Barbara Harriss*   276
20 Comparing Twelve South Indian Villages: in Search of
    Practical Theory   *Robert Chambers and John Harriss*   301
21 Hydrological Consequences of Agrarian Change   *C. M.
    Madduma Bandara*   323
22 Men and Water: the Organisation and Operation of
    Irrigation   *Robert Chambers*   340
23 Problems of Water Management in Hambantota
    District   *John Harriss*   364
24 The Crisis and the Future   *Robert Chambers, H. D. Dias,
    Barbara Harriss and John Harriss*   377
25 Challenges for Rural Research and Development   *Robert
    Chambers*   398
26 Perceptions, Technology and the Future   *Robert Chambers
    and B. H. Farmer*   413
    Index   423

List of Figures

Figure
2.1 The study area in North Arcot District, Tamil Nadu, India   8
2.2 The study area in Hambantota and Moneragala Districts, Sri Lanka   9
4.1 India: distribution of agrarian research reported in the *Economic and Political Weekly*   31
6.1 Sri Lanka: the area under different categories of paddy varieties   61
6.2 Sri Lanka: gap between production of paddy and estimated requirement   64
6.3 Sri Lanka: variation in yield per acre, 1957–73   67
6.4 A. Distribution of cultivators in each cultivation committee area classified according to yield, Maha 1973–4   74
     B. Distribution of cultivators according to cultivation committees obtaining a particular yield, Maha 1973–4   75
6.5 Sri Lanka: the study area showing location and nature of sample areas   76
8.1 North Arcot: number of HYV adopters and number who adopted HYVs for the first time by year of adoption   98
8.2 North Arcot: price in rupees of different varieties of paddy in sample villages, 1973–4   107
8.3 North Arcot: adoption of HYVs by deciles, 1972–3 (A and B)   110
9.1 Number of pump-sets in Randam   125
9.2 Adoption of new varieties in Randam   130
10.1 Labour utilisation and net income per acre   151
12.1 Operational intensity and profits   171
12.2 Rates for field preparation, Hambantota District   177
13.1 Models of innovation diffusion   184
13.2 Diffusion of electric pump-sets, District level   185
13.3 North Arcot District: the diffusion of rural electrification   186

13.4 Planned installations   188
13.5 Sales profiles of sample traders in North Arcot District   190
13.6 Locations of sources of pump-sets for sample villages   194
13.7 Adoption of electric pump-sets, sample villages   196
13.8 North Arcot District: operational holding size and the
      adoption of pump-sets   200
14.1 North Arcot District: composition household   206
14.2 Number of person-days of agricultural labour among
      sample households, 1973–4   214
15.1 Demand for male casual labour in Randam   230
15.2 Demand for female casual labour in Randam   231
17.1 Formal marketing systems:
      A. Fertiliser in Tamil Nadu   258
      B. Agrochemicals in Sri Lanka   259
17.2 Fertiliser: prices per 50 kg bag, North Arcot District   264
18.1 Hypothetical example to show various possible market
      reactions to increase in levy percentages, assuming one
      variety of paddy and no changes in supply and demand   270
18.2 Actual price behaviour, Rosekar paddy and rice in
      Vellore market in response to changes in levy   272
19.1 Systems of paddy processing.
      A. Cheyyar Modern Rice Mill
      B. Traditional mills   278
19.2 The mills in Cheyyar taluk, North Arcot District, 1973   280
19.3 Fixed-cost curves for MRM, URD shellers and hullers   284
20.1 Demographic trends showing growth from 1871 (not
      including Randam, Duli and Sirungathur, which
      cannot be shown on this scale)   306
21.1 The expansion of the irrigated area in North Arcot   324
21.2 The development of lift irrigation in North Arcot   325
21.3 Rainfall fluctuations in North Arcot District   329
21.4 The changing relationship between rainfall and discharge
      of Cheyyar   332
21.5 Seasonal regime of the water-table in North Arcot   334
21.6 The changing relationship between seasonal rainfall and
      fluctuation of the water-table in North Arcot District   336
24.1 Relation between yield and cost per bushel:
      A. Before price increase
      B. After increase of GPS price to Rs33   384

Foreword

Those who have been concerned with the social and economic development of South Asia have good reason to regret that the term 'Green
Revolution' was ever thought of. It has given rise on the one hand to hopes
of economic gain that cannot be realised, and on the other, to allegations of
social loss beyond what can be supported by the evidence. Yet if this term
had not been coined, some other would have been, for we have witnessed a
technological change in the rural scene that has come about very rapidly
and has had far-reaching consequences. And to give it a name is much
easier, and a much more human response, than to undertake the laborious
and exacting task of learning to understand it.

The volume of literature generated by the Green Revolution is very
large. From the accounts of the plant-breeding triumphs embodied in the
new high-yielding cereal varieties to the very critical analyses of the social
consequences of the new technology, it is dominated by the grand-scale
approach. It is not just that thinking about the Green Revolution has been
predominantly in terms of new seeds bred by international teams, but
rather that it has been accepted as the achievement of a massive
international effort, financed and organised to bring the whole weight of
Western research to bear on a continental scale upon the problems of the
poor and populous countries.

The rising food prices of the 1960s favoured the exploitation of cheap
energy supplies and cheap fertilisers by the use of fertility-responsive new
varieties, and made possible a very widespread technological change
within a decade. The circumstances of the mid-1970s are very different.
Not only is energy expensive and fertiliser scarce; it is now apparent that
internationally bred cereal varieties do not necessarily fit into district, or
even regional, farming patterns. This first became evident when the
contrast appeared between the sweeping success of a few wheat varieties on
India's irrigated alluvial lands, and the much more limited success of the
new rice varieties on the great diversity of India's rice lands.

The mixture of spectacular success, modest improvement and critical
disillusion has led to endless, but inconclusive, debate – inconclusive
because of the lack of real information on what actually goes on in the

farmers' fields. On the initiative of the Centre of South Asian Studies in Cambridge, and with the co-operation of the Universities of Madras and Sri Lanka and of the Agrarian Research and Training Institute, Colombo, an inter-disciplinary study group was assembled to provide some of this information. The members of the team undertook comparative field studies of the impact of the Green Revolution technology on rice-farming in two areas, one in Tamil Nadu and one in Sri Lanka.

This volume is the report of the group, and it carries the debate a stage further, in that it puts on record a great range of material and shows how inadequate a simple international concept of agricultural advance can be. Diversity is a basic characteristic of all agricultural enterprise, and we have ignored it to our cost. In the formulation of research objectives, in plant-breeding, in soil fertility, in water conservation and management, in the planning and execution of economic policy, and in the amelioration and reform of social practice and custom, the fundamental importance of local circumstances is brought out.

This is not a reassuring book. It destroys the illusion that agricultural problems can be solved by massive centrally planned research, and directs the investigator to the village and the field as the places where understanding must be gained if progress is to be made. But surely we knew that we were deluding ourselves, and that in the long run we must go back to the field. This project brings a sense of realism into the debate that all concerned scholars will welcome.

Editor's Preface

As will be made clear in the pages that follow, this book is based on a field research project focused on rice-growing and undertaken in parts of North Arcot District in Tamil Nadu (India) and of Hambantota and Moneragala Districts, Sri Lanka. We use 'S.E. Sri Lanka' as shorthand for the whole of the latter study area, and 'Hambantota District' for the part of it which falls in that District. Except where the context requires otherwise, the present in our book refers to 1973–4; while 'Randam' and 'Pahalagama' are fictitious names for real villages.

The project was an inter-disciplinary one, involving workers qualified in economics, geography, hydrology, sociology, statistics and the study of the administration of development.

At the time of writing data-processing and analysis are still in process: we only report here on work already completed, which for reasons inseparable from the operation of a complex research project have reached a more advanced stage in some directions (e.g. on cultivation data for North Arcot) than in others (e.g. on similar data for Sri Lanka). We report now, rather than waiting until more results emerge, and report mainly in the form of amended and augmented versions of papers presented at a seminar held in December 1974, because we believe that our results have urgent practical consequence for the people of our study areas and (though we do not make wildly extrapolative claims) in other rice-growing regions too. If we had taken more time, much more time, we could have produced additional results and, perhaps, a more comprehensive and cohesive book. But if, with one ear, we were conscious of potential academic critics (especially those nurtured in a single discipline, who may have difficulty in appreciating all of our approaches), with the other we were even more conscious of time's wingèd chariot hurrying near – not for us, but for the people of our villages, whose need is great.

If we appear to prescribe remedies, then, on the basis of incomplete results, let it be understood that we do it modestly, with a real sense of urgency and commitment. The busy practical man who wishes to know what we suggest in his field is advised first to read our concluding chapter and then to refer back to earlier chapters, using the index if necessary.

Some of us have worked full-time on the project and others, like myself, very much part-time; and since some have administered or computed while others wrote, output per author does not necessarily measure contribution to the project. In particular, Dr Kusuma A. Gunawardena, of the University of Sri Lanka, is not a contributor but has done sterling work in the field and in data-processing; while A. J. N. Richards and Mrs J. Ceresa have cheerfully carried a heavy load, respectively administrative and secretarial, in Cambridge. U. Aiyasami bore similar burdens in Madras.

All of us would like to express warm appreciation for the help and encouragement we have received from Professor Sir Joseph Hutchinson, FRS, who kindly consented to act as Scientific Adviser to our project, and who contributes a foreword to this book. Remaining scientific solecisms are, however, ours not his.

There are a large number of field and other assistants without whom our work would have been quite impossible. In Tamil Nadu the sample survey was supervised by K. Ramachandran and V. Rengarajan, assisted by M. Asokan, C. S. Janakarajan, N. G. Jeyaprakesh, A. Kanagaraj, A. Kumanan, Tom Mighty, M. Sadagopan, M. Subramanian and S. Subramanian, while the following helped with processing: Miss Shereen Begum, R. Janarthanan, Miss M. L. Kausalya, R. Netyanandan, Miss.T N. Usha and Miss K. Vijayalakshmi. In Sri Lanka fieldwork was supervised by B. W. E. Wickremanayake (a contributor to this volume) assisted by W. D. Ariyasena, V. Banduwansa, A. H. Dhanapala, Basil Perera, Mervyn Perera, M. Seneviratna, K. Amarasiri Silva and M. Sirisena. The last four also assisted with processing, in which they were joined by P. V. Dasenayake, Miss W. Dayawathie, Miss S. Gunawardena, Miss P. Hemalatha, Miss R. Hewamadihage, Miss R. Jayalath, Miss U. L. Kamalawathie, Miss N. Rajapakse, Miss S. T. Mr. de Silva and W. N. Wilson.

Invaluable help with our computer work was provided by Dr S. Natarajan and his staff at the Government Data Centre, Guindy, Madras; Dr J. A. Gunawardena at the University of Sri Lanka, Peradeniya, assisted by R. Dayasundera, N. C. Fernandez, L. D. Jayakody, M. Thillai Nadesan, S. Paramaguru and M. Sreetharan; and by the University of Cambridge Computing Service, and Dr G. P. Chapman.

Barbara Harriss was assisted in the field by C. S. Balasubramaniam, S. Gamage, S. Leitan, Jayaprakash P. Narayan, K. Narayanan and J. Wickramanayake.

All of us wish to thank the many government and other institutions in both India and Sri Lanka who are far too numerous to list but who provided help, information and encouragement; and, above all, the farmers, traders and others whom we subjected to interviews and to interminable questionings. They are the real contributors to this book.

All of us also wish to express warm gratitude to the bodies that provided the finance for the project: the Ministry of Overseas Development and the Social Science Research Council in the United Kingdom, the Fertiliser Corporation in Sri Lanka. The Universities of Cambridge, Madras and Sri Lanka made available the services of a number of contributors to our work as did the Agrarian Research and Training Institute, Colombo; while the Leverhulme Trustees, the Ministry of Overseas Development and St John's College, Cambridge, financed the seminar held in Cambridge in December 1974 at which preliminary drafts of many of the chapters in this book were discussed, to our great benefit.

Finally, I personally would like very warmly to thank all of my colleagues, whether contributors to this book or not, for their help, friendship and co-operation during the period of the research project and of the writing of this book. Between them they have made the editing of it a much lighter task than it might otherwise have been.

January 1976   B. H. FARMER

Glossary

ande (Sinh.)	share-cropping system of land tenure (Sri Lanka)
anicut	a dam or weir to direct river water into channel
asweddumise	to prepare land for paddy cultivation by levelling and construction of bunds
ayacut	the irrigable command of an irrigation work
bethma (Sinh.)	custom whereby only part of the village paddy fields are cultivated in drought
chena	anglicisation of hena (q.v.)
cheri (Tam.)	Harijan quarter or hamlet in a village
cholam (Tam.)	sorghum; *Sorghum vulgare* (jowar in N. India)
collector	chief revenue officer of a District (India), now invested with many other functions
cumbu (Tam.)	the millet *Pennisetum typhoideum* (bajra in N. India)
dry land	unirrigated land (Revenue classification, Tamil Nadu)
eri (Tam.)	a tank or reservoir for irrigation
etram (Tam.)	a man-operated irrigation lift
gambāra	system, common in Hambantota District of Sri Lanka, of operating land through agents or intermediaries (but see pp. 251–4)
gambāraya	man acting as agent, etc., in gambāra system (q.v.)
garden land	dry land (q.v.) irrigated by using wells (Tamil Nadu)
godown	warehouse, storage shed
goiya (Sinh.)	cultivator
Government Agent	chief revenue officer of a District (India), now invested with many other functions
Gram(a) Sevak	village-level worker (VLW) under community development programme (India)
Harijan	name given by Gandhi to untouchables
hena (Sinh.)	plot cultivated by shifting cultivation
high land	unirrigable land (Sri Lanka)

HYV	loosely – high-yielding variety. Strictly (in India) – variety officially released under the high-yielding varieties programme (HVP or HYVP)
IADP	Intensive Agricultural District Programme (India), carried out in certain Districts only, which were chosen because of supposedly superior resources
IV	improved variety, not necessarily an HYV (q.v.) in strict sense (see p. 93)
jajmani	system of reciprocal patron–client relations in Indian village, with division of labour by caste (see pp. 236–7)
kachcheri	District offices of government in Sri Lanka
karnam	village accountant (Tamil Nadu)
kattadia (Sinh.)	practitioner in black magic
kattimāru (Sinh.)	system of cultivation by rotating plots between share-holders
kavalai (Tam.)	bullock-operated lifts for irrigating from wells
kurakkan (Sinh.)	finger millet, *Eleusine coracana*; ragi (Tam.)
kuttali (Tam.)	attached labourer who receives a share of the crop rather than wages
kuzh (Tam.)	gruel made of ragi (q.v.)
KVS	Krushikarma Vyāpthi Sevak; lowest level in agricultural extension staff (Sri Lanka)
landu	abandoned chena (hena, q.v.) less than ten years old
MPCS	Multi-purpose Co-operative Society (Sri Lanka)
mammoti	hoe (Sri Lanka and Tamil Nadu)
mandi	market-place (India); foodgrain trader's shop (Tamil Nadu)
munsiff	village headman (India)
padial (Tam.)	attached labour paid a fixed wage, usually per season, who may be called on to do housework as well as agricultural work (cf. kuttali)
paddy	unhusked rice
panchayat	local or village council
pangu	a share in land
parboiling	a process by which paddy is steeped in water and then boiled, simmered or subjected to steam at low pressure, before drying and milling
patta	a written document settling title and/or land revenue
pongal	festival held in January (Tamil Nadu)
poromboke	land in a village (Tamil Nadu) reserved for purposes other than cultivation
purāna gama	ancient village, usually nucleated (Sinh.)
rabi	'winter' or north-east monsoon cropping season

ragi	finger millet, *Eleusine coracana* (Tam.); kurakkan (Sinh.)
ryot	peasant or cultivator
seru (Tam.)	muddy soil, literally 'ooze' (see p. 134)
taluk	an administrative sub-division of a District (S. India)
thattumāru (Sinh.)	system of cultivation by share-holders of an undivided plot, each cultivating in rotation
TV	traditional variety (see p. 98)
ur panchayat	caste council
varam (Tam.)	land leased on an informal basis
Vel Vidane (Sinh.)	irrigation headman
VLW	village-level worker (Gram Sevak) under community development programme (India)
watte (Sinh.)	garden land
wet land	land irrigated by tanks, canals or rivers (Revenue classification, Tamil Nadu)
yaya (Sinh.)	a tract of paddy land

GREEN REVOLUTION?

1 Technology and Change in Rice-growing Areas

B. H. Farmer

For three out of five people in the world, rice is the staple food: the main source of calories, the main means of keeping alive (all too often only just alive). The vast majority of the world's rice-eaters live in monsoon Asia, in the countries that lie in an arc from Pakistan on the west, through South and South-East Asia to China and Japan. Within South Asia, rice is the basic foodstuff of Bangladesh and Sri Lanka and of a majority of the vast population of India; and it is not unimportant in Pakistan. All of these South Asian countries suffer in varying degrees, and nowhere more ominously than in Bangladesh, from rapid rates of population increase, from pressure of man on land, and from extreme poverty and hunger among the less privileged strata of society; and hardly anywhere in the world is it of greater urgency to improve crop yields by modernising technology and to spread the resulting benefits, in food and income, to the poor.

All this is well known. It is also well known that, five years or so ago, there was abroad a cruel and facile optimism that would be simplistic if it were not so obviously self-justificatory. One author wrote of IR.8, the 'miracle rice' which was proclaimed as the spearhead of the Green Revolution:

> The development of IR.8 and its dissemination throughout Asia is . . . literally helping to fill hundreds of millions of ricebowls once only half full (Brown, 1970, p. 4).

The Green Revolution was to lift South Asia out of the gloom of the mid-1960s, when there was widespread crop failure; and this, as the quotation shows, was to affect rice as well as wheat, spectacular increases in whose production had indeed been recorded in Pakistan and North India.

But now, in 1975, we have descended once again into gloom and despondency (Klatt, 1975a). Quite apart from the effects of short-term phenomena like floods and drought, there is a large question-mark, as in the title of this book, against the Green Revolution as a means of overcoming in the longer term the basic South Asian problems of food supply and increasingly intolerable poverty. The question-mark hangs heavily over the Green Revolution in general, over wheat and the millets as well as over rice. But it hangs heaviest of all over rice. (In this connection, see Sen, 1974, which came to hand too late to receive detailed comment in the present volume. The same applies to IRRI, 1975, which includes (pp. 71–91) a report by V. Rajagopalan on changes in rice-farming in North Arcot District, based, however, on data collected in three villages only for 1971–2, before our project started.)

True, there appears to have been spectacular increases in rice production locally, notably in Sri Lanka, where it is claimed that increased area and higher yields together led to a 50 per cent rise in production between 1964 and 1970 (Corea, 1973). But, over South Asia as a whole, rice has tended to lag well behind wheat. According to official Indian statistics, wheat production more than doubled between 1964–5 and 1971–2, from 12,290,000 tonnes to 26,410,000 tonnes; but over the same period rice production rose only from 39,034,000 tonnes to 43,068,000 tonnes, an increase of under 10 per cent. The same figures illustrate the greater importance of rice to the Indian economy and food supply.

Yet it is still true that the Green Revolution in rice-growing in South Asia remains less studied than that in wheat, though rather less so than was the case five years ago. This is in spite of the work being done by the All India Co-ordinated Rice Improvement Project (AICRIP) and by other agronomic and plant-breeding institutions in India, Sri Lanka and elsewhere in South Asia; in spite too, of the growing volume of literature which reports on new technology and agrarian change in rice-growing areas (see, for example, the bibliography in Byres, 1972). Moreover, some of this literature is simplistic in its attribution of reasons for the lag in rice; or derivative, one or more degrees, or completely removed from empirical research in the paddy fields themselves, where much of the truth must necessarily lie; or slanted, as John Harriss shows in chapter 4, towards Indian deltaic areas which, for all their teeming populations and huge rice production, have particular environmental and other features such that their conditions in them cannot necessarily be extrapolated to the non-deltaic areas which cover almost the whole of Sri Lanka and much of the interior of South India, with its terrible insecurity and poverty. Nor can they necessarily be extrapolated to Bangladesh, deltaic in all conscience, but no place for 'miracle rice' when it is deeply flooded every year.

There seemed very good reason, then, for a research project which should examine the Green Revolution in rice-growing in non-deltaic areas in South Asia. As the Preface has indicated, this book in fact records the early policy- and practice-oriented results of such a project: an inter-disciplinary project undertaken by workers drawn from India, Sri Lanka and the United Kingdom and based on the University of Madras, the Agro-Economic Research Centre (Madras), the University of Sri Lanka, the Agrarian Research and Training Institute (Colombo), and the Centre of South Asian Studies in the University of Cambridge. For the negative reason that we wished to avoid delta bias, and the positive reasons to be explained in chapter 2, the study areas chosen were parts of North Arcot District, Tamil Nadu and of Hambantota and Moneragala Districts, Sri Lanka. In these areas we combined rigorous sample surveys with study in depth in two villages whose identity is concealed – in the style of the social anthropologists – behind the pseudonyms 'Randam' and 'Pahalagama'. Our work was firmly set in the paddy fields themselves: all of us have seen our data growing, or flowing, or walking about in the villages. We do not claim, indeed it would be contrary to some of the more important of our tenets to do so, that our results are typical; and our two study areas turned out to be very different. We do stake the modest claim, however, that they, like other micro-studies, provide a necessary corrective and complement to macro-studies, some of which nobly attempt an overview by bringing together a great amount of varied data and literature (for example, Byres, 1972, and Griffin, 1974), but have been criticised for seeing the 'agrarian scene in a simplified way' and for being 'too sweeping' in their judgements, sometimes because of an ideological bias more obvious, but no less real than delta bias (Klatt, 1975b, reviewing Griffin, 1974; see also Deepak Lal, 1975).

Our central theme is that of technology and change. The Green Revolution in rice-growing tends to be envisaged as a single, transferable, indivisible package that includes not only the seeds of the new varieties, but also chemical fertilisers, pesticides and weedicides, combined with the improvement of irrigation and the adoption of new agricultural practices. This view has held whether the package has emanated from national, regional or local research stations, or crossed international frontiers through the agency of institutions like the International Rice Research Institute (IRRI) in the Philippines. (Given the expected increases in rice production, another such package offers the Modern Rice Mill, a complete mechanised technology, to replace traditional methods.) In practice the farmer finds only some part of the package acceptable or practicable. The prescribed 'miracle rice' may not suit his conditions of soil or length of growing season: Gilbert Étienne has pointed out that IR.8 is 'ill-fitted to monsoon conditions' when perforce much of South Asia's rice is grown and when little else can be grown over much low-lying land (Étienne, 1973, p. 201). (We shall show that IR.8 is particularly ill-adapted to the main rice-growing season in Tamil Nadu.) The farmer, again, may adopt the latest varieties to the exclusion of older ones, but neglect other parts of the package to such an extent that he secures nothing like potential yields. In this context, H. D. Dias speaks of 'over-adoption' of high-yielding varieties (chapter 6) and, indeed, advocates a policy of deliberately selective adoption with local variation. Again, mechanisation may mean the wholesale electrification of pumping from wells (with adverse effects on the stability of the water-table) and the almost complete neglect of tractors, as in North Arcot; or it may mean a very high level of tractorisation but the complete neglect not only of the possibilities of mechanised pumping but even of underground water itself, as in the Sri Lanka study area. Our principal concern is, then, with the pattern of this selective adoption of a transferred technology, and with the reasons for selectivity. As our work developed, however, our interest spread from paddy-growing itself to other aspects of technological transfer – all, however, related to the Green Revolution in rice.

We had a number of initial hypotheses, whose number grew and formulation varied as our fieldwork progressed and as ideas flowed between what we tried to maintain as a coherent, integrated and self-reinforcing team. Thus there was the proposition derived from some, though not all of the technical literature that independent control of adequate water in the paddy fields is of critical importance in the successful introduction of new practices and new varieties. Again, given our inter-disciplinary scepticism about simplistic or dogmatic solutions, we did not set out to prove the case for a particular relationship between, say, size of farm or tenurial status on the one hand and 'adoption' on the other. Rather did we have an initial and flexible hypothesis that there is *some* relationship between the acceptance of new practices and varieties on the one hand and, on the other, such factors as size of holding, owner-occupancy and owner-cultivation, the cultivation of land other than paddy land, the method of cultivation and planting, inputs of labour, fertiliser and pesticide, and access to water and markets; but that the relationship is by no means simple. However, we admitted other factors that became evident in the course of fieldwork: for instance, the varying pressure of population on land, with apparent consequences as in terms of differing traditional intensities of cultivation (Boserup, 1965), as between long and densely settled North Arcot and recently and sparsely settled Hamban-tota – Moneragala. Again, possible competition between paddy and other crops means, in North Arcot, competition with groundnut on 'dry' land, in Hambantota – Moneragala with shifting (chena) cultivation of a number of crops under 'frontier' conditions of land availability. Another hypothesis whose testing was to some extent made possible by the two-country nature of the project, was that differences in the organisation of extension and other support services make for critical differences in acceptance of the new technology as between Tamil Nadu and Sri Lanka (this was the claim of officials – see chapter 11).

We were also concerned with the economic and social changes that accompany technical innovation: with technology *and* change. We sought to establish, as objectively as possible, the answers to such questions as 'Who benefits from the technical changes, and to what extent? What are the social concomitants? Are, for instance "traditional" patron—client relationships, linked to caste, being replaced by a class structure, complete with capitalists, rich peasants, middle and poor peasants, and landless labourers, as some hypotheses and models would have it?'

If technology and change is our main theme, a sub-theme that emerged with equal clarity in the course of our work was the unreliability and confusion of the official statistics in which so many writers have shown such touching faith. For example, we found that official figures for the area under high-yielding varieties of paddy in North Arcot District were exaggerated at least threefold. (What if this disparity is reproduced at the All India level?)

A book such as this, dealing with situations in which many interlocking factors are at work, could be arranged in various ways. It may be helpful briefly to explain the layout adopted. The first five chapters are introductory: chapter 3 is a commentary on the official statistics on paddy and rice in Sri Lanka, and reaches practical conclusions on the gap between production and self-sufficiency; chapter 4 elaborates the point on bias in the perception of agrarian change in India to which reference has already been made; while chapter 5 describes our research methodology in sufficient detail to enable the reader to understand how we arrived at our data and what their reliability and limitations are (I hope that we can say, without the self-righteousness of which the Indian sub-continent has had more than enough, that we have tried to be honest about our methods).

The core of the book is in chapters 6 to 13, which present our results to date on the pattern of – and reasons for – the selective adoption of the new technology in the two study areas; they examine the ways in which farmers behave when confronted with it (in chapters 9 and 10 relying on village depth studies), and explore agricultural extension as it actually operates in a context of selective adoption. Chapters 12 and 13 centre on the two very different forms of mechnisation, tractors in Sri Lanka (with special reference to levels of profitability and rural indebtedness) and electric pump-sets in North Arcot (with emphasis on the diffusion of this innovation).

Discussion in chapters 14 to 19 turns to some of the economic and social implications and concomitants of the differential innovation by now thoroughly exposed. First, the implications at village level for employment and income, and for social relations; then, at a larger scale, patterns of marketing for agrochemical inputs; the discussion then proceeds to the disposal of the rice surplus generated (or so it is hoped) by the technical changes, chapter 19 extending to the Modern Rice Mill, its relevance and economics.

Chapter 20 brings together important material on inter-village variation, a theme running through many of the foregoing chapters. Then follow three chapters on the major topic of water: chapter 21 on the evidence for a secular decline of the water-table in North Arcot as a result of over-pumping; chapters 22 and 23 on often-neglected aspects of the management of irrigation systems.

Chapter 24 reviews, sometimes in necessarily speculative fashion, the consequences of the recent enormous increases in fuel, power and fertiliser prices, and possible alternative technologies to meet this situation and the future – the study of inter-village variation contributes notably here. Chapter 25 examines the challenges for rural research and development, as one looks back over the project and its implications for so many inter-related fields; particularly, the need for interaction between the natural and social sciences.

Finally, an attempt is made in chapter 26 to draw the threads together and, in the light of the book as a whole, to turn our results to some account in terms, broadly, of research, policy and practice: policy *and* practice because none of us has ever been long unaware of the stark need of many of the peoples in our study areas – as elsewhere in Asia's rice-growing areas – and, above all, of the hunger and hopelessness of the poor.

REFERENCES

Boserup, Ester (1965). *The Conditions of Agricultural Growth: The Economics of Agrarian Change under Population Pressure*, London, Allen and Unwin.

Brown, L. R. (1970). *Seeds of Change: The Green Revolution and Development in the 1970s*, London, Pall Mall for Overseas Development Council.

Byres, T. J. (1972). 'The Dialectic of India's Green Revolution', *S. Asian Rev.*, 5, 99–116.

Corea, G. (1973). 'Economic Planning, the Green Revolution and the "Food Drive" in Ceylon' in W. L. David (ed.), *Essays in Honour of Ursula Hicks*, London, Macmillan.

Deepak Lal (1975). 'The Agrarian Question', *S. Asian Rev.*, 8, 389–400.

Étienne, G. (1973). 'India's New Agriculture: A Survey of the Evidence', *S. Asian Rev.*, 6, 197–213.

Griffin, K. (1974). *The Political Economy of Agrarian Change: An Essay on the Green Revolution*, London, Macmillan.

IRRI (1975). *Changes in Rice Farming in Selected Areas of Asia*, Los Banos, International Rice Research Inst.

Klatt, W. (1975a). 'Asia after the World Food Conference', *International Affairs*, 51, 344–57.

Klatt, W. (1975b). Review of Griffin, 1974 in *International Affairs*, 51, 284–5.

Sen, B. (1974). *The Green Revolution in India: a Perspective*, New Delhi, Wiley Eastern.

2 Setting the Stage

B. H. Farmer, C. M. Madduma Bandara,
V. Shanmuga Sundaram and W. P. T. Silva

THE STUDY AREAS (BHF AND CMMB)

The previous chapter emphasised the need, in choosing study areas for our research project, to avoid 'delta bias'. Further, we wished to explore the benefits of inter-country comparison between Sri Lanka and India. In Sri Lanka it was important that the area should be in the non-deltaic dry zone lowlands where, rather than in the wet zone, the Green Revolution in rice-growing had taken root. Since we wanted to compare the agrarian impact of different political and administrative systems, including different approaches to agricultural research and extension, it was important that the natural environment of the Indian study area should not be grossly dissimilar from that of the Sri Lanka dry zone: otherwise comparability would be obscured by the consequences of, for example, greatly differing cropping seasons and hydrological conditions. Tamil Nadu seemed an obvious Indian State to choose for reasons of propinquity; and within Tamil Nadu, field reconnaissance indicated the advantages of North Arcot District, or rather that part of it east of the Javadi hills and south of the sandy belt along the Palar (Fig. 2.1). For here was a traditional and reportedly progressive ricebowl area within reach of, yet not over-shadowed by Madras, which, like the Sri Lanka dry zone, was floored by crystalline rock overlain by an aquiferous layer of weathered material and soil and subject to a north-east monsoon rainfall maximum. Within Sri Lanka the choice fell in the south-east on that part of Hambantota District which lies in the dry zone, together with the southern portion of the adjacent Moneragala District (Fig. 2.2), a rice-growing area known to be influenced by the new technology but relatively untouched by the insurrection whose effects were, at the time of reconnaissance, still to be felt in northern parts of the dry zone. (The insurrection of April 1971, was basically an armed uprising of certain frustrated groups of educated unemployed.)

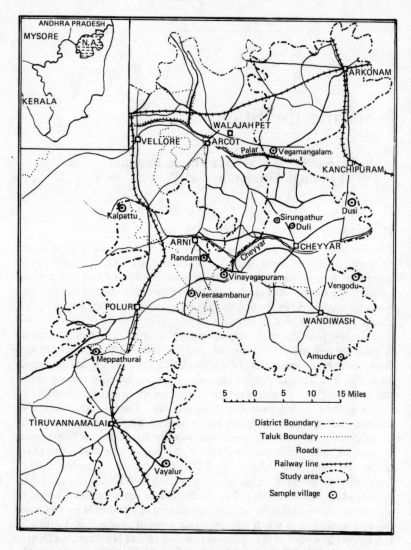

FIG. 2.1 *The study area in North Arcot District, Tamil Nadu, India*

But the two study areas, chosen for broad environmental similarity, are by no means identical, and it is important to an understanding of this book that the salient features of each should now be sketched, not least to avoid its findings being applied uncritically to dissimilar areas elsewhere.

The Aquifer

In both areas the water-table is sensitive to recharge from rainfall, fluctuating seasonally with it, and also to inflows of water from surface irrigation and rivers; it may be tapped by relatively shallow open wells.

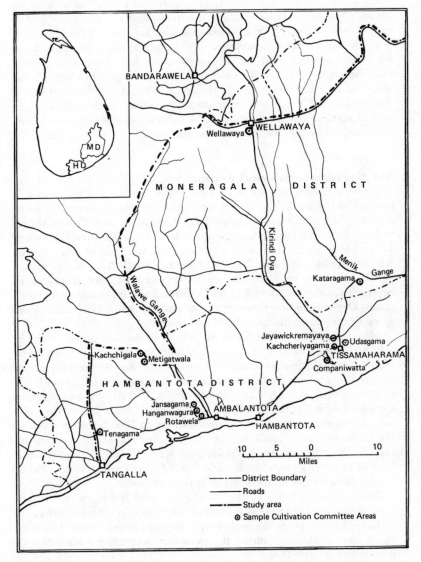

FIG. 2.2 *The study area in Hambantota and Moneragala Districts, Sri Lanka*

The aquiferous zone of weathering appears usuallly to be a great deal thicker and more continuous spatially in Tamil Nadu than in the dry zone of Sri Lanka (Farmer, 1956a, 1956b), so that in spite of lower rainfall the potentialities for well irrigation are higher in the former than the latter, though liable to over-exploitation by heavy pumping (Ramachandran, 1975, and see below, pp. 332–7). The potential in Sri Lanka is by no means negligible yet remains largely untapped: we have both advocated its exploitation (Farmer 1956a; Madduma Bandara, 1973, 1974).

Wells dependent on the weathered-rock aquifers of our two study areas are vastly different from the tube-wells which have been such notable contributors to the Green Revolution in the alluvial plains of North India and Pakistan; and which tap far greater supplies of underground water. The wells of the 'hard rock' areas are all too prone to exhaustibility, to a precarious balance between inflow from rain and surface water on the one hand and extraction for irrigation on the other.

The Hydrometeorological Regime

The two study areas share a broadly similar regime but one which is anomalous for South Asia as a whole. Mean monthly temperatures are in excess of 20°C at all seasons; and in North Arcot are over 30°C from March to June. In both areas the rainy season falls in the period from October to January with a maximum in October in North Arcot and in November in S.E. Sri Lanka (see Table 2.1). Over most of South Asia, of course, this period is dry – the rains fall during the south-west monsoon, from June to September, a dry season in S.E. Sri Lanka and to a lesser degree in North Arcot. Dry seasons are, however, seasons of strong sunshine, favourable, given irrigation, to photosynthesis and ripening.

Mean annual rainfall in North Arcot is lower than almost anywhere in S.E. Sri Lanka (Table 2.1). Further, higher evaporation in North Arcot renders rainfall less available for crops and for the recharging of underground water: it reaches a maximum in the hot period from March to June. North Arcot has an average of 100–150 dry days per annum compared with 40–100 in S.E. Sri Lanka. North Arcot has, further, one long dry season, in mean terms from January to June, whereas much of Hambantota–Moneragala has two shorter dry seasons punctuated by rains in March and April. Preliminary work (CMMB) suggests that rainfall reliability generally is higher in S.E. Sri Lanka than in North Arcot, though in both areas failure is not unknown.

River-gauging records for the Cheyyar in North Arcot and the Kirindi Oya in S.E. Sri Lanka show the impact on streamflow, and therefore on surface irrigation potential, of these climatic parameters (Table 2.2). Both rivers have peak flows during the rains but, whereas the Kirindi Oya maintains a sizeable flow at other seasons, the Cheyyar is effectively dry for seven months of the year; the former's mean annual flow is eight times that

Table 2.1 *Mean rainfall, North Arcot (NA) and S.E. Sri Lanka (SESL), in mm*

	Jan	Feb	Mar	Apr	May	June	July	Aug	Sept	Oct	Nov	Dec	Year
NA	26·8	9·0	12·9	24·7	68·3	66·3	89·0	132·7	149·1	181·2	155·7	65·5	981·3
SESL	102·9	66·1	115·5	141·9	109·7	44·4	41·8	42·1	61·9	170·3	236·3	156·3	1289·3

Based on twelve stations in North Arcot District and fourteen stations in S.E. Sri Lanka, 1921–70.

Table 2.2 *Mean monthly streamflow, Cheyyar and Kirindi Oya, in mm*

	Jan	Feb	Mar	Apr	May	June	July	Aug	Sept	Oct	Nov	Dec	Year
Cheyyar	1·14	0·10	0·16	0·00	0·09	0·05	0·40	0·84	2·82	10·00	23·01	11·30	49·91
Kirindi Oya	38·60	19·80	30·48	76·45	39·12	11·43	7·37	5·84	5·33	25·15	79·76	68·07	407·40

A flow recorded as 1 mm per month is equivalent to a volume of water which, if distributed evenly over the catchment, would cover it to a depth of 1 mm.

of the latter. North Arcot's 'rivers without water' are proverbial, and water is there the prime constraint on agriculture.

Soils

Soil maps of India, even of relatively small regions are apt to depict large areas as having 'red soils' or 'black soils'. Hence the quite mistaken belief that areas like North Arcot have uniform soil conditions. At the scale of the village or the individual paddy tract – the scale at which farmers make decisions – there is great variety of soils. The key to the large-scale soil map is that there is a sequence, starting with bare rock or thin infertile soils on watersheds, and grading through poor, often sandy, red soils to heavier loams or clays, sometimes waterlogged or even alkaline, in the valley bottoms.

In S.E. Sri Lanka the same operational scale, a similar sequence, holds good but soils run from rock-knobs, through wide belts of reddish-brown earths, to low-humic gley soils (with some alkaline patches) in the paddy-growing valley bottoms (De Alwis and Panabokke, 1972–3). The reddish-brown earths, by no means uniform but relatively fertile as tropical soils go, have no analogue in North Arcot.

It is clear, then, that S.E. Sri Lanka, though not without its difficulties, is better endowed than North Arcot in terms of rainfall, streamflow and in some respects soils. North Arcot on the other hand appears to have superior resources of groundwater. But it has long supported a dense agricultural population whereas S.E. Sri Lanka is essentially a pioneer fringe of comparatively recent settlement (see below, pp. 145–53). The consequence, a greater intensity of cultivation in North Arcot, has to be considered in almost all aspects of our study, and pressure of population has made far greater inroads on resources in North Arcot than as yet in S.E. Sri Lanka. Thus, in North Arcot, there has been a secular decline in the level of the water-table (chapter 23), with streamflows depleted both because of this and by abstraction for surface irrigation; soils on dry land, have lost fertility through lack of the careful attention to manuring bestowed on the paddy fields and gardens; and soil degradation has been hastened by goats destroying the vegetation. The visible bleakness of the bare, often eroded interfluves of North Arcot indeed contrast with the still often jungle-covered, slopes of Hambantota – Moneragala: the reasons are man-made as well as natural.

Rice-cropping Seasons (BHF)

The hydrometeorological regimes serve to explain the annual calendar of rice-cropping in the two study areas. In Sri Lanka the Maha season (September/October to March) is clearly related to the rainy season, the irrigation-dependent Yala (March or April to July or August) to the south-west monsoon drought. A Meda crop is sometimes taken, overlapping late Maha and early Yala. In North Arcot, Samba, generally sown in July or

August and harvested in December or January, is the rainy season crop. Navarai (locally Kar) stretches from December or January to May, the dry season, and Sornavari from May or June to September, partly during the period of light, ineffective south-west monsoon rainfall. Traditional varieties of rice in both countries are adapted in duration to one or other of these seasons – but newer varieties do not necessarily fit local seasons (see below, pp. 99–100).

NEW RICE VARIETIES IN TAMIL NADU AND SRI LANKA (BHF)

Contrary to a popular misapprehension, rice-growing in South Asia was not sunk in the primitive cultivation of low-yielding indigenous varieties until, suddenly, new high-yielding varieties (HYVs) became available. Rice-breeding, like plant-breeding in general, is a continuum. A long process of selection was undertaken by farmers through the ages, and the modern period of scientific rice-breeding has a respectably long history, stretching back in India to the early years of this century (Shastry and Sharma, 1974). Since the early years after independence, and well before the advent of the dwarf 'miracle rices' from the International Rice Research Institute (IRRI) in the Philippines, both India and Sri Lanka had been experimenting with further improved varieties, notably the long-strawed ADT.27 (bred in Tamil Nadu) and H.4 and H.8 (bred in Sri Lanka). HYVs, then, are no revolutionary phenomenon.

There is, however, a technical sense in which high-yielding varieties did suddenly become available. For in 1963 the government of India launched its high-yielding varieties programme (HVP or HYVP) and designated specific varieties to be disseminated under the programme. (ADT.27 is not such a variety, but in Tamil Nadu was included in statistics as an HYV until 1971–2; and, in spite of a directive to the contrary, still tends to be so included.) It is also true that the dwarf rices emanating from IRRI did represent a significant breakthrough. Long-strawed rices like ADT.27 and H.4 were limited in their response to nitrogenous fertilisers and tended to lodge. But short-strawed rices like IR.8 and its successors are more efficient in response to fertiliser and, also, able to carry their heavier ear without lodging.

The improved varieties actually encountered in North Arcot and S.E. Sri Lanka in the course of fieldwork are recorded in chapters 6 and 8.

RICE IN THE ECONOMY OF TAMIL NADU (VSS)

Tamil Nadu has 7·5 per cent of the total population of India and contributes 12 per cent of the country's rice output. Formerly deficit in rice, in the last two years it has produced enough paddy to allow 20–25 per cent of its output to be available for other States. This was made possible largely by spectacular increases in production in a few IADP Districts, subsequently followed by other Districts in the State. Out of the geographical area of 13m. hectares, 6·3m. (48·3 per cent) is the net sown area. The *per capita* arable land in Tamil Nadu works out at 0·15 hectare, which is lower than that of most other States in the Indian Union. Thus the State has to depend on intensive use of land – 76 per cent of the area was under food crops and 24 per cent under non-food crops in 1973–4. There are two lines of action open to the economy of Tamil Nadu. First, the production of crops other than foodgrains could be increased, given the present surplus of foodgrains in the State and the fact that such crops appear to be profitable to the farmers. However, if sufficient improvements in the fixation of rice prices could be effected, one could think alternatively of inter-regional specialisation in agricultural production: Tamil Nadu and Andhra Pradesh could become the surplus producers of rice, groundnut and chillies, and exchange them for cotton and pulses from the other States of India. But the obstacles to inter-regional trade are many, and one cannot be sure of long-term predictions as to the statutory regulations in the way of movement of agricultural commodities within the country.

The place of rice in the overall economy of Tamil Nadu has to be viewed in terms of (i) providing a balanced diet for the growing population, (ii) increasing the supply of agricultural raw materials, and (iii) increasing the incomes of the rural population and provision of additional employment opportunities. Pulses, oils, fats, fruits and vegetables have to be produced in larger quantities because the output of these commodities has been stagnant in the past decades. The Tamil Nadu textile industry consumes 1·1m. bales of cotton and produces 0·4m. bales. The sugar factories work only for short periods in the year. Thus, problems arise in planning and over the farmers' choice of land use.

Table 2.3 gives the projection of foodgrain requirements by the State Planning Commission. The demand for rice will taper off from 1975 onwards and there should be a net surplus of rice in the following years. The assumptions behind this projection are (i) the total area under paddy would be maintained throughout the perspective plan period (1972–3 to 1983–4) at the same level as in 1972–3, (ii) the share of the area under HYVs of rice would be increased by 80,000 hectares up to 1978–9, 200,000 hectares during the Fifth Plan, and 120,000 hectares during the Sixth Plan, (iii) the productivity of the existing area would be increased by a fertiliser input from the present level of 50 kg of N to 125 kg per hectare during the period ending 1983–4. When some 5–7 per cent of foodgrain production for industrial use, seeds, waste, etc. is allowed for, Tamil Nadu is expected to have a surplus of 1·3m. tonnes in 1983. The competition in the use of land arises on account of the demand for cholam, cumbu, maize, ragi and other millets. An increase in total output of these is sought, from 1·6m. tonnes in 1973 to 2·6m. tonnes in 1983, while slightly reducing the area under cultivation of these crops from 2·1m. to 1·9m. hectares. The consumer preference for rice, millets and wheat is assumed to be broadly in the pattern given in Table 2.4. Due to the increasing awareness of nutritional potentialities of millets, it is likely that occupational shifts would increase demand for rice only marginally.

Table 2.3 Perspective plan for food grain consumption excluding requirements of animal husbandry

Year	Population (millions)	Per capita consumption per day		Total cereals (million tonnes)	Pulses (million tonnes)	Total foodgrain (million tonnes)
		Cereals	Pulses			
1970–1	41·1	397	48	6·0	0·7	6·7
1973–4	44·4	397	48	6·4	0·7	7·1
1978–9	48·9	369	71	6·6	1·2	7·8
1983–4	53·7	340	85	6·8	1·7	8·4

Table 2.4 Occupational status and consumption of cereals

Occupational status	Daily consumption of cereals per adult (g)			
	Rice	Millets	Wheat	Total
Non-working cultivators, moneylenders etc.	493	17	20	530
Working cultivators	354	272	3	629
Agricultural labourers and coolies	286	252	3	541
Village artisans, etc.	362	145	3	510
Industrial workers, etc.	482	28	37	547
Weavers	411	105	3	519
Small traders	439	77	3	519
Salaried persons – clerks	456	17	14	487
Postmen – lowest grade government servants, etc.	468	85	6	559

Source: Data collected for the Committee on the Cost of Agricultural Commodities, 1974 (Madras, Government of Tamil Nadu)

Tamil Nadu as the producer of increasing surpluses of rice, and India as a net exporter of rice in the 1970s and 1980s, could be models for agricultural planners in India. A brief reflection on the world position of rice reveals that India is the largest producer of rice in the world apart from mainland China. India's rice output has been fluctuating between 59m. and 69m. tonnes in two consecutive years, 1972–4. Bangladesh, Indonesia, Japan and Thailand produced in the range of 13–21m. tonnes. The total world output has grown during these years from 201m. to 208m. tonnes excluding the output of China (estimated at about 100m. tonnes) and that of the USSR (estimated at 1·8m. tonnes). The United States, which has been the largest supplier of wheat to India (in the range of 2–10m. tonnes per annum). cannot meet the rice requirements of India. The USA output is at about 5 per cent of the total rice output of India; and America may have to meet the market requirements of any one of the 45 rice-producing countries when they face marginal deficits. Pakistan, which produces 3·6m. tonnes, could continue to have a world market for the fine-variety rice and hence the contemplated trade this year between Pakistan and India would be in the face of world competition for its rice. Rice output of India, therefore, should provide for a large storage and surplus capacity. If there is a steep fall in rice output there is no country in the world which can readily meet the shortage. Five countries of the South Asian region – Pakistan, India, Bangladesh, Burma and Sri Lanka – produce about 100m. tonnes out of the world output of 208m. tonnes, excluding Chinese output of about 100m. tonnes. Those countries of South Asia have large populations and limited scope for trade in rice between them. Therefore India has potentially to be a rice-surplus country in all normal years, to provide for unexpected seasonal variations in output at home and in neighbouring countries.

Food shortages in India have so far been chronically associated with wheat production and wheat imports. However, when major calamities like the Great Famine of Madras in 1876–8 or the Bengal famine of 1943–4 occurred the rice belts were most severely hit. The rice-growing areas of India, are indeed, prone to shortages and it is necessary for India not only to have a clear agricultural policy of large surpluses and storage facilities in normal years, but also particularly to ensure increased productivity and rational price policy in respect of rice.

The broad issues in pricing policy are (i) the resilience with which the price of rice and other foodgrains can be fixed so that the farmers do not substitute other commodities in place of paddy production, (ii) the supply in adequate quantity and at reasonable price of fertilisers and pesticides on the one hand and the economic gains on the other, (iii) the resolution of the conflicts between labour and machinery, employment and income; the price of rice has fluctuated in the range of Rs40–112 within a short period of eight months and this happens not infrequently.

The policy of the Union government is to declare a procurement price for wheat, rice and certain other agricultural commodities. Similarly the State governments, following the All India price, often seek to fix the procurement prices. The timing of these announcements can never be the most appropriate, because the harvesting under well irrigation can vary considerably even in the same State. The prices of inputs and regional variations in wages, transport costs and natural endowments have been such that All India prices have often satisfied the criteria of political control and bureaucratic uniformity rather than economic justice to the farmer or the balancing of supply and demand.

RICE IN THE ECONOMY OF SRI LANKA: THE NEW ENVIRON-MENT (WPTS)

Rice is the staple food of Sri Lanka and its most important food crop. Given the export economy inherited from colonial times (Snodgrass, 1966) and that the country is heavily dependent on imported foodstuffs, and given post-independence foreign exchange difficulties, government has under-standably thought in terms of a drive towards self-sufficiency in food supply, particularly in rice. The contributions of increased area and yield to this drive are explored in chapter 6, while chapter 3 comments on problems of official statistics in this connection. All that need be done here is to outline, as an important part of the setting for the Green Revolution in Sri Lanka, the steps taken to create an environment which would help paddy farmers to raise the productivity of their lands (paddy is essentially a small-holders' crop), as at the time of our fieldwork. (Note that 2·47 acres = 1 hectare, and that 1 bushel of paddy per acre may be taken as 52·77 kg per hectare)

1   *The Guaranteed Price Scheme (GPS)* which goes back to 1948 and provides not only a fair and stable official price (Rs33 per bu. since July 1974) but also a marketing outlet, since government organises purchase at its guaranteed price. The proportion of output so purchased has fluctuated, reaching a peak of 61 per cent in 1960 but falling to 21 per cent in 1969 when open-market prices were high. In 1973 (when project fieldwork took place) paddy purchase was made a government monopoly, inter-regional transport of rice and paddy was curbed, and fertiliser was issued only to those selling to the Paddy Marketing Board. (In October 1975 these restrictions were relaxed.)

2   *The fertiliser subsidy scheme* was started in 1951 and has been modified from time to time. During project fieldwork there was a 50 per cent subsidy on both cash and credit purchases. Fertiliser consumption increased from 14,000 tonnes in 1957 to nearly 90,000 tonnes in 1971.

3   *Agricultural credit* has been provided under a variety of schemes since before independence. The comprehensive rural credit scheme began in 1973 and was designed to meet in a consolidated manner all the requirements of the rural sector (Central Bank of Ceylon, 1973). In 1973, Rs80·1m. were loaned for paddy cultivation. In Maha 1973−4 there was an appreciable increase in the number of people utilising institutional credit.

4   *The Paddy Lands Act (1958)* was designed to promote production by giving tenants a permanent and secure title to land, and to eliminate unlawful eviction and regulate rents. It also established elected village-level cultivation committees to promote the development of paddy

cultivation and to secure tenants' rights (Commissioner of Agrarian Services, 1967). Hambantota District was one of the first Districts in which the Act was implemented.

5 *Crop insurance* was inaugurated on a pilot basis in 1958–9 and, since higher cover without increased premium was afforded to those who followed specified practices, it has been used to popularise improvements such as row sowing and transplanting.

6 *Improved varieties* are discussed below (pp. 57–8).

7 *Extension services* go back to the 1920s but only after 1973 did the District Agricultural Extension Officer become free to concentrate on extension work. The entire service has been progressively streamlined and has no doubt played an important role in the spread of new practices (see, however, pp. 155–66 below).

It is of course difficult to gauge the precise effects on productivity, of any one of the above measures. For example, while fertiliser issues through co-operatives have increased significantly, it is not known how much was devoted to paddy, increased yields of which are the outcome anyway of a number of factors operating simultaneously. Further, farmers have not received the full benefits of these measures because of weaknesses in the services provided: for instance, malpractices in GPS purchasing; the inadequacy of the incentive provided by the crop insurance scheme, especially in high-risk areas (Jayaweera, 1973); and weaknesses in the operation of the Paddy Lands Act (Sanderatne, 1974).

However, it seems reasonable to assume that the various measures taken together must have played their part in the notable increases in average paddy yield that have taken place (26 bu. per acre in 1950, 51 in 1970, 45 in 1973). But it must not be forgotten that rises in free-market prices have also formed part of the economic environment.

REFERENCES

Central Bank of Ceylon (1973). *Annual Report*, Colombo.

Commissioner of Agrarian Services, Government of Sri Lanka, 1964–5 to 1968–9. *Administration Reports*, Colombo.

De Alwis, K. A. and Panabokke, C. R. (1972–3). 'Handbook of the Soils of Sri Lanka (Ceylon)', *J. Soil Sci. Soc. Ceylon*, 2, 11–97, with map.

Farmer, B. H. (1956a). 'Land Use Lessons Learnt in Madras and Applicable to the Dry Zone of Ceylon', *Bull. Ceylon Geogr. Soc.*, 10, 9–19.

Farmer, B. H. (1956b). 'Rainfall and Water Supply in the Dry Zone of Ceylon' in R. W. Steel and C. A. Fisher (eds), *Geographical Essays on British Tropical Lands*, London, Philip, pp. 225–68.

Jayaweera, N. (1973). 'Credit Support for High Yielding Varieties of Rice in Sri Lanka', *Marga*, Colombo, 2, No. 2, 18–44.

Madduma Bandara, C. M. (1973). 'Groundwater Resources in the Dry Zone Hard Rock Areas', *Proc. 29th Ann. Session, Ceylon Assoc. Advmt. Sci.*, part 1, 98–9.

Ramachandran, R. (1975). *Spatial Diffusion of Innovations in Rural India*, Mysore, Institute of Development Studies, University of Mysore.

Sanderatne, N. (1974). 'Leading Issues in Sri Lanka's Land Reforms', unpublished paper read at Conference on Agriculture in the Economic Development of Sri Lanka, Peradeniya.

Shastry, S. V. S. and Sharma, S. D. (1974). 'Rice' in Sir Joseph Hutchinson (ed.) *Evolutionary Studies in World Crops*, Cambridge University Press, pp. 55–61.

Snodgrass, D. R. (1966). *Ceylon: an Export Economy in Transition*, Homewood, Ill., Irwin.

3 Paddy and Rice Statistics in Sri Lanka

Barbara Harriss

PADDY PRODUCTION

According to the Ministry of Agriculture and Lands (MOAL) *Cereal Balance Sheet* (1974), production of paddy in Sri Lanka amounted to 898,000 rice tons in 1972 and 885,051 in 1973 (1 ton=1016 kg). After accounting for seed and wastage, the net domestic supply was 790,800 rice tons in 1972 and 728,846 in 1973. However, the District-level data from MOAL for 1972 (1973a) sums to 987,288 tons if a standard paddy/rice conversion of 67 per cent is used (as in PMB, 1974, p. 24). There is thus a 10 per cent error margin between these sets of figures, and some of the assumptions behind the MOAL figures must be examined.

Production is based on the 'net extent harvested' multiplied by 'average yield per acre' in bushels (46–48 lb or 20·9–21·8 kg). Net extent harvested is always taken as 85 per cent of gross extent harvested (in order to account for land 'wasted' in bunds, ridges and threshing places). Gross extent harvested appears to be 97 per cent of gross extent sown where 100 per cent would be the total holding size. So the net extent harvested is 82·5 per cent of the gross extent sown.

Yield is estimated from crop-cutting surveys. The probability of inclusion in the survey varies directly with the size of holding. Yield, however, often varies inversely with holding size (see ARTI, 1974, p. 100), although the evidence is somewhat equivocal (Dias, 1973). If 'yield per net acre' used by MOAL is 'average yield' for 82·5 per cent of gross area, it may be an underestimate.

Accuracy would improve if there were District-specific conventions for the differences between gross and net acres. For a 1 per cent difference here has as much effect on official accounts of rice availability as would probably, for example, a change in rice-milling technology. In the same way the conventions of out-turn of rice from paddy should periodically be checked, co-ordinated and revised; for instance, if out-turn had been 70 per cent in 1972 the second estimate of rice production would be 1·031m.

tons and the margin of error between the two sets of official statistics, 15 per cent.

It seems most likely that the production figures for 1972 (898,000 rice tons) and 1973 (885,051 rice tons; 62,450,152 paddy bu. and 61,549,631 paddy bu. respectively) are underestimates. In further estimates, e.g. of marketable surplus, the higher set of 1972 statistics (MOAL, 1973a) will be used. Of this production about 69 per cent was in parts of Sri Lanka which have parboiling facilities.

MARKETABLE SURPLUS

Paddy Marketing Board (PMB) Guaranteed Price Scheme (GPS) purchases for 1972 amounted to 469,816 rice tons (Table 3.1). This was 31·96 per cent of total production according to MOAL. If total production was 987,288 rice tons and 12 per cent was used for seed and wastage then available rice accounted for 868,788 rice tons.

In a situation where 4 lb of rice was given on the ration, Sagar (1969, p. 1) estimated that 'the entire quantity except what is required for seed, payment to village artisans etc. could be treated as marketable surplus' (1 lb=0·45 kg). When the ration was reduced by 50 per cent the quantity procured by the GPS dropped from 56·9 per cent of total production to 31·2 per cent. Some 12m. bu. were retained for home consumption. When the ration quantity is reduced by the government, the PMB is unable to reach its own procurement targets, which apparently have to be set regardless of this rather crucial factor. In Sagar's model (considering seed and wastage, ration size, wages and rents, holding size and family size), marketable surplus in 1969 with a 2 lb ration varied between minus 400 per cent of production on holdings of under a quarter-acre to 65·6 per cent on holdings above 5 acres; the average was 41 per cent (ibid., p. 4).

Crudely, then, in 1972 with a 2 lb ration, marketable surplus should have been 356,203 rice tons. In fact GPS purchases amounted to 464,816 rice tons or 54 per cent of production. Either the estimate provided by Sagar is 13 per cent too low, factors not considered by him shaping producers' responses; or GPS purchases exceeded marketable surplus. Research on sales of paddy to the PMB when GPS prices change, when ration quantities change, and in response to factors such as seasons, holding size, tenure status and input intensity would be very useful.

The Sagar estimate for marketable surplus seems reasonable given the ARTI 1974 data for Hambantota District, which give marketed surplus as 48 per cent of production in Maha and 40 per cent in Yala. On this basis, all island marketable surplus would be 444,279 rice tons, virtually the same as the GPS purchases. But observations during fieldwork suggest that a further 5 per cent of paddy production was traded illegally as rice or semi-officially as flour.

In Hambantota District GPS purchases expressed as a percentage of 'marketable surplus' using ARTI (1974) criteria have increased from 32

Table 3.1 Statistics on production and consumption of rice

District	Production in rice tons 1972 (MOAL)	GPS purchases in rice tons 1972 (PMB)	Weekly ration at one measure (tons)	Annual need at 103 kg per person (tonnes)	Population 1972, from ration cards (PMB)	Population 1972, from Census (Food Commission)
Mainly raw rice						
Amparai	78,864	41,355·9	228	23,910	232,145	272,790
Raw rice						
Badulla	28,703	7,994·2	578	60,616	588,509	616,315
Hambantota	41,776	21,979	314	32,930	319,709	341,005
Matara	41,704	3,461	558	58,518	568,145	588,254
Galle	32,155	3,738·9	780	81,800	794,181	737,451
Moneragala	12,870	7,369·4	162	16,989	164,945	171,505
Ratnapura	40,568	11,789·7	504	59,143	574,254	661,710
Kalutara	27,769	1,791	676	70,893	688,290	731,824
Raw sub-total	304,409	99,478	3800	404,799	3,930,178	4,120,854

District	Production in rice tons 1972 (MOAL)	GPS purchases in rice tons 1972 (PMB)	Weekly ration at one measure (tons)	Annual need at 103 kg per person (tonnes)	Population 1972, from ration cards (PMB)	Population 1972, from Census (Food Commission)
Mainly parboiled rice						
Batticoloa	44,695	11,082	238	24,959	242,327	258,104
Kandy	66,007	15,456	1,165	122,278	1,187,170	1,187,170
Vavuniya	21,945	152,349	98	10,277	99,781	95,536
Trincomalee	24,807	18,619	160	16,779	162,909	191,989
Anuradhapura	86,471	39,081	380	39,851	386,909	389,207
Parboiled rice						
Kurunegala	90,426	23,075	958	100,468	975,418	1,028,107
Matale	21,513	89,169	290	30,413	295,272	316,342
Mannar	99,198	12,086·9	64	6,711	65,163	77,882
Jaffna	29,681	12,342	724	75,927	737,163	704,350
Colombo	38,842	352	2,266	237,641	2,307,200	2,672,620
Kegalle	29,509	1,754·3	596	62,504	606,836	652,094
Puttalam	8,513	3,689	352	39,552	384,000	379,787
Nuwara Eliya	33,666	1,692·6	376	34,188	331,927	453,243
Polonnaruwa	88,326	64,843	142	14,891	144,581	163,858
Parboil sub-total	682,879	365,338	7,809	816,439	7,926,656	8,570,289
Total	987,288	464,816	11,609	1,221,238	11,856,834	12,711,143
Percentage parboiled to total	69·16	78·59	67·27	64·27	66·88	67·42

Note: The production of, and demand for, parboiled rice is much more matched than are GPS purchases.

per cent of production in 1967–8 to 120 per cent in 1972, with a 13 per cent decline in production over the period. The GPS *target* for 1972 was 3m. bu. in Hambantota District when *total production* amounted to 1,308,400 bu. These targets need to be set realistically against production (in view of farmers' home consumption under different sizes of ration, paddy payments for rent, tractors, donations and requirements for seed and wastage). Otherwise the targets are meaningless as aids to the planning of storage, milling and distribution, which must be part of their function.

RATION REQUIREMENTS
At one measure per person (adult or child) per week, raw-rice consuming Districts require 3800 tons according to PMB data sheets (1973b). The ration for Districts where parboiled rice is eaten is 7809 tons per week. Per annum this is:

	tons rice	bushels rice	bushels paddy
Raw	197,600	9,621,144	13,738,993
Parboiled	406,068	19,775,511	28,239,429
Total	603,668	29,396,655	41,978,422

Thus, ideally, 67·3 per cent of the ration should be parboiled. There is considerable congruence between production of and need for the two forms of rice in Sri Lanka. When people in parboiling zones have to eat raw rice, it is likely to be due to institutional factors rather than to environmental or technological ones.

Nutritional Need/Apparent Consumption
Sagar (1971, p. 9) calculated that during the years 1952–66 when there was no serious rice supply problem and when the rice ration was two measures free per week, average *per capita* consumption rose from 84·8 to 101·9 kg per year. According to the MOAL *Cereal Balance Sheet* (1974) rice consumption rose from 87·8 kg to 105·4 kg *per capita* per year. If we work out the consumption on the basis of the total adult population (since 30 per cent of the population is under 10 years of age and is therefore eating 50 per cent of adult requirements, the total adult population is 85 per cent of total population) average rice consumption rose during the period from 100 to 112·8 kg.

It has been calculated in India that 10 oz of rice *per capita* per day (or 12 oz in this case per adult) is nutritionally sufficient (*Indian Express*, 7 September 1973; Ryan *et al*; 1974); 10 oz (0·28 kg) per day represents 103 kg per annum. Average Ceylonese consumption during the period 1952–6 was 9·65 oz, so that this 10 oz standard seems a fair approximation to reality in a situation when there was no food shortage in Sri Lanka, and also meets nutritional sufficiency. The PMB rice distribution simulation model (1973b) is based on a total population of 11,856,834. At 103 kg *per capita*, nutritional need is approximately 83·6m. paddy bu:

	tons rice	tons paddy	bushels paddy
Raw	398,433	568,962	27,705,710
Parboiled	803,587	1,147,522	55,884,352
Total	1,202,020	1,716,485	83,590,063

The MOAL *Plan for Self Sufficiency* (1973b) gives a total population of 13,185,000 for 1972–3 so that total need is more like 1,336,668 tons rice (1,908,762 tons paddy, or 92,956,723 bu. paddy without seed and wastage). The same plan, however, gives demand for paddy as 109·23m. bu. – 118 per cent of nutritional need. This exceeds the 12 per cent wastage allowance but is less than the total *per capita* consumption of all cereals including wheat (discussed later) and maize. It is difficult to understand why 'demand' is set at this level.

Finally, if we use the Census Department estimate of 13·480m. population in 1972–3 and assume that the ration remains at 2 lb per week, or 0·047 rice tons per card-holder per year, the ration requirement totals 620,080 tons of rice while the total need is 1,366,574 rice tons or 94,978,700 bu. of paddy. Either the ration must be supplemented or current trading restrictions relaxed so that the necessary foodgrains can be bought legitimately.

SHORTFALLS AND THE ROLE OF IMPORTS

The magnitude of the shortfall can be viewed in two ways: (i) theoretically, as the difference between production (less seed and wastage) and nutritional need, (ii) empirically, as the quantity of rice imported each year. The present nutritional need for rice is currently at 94·98m. bu. of paddy. This would require a production of that quantity

Table 3.2   Rice Imports ('000 tons)

Year	Ceylon Trade Jnl (1)	Food Commission (2)	Customs returns (3)	Highest (4)	Lowest (5)
1964	639	547	648	648	547
1965	257	642	286	642	257
1966	564	485	682	682	485
1967	339	375	349	375	339
1968	364	334	364	364	334
1969	303	260	304	304	260
1970	522	525	472	525	472
1971	289	334	289	334	289
1972	262	293		293	262

plus the 12 per cent conventionally allowed for seed and wastage, i.e. 106,376,144 bu. In fact the production level appears to be around 60 to 70m. bu., that for 1972 being some 71·2m. bu., leaving a shortfall of some 35m. bu. of paddy – approximately 500,000 rice tons. Although import data should be more accurate than production figures, a series of figures for rice imports have been collected and are ordered in Tables 3.2 – 3.4 to show their internal variation. At the least this variation between sets of official figures is 15,000 rice tons (3·5m. paddy bu.), at most it is 395,000 rice tons or 27·5 paddy bu.

Table 3.3   Rice production ('000 tons)

Year	Rice Production Central Bank, 1973 (6)	MOAL (7)	Total availability highest (8)	Total availability lowest (9)	Low, as percentage of high (10)	Population (Census) (11)	Demand at 103 kg per capita per year '000 tons (12)
1964	727	707	1,369	1,254	91		
1965	518	508	1,160	765	65		
1966	654	641	1,336	1,126	84		
1967	786	770	1,161	1,109	95	12,072	1,216
1968	923	902	1,261	1,246	98	12,341	1,243
1969	941	922	1,245	1,171	94	12,616	1,271
1970	1,092	1,084	1,618	1,556	96	12,896	1,294·9
1971	956	936	1,290	1,225	94	13,185	1,329
1972	896	898	1,190	1,158	97	13,480	1,358

Table 3.4   Demand ('000 tons)

Year	Demand minus highest estimate of availability (13)	Demand minus lowest estimate of availability (14)	Demand MOAL ('000 rice tons) (15)	MOAL demand minus highest estimate of availability (16)	MOAL demand minus lowest estimate of availability (17)	Imports of flour ('000 tons) Ceylon Trade Jnl (18)
1963						137
1964						296
1965						214
1966						218
1967	− 55	−107	1,427	−266	−318	492
1968	+ 18	+ 3	1,436	−175	−190	469
1969	− 26	−100	1,469	−224	−298	260
1970	+319	+257	1,502	+116	+ 54	526
1971	− 39	−104	1,535	−245	−310	334
1972	−167	−200	1,570	−380	−412	

Column 11 gives population as estimated by the Census and column 12 gives the need for rice at 103 kg per person per year. Columns 13 and 14 compare the difference between this demand and the highest and lowest estimates of rice production plus rice imports. On the most generous figures the difference between production *plus* imports and need is increasing, although to be fair, two aberrant years 1968 and 1970 had a clear surplus under all conditions of data. Strictly speaking, and under generous assumptions about data, there was enough surplus in rice alone to tide the country over the two following years and longer. Using the lower sets of data the country could have lasted for eighteen months on 1970's production *plus* imports. If we ignore the possibility of stocks, in the year on which this paper concentrates (1972), at best the deficit was 167,000 rice tons or 11·6m. paddy bu., at worst 200,000 rice tons or 13·9m. paddy bu.

The picture is different if we compare production and rice imports with MOAL's 'demand for paddy', which is 118 per cent of the nutritional sufficiency. In 1972 at best the deficit was equivalent to 26·4m. paddy bu. and with low data it was 28·6m. paddy bu. Average shortfalls in 'theoretical' terms over the period 1967–72 at best have been 195,000 rice tons (13·5m. paddy bu.), and at worst 245,666 rice tons (17·7m. paddy bu.).

We may, then, perhaps conclude that to achieve self-sufficiency, paddy production needs to be increased by some 35m. bu. or by about 50 per cent, and that at present imports of rice make good about half of this deficit.

FLOUR IMPORTS AND TOTAL CONSUMPTION

The other half of the deficit is made up by flour imports and, since Sri Lanka has its own mills, imports of wheat. Although wheat is of considerable importance in balancing the foodgrains equation (indeed it more than balances it), little is known about wheat relative to rice consumption.

Sagar (1969, p. 4) has calculated 'average apparent consumption' of cereals. Over and above the adequate 103 kg of rice in the comfortable years, 21·5 kg *per capita* of wheat flour were eaten each year (strictly, this 21 kg was not nutritionally necessary: it was in excess). His main observation was that this wheat was mainly consumed in urban areas, and that people in rural areas would probably compensate by eating more rice than the average. This implies that wheat is a superior good in comparison with rice. In fact to a very great degree the Sri Lankan government is able to control whether or not this is so, and it is impossible to discover what 'natural' behaviour with regard to wheat consumption patterns would be. When rice is freely available its *per capita* consumption rises relative to that of wheat simply because the import of the latter is strictly controlled. Wheat consumption varies very greatly from year to year, e.g. from 28 kg *per capita* (1966) to 40 kg *per capita* (1967). The long-term mean is 21·5 kg and there is no detectable trend in consumption above an increase following that of population.

Total urban population according to the Census Department was, in 1971, 2,842,072 out of the total of 12,711,143 – some 22·35 per cent. Assuming the same percentage in 1972–3, urban population was 2,946,847. If all the flour imported were consumed by the urban population exclusively, the *per capita* consumption of flour would have amounted to 115 kg. This means that in theory the urban population did not need rice at all. If we further assume that rural people ate all the rice (production plus imports) *per capita* annual consumption amounted to 118 kg. Two points emerge from this:

1 The assumption of rural–urban contrasts in diet is a false one, as shown by survey evidence presented by the Central Bank (1970). In urban areas actual wheat consumption, on and off the ration, varied from 6·49 lb per month (2·95 kg) in the income group below Rs200 per month, to 8·50 lb per month (3·95 kg) in the bracket over Rs1000. In rural areas the corresponding figures are 5·6 lb (2·54 kg) and 6·04 lb (2·75 kg). Wheat consumption does not appear to be highly income-elastic under these artificial conditions, nor does there seem to be a highly significant difference between wheat consumption patterns of urban and rural areas.

2 If we calculate the consumption per adult, total cereal consumption in 1972 was in the region of 154 kg *per capita* as against the nutritional requirement of 121 kg per year, so that about 30 kg per adult of present consumption (or 25 kg *per capita*) appears to be in excess of nutritional requirement.

These are controversial figures because the nutritional requirement varies between authorities. That of India has been used, but MOAL's 'demand for rice' is different, and the Medical Research Institute in Colombo gives 131 kg of cereals as the minimum necessary for health (Sagar, 1971, p. 12). On the basis of the Indian figure, the 'shortfall' made good by flour imports is excessive by 50 per cent. It would even seem that in nutritional terms, in most years since 1966 (even on the lowest data), there should have been a total food surplus. The MOAL self-sufficiency targets are probably in the region of 12–15 per cent too high.

CONCLUSIONS

1 Generally the tighter the government's control the more accurate the statistics necessary. Some conventions regarding the statistical treatment of data should be periodically rechecked and if necessary be made District-specific; more realistic procurement targets should be set; the self-sufficiency programme is probably pursuing a high, rather than low, estimate of cereal requirements.

2 If there has been real shortage of food in Sri Lanka in the last few years it is not revealed by annual figures and so must be seasonal, regionally

sporadic, and unpredictable. This does not mitigate its seriousness when it does occur, but puts emphasis on the careful control of storage and distribution.

3   Paddy production is variable from year to year, but the quantity marketed via GPS has in the past been even more variable. Rainfall is not easily predictable, and there is at the very least a two-month lag between ordering rice from abroad and its arrival at the granaries in Colombo. Buffer stocks in Sri Lanka are, in practice if not intentionally, short-term; there is no attempt to create a separate buffer stock on the lines of that in India. A buffer to tide over two consecutive seasons of production at one standard deviation below average trends ought to be considered as an ultimate goal.

REFERENCES

Agrarian Research and Training Institute ARTI, (1974). *The Agrarian Situation Relating to Paddy Cultivation in Five Selected Districts in Sri Lanka:* part 1, *Hambantota District*, ARTI Research Study no. 6, Colombo.

Central Bank of Ceylon (1970). *Socio-Economic Study*, Colombo.

Dias, H. D. (1973). *A Land Reform Policy in the Context of High Yielding Varieties*, ARTI/IDS Seminar on the Social and Economic Consequences of the Introduction of the New Varieties, Colombo, ARTI.

Ministry of Agriculture and Lands (MOAL), (1973a). *District Level Agricultural Statistics from 1967–1972: Targets and Achievements*, mimeo.

Ministry of Agriculture and Lands, (1973b). *Plan for Self-Sufficiency*, mimeo.

Ministry of Agriculture and Lands, (1974). *Cereal Balance Sheet*, mimeo.

Paddy Marketing Board PMB, (1973a). *Minutes of Regional Managers' Meeting, January*, mimeo.

Paddy Marketing Board, (1973b). *Transportation Model for Paddy-Rice Distribution: Data Sheets*, mimeo.

Paddy Marketing Board, (1974). *Report of the Committee appointed to prepare a Scheme for the Co-ordination of Procurement of Paddy and Distribution of Rice by the Paddy Marketing Board in Sri Lanka*, Colombo.

Ryan, J. G., Sheldrake, R. and Yadav, S. P. (1974). *Human Nutritional Needs and Crop Breeding Objectives in the Semi-Arid Tropics*, Economics and Statistics Unit, ICRISAT, Occasional Paper no. 4, Hyderabad ICRISAT.

Sagar, Vidya (1969). *Trends of Rice Consumption in Ceylon*, MOAL, mimeo.

Sagar, Vidya (1971). *Cereal Consumption in Ceylon: Patterns and Demand Estimates*, UNDP/FAO Special Programme on Agriculture, MOAL, mimeo.

4 Bias in Perception of Agrarian Change in India

John Harriss

BIAS RELATED TO THE DISTRIBUTION OF RESEARCH

The sites of research and data referred to in articles and special studies in the *Economic and Political Weekly* or other key publications listed in Byres' bibliographical paper (1972) and in subsequent issues of the *EPW* (to September 1974) are shown in Fig. 4.1. My analysis of the literature is thus restricted, and this obviously introduces the possibility of serious bias in the impression conveyed by the map. But the journal that has been my main source is a particularly influential one, so that the bias that it imparts is of special interest in itself. In addition, it has been the general experience of project members that the studies we know of have nearly all been carried out in the areas shown on this map. Farmer mentions 'delta bias' in studies of HYVs of paddy in explaining the reasons for his choice of North Arcot District as the locality for our research. My search of the literature suggests that this pattern is related to a more general bias towards IADP Districts, while the map also reveals the efforts of particularly energetic centres of research: the Punjab Agricultural University at Ludhiana; the Agro-Economic Research Centres (AERCs) at Sardar Patel University, Gujarat, at Waltair in Andhra Pradesh and at Delhi; and work by Ashok Rudra in West Bengal. Another source of bias, not shown on the map but familiar to those who have used the results of AERC Farm Management Surveys and Village Studies, is the practice of concentrating studies over time in particular villages and localities. There are, of course, ways in which this practice is extremely valuable, and we ourselves have been able to make use of the earlier studies of one village (Dusi) in North Arcot District. But equally it is evident that the practice of doing 'follow-up' studies can easily become mere ritual because it makes it easier to operate on stringent budgets, and often with a short time in the field.

We can be fairly certain, then, that our perceptions of agrarian affairs in India are subject to considerable geographical bias, and that since the bias

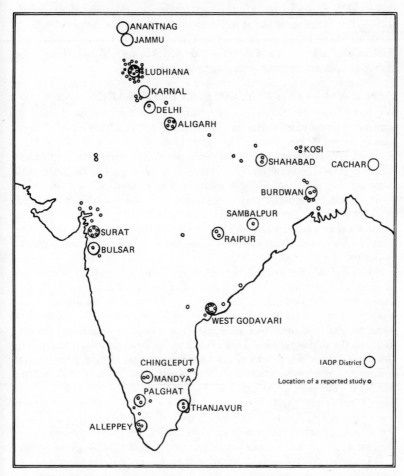

FIG. 4.1 *India: distribution of agrarian research reported in the* Economic and Political
    Weekly

is related to the IADP Districts, our perceptions are modelled on areas
particularly well endowed with government services. It is not at all clear
that the Districts selected for IADP were as well endowed in terms of
infrastructure provision and assured water supplies as they were supposed
to have been, and indeed the performance of some of the Districts implies
that the criteria were not always met (for criteria of selection, see Brown,
1971, p. 12). Examination of the tables in Brown's study of the IADP shows
that over the period 1956–7 to 1965–6 increases in output and yield were
lower than the State averages for the same period in five of the IADP
Districts, and it is interesting to observe that the same Districts are just

those IADP Districts that are least well represented among the research studies. But, whether or not as well endowed as they were supposed to have been, all IADP Districts had additional management and extension staff. 'Urban bias' is less marked than the tendencies already noted, though the choice of specific research sites might well show it up.

IMPLICATIONS OF SPATIAL BIAS IN RESEARCH

We have more information concerning Districts in which density of administrative and infrastructural provision for agriculture is rather high, which probably amounts to the same kind of selective feedback from research as that observed by Blaikie with regard to family planning studies 'on the relation between the level of administrative facilities and performance' (1972, p. 442). A similar criticism is made with regard to some studies of agricultural innovation in India, by Chambers and Wickremanayake (see chapter 11). Because most research is done in relatively developed areas with high levels of infrastructural provision 'the effect of these variables upon response rates' (Blaikie) is not properly evaluated.

Secondly, we evidently have relatively little information about the progress and problems of agriculture in the agriculturally poorer parts of the country. The vast gaps on the map (Fig. 4.1) include, significantly, the 'disaster areas' of northern Karnataka and Maharashtra, the expanses of Madhya Pradesh, much of Eastern Uttar Pradesh, Bihar and Orissa, and – on the smaller scale of Tamil Nadu which is of immediate concern to this book – there is a dearth of research information for the great area of traditional 'dry' cultivation including North and South Arcot, Salem, Madurai, Thiruchchirappalli and Thirunelveli. Exceptions are reports from Chingleput (Joan Mencher, 1974) and from Coimbatore (where Tamil Nadu's Agricultural University is located). Work has been done in the 'blank' Districts, for example by the AERC in Madras (reviewed by Aiyasami, 1974), but has not yet been reported in accessible publications.

It has been fairly widely accepted that we can only speak of 'pockets' of Green Revolution, principally in Punjab and Haryana. But the absence of studies in areas outside the most favoured localities is important not simply because of the inflated image of progress conveyed by spatially biased reporting. Much more serious is the dearth of information about conditions in poorer areas. There is perhaps an important self-reinforcing process going on here. Plant-breeding research appears to have tended to serve the needs of the most favoured areas, about which there is more agro-economic information. Hence varieties are produced which are, for example, unsuitable for North Arcot conditions (the variety known as Karuna is a possible example), while agricultural scientists are most interested in results from the favoured areas which first adopt their innovations.

The bias towards the relatively richer areas has often been defended by researchers on the grounds that by studying the 'spearheads of change' it is possible to identify trends that will eventually obtain in other areas: it should be possible then to show up the obstacles to their development and thus to speed it up. The fallacies of this argument are comparable to those which support the argument that, because HYV technology is theoretically scale-neutral, all cultivators have equal access to it. It is an attractive argument, perhaps partly because it justifies the interest of the researcher in areas where 'something is moving', and also happens to be gratifying to the administration (Blaikie, too, refers to this tendency). But it is very doubtful if any social processes are so predictable as to enable us to say that the experience of one area will be replicated elsewhere. The conditions which have made some Districts poorer than others are likely to make their requirements and response to particular programmes different too, as has been suggested in connection with plant-breeding and, as Blaikie suggests, with regard to the diffusion of information (1972, p. 441).

The practical research and policy problems raised here are of great importance, and have not been given sufficient recognition. With limited research funds and manpower, how is it going to be possible to build up better understanding of agriculture throughout India, and to give due weight to the differences between Districts and regions? Is it possible to generalise in such a way as to predict the management and research requirements of agriculture at different phases of development? Can we make use of the 'spearhead' argument by using it more critically, as some speakers advocated in discussions during the project seminar? These problems might be tackled on the following lines – among others no doubt:

1   While it might seem to be worthwhile to divert research funds to the blank areas on the map, there is no particular merit in merely claiming new territory for agro-economic research, especially if it becomes a new research ritual ('we never go to the same place twice for spatial coverage' rather than 'we always study the same places for time-depth'). True, if we knew more about the problems of the poorer areas we would probably be in a better position to make use of the experience of the 'spearheads'; but the scale and geographical diversity of India is such that some spatial bias in research is inevitable. Recognition of the bias that the location of research imparts will sometimes suggest the need for a 'new' or different area in which to try out established ideas – which was why we went to North Arcot. A corollary is that it should be the responsibility of researchers to give great emphasis to the peculiarities of the areas they study. For example, some strongly held popular views concerning the social effects of the Green Revolution are largely based on events in Thanjavur (Tanjore) District (see below, pp. 241–2). Yet the processes considered to obtain very widely may have been largely restricted thus far to certain taluks of Thanjavur, because of peculiar conditions recently analysed by Béteille (1974). A

keener awareness of uniqueness may be a valuable antidote to sloppy generalisation.

2 It seems important to view the bias discussed here in the context of research strategy and organisation as a whole. It is doubtful, for example, whether the 'farm survey' approach so often used is necessarily the best tool. Perhaps flexible combinations of locality studies, which would ideally involve natural scientists as well as social scientists, and rather broad-ranging surveys will prove to be more effective. Nevertheless, methods and sites for research should follow from the definition of *problems*. It is here that social scientists have so often been tied by rigid disciplinary thinking, and it is because of this that social scientific research in the agrarian field will benefit from closer links with natural scientists. One requirement is for more social scientists to begin to 'speak the language' of the natural scientists engaged in plant-breeding and in crop production (for further discussion of research organisation see pp. 398–411). So the significance of 'bias in the distribution of research' lies rather in what it tells us about the whole research process, than in the bias itself.

BIAS IN THE INTERPRETATION OF FACTS: FALLACIES OF WISHFUL THINKING?

' . . . the fact of change is so much taken for granted by most of us that any likelihood, or any unverified statement will pass for proof' (Dumont, 1964, p. 13)

I can best illustrate bias of this kind by reference to the much-quoted work of Francine Frankel (1971) and to a recent paper by Joan Mencher (1974) concerned with developments in Chingleput District, immediately adjacent to our own area of study. Mencher (p. 311) states, 'It is undeniable that, at least in the rice regions, the Green Revolution along with increasing agricultural production has increased economic class differences, and (at least covert) inter-group tension', but, at no point in that paper is there any substantiating evidence; later, she remarks 'What is striking on the whole is the relative lack of overt tension'. The distinction between 'overt' and 'covert' is not discussed, and her second statement is followed by an attempt at *ex post facto* explanation of the absence of 'overt' tension. The discussion is marked by an expectation of change in the direction of increased perception of class interest. Stokes (1973) has recently pointed out that such expectations have a pedigree extending back as far as Marx's writings on India. If Stokes finds that the evidence for such changes during the colonial period is insubstantial, the somewhat baffled discussion of Mencher and others may imply that there is uncertainty for the present as well.

Mencher does assert that 'there is a great deal of resentment and hostility on the part of the landless and poorer tenants'; even though there has only been one substantial 'incident' in the area she studied. That such incidents were described by Kathleen Gough twenty years ago, and that they form the principal theme of a monograph by Sivertsen, based on fieldwork carried out more than fifteen years ago, is not mentioned. The omission is pardonable since Mencher is writing with reference to Chingleput, whereas Gough and Sivertsen were both writing about Thanjavur District. But similar omission by Frankel (1971) is less excusable, since she writes specifically about Thanjavur and makes much of violent incidents there in her overall thesis. Mencher, and Frankel before her, tend to impute a significance to conflicts between farmers and labourers and between landlords and tenants that is not justifiable, for such conflicts are not a new phenomenon. And even though they are now endemic in parts of Thanjavur District, there seems little evidence to justify an assertion that it is 'undeniable' that 'economic class differences and inter-group tensions' have everywhere incréased. Even in Thanjavur it is not possible to link agrarian conflicts specifically with the Green Revolution in the way that Wharton suggests in a widely quoted article (1969) '. . . Tanjore District, Madras has been one of the prize areas where the new HYVs have been successfully promoted. Yet one day last December (1968) 43 persons were killed in a clash there between the landlords and their landless workers who felt that they were not receiving their proper share of the increasing prosperity brought by the Green Revolution'. The Kilvenmani incident referred to here has been made the basis for optimistic predictions about the likelihood of the 'green revolution turning red' by a kind of 'rapportage overkill' which has used one incident many times over as evidence of the imminence of revolution.

Presumably Mencher intends us to link up her observation that there is 'a great deal of resentment and hostility' with her earlier generalisation about increasing economic and class differentiation. But there are many indications that such hostility has been a feature of Indian society over a very long period indeed; and the notion that tensions between landowners, tenants and labourers is in any way a new phenomenon seems to imply an 'acceptance by reversal' of the myth of the 'Village Republic', and that the 'hierarchised interdependence' of Dumont's model of Hindu society really worked out in practice (cf. Dumont, 1966). Indian history suggests that the model itself has been opposed vigorously by certain groups and movements which have asserted values of individualism and equality, over a very long time indeed. Surely the initial successes of a movement like Veerasaivism can be explained in part by its capacity for articulating 'resentment and hostility' to 'hierarchised interdependence'?

This case illustrates only one kind of bias in the interpretation of facts. It would be easy to find examples also of the selection of facts to support theories (much of the literature on the relationship between farm size and productivity would provide one set of examples); and even bland acceptance of covariance without analysis, which is not so much a 'bias' as a sign of intellectual impoverishment.

It is appropriate to conclude with quotation of a charge laid at the door of the historians by Stokes, which applies just as well to social scientists in their studies of the present agrarian situation: 'The science of history proceeds no doubt as the detailed criticism of sociological generalisations, but of generalisations so rudimentary and so little analysed that they constitute primitive archetypal images lurking in the background of the historian's consciousness rather than a formed system of ideas' (Stokes, 1973, p. 136).

Acknowledgement: This paper owes much to discussion at the project seminar, and particularly to Ingrid Palmer, to whom I am very grateful for helpful criticism.

REFERENCES

Aiyasami, U. (1974). *A Review of Agro-Economic Research in Tamil Nadu with particular reference to Agrarian Change* (unpublished).

Béteille, A. (1974). *Studies in Agrarian Social Structure*, Delhi, Oxford University Press.

Blaikie, P. M. (1972). 'Implications of Selective Feedback in Aspects of Family Planning Research for Policy Makers in India', *Population Studies*, 26, 437–44.

Brown, D. D. (1971). *Agricultural Development in India's Districts*, Cambridge, Mass., Harvard University Press.

Byres, T. J. (1972). 'The Dialectic of India's Green Revolution', *S. Asian Rev.*, 5, 99–116.

Dumont, L. (1964). 'Change, Interaction and Comparison', *Contributions to Indian Sociology*, 7.

Dumont, L. (1966). *Homo Hierarchicus*, Paris, Gallimard.

Frankel, Francine (1971). *India's Green Revolution: Economic Gains and Political Costs*, Princeton University Press.

Mencher, Joan P. (1974). 'Conflicts and Contradictions in the 'Green Revolution', *Econ. Pol. Weekly*, annual number, 309–23.

Stokes, Eric (1973). 'The First Century of British Colonial Rule in India: Social Revolution or Social Stagnation?', *Past and Present*, 58, 136–60.

Wharton, C. R. (1969). 'The Green Revolution, Cornucopia or Pandora's Box?', *Foreign Affairs*, 47, 464–76.

5 Research Methodology

Robert Chambers, B. Nanjamma Chinnappa,
Barbara Harriss and B. W. E. Wickremanayake

The previous chapters have made it clear that this book records some of the results of an inter-disciplinary research project which operated in parts of North Arcot District, Tamil Nadu and of Hambantota and Moneragala Districts, Sri Lanka; and that our field methods involved both rigorous sample surveys and village studies in depth. The purpose of the present chapter is to describe our research methodology in such a way that the reader may understand how we arrived at our data and what their reliability and limitations are. It does not, however, deal with our methodology in the detail or at the depth that would, for example, be required in a comprehensive guide to field methods for future surveys: that purpose will, we hope, be fulfilled in other publications.

THE NORTH ARCOT SAMPLE SURVEY (BNC)

Since the major focus of the project was rural paddy cultivation, villages with a population of less than 50 or more than 5000, or in reserved forests or hilly regions, were excluded from the sample (Table 5.1). The pilot survey (to test and modify the schedules, to train investigators and to provide test tabulations) was conducted in January 1973 in three villages, and in a sample of 126 differing households. The main survey was conducted in the period February 1973 to June 1974, phase 1 in February to March 1973 and phase 2 in April 1973 to June 1974 (Table 5.2).

The Sample Design

A two-phase, two-stage design was used with the same essential structure as that for the Sri Lanka sample (see pp. 44–5). Basic information was collected in the much larger phase 1 sample and used to select an efficient phase 2 sample. In the two stages of each phase, villages were the first-stage sampling units and households the second. A village was taken as a 1971 Census village. A household was defined as a group usually living together,

Table 5.1 Some basic statistics for the study area

Taluk	Total no. of Census villages	No. of villages excluded because they were			No. of villages in study area	For villages included in study		
		uninhabited or population <50	forest or hilly areas	population >5000		total population	No. of cultivators	No. of agricultural labourers
Arkonam	147	2	3	4	138	230,309	36,118	39,020
Cheyyar	223	6	1		216	210,868	41,429	29,092
Wandiwash	217	1	6	3	207	217,875	40,783	37,143
Arni	77			12	65	77,889	18,794	18,323
Polur	205	3	33	8	161	211,444	38,589	26,471
Tiruvannamalai	218		13	3	202	223,103	50,543	25,115
Total	1,087	12	56	30	989	1,171,488	226,256	175,164
Average per village						1,185	229	177

Source: Population data from 1971 Census.

Table 5.2   Subject coverage of the main survey (North Arcot)

Schedule	Frequency	Title	Subject coverage
Phase 1			
0	Once – at beginning of survey	List of households	List of households: hamlet, street, name of head of household, age, sex, occupation and literacy of each member and relationship to head; area owned and operated in 1972–3, maximum area under paddy in any season of that year; religion, caste; ownership of radio, cycle; type of house
1	Once	Farm survey	Agricultural implements, loans, details of land-holdings and land utilisation in 1972–3, sources of irrigation, pattern and history of use of modern inputs, labour use, and extension contact
Phase 2			
2	Twice – at beginning and towards end of survey	Basic schedule	Buildings, wells, livestock, farm equipment, stores and financial assets, parcel-wise particulars of land holdings, marketing practices for paddy, use of attached labour
3	Thrice – once every season	Cultivator schedule	Area cultivated in each season under different crops and details of dates of operations, inputs used (human, animal and material), access and information, costs, credit, output, marketing and post-harvest operations
4	Thrice – once every season	Cultivator opinion	Opinions on high-yielding and traditional varieties of paddy, reasons for crop combination adopted, problems in cultivation, water supply from different sources, soils
5	12 times – once every month	Livelihood	Income, employment and expenditure particulars for the month preceding the date of survey and details on the diet for the day and week preceding the date of survey

Note: The frequency refers to the number of schedules filled in for each informant. The number of interviews required per schedule for each informant was invariably more than the frequency, e.g. for schedule 3, data for each season was collected over a series of repeated interviews during the period of cultivation.

eating from a common kitchen and contributing to and drawing from common resources.

The sampling frame for the first-stage units was the 1971 Census list of villages. For the second-stage units, a complete list of households was compiled for each sample village. The sample size for the phase 1 was twelve villages and all their 2563 households for the list of households (schedule 0); and 785 cultivator households (cultivating a quarter-acre or more land) for the farm survey (schedule 1). The sample size for phase 2 was the same twelve villages – 200 paddy-cultivator households, 10 non-paddy cultivator households and 150 non-cultivator households for the basic schedule (schedule 2); 200 paddy-cultivator households for the cultivator and opinion schedules (schedules 3 and 4); and 80 paddy-cultivator households, 10 non-paddy-cultivator households and 80 non-cultivator households for the livelihood schedule (schedule 5).

A simple systematic sample of eleven villages was selected with equal probability, from the 989 in the sampling frame. (An equal-probability simple systematic sample is obtained by selecting every kth unit from an arranged list, the first selection being at random from the first set of k units in the list. The interval of selection, k, is determined as the inverse of the sampling fraction desired.) The villages were arranged in the following order before selection: (i) by contiguous taluks; (ii) by distance from towns within the taluks in four classes, (iii) by 1971 population size-classes, (iv) by proportion of agricultural labourers to cultivators (whether lesser than or greater than one), and (v) by spatial proximity (as indicated by village location codes given by the 1971 Census). The twelfth village, Dusi of Cheyyar taluk, was purposively included in the survey because it had time-series data for 1916 (Slater, 1918), 1936 (Thomas and Radhakrishnan, 1940), 1959 (Agro-Economic Research Centre, Madras, 1960) and 1961 (Haswell, 1967).

A 50 per cent equal-probability simple systematic sample of the 1673 cultivator households was selected after arranging them in four classes: those with:

1 Cultivation as principal means of livelihood, growing paddy.
2 Cultivation as principal means of livelihood, not growing paddy.
3 Other than cultivation as principal means of livelihood, growing paddy.
4 Other than cultivation as principal means of livelihood, not growing paddy.

Within each class, households were arranged by the hamlets in which they lived. Of the 835 households thus selected, 50 were found to have leased out all their land, to have been misclassified as cultivator households, or to have migrated. The final sample for the farm survey was, therefore, 785 households. Of these, 694 were found to be potential paddy-cultivator households (those having some wet and/or garden land). These households were arranged in the following order:

1 Those growing high-yielding and other varieties of paddy.
2 Those with pump-sets, those without pump-sets but with iron ploughs, and those with neither pump-sets nor iron ploughs.
3 In decreasing order of area operated.
4 In decreasing order of maximum area under paddy in any season.
5 By tenure status – owners, owner-cum-tenants, and tenants.

The sample of 200 households was selected from the arranged lists in the villages by circular systematic sampling, with equal probability, using the same sampling interval in each village. The sample of 80 paddy-cultivator households for the livelihood schedule was selected systematically from the original sample of 200, using the arrangement described above. (In circular systematic sampling, as opposed to simple (linear) systematic sampling, the first unit is selected at random from all the units in the universe to be sampled and every kth unit is selected thereafter by proceeding in a circular manner, i.e. treating the first unit in the arranged list as the unit following the last unit in it. This method is convenient for systematic sampling from small populations.)

Among the households listed in phase 1, some 890 belonged to the category 'non-cultivator households'. These households were arranged by the hamlets in which they lived, and within them in the following order:

1 By principal means of livelihood.
2 By religion and caste.
3 By household size.

The total sample of 150 households was selected at random from the arranged lists of households within the villages by circular systematic sampling, with equal probability, using the same sampling interval in each village.

The reduced sample of 80 non-cultivator households for the livelihood schedule was selected from the 150 simple-systematically, using the arrangement described above.

The sample of 10 non-paddy cultivator households was selected by simple systematic sampling with equal probability from the 110 cultivator households in the twelve villages having only dry land, after arranging them in increasing order of area of operated land, in land tenure classes, and by household size.

An equal-probability systematic sample design was adopted at both the stages, with equal intervals of selection within each village, to ensure (i) a self-weighting design (so that all the estimates and tables from the survey could be obtained directly without using different weights or multipliers for different units), and (ii) representation of different types of units at each stage.

Substitution for an informant was allowed only if he had left the village or did not belong to the required category. He was then replaced by the next household in the arranged list for systematic sampling.

Data Collection

This was by the interview method, using schedules and instructions in English and Tamil for the interviews, which were conducted as conversations, the informant being allowed to elaborate or to digress into topics that interested him. The information thus collected was noted separately for each informant and was transferred daily to the schedules. Checks on accuracy and completeness were made by further visits. Sufficient space was provided on the schedules for additional observations: these threw much light on the data and opened up new areas of interest. The schedules were kept flexible, additions and corrections being conveyed in supplementary instructions to the investigators.

The investigators were subjected to intensive training for a week before the pilot enquiry and to selection on the basis of performance during the pilot enquiry. There was another week of training before phase 2. Investigators, who were each allotted either one or two villages for survey, resided in or near their villages. The quality of data improved when the investigator actually lived in his village, and investigators who came from farming communities in rural areas proved superior.

Experienced supervisors were appointed, one for each half of the study area. They were responsible, in addition to supervision, for monthly data on prices of crops and inputs, on agricultural wages, crop condition, rainfall, labour, pest attacks and the availability of inputs. They collected completed schedules and spent about a week at Madras every month, scrutinising data and discussing problems met. They also trained replacement investigators.

Switching investigators between villages after phase 1 was found to be most useful in checking data. Occasional meetings were arranged between all the investigators and the research team for the discussion of problems, the exchange of information and discussion of changes in instructions or in the programme of work.

Accuracy of Data

Methods used to improve the quality of the data included cross-checks built into the schedules, checks on consistency between schedules, checks conducted by different investigators, resurveys, and external checks prompted by observations made during scrutiny of schedules and by supervisors and members of the research teams during the field survey. Thorough checks were made of the coding and transfer of data to the coding sheets. Major errors in coding sheets were, if missed in checking, picked up by a computer programme on logical checks. Punching of all cards was checked using card verifiers. A sample of the computer output tables was checked using hand tabulation. Whenever an error was picked up on the coding sheets or tables, all the sheets or tables were checked for that error. Doubts raised on the accuracy of data during the field survey were referred back to the investigators. At the final stage of coding, the investigators scrutinised and coded the data themselves, exchanging schedules. Errors were rectified by reference to the notes kept during the survey.

Table 5.3   Land owned per household as reported in schedules 0, 1 and 2

Village	Sample size	Land owned per household in acres as per		
		schedule 0	schedule 1	schedule 3
Vegamangalam	17	2·73	2·61	4·35
Sirungathur	12	2·86	3·92	4·05
Duli	10	3·71	2·69	2·69
Vengodu	19	2·72	3·20	3·27
Vinayagapuram	15	3·06	3·13	3·13
Amudur	17	2·28	2·28	2·76
Randam	17	3·67	4·15	3·96
Kalpattu	21	2·68	2·92	3·13
Veerasambanur	10	3·06	3·72	3·54
Meppathurai	11	3·48	3·90	3·96
Vayalur	12	2·25	2·25	2·36
All villages, excl. Dusi	161	2·91	3·10	3·39

The study of Randam by John Harriss focused attention on important phenomena to be studied in sample villages, and provided checks on sample data which led to rechecks in other villages. For example, he showed that overall underestimation of area owned was of the order of 36 per cent, bigger cultivators underestimating the most. Considerable efforts were then made in phase 2 to ensure that all the area owned and operated by the sample cultivators was reported accurately (Table 5.3). The underestimation was of the order of 14 per cent at the listing stage and of 8 per cent at the farm survey stage, for all the sample villages taken together. Panse (1958, p. 224) observed, on the basis of a study of all-India surveys, that the average reported size of the operational holding increased with the duration and nature of the enquiry. Our main difficulty here resulted from the focus of the survey on the cultivator. If the objective had been simply to estimate the area and yield of different crops (and not to relate them to the sample of cultivators) it would have been possible, and better, to select a random sample of plots (cf. Mahalanobis, 1958, p. 215).

Data-processing

Scrutiny of data, coding, punching and computer-processing was involved, with checks as necessary at each of these steps. Preliminary hand tabulations of phase 1 data and tabulations of the data from the pilot survey helped considerably in finalising the scrutiny and coding programmes, in drawing up the tabulation plans and in checking the computer output. Later came the scrutiny of schedules, coding, and test tabulations. The coding programme was devised to suit the data analysis planned. Close liaison between the graduate assistants concerned and the computer programmer in charge if the data-processing was found to be very useful.

Two of the major lessons learnt from the survey were, first, the need for careful planning and allocating of the time, manpower and financial resources for both data collection and the various steps in data-processing, and secondly, the need for careful checking of the accuracy of the data at the various stages of data collection and processing.

THE SAMPLE SURVEY IN S.E. SRI LANKA (BWEW)

Basis for the Selection of Sample Areas

In Sri Lanka cultivation committee (CC) areas – not villages – were taken as the basic unit in selecting the sample. Village households are often widely scattered while, in terms of paddy cultivation, CC areas are more homogeneous and manageable units than villages: particulars of paddy cultivators were easily obtainable for the CC areas, but not for the villages. At the time of the survey, the jurisdiction of the CCs did not, however, extend to the high land. Colonisation schemes (Farmer, 1957) were purposely excluded, since they might produce a distorted picture.

The Sample

A two-stage sample design was adopted for the selection of the sample, CCs constituting the first-stage units and households the second. The sample frame for the first stage was the list of 127 CCs in the area. Data on the area under paddy and number of *ande* (tenant) and owner cultivators in each area were also included in the sample frame. The sampling frame covered six Divisional Revenue Officers' (DROs) Divisions: these were arranged by geographical contiguity, by coastal and inland areas, by proportion of wet to dry land and by proportion of cultivated land to total land. Within each DRO's division the CCs were arranged in increasing order of percentage of owners among cultivators. A circular systematic sample of twelve CCs was thus selected, with equal probability.

Two samples, one of 200 paddy-cultivator households and another of 150 non-cultivator households, were selected for phase 2. The total sample of 200 was allocated to the twelve CCs in proportion to the number of paddy-cultivator households in them. Within each sample CC, the households were arranged by four criteria:

1 By tenure.
2 Within each tenure class by adoption patterns of different innovations.
3 Within each 'tenure by adoption pattern' group, the households were arranged in increasing order of total area operated.
4 Within these by area under paddy.

In this way an equal-probability systematic sample of the allocated number of households was selected.

The total number of non-cultivator households (all households other than those operating a quarter-acre or more of paddy land) listed during phase 1 in the twelve sampled CCs was 595. This list was used as the sample frame for selecting a non-cultivator sample of 150 households for phase 2. The households within each CC were arranged in the following order:

1 By principal means of livelihood.
2 Within that by religion.
3 Within 'means of livelihood by religion' classes, by household size.
4 By total number of literates in the household.

An equal-probability circular systematic sample of the allocated number of households was selected from the CC using the sample interval of four.

Pilot Survey
In order to test the schedules a pilot survey was conducted in January 1973, in two contrasting CC areas. Certain unsuitable sections of the original schedules were then modified for the main survey.

Main Survey
During phase 1 of the survey, the farm survey schedule was administered to the sample cultivator households, and a list of non-cultivator households was prepared. Phase 2 of the survey started in May 1973 and ended in July 1974. The cultivator schedule was administered to all the paddy cultivators in the sample who cultivated during Yala 1973 and Maha 1973–4; the livelihood schedule, after a trial run, to 80 selected cultivators and to 80 non-cultivators; a modified livelihood schedule to the cultivators not covered by the livelihood schedule; the basic schedule, at the last stage of the survey, to all the cultivators and the non-cultivators of the sample; the supplementary schedule to those who were self-employed in trade, services and other fields; and a chena schedule to cultivators engaged in shifting cultivation (see chapter 7). Except for the farm survey schedule, in English, all other schedules were in Sinhala.

Methods of operation: some Comparisons with those in North Arcot

In order to achieve better supervision, control and communication between the investigators, the supervisor and the members of the research team – and given the remoteness, transport problems and scattered residential pattern of the sample areas – the investigators and the supervisor were stationed at Hambantota. The team of investigators visited each CC area together: no particular areas or informants were assigned, as in North Arcot, to any one investigator. The team was able to discuss problems as they arose and to work out uniform solutions, also, to compare the situations prevalent in different areas. However, all investigators had to know all twelve sample areas and about 280 individuals: this indeed limited the opportunity for them to get thoroughly acquainted with a particular area and its people and to cross-check. Moreover, it was not possible to spend more than two or three days a month in any one area, when an all-out effort had to be made to meet all the informants. This left very little time to meet people who were not in the sample. As in North Arcot the interview method was followed, but in Sri Lanka the investigators filled in the schedules while conducting the interviews. The team approach, however, ensured that no area was subject to the individual bias of any one investigator. Completion of the schedules in the field had the advantage that the investigators could check the completeness of information, and avoided copying errors.

The restriction of the CC areas to the paddy tract created a problem in listing the non-cultivators to whom the livelihood schedule only was administered. Arbitrary boundaries had to be demarcated on the high land, using aerial photographs of the settlement areas there.

To bring it to a manageable level the sample for the livelihood schedule had to be reduced to 160 – 80 selected cultivators and 80 non-cultivators.

At a late stage, some cultivators said that the area they cultivated was less in some cases, slightly more in other cases, than that given in the Paddy Lands Register. It was not possible to come to a firm conclusion, cultivators' estimates not being completely accurate and there being no proper survey. Discrepancies in areas occurred also for other reasons: for example, when owner or gambaraya (see Dias and Wickremanayake, 1974), while registering tenants, exaggerated so as to collect a higher rent; when high-land plots used as threshing floors or house sites were included with the paddy-land figures; or when the Mandala Sevakayan (Administrative Secretaries) of CCs deliberately included higher figures so as to collect higher acreage tax.

Accurate yield figures are difficult to obtain in a survey where investigators have to depend on what cultivators say. However, because of the investigators' rapport with the informants, more reliable figures could be obtained than might otherwise have been the case.

In spite of all the difficulties, the information collected in this survey was reliable to a great extent because of the frequent contacts with the informants over a long period of time. But the discrepancies between information collected at the initial stage and that derived from the later stages prove the difficulty of obtaining accurate data during one short survey. Especially in paddy cultivation, in which there are many complications and regional variations in operations, thorough familiarity with the situation is desirable. This needs a longer survey period, which would, of course, be more expensive.

STUDYING MARKETS AND TRADE (BH)

In order to undertake research in depth into the delivery systems for agricultural inputs (fertiliser, agrochemicals, pump-sets, tractors and money) and for paddy and rice, it was first necessary to study the pattern of marketing. Until the nature of market structure and conduct is known, one cannot conjecture the effects either of potential increases in marketable surplus resulting from the acceptance of new agricultural technology, or of externally induced conditions of scarcity such as those following the 'oil crisis'.

The analysis of market performance is centred conceptually on its relative efficiency in terms of five measures: (i) productive efficiency based on considerations of capacity utilisation and operational scale (see chapter 19), (ii) pricing efficiency (chapter 12), (iii) spatial efficiency – the extent to which geographical coverage is achieved at minimum social transport costs (chapters 12 and 13), (iv) operational efficiency – stock control and management practices at the level of the firm (see pp. 287–8), and (v) 'social' efficiency, an assessment of firms in terms of output/labour ratios and of the creation of employment. The spectrum of institutions (co-operatives, parastatal boards, private trade in various combinations) in Tamil Nadu and Sri Lanka represent an excellent laboratory for this kind of research.

Preparations

In both countries it was necessary to gather, at State and District levels, such data as official statistics on paddy and rice prices, levies and taxes, milling margins, and storage and warehousing capacities; prices of fertiliser, agrochemicals, pump-sets and mill machinery; and co-operative credit. Frequent interaction with the various sectors of private trade and government was an invaluable preparation for fieldwork.

It was also essential to list the addresses of the population of firms to be sampled: a slow process in both countries. Details of the samples have been summarised in Table 5.4. All samples were equal-probability stratified random samples. For the sample of branch co-operatives in India those 18 nearest the 12 randomly selected villages of the main project survey were chosen; in Sri Lanka, those 12 branches nearest the sample villages and 12 others were randomly selected.

Fieldwork Method

Private traders are reputedly liars and very hard to interview. Great pains

Table 5.4 Sample details

Type	India			Sri Lanka		
	Source of data	Popu-lation	Sample	Source of data	Popu-lation	Sample
Co-operatives	Department of Co-operation:			Department of Co-operation:	8	8
	taluks	7	7	MPCS		
	branches	160	18	branches	154	24
Panchayat union	District Development Office	17	17			
'Paddy and Rice Traders'	District Development Office	451	75			
'Rice-millers' (Private)	Civil Supplies	1,124	25	PMB	155	22
Government	Civil Supplies	2	2	PMB	36	18
Private Fertiliser and/or agrochemical traders	Private companies	122	74	Urban surveys and private companies	19	19
Pump-set Traders	District Development Office	69	23			
Car/tractor repair	Urban survey	71	5	Urban survey	37	3
Tractor stockists	Urban survey	4	4	Urban survey	7	7
4-wheel tractor owners	Government Tractor Depot, Vellore	about 500		Licences Massey-Ferguson	387 550	42
2-wheel tractor owners				SLTC estimates SLTC estimates	900 2,000	19
Lorry owners	District Development Office	14	10	Licences	100	16

Note: MPCS=Multi-purpose Co-operative Society, PMB=Paddy Marketing Board, SLTC=Sri Lanka Tractor Corporation.

were taken to establish rapport and obtain accurate data. Advance letters sent in English and the local language, explaining the objectives of the project and my survey, the random nature of selection – and assuring confidentiality – were a useful investment. A standard skeleton schedule calling for family, historical, social, economic and management data was used for all types of interview, but never displayed at interviews. The interview was started at any suitable point, proceeded in any order, and covered about 90 per cent of the questions (up to 150) in the average time of $1\frac{1}{2}$ hours allowed by a trader; a second visit was usually easy to arrange. An assistant was necessary to facilitate a businesslike communication: he fired questions in the local language and I, having mastered at least 700 relevant words, translated and noted the replies. Care was taken to minimise the use of English, and time taken at the beginning and end to explain the project and talk generally. It was important to follow up leads and to have a relaxed attitude to the programme and the questions asked. My assistant and I ate at traders' houses, met their families, visited their farms and thereby learned about moneylending activities, illegal trade and the organisation of labour. I am convinced of the advantages in accuracy and comprehensiveness of collecting data personally at the expense of speed, as well as the advantages of attempting to speak the local language as a social lubricant and as a check on assistants.

Living style was also moulded to the survey. Living in the same hotels as visiting traders paid dividends; identification as the wife of the 'white man' living in a local village helped to establish general credibility.

Quality of Data

In all cases the populations, and therefore the original samples, were found to be defective and randomly selected reserves were enlisted. Functional mapping of all urban areas exceeding 10,000 in population has established the precise population of all relevant traders save those in paddy and rice, who are geographically dispersed and sometimes unlicensed. Paddy and rice traders in Tamil Nadu are, therefore, the population known to the Civil Supplies Department of the government. (In Sri Lanka the problem did not arise.)

Of the data supplied in interviews, relatively little concerned aspects of trade where concealment was a common response, although 'hot' questions were asked. 'Hot' data for private fertiliser traders in India was cross-checked with their firms' regional representatives and with company records, and proved generally accurate. Similarly, in Sri Lanka, headquarters offices verified data supplied by the managers of branch co-operatives and contract mills. So it is data on private paddy traders and millers in India and Sri Lanka whose accuracy can least be known. The accuracy of an interview, intuition apart, can be judged by the internal consistency of the schedule. In time this became a binding principle; and sets of cross-checking questions were built in. Many traders remained consistent throughout, others showed awareness that they were 'cornered' and 'came clean', giving consistent replies; few who became aware of the traps remained inconsistent, and very few unaware and inconsistent. Under-declaration of profit or over-declaration of costs is, with experience, easy to spot, and corrections can be thrashed out in the interview. One can also build on dealer to dealer consistencies. Less than 5 per cent of the schedules are so distorted as to be useless.

Integration

From official data, international comparison is limited by differences in the statistical base: for example, good price data in India, little in Sri Lanka; good trading data in Sri Lanka, little in India. But it has been possible to compare and contrast rice-milling technologies and the reaction of marketing institutions to input scarcities.

As regards the fitting of my survey to the project survey, only in respect to co-operatives was my sample related to the project samples. And, except for one individual in Sri Lanka, the two surveys were mutually exclusive. However, the sample survey itself contains questions about the installation and marketing of inputs and paddy which are complementary to my own survey; and it may be that the reverse holds true.

OPPORTUNISM IN RURAL RESEARCH (RC)

The Experience

Conventionally, rural social science research tends to involve either deep but narrow case studies or shallow but extensive surveys. In combining these two approaches the project has provided an environment for 'opportunist research': I have been both opportunist and exploiter, taking advantage of the survey and of my colleagues so as to conduct research quickly and somewhat unconventionally. This approach does not have a rigorous methodology but, as it is widely practised, notably by senior academics and officials, its techniques and dangers deserve description.

Research opportunism was forced on me. A social anthropological approach was out of the question for reasons which included training and language. The extensive survey was already being handled by the Madras and Colombo teams. With only about a year for field-work, divided between two unfamiliar countries, I had to use my time efficiently. It was impossible to learn Sinhala or Tamil well enough for the conduct of interviews. I could use English in examining seed-breeding and agricultural research. But more methodologically interesting are three other areas requiring rural fieldwork – agricultural extension, water management and inter-village comparisons.

Agricultural Extension

The main question initially was the extent to which differences in agricultural extension could account for differences in adoption of HYVs in the two countries. The method proposed involved, first, questions in the farm schedule (applied early in the survey) and intended to identify the sources from which cultivators gained knowledge of new practices. They were unsatisfactory because (i) the questions, drawn up without prior field interviews, were not sufficiently specific to the extension programmes, (ii) I could not be present till after the modification of the schedule following the pilot survey, (iii) in the final questionnaire, questions late in the sequence were polluted by earlier questions, thus influencing the responses, (iv) the questions were not sufficiently thought through in terms of detailed instructions to investigators, coding or analysis. When completed schedules were examined, about half the questions were rejected as unusable: more were abandoned later. The lessons are obvious.

The second approach was to try to find out from extension staff the current extension programmes and activities. This proved surprisingly difficult. While outwardly co-operative, staff suspected we might report on them to higher quarters. Junior staff were especially suspicious of my desire to see their daily diaries (which, it turned out, were systematically falsified). I never had frank discussion with them: B. W. E. Wickremanayake was more successful.

These failures point to the difficulty of studying the lower levels in any hierarchical organisation, especially when staff have something to hide. This sort of research cannot be carried out when time is short: a single researcher making brief visits is unlikely to gain an accurate impression of what junior government staff in rural areas really do.

We found, however, that by pooling our findings and using material from various sources – interviews with staff and farmers, visits to agricultural instiutions, the in-depth work in villages, survey investigators and secondary material – some useful findings emerged.

Water Management

Water management differed, first, because it was not a major interest at the start of the project, but became so through discussions and observations in Sri Lanka. Secondly, it did not have much of an existing literature, so that reconnaissance research was needed to open up the subject. C. M. Madduma Bandara, as a geographer – hydrologist, John Harriss as a social anthropologist, B. W. E. Wickremanayake (in charge of the survey) and I, as a research opportunist, all variously explored the subject. The main methods used were interviews with staff concerned; field visits, including inspection of systems and practices on the ground, and interviews with local leaders and farmers; the design, pilot testing, modification and then application of questions about water management in the survey questionnaire in Sri Lanka; observations of actual water management practices over time (by John Harriss); searching the literature (largely drawing a blank on the most important issues); and discussion, and exchange of letters with the team.

A weakness here, partly overcome through continuous field observation by John Harriss, was the difficulty of being sure that the water allocation and distribution system as described to us was the real one. But the combination of techniques did help to explore the subject fairly rapidly, identifying issues for government policy and future research (see pp. 340–75).

Village Comparisons in India

Every member of the project who was exposed to the villages in North Arcot was struck by their diversity in terms of population size, caste composition, water supply system, cropping pattern, wage rates, land values and geographical accessibility. Farm survey data showed major differences in the adoption of improved varieties and in other characteristics (see pp. 301–22). John Harriss later visited most of the villages and circulated notes on differences in resource base and exploitation, in caste, in leadership, in socio-economic relationships, and in many other factors. It was an intellectual challenge to understand how and why the villages differed and whether any policy issues might arise from the observed differences.

As with water management, the approach was eclectic and opportunist. Some of the more important sources of information were:

1   Open-ended interviews, typically taking half a day to a day for one village, and typically with one or two revisits of a similar length.
2   Analysis of data from Census volumes (this proved difficult and was corrected and supplemented from the records of karnams and schoolteachers, through interviews and through field inspection).
3   Examination of resettlement registers, about 60 years old, which gave a wealth of information.
4   Recent crop and land acreage from karnams' records.
5   Having investigators mark on maps for each village the land and water use categories, wells, and the water-lift system used.
6   Having investigators collect comparable data for their villages, for a number of characteristics.
7   Written dialogue between researchers 'on the run' (with a mixture of mutual stimulation and collaborative urgency in getting to the root of things).
8   Early processing of survey data so that it could generate questions for further exploration.

The ways we have tackled the above three topics differ in detail, but they have in common (i) a research-sparing character (in general they have

not been research-intensive), (ii) *ad hoc* collaboration, (iii) eclectic
opportunism in choice of methods forced on us, and particularly me, by
shortage of time, and permitted by the research environment, the
generosity of my colleagues, and the flexibility of the project.

REFERENCES

Agro-Economic Research Centre, Madras (1960). Mimeographed report on Dusi.

Dias, H. D. and Wickremanayake, B. W. E. (1974). 'Gāmbara System in Hambantota District', paper to Conference on Agriculture in the Economic Development of Sri Lanka, Ceylon Studies Seminar, Peradeniya, mimeo.

Farmer, B. H. (1957). *Pioneer Peasant Colonization in Ceylon: a Study in Asian Agrarian Problems*, London, Oxford University Press.

Haswell, M. R. (1967). *Economics of Development in Village India*, London, Kegan Paul, Ch. 3.

Mahalanobis, B. (1958). 'Some Observations on the 1960 World Census of Agriculture', *Bull. Intern. Stat. Inst.*, 36, 214–221.

Panse, V. G. (1958). 'Some Comments on the Objectives and Methods of the 1960 World Census of Agriculture', *Bull. Intern. Stat. Inst.*, 36, 222–227.

Slater, G. (ed.) (1918). *Some South Indian Villages*, University of Madras, *Econ. Studies*, vol. 1, London, Oxford University Press.

Thomas, P. J. and Radhakrishnan, K. C. (1940). *Some South Indian Villages: A Resurvey*, University of Madras.

6 Selective Adoption as a Strategy for Agricultural Development: Lessons from Adoption in S.E. Sri Lanka

H. D. Dias

SELF-SUFFICIENCY: CULTIVATED AREA AND YIELD

High-yielding varieties of paddy form one prong of a three-pronged attack on the problem of self-sufficiency in Sri Lanka. The other two prongs are increases in the area of paddy land and in the production of substitute food crops such as manioc and sweet potatoes. Although the desire for self-sufficiency has prevailed for many years, a new urgency has been induced by the worsening foreign-exchange position, and by steep rises in the prices of imported cereals, of other food commodities, and of agricultural raw materials. It is thus necessary to produce locally as many of these agricultural commodities as possible. This increases the competition for scarce resources, especially that for land. As a substitute for scarce land, HYVs assume a very significant role. Their importance may be considered with reference to food requirements and to the area of land required to produce them.

B. Harriss estimated the 1972–3 requirement of paddy at 106,376,144 bu. on the basis of 103 kg per head nutritional need plus 12 per cent for seed and wastage (see above, pp. 25–6). She also quotes the MOAL estimate of 109·23m. bu. If one takes 13 measures of rice per week as the amount that might be expected to be consumed in an average household (approximately 5 adult equivalents), needing 103 kg per head or 123 kg *per capita* adult equivalent, I estimate that 94,921,671 bu. of paddy were required. Allowing 12 per cent for seed and wastage then gives the total production requirement as 106,312,271 bu. If we project, on the same basis, the requirement for 1983 when the population will reach 17·04m. on a medium projection (Selvaratnam and Jones, 1972, p. 44), the amount of paddy required would be approximately 128,956,000 bu. If all of this were to be produced locally, what acreage would be required?

This clearly depends on the productivity assumed. The average yield per acre in 1957, before HYVs had made any appreciable impact on the levels of productivity in the country, was only 32·3 bu. (bu. per acre can be converted approximately at 52·77 kg of paddy or 35·35 kg of rice per hectare.) At that level of productivity 3,291,401 acres were needed in 1972–3, and 3,992,460 acres in 1983. This includes land cultivated both in Maha and Yala, so the actual amount of asweddumised land would be less. If 34 per cent of the area cultivated during the year is cultivated in Yala (as was the case on average in 1967–2), the asweddumised area required was 2,172,325 acres in 1972–3 and would be 2,635,024 acres in 1983. However, the introduction of HYVs in the period following 1957, together with improved methods of cultivation, led to increased productivity. The highest average yield officially recorded up to 1974 was 51·3 bu. per acre in 1970. Given productivity at this level, the required cultivated area in Maha was 1,367,760 acres for 1972–3 and should be 1,659,083 acres for 1983; and in Yala, 704,603 acres in 1972–3 and 854,679 in 1983 (see Table 6.1).

Table 6.1   Area of paddy land required to be cultivated to be self-sufficient in rice (acres)

	Maha		Yala	
	1972–3	1982–3	1973	1983
Pre-HYV productivity	2,172,325	2,635,024	1,119,076	1,357,436
Maximum productivity (1957–74)	1,367,760	1,659,683	704,603	854,679
Actual area cultivated	1,178,969		613,133	

The increase in productivity between 1957 and 1970 had thus reduced the acreage required in 1972–3 by 804,565 (Maha) and by 414,473 in Yala. The actual acreage cultivated in 1972–3, however, fell short of these figures by 188,791 acres in Maha and 91,470 acres in Yala. But the yield for 1972 was only 46·8 bu. per acre; so the actual deficit was much more (Table 6.2).

The decrease in yield of 4·5 bu. per acre between 1970 and 1972 had increased the requirement of land by 131,515 acres in Maha and 76,751 acres in Yala. Self-sufficiency could have been achieved in 1972–3 on the actual area cultivated if the average yield had been 59·3 bu. per acre – 24·6 per cent higher than it was.

We can now project forward to 1983 (Table 6.3). The asweddumised area increased by 17 per cent from 1961–64 to 1970–73 (Census and

Table 6.2   *Area of paddy land required in 1971–2 for self-sufficiency at the 1972 level of productivity (acres)*

	Acreage required at 1972 yield	Acreage cultivated	Deficit acreage	Additional acreage required due to decrease in yield between 1970 and 1972
Maha	1,499,275	1,178,969	320,306	131,515
Yala	722,354	613,133	159,221	67,751

Statistics, 1973). If the asweddumised area increases by a similar proportion between 1973 and 1983, the acreage in 1982–3 will be 1,684,656 – 1,376,364 in Maha and 719,348 in Yala – a total of 2,095,712 acres (assuming 81·7 per cent of the asweddumised area is cultivated in Maha and 42·7 per cent in Yala – as in 1964–5 to 1971–2). While irrigation schemes such as Mahaweli Ganga and Uda Walawe will add to the asweddumised and double-cropped area, it is doubtful if the cultivated area will be as much as 2,095,712 acres in 1982–3. Even if it is, the yield necessary to produce the estimated requirement of paddy would be 61·53 bu. per acre, 23·9 per cent above that in 1972; if it is not, then the yield will have to increase even more. If some newly cultivated land is utilised for crops other than paddy, then paddy yields must be higher still.

Table 6.3   *Area of paddy land required for self-sufficiency in 1983 at varying levels of productivity*

Level of productivity (bu. per acre)	Total	Maha	Yala
Pre-HYV (32·3)	3,992,460	2,635,024	1,357,436
1957–74 max. (51·3)	2,513,762	1,649,083	854,679
1960	2,149,267	1,418,516	730,751
1965	1,983,938	1,309,399	674,539
1970	1,842,229	1,215,870	626,357
1975	1,719,413	1,134,813	584,600
1980	1,611,950	1,063,887	548,063

The contribution that HYVs can make to food production must be viewed in this context. The area needed in 1983, relying on the varieties cultivated prior to the advent of HYVs, would be 3,992,460 acres – more than double that available if past trends continue, and thus unattainable. So with the productivity level prevailing prior to the introduction of HYVs, it is impossible to envisage self-sufficiency in 1983. Even if asweddumised land increases at the same rate as during the past decade, an unrealistic expectation, the production of paddy would fall short of requirements by 35 per cent.

The increased productivity made possible by HYVs and by improved cultivation methods provides an alternative solution. The level of productivity must, however, be greatly increased. But without an increased cultivated area, the necessary increase in productivity appears equally unattainable. If the area cultivated remains at the 1972−3 level, an average yield of 72 bu. per acre would be required in 1983 to achieve self-sufficiency. Although the yield increased by 58·8 per cent to 51·3 bu. per acre between 1957 and 1970, it is very unlikely that it will increase by a further 40 per cent to 72 bu. per acre by 1983. The initial increases were made possible by the HYVs and improved cultivation methods, exploiting an under utilised potential in the ecological and socio-economic environment: further increases are less easily attainable. This argues for a dual approach to the problem of self-sufficiency:

1 An increase in the area cultivated.
2 An increase in the level of productivity.

THE AVAILABLE HIGH-YIELDING VARIETIES

Early efforts in the 1940s concentrated on the selection of the best strains from among the indigenous varieties cultivated in different parts of the country (Peiris, 1973), and produced *improved traditional varieties* capable of yields up to 60 bu. per acre. Then came cross-breeding between some of these varieties and high-yielding foreign strains. One outcome, H.4, proved to be an outstanding success, although tall and susceptible to lodging. H.4 was released for general cultivation in 1953. A study made in 1969 among cultivators in the Parakrama Samudra scheme (Polonnaruwa District), revealed that 77 per cent of the cultivators were growing this variety (Gunawardena *et al.*, n.d., p. 20). H.4 was followed by H.7 and H.8 in the early 1970s and by H.10 later. During this period IR.8 had also been introduced, but did not spread widely. The 'H' series predominated until the 1970s; and with Podiwee A-8, 62-355 and Pt.16 (obtained from India) constitute the *early high-yielding varieties*. While most of these were capable of yielding 40−60 bu. per acre, some yielded as much as 80 bu. and H.4 could yield over 100 bu. Yamada has estimated its potential at 160 bu. per acre under favourable circumstances (Peiris, 1973, p. 2), but its ruggedness enables farmers to obtain high yields even at a comparatively low level of management.

The most recent phase has seen the crossing of high-yielding local varieties with dwarf varieties such as IR.8 and TN.1, then selection of natural or irradiated dwarf mutants of high-yielding local varieties. These varieties overcame H.4's tendency to lodge, particularly at higher levels of fertiliser application and under wet-weather conditions. Varieties thus produced fall into three age groups:

3 months: BG.34-8, BG.34-11, BG.34-2, BG.33-2
$3\frac{1}{2}$ months: IR.262, BG.34-6, BG.35-2, A.9-48
$4-4\frac{1}{2}$ months: BG.11-11, MI.272(m), LD.66, A.11-15, A.11-40
      BG.66-1, BG.90-2

These constitute the *new high-yielding varieties*. Most of them can yield over 100 bu. per acre: the 3 and $3\frac{1}{2}$ month varieties, 120–140 bu. Among the $4-4\frac{1}{2}$ month group, BG.11-11 has yielded 140–150 bu., even at low levels of fertiliser application. In extensive field trials many of these varieties yielded 90–100 bu. per acre.

The development of HYVs in Sri Lanka has thus progressively pushed the ceiling of the potential yield per acre from 40 bu. for traditional varieties, to 60 bu. for improved traditional varieties, 80–100 bu. for early HYVs and 120–140 bu. for the new HYVs.

But HYVs depend on several complementary factors and conditions to produce these potential yields. Soils and supply of water are very important: HYVs have produced their best results with fairly well-drained soils, an assured water supply, plenty of sunshine, and dry conditions immediately preceding harvest. Rain and excessive wind during flowering are harmful. These requirements place a premium on areas with an assured supply of irrigation water, good drainage and timely cultivation. A package of cultural practices is also required for high yields. New HYVs at maximum yield levels have a much higher nutrient requirement than the proved traditional varieties, removing 2·5 times more nitrogen and phosphorus and 4 to 4·5 times more potassium (Nagarajah, 1973, p. 8). Weed control is very important, as the shortness of the varieties and the application of fertiliser encourage weed growth (Weeraratne, 1973, p. 5). Timely application of fertiliser, weedicides and pesticides also necessitate good water management. The HYVs, together with the cultural practices which allow them to produce their yield potentials, constitute a new agricultural technology – sometimes referred to as the 'high-yielding package' – which makes paddy cultivation a full-time occupation. Although the best results are obtained with the adoption of the complete 'package' the individual components produce an increase in yield, provided other practices remain constant. Application of fertiliser even to the traditional varieties produces increased yield, although excessive application can cause a decline due to lodging. Weed and pest control have a very beneficial effect regardless of variety or fertiliser use. Transplanting increases yields, particularly with improved traditional varieties and the early HYVs. Even improved varieties by themselves can increase yields, because they process plant nutrients in the soils more efficiently. Similarly, good water management is very beneficial: apart from its influence on weed and pest control, water at certain critical times, and draining at other times, have a favourable effect. Where these various cultural practices are adopted in combination, the yields increase more according to the combination adopted. Cultivators range throughout the continuum from those who have not adopted any of the improved cultural practices to those who have adopted the entire package.

As a whole, the two Districts studied, Hambantota and Moneragala, are areas in which improved cultural practices are adopted very widely. To quote official data from the Ministry of Agriculture and Lands, in Maha 1973–4 some 96 per cent of the cultivated area in Hambantota and 88 per cent in Moneragala were reported to be under the early and new HYVs. They ranked second and ninth respectively among the country's twenty-two Districts. In Hambantota 81 per cent of the area was under the new HYVs, ranking it first: Moneragala, with 58 per cent, ranked eighth. Similar information is not available for fertiliser application. However, in Maha 1973–4, the issue of fertiliser per acre was highest in Hambantota, but Moneragala ranked very low. There are no data on a national scale for the practice of weed, pest and disease control. Only 18 per cent of the cultivated area was transplanted in Hambantota in Maha 1973–4 (Moneragala had transplanted 44 per cent). As, however, the practice of transplanting had been adopted to a limited extent except in a few Districts, Hambantota ranked eighth. Hambantota does not fall into the top category taking all improved practices together, because of the small proportion of cultivated land which is transplanted. (Transplanting is included here as an improved practice because it produces demonstrably higher yields with improved traditional varieties and early high-yielding varieties. Whether it can be considered equally important for the new high-yielding varieties is contested by many local agronomists.) Moneragala ranks lower.

It is clear, then, that Hambantota is not representative of the spread of improved cultural practices. It represents, for most practices, the areas in which the new technology has been introduced more successfully. The dry zone Districts with extensive areas under major irrigation, together with a few of the Districts in the central highlands such as Kandy and Kegalle, fall into this category. Moneragala is more representative of the 'average' conditions of dry and intermediate zone Districts dependent more on minor irrigation; the remaining Districts in the central highlands fall into this category. Some of the wet zone lowland Districts represent areas where the new technology has not yet made a substantial impact, for several ecological and socio-economic reasons. (The extrapolation of the conditions in Hambantota and Moneragala to other Districts is not based on any objective analysis, which would be beyond the scope of this work. It is included here only to give some perspective.)

The information obtained from our study relates mainly to conditions in Hambantota District, since a majority of the sample fell within that District. Only two of the twelve cultivation committee (CC) areas – Wellawaya and Kataragama – fell within Moneragala District. The initial phase of the study covered 1432 households with a population of 9192.

Most of these households reported agriculture as their major source of income (Table 6.4).

Table 6.4   Distribution of households in the sample, according to major source of income

Major source of income	Distribution of households	
	No.	Percentage
Agriculture	1,054	73·5
Trade	106	7·4
Rent from property	6	0·3
Village industry	23	1·6
Professional service	51	3·6
Other non-agricultural employment	184	12·9
Charity	10	0·7
Total	1,434	100·0

The sample population may be considered quite young, as many as 59 per cent being less than 21 years of age. Only 12 per cent of the population were over 45 years old. About half the population were of working age (15—65 years). Some 70 per cent were literate – as many as 31 per cent had received formal education for over five years. Of the 6743 persons aged 10 years and over (i.e. 23·8 per cent,) 1606 reported their major occupation as agriculture. This, however, does not give a realistic picture, for many women did not so report, even though they engaged in various agricultural operations. Some 39·5 per cent of the males aged 10 years and over reported agriculture as their major occupation.

The average age of those occupied in agriculture was 38·4 years. The level of literacy among the agriculturally occupied was similar to that of the population generally, but the average level of education was lower: those with only primary education represented 48 per cent as against 37 per cent; those with secondary education, 26 per cent as against 37 per cent. This agriculturally occupied population was thus middle-aged and literate. If these farmers took to agriculture at the age of 14—15 years, most of them would have started after the early HYVs had been released for general cultivation.

Although the agricultural extension services use several mass media, and in spite of a high level of literacy, information about new cultural practices appears to be transmitted mainly through inter-personal communication. The commonest sources from which farmers heard about new varieties of paddy were other farmers, farmers' meetings, cultivation committee officials and agricultural extension personnel. Among impersonal sources of information, demonstration plots, farm radio programmes, extension literature, newspapers and films figure prominently. Most farmers had been exposed to several sources of information. It is obvious that the information media together constituted a very effective communication network, partly formal and partly informal, which reached the whole farming community. Nearly all cultivators were aware of HYVs and of most of the advantages of using fertilisers and pesticides. Whatever deficiencies there may be qualitatively in the information they received, nearly all the farmers are aware of improved cultural practices.

The level of adoption among the cultivators in our sample not only confirms the official data, but makes it clear that cultivators have gone beyond the stage of mere awareness. Among the 1432 households enumerated, 802 were paddy-cultivator households (i.e. cultivating 0·25 acres or more in paddy). Of these, 734 had cultivated paddy in Maha 1972−3, the study year. Only 21 farmers (3 per cent) had confined themselves to traditional varieties. The remaining 97 per cent had cultivated an HYV on at least some part of a field (Fig. 6.1). Altogether, 95 per cent of the cultivated area of 2083·8 acres was reported to be under HYVs, both the early varieties, such as H.4, H.8, H.10, H.501 and 62-355, and the new varieties, such as BG.11-11, BG.34-6, BG.34-8, LD.66 and IR.8. Already by this season, two years after they had been released for general cultivation, the new HYVs occupied a major portion (54 per cent) of the area cultivated under HYVs (Table 6.5). To illustrate the rapid spread of these new varieties: the number of farmers who reported cultivating BG.11-11 increased from 31 in 1970 to 97 in 1971 and 227 in

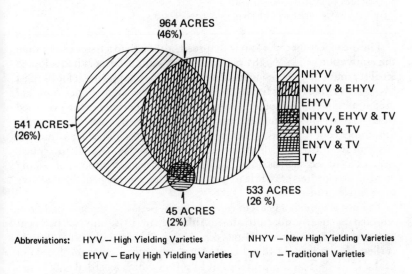

NHYV	New High Yielding Varieties
NHYV & EHYV	
EHYV	
NHYV, EHYV & TV	
NHYV & TV	
ENYV & TV	
TV	

964 ACRES (46%)

541 ACRES (26%)

45 ACRES (2%)

533 ACRES (26 %)

Abbreviations: HYV − High Yielding Varieties   NHYV − New High Yielding Varieties

EHYV − Early High Yielding Varieties   TV   − Traditional Varieties

FIG. 6.1 *Sri Lanka: diagrammatic representation of the area under different categories of paddy varieties*

1972 – 28 per cent had switched over completely to the new varieties, while a further 26 per cent cultivated both the new and the early HYVs.

Table 6.5   *Distribution of cultivators and cultivated area according to paddy varieties, Maha 1972–3*

Category of paddy variety	Cultivators		Category of paddy varieties	Cultivated extent		
	No.	Percentage		Acres	Percentage*	Percentage†
New high-yielding only	202	27·5	New high-yielding	1,054·43	50·6	53·5
Early high-yielding only	281	38·3	Early high-yielding	915·57	43·9	46·5
Early and new high-yielding	190	25·8	All high-yielding	1,970·00	94·5	100·00
High-yielding and traditional	40	5·5				
Any high-yielding	713	97·1				
Traditional only	21	2·9	Traditional	113·80	5·5	
Total	734	100·0	Total	2,083·80	100·0	

* Total area cultivated = 100 per cent.
† Area cultivated under high-yielding varieties = 100 per cent.

The use of fertiliser was also widespread, although to a lesser extent than the cultivation of HYVs – 84 per cent of our sample farmers had adopted fertiliser, most of them reporting that they had been applying it for the past five years or more. The fertiliser used by most was urea: 78 per cent had used it at some time or other. Only 30 per cent reported having ever used basal fertiliser but the number using it has increased, especially recently. Only 4 per cent reported using top dressing mixtures. (The Department of Agriculture introduced fertiliser mixtures in Maha 1971–2 to replace straight fertilisers such as urea. Basal and top dressing mixtures containing varying proportions of N:P:K to suit different agro-ecological regions have been introduced.)

The use of agrochemicals to control weeds, pests and diseases had been adopted by nearly all cultivators. Although in 1972 only 72 per cent reported their use, almost 94 per cent had used them either that year or earlier. However, only 18 per cent of the cultivators had transplanted in Maha 1972–3. This confirms the ARTI survey which recorded only 17 per cent in Maha and 9 per cent in Yala (ARTI, 1974, p. 82).

These figures thus reveal a very high level of adoption of HYVs and of some other components in the high-yielding package in the area studied and at the same time give credence to the official data regarding the spread of the new technology (compare the situation in North Arcot District, pp. 93–7).

It is necessary, however, to know not only the extent of the adoption of various individual components in the high-yielding package, but also that of combinations of the components (Table 6.6). Most of the cultivators have adopted three components – fertilisers, weedicides and pesticides. Transplanting was the least adopted of the improved practices (cf. above, p. 59), and most of the transplanting cultivators had adopted the other components also. Some 85 per cent of those who transplanted in Yala and/ or Maha had adopted all four components. Very few cultivators have adopted only a single component: of these, 64 per cent had used only fertiliser and 28 per cent only pesticides. It is interesting to note that few cultivators had adopted HYVs without adopting any of the other components: they were more common in Yala. Farmers realise the need to complement the adoption of HYVs with other components of the new technology, although they have not adopted it in its entirety or uniformly – perhaps for very justifiable reasons.

Table 6.6   *Adoption of the high-yielding package singly and in combinations of components by farmers cultivating high-yielding varieties of paddy*

Seasons	Total	No adoption		One component		Two components		Three components		All four components	
		No.	Per-cent-age	No.	Per-cent-age	No.	Per-cent-age	No.	Per-cent-age	No.	Per-cent-age
Yala	408	19	4·7	18	4·4	48	11·8	262	63·9	67	15·2
Maha	713	23	3·2	41	5·7	125	17·5	414	58·1	110	15·4
Yala and/or Maha	731	39	4·8	50	6·1	137	16·7	470	57·4	123	15·0
Yala and Maha	390	3	1·0	9	3·0	36	11·9	205	67·9	49	16·2
Yala only	18	16	15·1	9	8·5	12	11·3	56	52·8	13	12·3
Maha only	323	20	4·9	32	7·8	89	21·7	209	50·9	61	14·8

Components included in this table are: application of fertiliser, application of weedicide, application of pesticides, and practice of transplanting.

What of the low adoption of transplanting? Transplanting contributed towards an increase in the yields with the earlier varieties that were prone to lodging: 'Under transplanted conditions, both varieties are identical in yield. However, under broadcast conditions, H-4 yields approximately 60 per cent of IR-8. The yield drop of H-4 under broadcast conditions is a direct result of early lodging. . . . Lodging resistance resulting from dwarfing elevated the yield of H-4 from 3·59 to 5·37 tons/ha.'. (Weera-ratne, 1973, p. 3). The development of shorter varieties which are lodging-resistant has virtually eliminated the advantages to be gained from transplanting. The package (minus transplanting) as adopted in our study area and several other parts of the country should, therefore, produce high yields. Has this expectation been realised?

Before dealing with this question, it will be useful to explain why this discussion on adoption does not follow convention and examine the

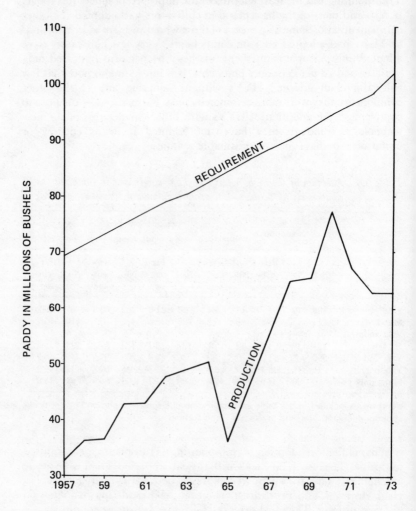

FIG. 6.2 *Sri Lanka: gap between production of paddy and estimated requirement*

influencing factors. During the formulation of this study, it was thought that the identification of such factors would contribute towards the development of agriculture and enable policy-makers to speed up the diffusion of the new high-yielding technology. But the information presented here more than adequately demonstrates that cultivators in at least this part of Sri Lanka are not only aware of HYVs and the other new cultural practices, but have also adopted them to a great extent. No real benefit is to be gained by delving into the relationship between adoption and variables such as literacy, income levels, size of holdings, water supply and so on. To the extent that this area represents conditions in other parts of the country, Sri Lanka seems to have had remarkable success both in getting the message across to the cultivators, and in persuading most of them to accept it. What is even more remarkable is the speed with which this diffusion now takes place. The new HYVs which were introduced only in Maha 1970–71 had spread to 81 per cent of the cultivated area in Hambantota by 1973–4 Maha, despite the serious dislocation of extension activity and administration that resulted from the disturbances of 1971 (see p. 7). The time gap between the farmers who adopted first and last is only a matter of a few seasons, and the identification of innovators and late adopters has little practical significance in Sri Lanka and is unlikely to speed up diffusion. What would be more relevant is the identification of non-adopters, but they constitute a small proportion of our cultivator sample – only 3 per cent had not adopted HYVs. Similarly, only a small proportion had not adopted any of the other components of the high-yielding package.

ADOPTION, OVER-ADOPTION AND SELECTIVE ADOPTION

With very high level of adoption and the increased potential of the new HYVs, Sri Lanka should be well on its way to self-sufficiency in paddy. Indeed, according to the Five Year Plan for 1972–6, 'if production during the Plan period keeps to schedule, domestic production of rice will meet nearly 97 per cent of the demand by 1976' (Ministry of Planning and Employment, 1971, p. 44). Some of the agricultural researchers have been even more optimistic and envisaged self-sufficiency as early as the end of 1974, provided that inputs of fertiliser and credit flowed smoothly and that adverse weather conditions were not met (Peiris, 1973, pp. 16–17). Despite these optimistic forecasts, production fell far short of expectations. The planned output for 1973 and 1974 according to the Five Year Plan was 94m. and 100m. bu. of paddy respectively, but the actual production was about 63m. and 76m. bu. – short of expectations by 33 per cent and 23 per cent (Fig. 6.2). What has gone wrong?

The new varieties rapidly replaced the earlier varieties, although not completely. HYVs occupied 82·5 per cent of the cultivated area in Maha 1973–4. Of the area under HYVs, 62·8 per cent was under the new HYVs: the area under these had increased by 57 per cent compared with the previous Maha. The issue of fertiliser increased also, by 47 per cent from 56,080 to 82,685 tons. This reflected a substantial easing in the supply of credit: loans for paddy cultivation in Maha 1973–4 amounted to Rs60·9m. compared to Rs20·3m. during the previous Maha. Maha 1973–4 was in several ways an unusual season: the government had mounted an intensive drive to increase production, weather conditions were more favourable than for several seasons before, and production was higher by 25 per cent on the previous Maha. But this exaggerated the achievement, as production in the previous Maha had been very adversely affected by drought. A more realistic comparison is with Maha 1969–70. Production in Maha 1973–4 was 3·1m. bu. higher than in Maha 1969–70 when the area cultivated was 9 per cent less, 76 per cent being under HYVs (mainly H.4); the fertiliser issued for paddy cultivation was only 58,378 tons (29 per cent less than in Maha 1973–4). Compared to both Maha 1969–70 and Maha 1972–3 the increased production in Maha 1973–4 was not commensurate with the larger area cultivated, the larger area under HYVs (particularly the new HYVs), and the larger quantity of fertiliser issued. It is clear from Table 6.7 that output has increased by a much lower proportion than inputs of fertiliser or high-yielding potential, or area cultivated. This is especially so compared to 1969–70, when weather conditions were as favourable as in 1973–4. The increase in production between 1972–3 and 1973–4 could well be due to better weather conditions, increased inputs having contributed little or nothing to increased output.

This raises important questions regarding the extent to which yields have increased because of investment in the high-yielding package. Despite fluctuations in yield due to adverse weather conditions and other factors, there has been a steady increase from around 32 bu. per acre in the early 1950s to about 47 bu. in the early 1970s. There is little doubt that this increase was achieved through the spread of the high-yielding package.

Table 6.7   A crude input – output analysis of paddy cultivation in three seasons

	Maha 1969–70	Maha 1972–3	Maha 1973–4	Percentage increase	
Total area cultivated (acres)	1,191,473	1,178,969	1,317,383	10·6*	11·8†
HYV area (acres)	905,519	879,994	1,087,070	20·1	23·5
New-HYV area (acres)	55,072‡	435,499	682,533	1,139·4	56·7
Fertiliser issues (tons)	58·378	56,080	82,685	41·6	47·4
Total production (m. bu.)	49·5	42·0	52·6	6·3	25·3
Yield (bu. per acre)	52·2	45·5	47·7	−8·6	4·8

* Increase in this column represents 1973–4 over 1969–70.
† Increase in this column represents 1973–4 over 1972–73.
‡ IR-8.

Although these hybrids H-4, H-7, H-8 were released several years ago and substantial information on fertiliser practices, weed control and pest and disease control were available, it was not until 1967 that their full impact began to be felt . . . In 1966 the government co-ordinated various activities such as intensified extension, better credit facilities, subsidised fertiliser etc. in an effort to improve production. The convergence of these efforts are reflected in the steep curve of increased production from 1,122,832 metric tons (54·96m. bu.) in 1966–7 to 1,581,282 metric tons (77·4m. bu.) in 1969–70 (Peiris, 1973, p. 3)

They were also reflected in a steep increase in the yield per acre (in bushels) as follows: 35·6 (1966), 41·3 (1967), 46·5 (1968), 50·3 (1969) and 51·3 (1970). This increase appears to have levelled off (Fig. 6.3), although the new HYVs had steadily replaced the earlier varieties. It is premature to be definitive as to whether the yield trend *has* levelled off, and almost impossible to predict its future behaviour. But it would clearly be unwise to project into the future the trends that have been observed in the past decade or two.

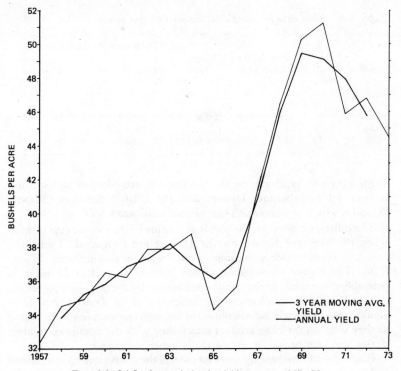

FIG. 6.3 *Sri Lanka: variation in yield per acre, 1957–73*

Adoption, then, despite its promise of high yields, did not set in motion a continuous process of self-perpetuating development in the paddy sector. HYVs, both the early varieties and the new ones, have a high yield potential; but it is clear that most farmers do not obtain potential yields. According to the ARTI (1974) survey, the average yield per acre reported by 147 cultivators in Hambantota was 33·8 bu. for Maha 1971–2 and 23·3 for Yala 1972. The yields according to the crop-cutting surveys for those two seasons were 63·4 and 55·2 bu. respectively for Hambantota and 50·3 and 54·6 for Moneragala. This wide divergence in the yield between the two surveys is difficult to explain. It is believed that cultivators tend to understate their yields to investigators. Although crop-cutting surveys are more objective, biases also affect them, and cultivators themselves state that they are not representative and tend to over-estimate yield. If we assume that the true yield lies somewhere in between, and nearer to the crop-cutting survey figure, these figures indicate a comparatively low yield. Our survey confirmed this (Table 6.8). While the yield was a little higher in Maha than Yala, it was low in both seasons compared to the potential of the HYVs.

Table 6.8   Yield data for sample cultivators (bu. per acre)

Season	No. of Culti-vators	Average yield	Median yield	Range of yield	Cultivators obtaining a yield of					
					over 70		over 80		40 or less	
					No.	%	No.	%	No.	%
Yala 1973	66	52·6	44·9	12·0 to 89·4	13	20·0	5	7·6	29	44·0
Maha 1973–4	173	56·3	50·0	40·0 to 122·5	35	20·0	16	9·0	59	34·0

Table 6.9 shows yields during the two seasons, according to crop-cutting surveys, for Hambantota District and the District Revenue Officers' Divisions within it into which our sample cultivators fell.

The difference between the yields according to the two surveys is small when the averaged figures for the District are compared. There are, however, considerable variations in the yields for smaller areas (Table 6.10). The bigger discrepancy at the level of the DRO Divisions is probably due mainly to the small sample used by the crop-cutting survey at that level. The smallness of the difference at the District level gives confidence in the yield figures obtained through our sample survey, based as they were on the close contact established with the sample cultivators during the long period of our carefully supervised survey.

It is evident from these figures that most of the cultivators have obtained yields substantially below the potential of the new technology. Among the

Table 6.9   Paddy yield for relevant DRO Divisions in Hambantota District, according to the crop-cutting survey

DRO Divisions	Survey area falling within DRO Division	Yield (bu. per acre)	
		Yala 1973	Maha 1973–4
Giruwa Pattu East	Ambalantota area	59·9	75·0
Tissamaharama	Tissamaharama area	57·4*	77·7
Giruwa Pattu South	Tenagama	54·2	44·8
Giruwa Pattu North	Kachchigala – Metigatwala	48·7	47·5
Hambantota District		53·5	63·3

* This figure is for Magam Pattu before it was divided into Tissamaharama and Hambantota Divisions.

20 per cent of the cultivators who obtained the lowest yields, 58 per cent in Yala and 74 per cent in Maha had cultivated new HYVs. This situation is not confined to this area of Sri Lanka or even to Sri Lanka itself: Chinnappa reports a similar situation for the North Arcot District of Tamil Nadu (see below, pp. 103–4). What is even more remarkable and relevant to policy-makers is that the yield obtained by 44 per cent of the cultivators in Yala and 34 per cent in Maha was 40 bu. or less per acre – well within the yield potential of improved traditional varieties. As many as 72 per cent in Yala and 67 per cent in Maha obtained 60 bu. or less per acre, within the yield potential of the early improved varieties. Some 20 per cent of the cultivators obtained yields in excess of 70 bu. per acre, and less than 10 per cent yields in excess of 80 bu. per acre.

Table 6.10   Comparative paddy yields for Maha 1973–4 obtained through survey and crop-cutting methods

Survey areas	Yield per acre (bu.)		Corresponding DRO Divisions
Ambalantota	58·5*	75·0†	Giruwapattu East
Tissamaharama	66·2	77·7	Tissamaharama
Tenagama	31·8	44·8	Giruwa Pattu South
Kachchigala	32·7		
	42·83	47·5	Giruwa Pattu North
Metigatwala	46·6		
Wellawaya	58·3		
Kataragama	55·9		

* This column derived from study survey data.
† This column derived from official crop-cutting survey data.

Only a small proportion of the cultivators were thus able to gain an adequate benefit from the new high-yielding technology. Now that adoption has come to be equated with agricultural progress, there is a tendency to consider that an area with a higher level of adoption is, *ipso facto*, more developed. The Green Revolution has produced a psychological environment that encourages the adoption of the new technology for its own sake and an unquestioning acceptance of the belief that adoption is beneficial.

B. H. Farmer has already spoken in this book of the 'cruel and facile optimism' (not yet dead) that was abroad in the first flush of the Green Revolution (above, p. 1; see also Brown, 1970, *passim*; Ahmed, 1973, p. 17, for Bangladesh; Swaminathan, 1973, pp. 5–6, for India; and Peiris, 1973, p. 17, for Sri Lanka). Such optimism engendered the drive to diffuse the new technology. The view that this new technology would mean freedom from dependence on food imports and bring prosperity to the rural areas was widely accepted. That every farmer should eventually adopt the new technology was almost unquestioned. The early adopters were undoubtedly the heroes of this crusade against hunger and poverty. The late adopters deserved our sympathy as they were prevented from adopting the new technology because of ignorance and other impediments. The process of winning them over had to be facilitated through research to remove these obstacles and by the provision of incentives. The results obtained through adoption, however, should raise some very justifiable doubts and make us think afresh about our strategy for agricultural development.

Now, there are several qualitative differences between the technology of traditional farming and the new high-yielding technology. The traditional varieties are more tolerant of unfavourable conditions.

The persistence of the undesirable plant type under low levels of management is an indication of their survival and competitive ability. Poor management practices in combination with low levels of nutrition resulted in an unconscious natural selection of plant characters best suited for competitive ability and low levels of fertility. With the least amount of inputs and attention, a farmer was assured of a marginal yield. In short, these types were tolerant of ill-treatment but not sufficiently responsive to better management practices. (Weeraratne, 1973, p. 3)

The HYVs are very much more demanding. Not only do they need a high level of management in terms of weed, water, pest and disease control, application of fertiliser, timely operations and constant attention, but they are more demanding with regard to ecological conditions, especially water, soil and light. These requirements make the new technology much more complex and sophisticated than that which our farmers had been accustomed to. Even more important, the farmer must depend on many factors beyond his control if he is to perform this complex operation successfully. This holds especially true for the basic requirement of water, even in irrigated areas of Sri Lanka, whereas in several areas of India, well irrigation under the control of individual farmers has enabled them to get very successful results from the new high-yielding technology. Getting the correct fertiliser to his field at the correct time is an equally complicated and precarious task. Farmers have first to acquire the necessary loans in time. Although the credit available from private sources is at very high interest rates, the State agricultural credit system is not a success because the borrower does not receive loans at the time he needs them most (Weerawardena and Collonnege, 1974, p. 238). Even if credit is available, inefficiencies in distribution may not get the fertiliser to the local co-operative store in time. The staggering of cultivation also makes it difficult for small co-operative stores without adequate storage space to keep the necessary stocks. Pest and disease control depends on timely accessibility to technical know-how and correct agrochemicals, and the availability of a sprayer in working order. Farmers are sometimes not sufficiently appreciative of the importance of timely application of fertiliser and agrochemicals, so that the benefits from application are reduced. Although the extension services have been successful in getting the new technology across to the farmers, it is doubtful if they are geared to upgrade the quality of management to the level required. Not only are socio-economic factors of vital importance for adequate benefits, but ecological conditions also play a vital role, e.g. the availability of water at the critical times, good facilities for drainage, absence of rain at particular times, freedom from floods (especially damaging to dwarf varieties), adequate light intensity and suitable soil conditions.

Adequate information is not available for a precise assessment of the extent to which sub-optimality affects the efficiency of the new plant types, but it is clear that, while ecological conditions may adversely affect all varieties of paddy, their effect on the more efficient plant types is worse, and that the conditions required to attain high potential yields are available to only a few farmers in some areas. Hence adoption by itself, or even an appreciation of the complexity of the new technology, may not provide the farmer with the expected results. The results obtained by the majority of farmers, therefore, fall far short of the potential, and well within the less complex and less demanding technologies available to them.

This implies that most farmers employed a technology which required a higher level of inputs when they could have obtained similar results with an alternative technology and lower level of inputs. From a national point of view this represents the employment of additional resources from which little or no benefit is gained. Table 6.8 shows that, while the production in Maha 1973–4 was only 6·3 per cent more than in Maha 1969–70, the yield per acre was actually lower. The increase in production may be attributed to the expansion in the area cultivated, which increased by 10·6 per cent. In the latter year, however, 42 per cent more fertiliser was used, the area under HYVs had increased by 20 per cent and the area under new HYVs had increased by 11·39 per cent. In other words there had been a big investment in the new high-yielding technology. The extra fertiliser alone was valued at Rs11·4m. (at the average cost of fertiliser imports in 1973): this represented scarce foreign exchange. Resources were also utilised to get the new HYVs to the farmers. To the extent that the new HYVs require more agrochemicals, more resources would have been utilised over the larger area cultivated with them. What returns were obtained from the employment of these additional resources? Probably little or none, because the production of Maha 1973−4 might have been possible with the technology employed in Maha 1969−70. Although the level of adoption achieved in the area we studied is a very creditable achievement if we consider the new technology inherently desirable, to the extent that resources have been employed which are yielding little or no return the process of adoption has gone beyond the level justifiable on economic grounds. In that sense, the situation in Sri Lanka is one of *over-adoption*.

There is another aspect also. The new technology, being more exacting in terms of ecological and socio-economic conditions, is more vulnerable to unfavourable conditions under the circumstances prevailing in most areas of Sri Lanka. From that point of view also, adoption has proceeded beyond justifiable limits.

Although there is an overall situation of over-adoption, it is clear that some farmers and some areas are capable of getting adequate benefits from the new technology. Adoption should, then, be seen, not as a process which is good in itself but as a result-oriented strategy for development. Seed varieties, fertilisers, agrochemicals and other components of the agricultural package should be considered for combined use in varying 'mixes'. They may be arranged along a continuum ranging from a fairly low input − low output simple technology, to a high input − high output complex technology. Thus:

low productivity − − − − − − − − *high productivity*

Traditional improved seed *plus* low fertiliser and agrochemical inputs *plus* moderate labour input *plus* low level of management	Early high-yielding seed *plus* moderate fertiliser and agrochemical inputs *plus* high labour input *plus* moderate level of management	New high-yielding seed *plus* moderate fertiliser and agrochemical inputs *plus* moderate level of management	New high-yielding seed *plus* high fertiliser and agrochemical inputs *plus* high labour input *plus* high level of management
40 or less bu./acre	40−60 bu./acre	60−80 bu./acre	Over 80 bu./acre

The problem is, then, one of selecting the appropriate technology or package to suit the prevailing conditions. The emphasis must change from adoption to adaptation, from mere diffusion of the new technology to *selective adoption*. That some farmers are capable of benefiting from the new technology is clear from Table 6.8. The increase in the overall production in Sri Lanka is probably due more to the large increase in productivity achieved by some farmers and in some areas, rather than to an overall uniform increase in productivity. In our study area we found that the higher levels of productivity were achieved only over a restricted extent of the cultivated area (Table 6.11).

Table 6.11   Study area classified according to paddy yields

Yield class (bu. per acre)	Yala 1973			Maha 1973–4		
	Acres	Percentage	Cumulative percentage	Acres	Percentage	Cumulative percentage
Over 80	9·0	5·91	5·91	52·75	10·13	10·13
71–80	11·75	7·71	13·62	54·5	10·47	20·60
61–70	23·75	15·59	29·21	103·3	19·84	40·44
51–60	31·5	20·67	49·88	102·0	19·59	60·03
41–50	18·25	11·98	61·86	92·5	17·76	77·79
40 or less	58·12	38·14	100·00	115·65	22·21	100·00
Total	152·37	100·00		520·73	100·00	

Only 14 per cent of the area in Yala and 21 per cent in Maha had produced yields that could be considered to have justified the adoption of the new technology. These areas were not uniformly distributed in our study area. As Table 6.10 indicated, the yield varied from 31·8 bu. per acre in Tenagama to 66·2 in Tissamaharama, which, with Ambalantota, Wellawaya and Kataragama, had the highest yields. This variation in yields is also reflected in the frequency of cultivators obtaining varying yields in the different cultivation committee areas studied by us (Fig. 6.4).

THE APPLICATION OF SELECTIVE ADOPTION: INTER-REGIONAL VARIATION

In implementing a strategy of selective adoption it is not possible to base it on the differences between individual farmers. A more realistic and practicable approach bases it on regional differences in the potential to benefit from varying levels of technology. It is thus necessary to identify the characteristics of regions or areas with a high productivity potential. The Department of Agriculture and the Land Utilisation Division (of the Ministry of Irrigation, Power and Highways) have already gone some way

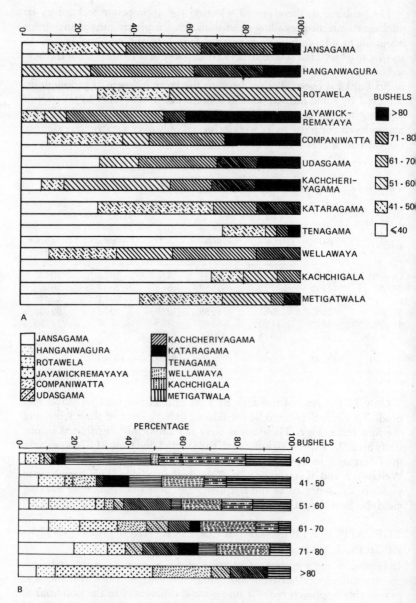

FIG. 6.4 A. *Distribution of cultivators in each cultivation committee area classified according to yield, Maha 1973–4*

B. *Distribution of cultivators according to cultivation committees obtaining a particular yield, Maha 1973–4*

along these lines, but our evidence indicates that it is necessary to refine the methods used to identify such areas, and to make them more comprehensive and rigorous. It is not sufficient, for instance, to base strategy simply on a criterion such as the type of irrigation. Nor is it sufficient to base it only on agro-ecological conditions, although these play a major role in determining the potential productivity of an area. It is more important to consider the totality of an area, paying attention to all the factors with significant impact on productivity. The availability of labour and draught-power, the efficiency of institutions and extension services are among factors that should be taken into account.

The inter-regional variations in our study area emphasise the importance of such an approach. Although the survey area was selected on the basis of general homogeneity, closer study has revealed important variations (Fig. 6.5). Each cultivation committee area is distinct in some way, but variations on that scale do not appear to play a significant role in determining either the extent to which the new agricultural technology has been adopted, or the returns from it. It is possible to group the twelve cultivation committees into four categories from this standpoint: these are representative of conditions typical of larger areas to be found in the intermediate and dry zones. They are:

1   Ambalantota–Tissa type: this includes Jansagama, Hanganwagura and Rotawela in the Ambalantota area, and Jayawickremayaya, Kachcheriyagama, Udasgama, and Companiwatta in the Tissa area;
2   Kachchigala–Tenagama type;
3   Wellawaya–Metigatwala type; and
4   Kataragama type.

The Ambalantota–Tissa area is outstanding: it has switched over almost completely to the new technology, and the cultivators are achieving better results than in other areas. Rotawela is the exception, probably due to less favourable soil conditions (Table 6.12). The low yield there depresses the average for the Ambalantota area. Excluding it, the average is almost the same as in the Tissa area (65·6 bu. per acre). The major characteristics that set these two areas apart are their more assured supply of water (particularly in Maha), larger holdings, tenant cultivators who operate under a somewhat exploitative gambāra system (Dias and Wickremanayake, 1974), compactness and easy accessibility. Located on the main coastal road in very close proximity to the service centres at Ambalantota and Tissamaharama, they are in the mainstream of life, including development activity. Although they are no different from the other areas in respect of the literacy and age characteristics of their population, they form the pioneer fringe for this part of the country, being areas of fairly recent settlement. The gambāra system and the service centres are manifestations of local entrepreneurship. In contrast to the other areas, paddy cultivation forms the mainstay of the economy and, because of the large holdings, cultivation is commercialised.

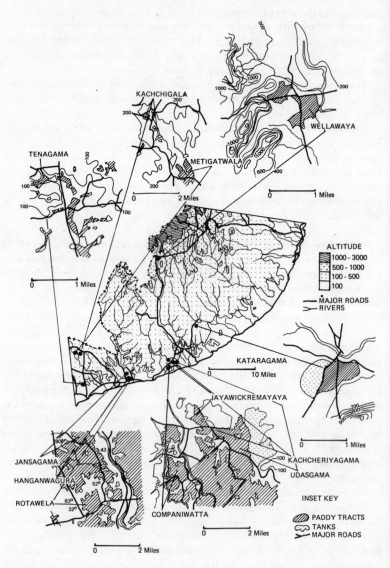

FIG. 6.5 *Sri Lanka: the study area showing location and nature of sample areas*

*Table 6.12   Average yield of paddy in the Ambalantota—Tissa area in Maha
1973—4*

Cultivation committee	Ambalantota area (bu. per acre)	Cultivation committee	Tissa area (bu. per acre)
Jansagama	63·7	Jayawickremayaya	74·4
Hanganwagura	65·9	Kachcheriyagama	63·8
Rotawela	45·7	Udasgama	65·4
		Companiwatta	62·4
Area average	58·5		66·2

The new HYVs had not spread to such a great extent in Tenagama and Kachchigala, and the proportion of farmers still cultivating traditional varieties – though relatively small – was higher here than in other areas. Most of the farmers, however, cultivated HYVs and, in Tenagama, most of them applied fertiliser. But only about half the cultivators in Kachchigala applied fertiliser. Despite this fairly high level of adoption, the yields were lowest in these areas (Table 6.10) suggesting an inability to benefit adequately from the new technology. This is not surprising when we consider the conditions. A poor and uncertain supply of water is almost an endemic problem: although the areas are in the intermediate zone the rainfall is variable and poorly distributed. Cultivation is dependent on numerous pocket-size tanks which cannot provide an assured water supply. Crop damage is caused both by inadequacy of water and by untimely rain. Problems of soil salinity and poor drainage also affect cultivation to some extent. These areas suffer from socio-economic disadvantages also. There is difficulty of access, especially in Kachchigala. Cultivation is carried on very largely by owner-cultivators on holdings smaller than 2·0 acres and is mainly for domestic consumption; the prevalence of joint ownership such as thattumäru and kattimäru adds to local problems – both are due to the long period of settlement and the limited availability of land suitable for paddy cultivation, given the prevailing topography. Because of the smallness of the holdings, income from paddy has to be supplemented from high-land cultivation or other employment, and paddy cultivation tends to be a part-time occupation. Poor transport facilities, bad roads and the absence of any dynamic service centres also add to the cultivators' problems.

Metigatwala and Wellawaya are intermediate between the Ambalantota—Tissa and Tenagama—Kachchigala types. Here, too, the holdings are relatively small, though bigger than in the latter area. Much more of the paddy land, however, takes the form of large tracts, and the supply of water is more assured. Both areas are better serviced by roads. The paddy tract at Wellawaya is adjacent to the main roads which radiate from Wellawaya, a fairly active service centre. Tenancy is common, but some of the cultivators own their land. There are no serious ecological constraints apart from the inadequacy of the water in Wellawaya and part of Metigatwala. The basic infrastructure is available to permit these areas to benefit from the new technology, but it needs to be upgraded.

Kataragama is a high-risk area as it depends on a tank that rarely gets enough water. Even when it fills, the water it stores is not sufficient for the Maha season unless supplemented by timely showers during the latter half of the season. There is no cultivation in Yala as there is no water. The soil and topographic conditions are satisfactory, and in seasons when adequate water is available – as in Maha 1973–4 – farmers obtain a good yield (Table 6.10) even though the new technology has not spread very widely; fewer farmers cultivated new HYVs and applied fertiliser compared to the other areas. Even those farmers who applied fertiliser used generally less than in other areas.

Comparison of the different areas shows that they vary considerably in their productivity potential. Ambalantota–Tissa is a low-risk, high-potential area while Kataragama is a high-risk, high-potential area. Tenagama and Kachchigala are high-risk, low-potential areas. Wellawaya and Metigatwala are of moderate risk and medium potential, and without incurring heavy investment can be upgraded to reduce the risk and increase the productivity potential. Even more important, however, than the variation in the nature and extent of adoption in the different areas is the variation in the results obtained from the new technology. Where conditions place constraints on productivity, the level of technology adopted should be adapted to the productivity potential of the particular area and so optimise the use of resources. To employ a very high-input technology in an area where the yields obtainable by using it are the same as those from a technology using a lower level of inputs is wasteful of resources that could be employed more productively elsewhere. From the individual point of view, the returns to the farmer would be reduced by using such an inappropriate technology. On the other hand it would be equally inappropriate and wasteful to employ a low-input technology in an area with a high productivity potential. The selection of an appropriate level of technology and the allocation of resources to take account of regional variations in productivity potential is particularly important in an economy where governmental activities impinge on the play of economic forces in various ways, e.g. through subsidies, guaranteed prices, credit policies, marketing restrictions, institutional support, irrigation facilities and extension services.

Another aspect of this problem is the possibility of changing the productivity potential of an area. For example, the availability of an assured water supply is a vital factor in determining productivity potential. This is a condition that is subject to modification; investment in improving the supply would, therefore, increase the ability of an area usefully to employ a higher level of technology. Resources that are now employed wastefully on inappropriate technology could thus be used more profitably to increase the productivity potential of areas with a lower present potential. The areas where the productivity potential could be increased at a lower cost should receive higher priority.

The strategy for increasing paddy production should, therefore, be based on appropriate technology and selective adoption. A primary need for this is a classification of the land used for paddy cultivation on the basis of its productivity potential and the investment required for increasing that potential. This is an area in which much work remains to be done. Some of the land now cultivated under paddy may eventually prove to be unsuitable and could be diverted to other crops.

APPROPRIATE TECHNOLOGY, SELECTIVE ADOPTION AND THE FUTURE

This has important policy implications in terms of the need to produce approximately 129m. bu. of paddy in 1983. It was stated earlier that, if the rate of increase in the area of asweddumised land continued at the same rate as in the period 1961–4 to 1970–73, it would amount to 1,684,656 acres in 1983. The author considers that this figure represents the maximum likely to be brought under cultivation. It is more reasonable to expect that the area would be some 1,586,568 acres. This estimate is based on the following assumptions (it is not proposed here to discuss their validity):

1 The area under major irrigation would increase from 454,805 acres in 1972 to 554,805 acres in 1983, due mainly to the extension of irrigation under the Mahaweli diversion and Uda Walawe schemes.
2 The area under minor irrigation would increase from 411,835 acres (1972) to 450,000 acres in 1983.
3 The area under rain-fed conditions would remain constant at the 1972 level of 581,763 acres.

It is further assumed that the areas that would be cultivated in Maha 1982–3 and Yala 1983 are as in Table 6.13.

On these assumptions, an average yield of approximately 68 bu. per acre would be required to achieve the target production of 129m. bu. of paddy. This yield represents an increase of 43 per cent on the 1973–4 yield and of 31 per cent on the highest yield recorded up to now (52·2 bu. per acre in 1970). In considering the strategy to achieve this production target it is obvious that, while it is necessary to increase the overall yield, the possible increase will vary considerably in different areas depending on the yield potential. The strategy that should be followed must not only adjust the agricultural technology to the existing productivity potential of the particular areas, but upgrade this potential to achieve the desired level of

Table 6.13   Estimated areas that would be cultivated under paddy in 1982–3, according to source of water

Source of water	Asweddumised area (acres)	Maha 1982–3		Yala 1983	
		Acres	Percentage*	Acres	Percentage*
Major irrigation	554,805	471,583	85	194,182	35
Minor irrigation	450,000	360,900	80	157,500	35
Rain-fed	581,763	488,681	84	221,070	38
Total	1,586,568	1,320,266	83	572,752	36

*Expressed as a percentage of asweddumised area.

productivity. Combinations of various levels of productivity could provide us with the required level of production.

It is not possible here to discuss the numerous alternative combinations possible or to attempt an optimal solution in the absence of both time and data. For the purposes of illustrating the issues involved, Table 6.14 presents one such combination. On the basis of these figures 422,486 acres in Maha and 103,095 acres in Yala must have a yield exceeding 80 bu. per acre, which requires a high level of technology to be used on areas of high productivity potential. As a proportion of the total area to be cultivated, this is equal to 32 per cent in Maha and 18 per cent in Yala. We do not have comparative figures for the Island as a whole, but we may use our survey figure of 10 per cent in Maha and 6 per cent in Yala. The implication is that the area over which high productivity should be achieved must increase at least threefold. The areas most suited to such high productivity are those that, like our Ambalantota–Tissa type, fall under major irrigation schemes in the dry zone. But conditions under major irrigation must be upgraded considerably to achieve this level of productivity. Of the anticipated irrigable area under major irrigation in 1973, some 76 per cent in Maha and 19 per cent in Yala must be brought up to this level to achieve the target. These areas must be identified and developed progressively during the next few years.

In 46 per cent (567,714 acres) of the area to be cultivated in Maha 1982–3 and 38 per cent (217,646 acres) in Yala 1983, the productivity should be 60–80 bu. per acre, with an average of 70 in Maha and 69 in Yala. In the study area the corresponding figures were 30 per cent in Maha and 23 per cent in Yala, indicating the necessity to increase the extent of land capable of this level of productivity by 50–60 per cent. Most of the remaining land under major irrigation, a fair proportion of the land under minor irrigation, and some of the rain-fed land should be brought to this level of productivity. This could perhaps be made up as follows:

Maha

85 per cent of remaining area cultivated under major irrigation	41,734	acres
80 per cent of area cultivated under minor irrigation	288,000	
49 per cent of area cultivated under rainfed conditions	239,454	
Total	569,188	

Yala

65 per cent of the remaining area cultivated under major irrigation	51,207	acres
55 per cent of the area cultivated under minor irrigation	86,625	
36 per cent of the area cultivated under rainfed conditions	79,814	
Total	217,646	

It will be necessary to use the new technology to achieve this level of productivity, but this could be suitably modified to suit the environmental conditions as well as to make the returns adequate. A very high level of inputs either of fertiliser or labour may not be required, but good water, weed and pest/disease control would be necessary. Supply of water would have to be improved greatly over much of the area under minor irrigation and rain-fed conditions. This would require supplemental irrigation perhaps from sub-surface water resources (Madduma Bandara, 1974 and pp. 9–10 above), or further development of facilities for minor irrigation. In some areas, improvement of drainage facilities may be required. Here again, the major task would be to identify the relevant areas and the nature of development required to increase their productivity potential to the desired level. Some of the areas in our Ambalantota–Tissa type and much of the Wellawaya–Metigatwala type come within this category as do some areas of the wet zone.

The categories considered above form the area that should receive top priority; 85 per cent of the production in Maha and 70 per cent in Yala is expected to be obtained from the land in those categories.

Achievement of self-sufficiency by 1983 calls for a reduction in the area of cultivated land where the yield is less than 40 bu. per acre; 22 per cent of the cultivated land in our study area in Maha and 38 per cent in Yala were in this category. At present costs of production, and given the scarcity of land, neither the country nor the farmers can tolerate such a low level of productivity. By 1983 this would be even more so. It is, however, unrealistic to think that it would be possible to eliminate that category altogether, as large areas under minor irrigation and rain-fed conditions have very low levels of productivity. The Tenagama–Kachchigala and Kataragama types in our study area fall into this category, as do the badly drained areas in the south-west lowlands and some other areas with poor or

Table 6.14   Desired levels of productivity to achieve the production target for 1983

Area (acres)	Percentage of total area	Yield (bu. per acre)	Production (bu.)	Area (acres)	Percentage of total area	Yield	Production
92,419	7·0	105	9,703,955	22,910	4·0	105	2,405,558
118,824	9·0	95	11,288,274	34,365	6·0	95	3,264,686
211,243	16·0	85	17,955,618	45,820	8·0	85	3,894,714
303,661	23·0	75	22,744,589	85,913	15·0	75	6,443,460
264,053	20·0	65	17,163,458	131,733	23·0	65	8,562,642
118,824	9·0	55	6,535,317	108,823	19·0	55	5,985,258
79,216	6·0	45	3,564,718	51,548	9·0	45	2,319,646
132,026	10·0	30	3,960,768	91,640	16·0	30	2,749,210
1,320,266	100·0	$x=70·4$	92,946,697	572,752	100·0	$x=62·2$	35,625,174

toxic soils. It is, however, necessary to reduce the area falling within this category. Table 6.14 envisages that this category would constitute only 10 per cent of the cultivated area in Maha and 16 per cent in Yala by 1983. A fairly low level of agricultural technology would be suitable for paddy land in this category. These lands should receive a very low priority when it comes to the allocation of resources.

Some of the land now in this category could be upgraded to produce 40–60 bu. per acre; 40 per cent of the cultivated extent in our study area came within this category in Maha and 34 per cent in Yala. Upgrading the level of productivity of the less productive areas would increase the proportion of land in this category. The proportion of this land, however, should be much less by 1983: 15 per cent in Maha and 28 per cent in Yala. Areas under minor irrigation and rain-fed conditions, and even some land under major irrigation, belong here. Much of this land would have to be developed through improvements in irrigation facilities, supplemental irrigation by tapping sub-surface water, and improving drainage facilities to raise its productivity potential. This yield could be obtained with early HYVs at moderate levels of fertiliser input. A high level of labour input for weed control and transplanting would increase the yields further. Consideration should also be given to socio-economic factors such as size of holding, the type of land tenure and the availability of labour in identifying these areas.

CONCLUSION

In summary, a case is made out for selective adoption, adjusting the level of technology to the varying productivity potential of different areas. There is undoubtedly a need for adopting the yield-increasing components of the new technology. The results obtained from this technology, however, have fallen short of the expectations that were entertained at the time it was introduced. It is the author's contention that the efficiency of any technology is influenced strongly by the ecological and socio-economic setting in which it is employed. This calls for the identification of

1   Regional differentiation in productivity potentials.
2   The appropriate level of technology for the particular potential productivity.
3   Factors which inhibit the potential in the lower productivity areas.
4   Methods of eliminating such constraints and upgrading the productivity potential.

Some work has already been done on these lines. Much more remains to be done, however. The focus of research should be on problems of this nature rather than on the process of diffusion. Concentration on diffusing the new technology without due regard to such problems leads to misdirection and a waste of resources. The early increases achieved through the new technology, which gave much hope and encouragement, might have been due to the utilisation of a potential that had hitherto been underutilised with the low productivity technology that then prevailed. A sudden burst of productivity would be quite natural under such circumstances, and the remarkable increase in yields in the past decade or so might have resulted from it. The spread of the technology appears now to have gone beyond the slack in the potential that had existed. We may have reached the limits of our capacity to utilise the new technology, and unless the limits themselves are widened, no further benefits can be expected from its spread. In fact, any spread beyond those limits would not only lead to a waste of resources but would make our agriculture more vulnerable to periodic fluctuations of a high magnitude. It is necessary to avoid this position and to utilise resources more productively. We must, therefore, approach the problem of agricultural development from two directions. One is the application of the appropriate technology for a given set of conditions. The other is the progressive upgrading of the potential of less productive areas to allow them to employ higher-yielding technologies more profitably. Such a policy is not without its own difficulties. There would be problems of implementation, problems both of an administrative and political nature. There would also be social problems resulting from regional inequalities that could be increased by such a policy. Consideration of these problems lie outside the scope of this chapter, but solutions to them must be sought if agricultural development is not to be an end in itself but the means to achieve more general development.

REFERENCES

Ahmed, I. (1973). *Use and benefits of the High Yielding Varieties of Rice Seeds in Bangladesh*, paper read at Seminar on The Social and Economic

Consequences of the Improved Seeds, Kandy; Seminar organised by the Institute of Development Studies (at the University of Sussex) and Agrarian Research and Training Institute (of Sri Lanka).

ARTI (1974). *The Agrarian Situation Relating to Paddy Production in Five Selected Districts of Sri Lanka, part I – Hambantota*, Agrarian Research and Training Institute Research Study Series no. 6, Colombo.

Brown, Lester R. (1970). *Seeds of Change* New York, Praeger.

Census and Statistics Department (1973). Statistical Pocket Book of the Republic of Sri Lanka 1973, Colombo.

Census and Statistics Department (1974). *The Population of Sri Lanka*, Colombo.

Dias, H. D. and Wickremanayake, B. W. E. (1974). *The Gambāraya System in the Hambantota District*, paper read at Conference on Agriculture in the Economic Development of Sri Lanka, Ceylon Studies Seminar, University of Sri Lanka, Peradeniya.

Gunawardena, K. A., Silva, W. P. T. and Dias, H. D. (n.d.) *Modernization of Peasant Agriculture in Ceylon*, Report no. 2, Department of Geography, University of Ceylon, Colombo.

Krishnamurti, S. (1972). *Agricultural Development of India*, V. Shanmuga Sundaram (ed.), University of Madras.

Madduma Bandara, C. M. (1974). *The Case for Recycling Sub-surface Water for Paddy Cultivation in the Dry Zone*, Ceylon Studies Seminar, 1974, Series no. 5, Serial no. 49, University of Sri Lanka, Peradeniya.

Ministry of Planning and Employment (1971). *The Five Year Plan 1972–1976*, Colombo.

Nagarajah, S. (1973). 'Selection of Fertilizer for Improved Rice Varieties' paper read at Seminar on Social and Economic Consequences of the Improved Seeds, Kandy.

Peiris, J. W. C. (1973). 'Recent Advances in the Development of High Yielding Rice Varieties', paper read at the Seminar on Social and Economic Consequences of the Improved Seeds, Kandy.

Selvaratnam, S. and Jones, G. W. (1972). *Population Growth and Economic Development in Ceylon*, Colombo, Hansa.

Silva, W. P. T. (1974). 'Rice in the Economy of Sri Lanka', paper read at Seminar on the Project on Agrarian Change in Rice Growing Areas of Tamil Nadu and Sri Lanka, Cambridge.

Swaminathan, M. S. (1973). 'Our Agricultural Future', Sardar Patel Memorial Lectures, 1973, at India International Centre, New Delhi.

Weeraratne, H. (1973). 'Rice: Biological and Environmental Features that Impinge on the Yield Potential', paper read at the Seminar on Social and Economic Consequences of the Improved Seeds, Kandy.

Weerawardena, I. K. and Collonnege, I. (1974). *A Short History of Credit for Peasant Agriculture in Sri Lanka*, Ministry of Agriculture and Lands, Colombo.

7 Chena–Paddy Interrelationships

W. P. T. Silva

Chena cultivation is the local name for the system of shifting agriculture which is generally practised on the unirrigable land of the dry zone of Sri Lanka (see Glossary; B. H. Farmer, 1954; E. F. L. Abeyratne, 1956). As seen in Hambantota District it constitutes the clearing and burning of the forest cover over a selected area of land, cultivating for one or two years in the Maha season with a variety of crops, and abandoning the clearing for five to eight years before using it again.

Chena cultivation is carried on by paddy cultivators as well as others, and for the former the chenas have always provided a useful subsidiary source of production and income. This income has increased substantially over the past few years because of the steady increase in the guaranteed price for several crops, the high open-market prices for most chena crops, and the efforts made by the government to encourage the cultivation of new cash crops on chenas. Crops such as chillies, pumpkins and even kurakkan, which were earlier grown largely for subsistence, are now grown on a commercial basis with new crops such as soya beans and cowpea; in consequence, the chena has become a very significant part of the farming enterprise. Many farmers in fact believe that chena cultivation, if successful, would provide them with a bigger income than paddy.

The paddy cultivator engaged in chena cultivation has to divide his labour, that of his family, and his cash resources between the two systems. The question which arises, therefore, is whether such a division has any adverse effects on paddy cultivation. In the past this was thought to be so. It is relevant to reconsider the matter at the present time, not only because of the changes that have taken place within the chena system over the past few years but because paddy cultivation has been subject to technological change and become more intensive with the introduction of HYVs and the increasing use of inorganic fertiliser, weedicides and pesticides. This

chapter therefore examines the interaction between the two systems of
cultivation, placing special emphasis on the way in which paddy
cultivators behave in relation to their chenas, and on any consequent
effects of chena cultivation on paddy cultivation, especially (in the context
of this book) those likely to affect the adoption of technological change in
the paddy fields.

DATA

The data for this analysis has come from a section of the sample farmers
selected for the broader study of agrarian change in the Hambantota
District. Of the ten cultivation committees from which the sample was
drawn, seven obtain water from major irrigation works while the
remaining three are dependent largely on minor works. Of the farmers in
the seven major irrigation areas, twenty-one in Udasgama, Kachcheriyagama, Jayawickremayaya and Companiwatta reported chena cultivation in the 1973—4 season. In Companiwatta, where eleven farmers had
reported chena cultivation, the Maha operations had started much earlier
than in other areas. Since a pre-Maha pattern of cultivation is not common
in the Hambantota District, it was decided to eliminate Companiwatta
and focus attention on the ten farmers in the other three areas. These were
interviewed at regular intervals from December 1973 to August 1974, and
the following analysis is heavily dependent on the data supplied by them.
As the study progressed, it appeared that the interrelationships between
the two systems might be different in the areas dependent on minor
irrigation works, because the agricultural holdings in such areas were
smaller and paddy cultivation less prosperous: given the limited amount of
time available it was decided to extend enquiries to one only of the minor
irrigation areas, that at Kachchigala. Information was obtained from the
twenty-three farmers reporting chena cultivation there.

THE CHENA AND PADDY CYCLES: COMPETITION OR COMPLEMENTARITY?

The paddy cultivator engaged in chena has to make a number of decisions,
the most important of which relates to the way in which he is to divide his
time between the two systems. The chena cycle usually lasts for about ten
months; and the different operations have to be carefully organised if the
possibility of a clash with paddy operations is to be minimal. The cycle
starts in early May with the selection of a plot, after which the farmer may
return to his paddy-holding, depending on whether or not Yala cultivation
is going to take place. If Yala cultivation does take place the preliminary
operations – including sowing or planting – are completed by mid-June,
and when the crop is a few weeks old the farmer returns to the chena to
commence removal of the forest cover. This operation takes from five to
fifteen days, depending on the size of the holding and the labour employed.
Once it is completed there is a slack period lasting two to three weeks which

enables him to attend to various operations on his paddy field, such as the application of fertiliser, pesticides and weedicides. Burning of the vegetation begins in mid-August and is followed by clearing and fencing. All three operations take *in toto* from one to two weeks, depending once again on the size of holding and labour force. When the clearing is over and the land prepared (about the end of August or the beginning of September), there is little work on the chena until planting, usually in late September or October, the precise timing depending on the arrival of the rains. In early September the paddy is ready for harvesting, and the second slack period gives the farmer enough time to complete his harvesting and threshing. The Maha paddy operations do not normally start until late October and, since the chena planting operations are completed by then, all that remains to be done until harvest time is weeding and protection. Competition can, however, in theory arise because of the steady demand for labour for weeding and protection. Weed growth is one of the major problems the farmer has to face and most of the chenas are weeded at least three times during the season, by members of the family as well as hired labourers. As in the preliminary operations, a very small proportion of farmers relied exclusively on hired labour. Since the first weeding takes place in November, a few weeks after planting, and is followed by a second weeding in December, there is always the possibility that either one or both weedings could clash with the Maha paddy operations, especially if the latter are delayed. The farmers admitted this possibility, but indicated that they would react either by postponing the weeding or, if this did not seem possible, by using hired labour. Either solution ensures that paddy does not suffer. Since subsequent weedings take place after the paddy planting operations and when the demand for labour from paddy is low, competition can in practice be ruled out.

Unlike weeding, protection is a continuous process which usually starts in mid-December when the plants are beginning to bear. By this time the paddy planting operations are over, but a chance delay could give rise to a competition for labour. Even if such a clash were to occur, paddy cultivation would not be seriously affected, partly because of the small amount of labour needed, partly because of the arrangements made between members of the family. If the chena is located close to the house, the most common arrangement is for one or two members of the family – very often the wife and one or two children – to look after the chena during the day and for the cultivator to take over in the night. If, on the other hand, the chena is located several miles away the farmer sends an adult male member of the household to live there, not only to protect the crops but to attend to other things such as weeding. Whatever the arrangement, there appears to be a neat division of labour among the members of the family, which ensures that the chena will be guarded without necessarily disrupting paddy operations.

The Location of Chenas

The farmers also try to reduce the possibility of a clash by locating their chenas in fairly close proximity to their houses. In the areas studied no virgin forest remains and, consequently, farmers have had no alternative but to rely on forest which is less than ten years old and referred to locally as 'landu'. Virgin forest, because of its greater fertility and the reduced weed growth, is obviously better suited for chena cultivation, but the farmers are reluctant to clear such forest, mainly because of its distant location. They prefer to clear landu forest nearer home in order to ensure that they can attend to work on both holdings without necessarily neglecting either of them.

The Concentration on Paddy

Under exceptional circumstances, such as a family illness, bereavement or wedding, or the inability to obtain tractors for Yala paddy cultivation on time, or lack of cash for preliminary operations, there could be a delay in either chena or paddy operations, and the ensuing clash would force the farmer to decide on one or the other. The evidence shows that farmers invariably decide to concentrate on the paddy and either to postpone chena operations or, if the necessary cash is available, to employ more labour on their chena.

The decision to concentrate on paddy rather than the chena is based on a number of considerations. The first and perhaps the most important is that most of the cultivators in the study areas do not own the paddy land they operate. Tenant farmers feel that they have certain responsibilities towards their landlords, especially when the latter provide the basic inputs. There is always the possibility that by paying greater attention to the chena the tenant farmer could cause the paddy to suffer. If this were to happen they would not only fail the owner, but might imperil their future tenancy. Secondly, as members of the yaya, they have to follow the schedule set by fellow cultivators. If they fell behind they would face three problems: (i) inability to take tractors into fields especially if they are centrally located, (ii) inadequate water for all the necessary operations, and (iii) considerable damage from birds which would find newly sown fields very attractive. Thirdly, paddy is considered a much less risky proposition since it depends mostly on irrigation water and, being less risky, could in the long run provide a larger and more stable income than the chena. The question of risk demands attention in rather more detail.

Risk in Chena Cultivation

The susceptibility of chena cultivation to the vagaries of rainfall makes it difficult for farmers to give it preference over paddy. If the rainfall is good the chena becomes a very productive enterprise, but if the rains do not arrive on time the farmer stands to lose most of what he has invested. Unfortunately the variability of rainfall is such that the farmers cannot predict whether the next season is going to be a good one (Farmer, 1956). Thus, according to most farmers, the 1972–3 season was a good one, whereas the 1973–4 season was poor because excessive rains at the start of the season were followed by a prolonged drought.

Farmers also run the risk of crop damage by wild animals. They attempt to minimise this risk through continuous protection and by planting closest to their watch huts those crops which are most susceptible to attacks from wild animals. But if the watcher is not alert or leaves the chena unprotected, particularly at night, considerable losses may be incurred.

Attitudes to Chena: Other Factors

Besides the risks involved, three other factors could help to explain the paddy cultivators' attitudes towards chena. First, the nature of the chena operations which are extensive when compared to preliminary paddy operations (though, unlike a paddy field, a chena is always cultivated by hand). Paddy operations, involving levelling, flooding and water control, have to be performed carefully and punctually and, although the labour may be hired, the operations are nevertheless carried out under the watchful eye of the operator, whose decisions are based on years of personal experience. Chena operations, on the other hand, do not require such careful supervision and therefore the cultivator is in a position to rely exclusively on hired labour if necessary, provided he has some trustworthy individual, preferably a member of the family to keep an eye on the labourers. Even if such an individual were not available, the location of the chena close to the residence always enables him to make a few quick trips to it while the paddy operations are in progress. Secondly, many farmers are of the opinion that, since the chena belongs to them, they can arrive at any decision without prejudicing others. If they wished they could postpone chena operations and could bear any resultant crop losses, without being answerable to anyone. Thirdly, many farmers seem to attach a recreational value to their chena. This does not mean that they discount the monetary benefits of chena cultivation and the hard work that goes into it; they certainly treat the chena as an economic enterprise, but at the same time point out that the best way to spend their slack periods from paddy is to 'go into the jungle and plant a few crops'.

It is evident therefore that chena cultivation does not compete for the farmer's labour because chena operations are invariably undertaken during the slack seasons in the paddy field and, in the event of an unexpected clash in operations, paddy cultivation is given priority. Chena, on the other hand, is considered a gamble and experience has convinced the farmers that there is no point in working out the probability of success.

Transfer of Funds from Paddy to Chena

Some farmers reported the use of hired labour, fertiliser and pesticides in their chenas, and it is therefore necessary to consider whether the expenditure on such inputs leads to a transfer of funds from paddy to chena. These inputs are no doubt costly, but it does seem unlikely that their use would lead to such a transfer, partly because of the farmer's desire to finish off his paddy operations first and also because he seldom maintains separate quanta of cash for paddy or chena, or for that matter, domestic consumption. Whatever cash is available is utilised for the current operation. If it is inadequate to complete the operation or to start on the next one, whether in chena or paddy, the farmer borrows.

Of the inputs mentioned above, hired labour is undoubtedly the most costly. The quantity of hired labour used depends on the size of the holding and the proportion of family labour employed, and the expenditure would under normal circumstances fall within the farmer's anticipated costs, which are usually met either from savings or by borrowing. However, if any operation has been delayed, necessitating its completion within a short period of time, or if the supply of family labour has been reduced, the farmer has to employ extra labour leading to an unexpected increase in labour costs. A few farmers did report unexpected increases but such exigencies were met, not by transferring what was reserved for paddy, but by borrowing from friends and relatives or through short-term loans.

Unlike hired labour, fertiliser and pesticides are not common inputs in chena cultivation. Few farmers reported their use and then only for specific crops such as chillies and pumpkins. For this reason, and because the quantities applied are usually small, expenditure on them is relatively low.

CONCLUSION

The evidence fails to confirm the view that in the study areas chena cultivation is detrimental to paddy cultivation, or to innovation in that cultivation. The strategy adopted by the paddy cultivator has enabled him to divide his resources between the two systems in a satisfactory manner; even if occasional clashes do occur, the solutions adopted ensure that the ill-effects on paddy cultivation are always minimised. Indeed it is possible to argue that chena cultivation, rather than being competitive, is complementary.

Chena cultivation is a risky enterprise, but its high income potential tempts farmers to invest some of their time and money in clearing a few acres of land in the hope that the next season will be a good one. Indeed, money earned by chena cultivation may supply funds for innovation in paddy cultivation. It is possible that, with the increasing number of non-paddy cultivators entering the chena scene, there could be a pressure on the forest land which would eventually force the farmers to incur extra expenditure on inputs such as fertiliser and weedicides. As John Harriss points out (see below, p. 145) there is already a trend in some areas and supported by regular use of fertiliser, towards semi-permanent cultivation of land typically used for chena cultivation. However, until this trend becomes more general, the farmers' interest in shifting cultivation will be reinforced by the mounting costs of paddy production and the increasing cost of living. The only way in which chena cultivation can be made to disappear is by the provision of water for permanent cultivation, or by a massive increase in the paddy acreage. Since neither is likely to happen in the foreseeable future and since chena cultivation as now practised appears to be ecologically well adapted to local environmental conditions, it is bound to remain a dominant form of agriculture on the unirrigable slopes in the Hambantota District. It does not, of course, follow that precisely the same conclusions can be drawn for other parts of the dry zone of Sri Lanka.

REFERENCES

Abeyratne, E. F. L. (1956). 'Dry Land Farming in Ceylon', *Trop. Agriculturist*, 112, 191–229.

Farmer, B. H. (1954). 'Problems of Land Use in the Dry Zone of Ceylon', *Geogr. J.*, 120–33.

Farmer, B. H. (1956). 'Rainfall and Water-Supply in the Dry Zone of Ceylon' in R. W. Steel, and C. A. Fisher (eds), *Geographical Essays on British Tropical Lands*, London, Philip.

8 Adoption of the New Technology in North Arcot District

B. Nanjamma Chinnappa

The technological innovations in paddy cultivation dating from the late 1960s in India are generally taken to include the use of HYVs, inputs of chemical fertilisers, improved cultural practices and the mechanisation of agricultural operations. Reports from agricultural research stations claim that an optimum package of these inputs leads to substantial increases in rice yields. More recently, following the oil crisis and subsequent fertiliser shortage, it has been claimed that an increase in the area sown with HYV seed, with low or even zero fertiliser inputs, would lead to increases in rice yields. Given the urgent need to increase rice production in India it is essential that the performance of this technology and the constraints on its spread be studied – not only in regions with assured water supply and high, stable yields (these contribute about 31 per cent to the area and 37 per cent to the production of foodgrains in India and include the much studied IADP Districts, see pp. 30–2), but in the more common and less studied regions which depend mainly on rainfall, are subject to periodic droughts, and produce medium and less stable yields (contributing 42 per cent to both the area and production of foodgrains); and again, in the rest of the cropped areas with low rainfall and unstable, low yields (classification of regions in these three categories as by Sen, 1967). Rice is confined mainly to the first two categories of region. The survey area in North Arcot District belongs to the second category.

SOME BASIC INFORMATION ON THE DISTRICT

According to official statistics, North Arcot contributes about 10 per cent to the total area and production of rice in Tamil Nadu. It ranks fifth in area, fourth in production and ninth in yield rate of rice among the thirteen Districts of the State (1972–3). Rice is grown on about 39 per cent of the total cropped area and groundnut on about 32 per cent of it. Rice is the staple cereal of the District and is consumed by all classes of people. Ragi, the other staple foodgrain, is consumed mainly by the poorer classes.

The mean annual rainfall is 850–1000 mm per annum, the major portion of which falls during the north-east monsoon (see above, pp. 10–12). North Arcot ranks seventh among the Districts of the State in quantum of rainfall and is nearest to the average rainfall for the State (946 mm). With 45 per cent of its net sown area irrigated, North Arcot ranks fourth in Tamil Nadu, by proportion of area irrigated. Tanks, wells and canals account respectively for 51, 42 and 7 per cent of the net area irrigated in the District. Wells supplement the irrigational sources in an additional 15 per cent of the net area irrigated. North Arcot has the largest number of wells and the highest density of wells: one well for every 2·4 hectares of net area sown as compared to one well for every 5·1 hectares in Tamil Nadu as a whole (1969–70). The District's intensity of cultivation (ratio of gross area sown to net area sown) is 1·26 (Director of Statistics, Tamil Nadu, 1969–70). The geographical characteristics of the District are as discussed in chapter 2.

North Arcot is a District of small farmers, the average holding being 1·43 hectares (1961 Census). It has the largest proportion of small cultivators among the Districts of Tamil Nadu (except for Kanyakumari), 52 per cent possessing less than 1 hectare, 80 per cent, less than 2 hectares and 91 per cent, less than 3 hectares each.

According to the sample survey (see pp. 37–47), 50 per cent of households in this area are mainly cultivators and 35 per cent are mainly agricultural labourers, so that 85 per cent of households depend on agriculture as a principal means of livelihood. Among cultivator households (cultivating some land), 85 per cent cultivate paddy. Of these, 20 per cent grow paddy only (the majority are small cultivators possessing less than 1 hectare each) and 80 per cent grow both paddy and groundnut.

THE OFFICIAL VIEW ON HYV ADOPTION AND COMPARISON WITH SURVEY ESTIMATES

Official statistics express the adoption of HYV paddy in terms of the proportion of paddy area under HYVs (Table 8.1). Since 1970–71 Tamil Nadu generally, and in particular the taluks and community development (CD) blocks covered by the survey have high official rates of adoption of HYV paddy, although there is considerable variation between taluks and CD blocks.

HYVs are varieties officially designated under the high-yielding varieties programme: those encountered in the survey area were IR.8, IR.20, IR.22, Jaya, Karuna, Krishna, IET.1991 and Bhavani (C-4) (compare above, p. 13). IVs are locally improved varieties developed in Tamil Nadu's agricultural research stations earlier than the HYVs. Varieties encountered in the survey were ADT.27 and Co.29. (The column 'HYV+IV' is included in the table because until recently IVs

Table 8.1 Percentage area under HYV and IV of paddy

Year	All India	Tamil Nadu		North Arcot District		In the six taluks covered by the survey		In the CD blocks within which the sample villages are situated
	HYV	HYV	HYV+IV	HYV	HYV+IV	HYV	HYV+IV	HYV+IV
(1)	(2)	(3)	(4)	(5)	(6)	(7)	(8)	(9)
1966–7	2·5		7·1		1·7	n.a.	n.a.	n.a.
1967–8	4·9	0·2	18·2	0·2	7·4	n.a.	n.a.	n.a.
1968–9	7·1	2·2	26·8	2·5	21·3	n.a.	n.a.	n.a.
1969–70	11·6	14·9	42·4	31·7	46·5	n.a.	n.a.	n.a.
1970–71	14·9	33·2	67·7	56·5	81·0	n.a.	70·0	73·0 (54·3–89·1 between CD blocks)
1971–2	19·3	47·9	84·1	59·4	89·6	n.a.	n.a.	n.a.
1972–3	24·0	55·1	82·5	n.a.	n.a.	39–48 (between taluks)	59–73 (between taluks)	n.a.
1973–4	n.a.	59·4	79·3	n.a.	n.a.	n.a.	n.a.	n.a.

Sources: Column 2 – papers read at the Symposium on the Green Revolution at the Indian Society of Agricultural Statistics, March 1972; *Indian Agriculture in Brief*, 1973.

Columns 3 and 4 – data from the office of the Director of Agriculture, Madras; *Tamil Nadu, An Economic Appraisal* (1974); *Season and Crop Reports*, Tamil Nadu. Columns 5–9 – data from the office of the Director of Agriculture, Madras, and from the District Agriculture Office, Vellore.

Table 8.2 Adoption of HYVs and IVs in the survey area, by season

Year	Sornavari				Samba				Navarai				All seasons			
	Paddy area (%)		Paddy cultivators (%)		Paddy area (%)		Paddy cultivators (%)		Paddy area (%)		Paddy cultivators (%)		Paddy area (%)		Paddy cultivators (%)	
	HYV	HYV+IV	HYV	HYV+IV	HYV	HYV+IV	HYV	HYV+IV	HYV	HYV+IV	HYV	HYV+IV	HYV	HYV+IV	HYV	HYV+IV
1972–3	13	23	12	22	4	4	5	5	26	35	30	41	13	18	29	39
1973–4	11	15	9	14	8	8	10	10	16	25	14	27	10	13	17	26

Source: Figures for 1972–3 are based on the farm survey data for 545 paddy cultivators collected in phase 1 from the 50 per cent sample of cultivators. Those for 1973–4 are based on the farm resurvey data collected towards the end of phase 2 from the same cultivators.

were grouped with HYVs in the official statistics for Tamil Nadu.)

Table 8.2 shows the percentages of paddy areas under HYVs and IVs in the survey area and the percentages of paddy cultivators adopting these varieties, by season, for 1972−3 and 1973−4 as estimated from the sample survey.

The proportion of the paddy land in the survey area under HYVs in 1972−3 (all seasons combined) is 13 per cent according to the survey estimates, which is much lower than the official taluk estimates for the area: Arkonam, 44 per cent; Tiruvannamalai, 39 per cent; Polur, 44 per cent; Cheyyar, 42 per cent; Wandiwash, 41 per cent and Arni, 48 per cent. Thus the overall official estimate for the proportion of paddy area under HYVs in the survey area is never less than 39 per cent and this appears to exaggerate the proportion, by a factor of 3 at the least.

The survey figures may tend to over-estimate the actual proportion of area under HYV paddy in the study area because the sampling frame excluded forest villages, uninhabited or very small villages, and very large villages, while the farm survey excluded very small cultivators with less than a quarter-acre of land; such villages and cultivators are the ones that are most likely to be poor adopters of HYVs.

On the other hand the survey estimates could be underestimates because of under-reporting of areas by the bigger cultivators in the farm survey. However, major distortions are unlikely because of the checks and corrections made. The survey estimates were further supported by the even lower adoption rates of 9 per cent for HYV and 12 per cent for HYV and IV areas for 1973−4 from the detailed study of cultivators in phase 2 of the survey; these estimates were based on repeated visits and on an effective sample size of 146 paddy cultivators. Also, even HYV adopters had devoted only 26 per cent of their paddy area to HYVs and this proportion decreased with increase in holding size (see Tables 8.10 and 8.11). While it seems improbable that there was any reluctance of farmers to declare areas under HYVs, it seems likely that at least during the first part of the year informants might have inflated their figures since, at that time, cards for the issue of fertilisers at controlled rates were given only to farmers cultivating HYVs.

Although there was considerable variation in the adoption rates between villages, the standard error of the estimate of proportion of area under HYV varieties was very low at 0·0018, and the coefficient of variation was 1·32 per cent so that the 99 per cent confidence interval for that estimate was (12·87 per cent, 13·93 per cent). This supports the reliability of the survey estimates. (This estimate of the standard error was an approximation obtained by assuming the sample to be a two-stage simple random sample and is expected to be higher than the actual standard error for the sample design adopted.)

Enquiries into the methods of compilation of the official figures revealed that area figures for HYVs are obtained from the village-level workers

(VLWs, or Grama Sevaks), each of whom reports on the HYV targets achieved for the six to ten villages under his jurisdiction. The high ratio of cultivators to VLWs and the heavy burden of the VLW's duties make it impossible for him to meet the cultivators individually to promote adoption of HYVs and collect data regarding it (see chapter 11). The VLW's reports are, therefore, often based on the quantity of seed distributed by official sources, the average seed rate per acre, and a factor to account for 'natural spread', i.e. from seed used from the farmer's own stocks or other non-government sources. The obvious biases in this method are due to faulty estimation of 'actual' area sown per kilogram of seed and of the factor of natural spread, and the possible tendency to over-estimate by officials anxious to report achievements of HYV target areas. Attempts to obtain data on the areas reported by the VLWs for the surveyed villages were fruitless. The VLW's records, where available, were not properly maintained.

The difference between the official and survey estimates of the rates of adoption of HYVs appears therefore to be explained mainly by the exaggerated reporting of the HYV area by the VLWs, who are expected to promote their cultivation and are judged by their reports on the targets achieved.

Now (and using simplified arithmetic), Sornavari and Navarai together only account for 25 per cent of the paddy area in Tamil Nadu State. Even if 100 per cent of the paddy area in those two seasons was under HYVs, to justify the official claim that 60 per cent of the total area for all three seasons is under HYVs would require 50 per cent of the Samba area to be under HYVs. That this achievement is not yet in sight is clear from many studies, including this one, which report low adoption rates in Samba. Using similar simplified arithmetic, Thanjavur District covers 25 per cent of the paddy area in Tamil Nadu; even if 100 per cent of its paddy area is under HYVs, 50 per cent of the paddy area in the other Districts must be under HYVs if the State percentage area under HYVs is to be 60 per cent, as required by the official statistics.

Having established that the HYV adoption rates in the survey area are low, the main task of this chapter is to investigate the causes for these low adoption rates and to discover whether non-adoption is rational. Some clues may emerge from the history of adoption, the popularity of the various paddy varieties grown, and the variation in adoption rates between years, seasons and villages. A comparative study of the yield rates and profitability of HYVs and traditional paddy varieties will indicate whether the farmer has an incentive to adopt HYVs. If HYVs indeed give higher yields than the traditional varieties and if they are more profitable, we will need to investigate the constraints on their adoption.

HISTORY OF ADOPTION OF HYVS AND IVS
Tamil Nadu has had a history of adoption for improved paddy varieties

that dates back at least to the early years of this century (compare p. 13). The first agricultural research station in Tamil Nadu was set up (at Saidapet, Madras) in 1863, and about 90 improved rice varieties have been developed since then. Many of the popular varieties that are referred to as 'traditional varieties' (TVs) in this chapter are themselves improved local varieties bred in the research stations of Tamil Nadu. For example, Kichili Samba is GEB.24 (introduced in 1924); Ottu Kichili is TKM.6 (introduced in 1963); Kullankar is ADT.23; Sirumani is Co.19 (introduced in the 1950s). Such IVs in fact account for more than 80 per cent of the area under traditional varieties. (Note: GEB=Government Economic Botanist, ADT=Aduthurai, Co=Coimbatore.)

The history of adoption of HYVs among sample cultivators is presented in Fig. 8.1. Evidently in the early years of adoption few of the adopters continued to grow HYVs in successive years. The proportion of 'de-adopters' seems to have decreased over the years. In 1972–3 almost all the adopters of 1971–2 appear to have continued to adopt, but in 1973–4 there was a sudden fall in adopters because of the poor rains.

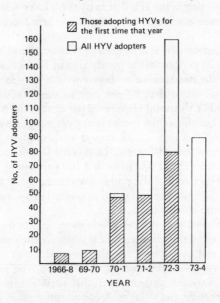

Fig. 8.1 *North Arcot: number of HYV adopters and number who adopted HYVs for the first time by year of adoption*
Note: Data on those adopting for the first time in 1973–4 are not available.

PADDY VARIETIES CULTIVATED AND VARIATION BETWEEN YEARS AND SEASONS

On comparing 1972–3 and 1973–4, it can be seen that the proportion of area under HYV paddy and of HYV adopters has fallen from 13 per cent to 10 per cent and from 29 per cent to 17 per cent respectively (Table 8.2). This is attributable to the steep fall in production during Navarai, the main season for HYV cultivation: the severe drought and to some extent the fertiliser shortage in Navarai 1974 appear to be the main reasons. The total paddy area itself dropped in Navarai 1974 to about half that of Navarai 1973, whereas the corresponding Sornavari and Samba areas had increased by 50 per cent and 10 per cent respectively over the two years. The fall in the HYV paddy area in Navarai 1974 reduced it to 30 per cent of that of Navarai 1973, in contrast to the increase in Sornavari and Samba HYV paddy areas by 25 per cent and 46 per cent respectively over the two years.

Although Samba is the main paddy season in Tamil Nadu and in the survey area, the highest rates of adoption of HYVs (see Table 8.2), and the largest HYV areas (see Table 8.3), are in Navarai. Non-availability of suitable HYVs that can be grown in Samba is one cause of the low overall HYV adoption rates. Abundant sunshine, favourable temperatures, low humidity and the greater possibility of controlling the water supply makes the dry season favourable to HYVs. Samba also has the disadvantage of a higher likelihood of pest attacks, and although it is the wet season, erratic rains make good water management difficult. There is also the problem that the IR varieties do not grow well in the seru soils which are more often met with in Samba (see p. 133). The higher price of paddy in the dry season could also be an incentive for growing it then, since a larger proportion of HYV paddy is sold as compared to other varieties (see, however, pp. 139–41).

Table 8.3   *Percentage of paddy area cultivated in the different seasons of 1972–3 and 1973–4, by paddy variety*

Paddy variety	Year	Sornavari	Samba	Navarai	All seasons
HYV	1972–3	15	12	73	100
	1973–4	26	43	31	100
Other varieties	1972–3	15	53	32	100
	1973–4	23	58	19	100
All varieties	1972–3	15	47	38	100
	1973–4	24	56	20	100

The popularity of the different varieties is shown in Table 8.4. Among the 32 non-HYV paddy varieties grown in the area, data on variety are presented only for the IVs ADT.27 and Co.29 and for the more widely grown TVs Kullankar, Kichili Samba and Sirumani. Kichili Samba or Arcot Kichili was the most popular variety in Samba and in all the seasons taken together. Its popularity was due mainly to its fine quality and the high price it fetched in the market. It is a long-duration variety (120 to 166 days among sample cultivators), suited to the wet Samba season when paddy takes longer to mature because of the cloudy monsoon days. A short-duration crop in Samba would risk the possibility of rain during harvest.

Kullankar, a short-duration variety (87 to 116 days among sample cultivators) was by far the most popular variety in the dry season of Sornavari and Navarai. The short duration of Kullankar is ideal for the dry season when water supply is limited. The survey data showed that none of the HYVs, although called 'short-duration' varieties, could compare with Kullankar in this respect. (Among sample cultivators the durations were IR.8, 105 to 152 days; IR.20, 109 to 150 days; C.4, 125 to 144 days). Similar experience in Randam is discussed in chapter 9. There is, therefore, a need for a long-duration HYV adapted to the wet Samba conditions, which can compete with Kichili Samba in the market, and for a water-economic short-duration HYV for the dry seasons, to compete with Kullankar.

Among HYVs IR.8 appeared to be losing ground to the more popular IR.20, the areas under these varieties being 43 per cent and 52 per cent respectively of HYV areas in 1972–3, and 18 per cent and 75 per cent of HYV areas in 1973–4. IR.20 has a fine-quality grain with good cooking qualities and fetches a better price than IR.8. It is less susceptible to pest attack and appears to be gaining favour in Samba. Official statistics for Tamil Nadu confirm the rising popularity of IR.20 over IR.8.

INTER-VILLAGE VARIATION IN ADOPTION OF HYV PADDY

Table 8.5 shows the variation in HYV adoption rates between the sample villages.

In 1972–3 Vegamangalam had the highest rates of adoption for HYV paddy area (27 per cent), followed by Randam (25 per cent), Dusi (18 per cent), and Amudur (17 per cent). In 1973–4 the picture was changed with Randam (26·5 per cent) having the highest rates, followed by Duli (19 per cent) and Vengodu (16 per cent). The higher rates of adoption in 1972–3 were mostly in those villages with assured water supply – Vegamangalam fed by a canal (Kasam) from the Palar river, Dusi fed by a major irrigation tank (Mamandur), Randam because of the preponderance of wells fitted with electric pump-sets, Amudur with a fairly equitable water-sharing system from the tanks, and Vinayagapuram with assured water supply from the Cheyyar river.

The sudden fall in the adoption rates in Vegamangalam between the two years stemmed from the joint decision of the cultivators owning the shared 'pangu' land (50 per cent of the wet land in the village fed by the

Table 8.4 Percentage of cultivators and of area of different paddy varieties

Variety	Sornavari				Samba				Navarai				In all seasons, gross area	
	Area		Cultivators		Area		Cultivators		Area		Cultivators			
	1972–3	1973–4	1972–3	1973–4	1972–3	1973–4	1972–3	1973–4	1972–3	1973–4	1972–3	1973–4	1972–3	1973–4
HYVs: IR.8	6	4	7	3	1	8	2	9	11	5	14	4	6	2
IR.20	5	6	4	5	2		3		13	10	16	8	7	8
All HYVs	13	11	12	9	4	8	5	9	26	16	31	14	13	10
Others														
ADT.27	2	1	4	2		<1		<1	1	1	1	1	<1	<1
Co.29	8	3	6	3		<1		<1	9	8	11	12	4	2
Kullankar	54	73	67	69	1		2		21	24	33	29	17	21
Kichili Samba	2	2	2		46	60	64	67	1	<1		<1	23	34
Sirumani					14	19	17	23	<1		<1		7	10
All non-HYVs	77	85	84	88	96	92	99	96	65	75	78	79	82	87
All varieties	100	100	100	100	100	100	100	100	100	100	100	100	100	100

Percentages of cultivators amount to more than 100 per cent because many grow more than one crop variety.

Table 8.5   Adoption of HYVs and IVs in the sample villages

Village	Year	No. of paddy cultivators	Percentage paddy area		Percentage paddy cultivators	
			HYV	HYV+IV	HYV	HYV+IV
Vegamangalam	1972–3	61	29·0	29·6	62·3	62·3
	1973–4	50	4·5	4·5	8·0	8·0
Sirungathur	1972–3	36	9·3	10·3	27·8	27·8
	1973–4	28	11·1	11·1	10·7	10·7
Duli	1972–3	33	7·3	8·5	15·2	18·2
	1973–4	33	18·8	19·7	24·2	27·3
Dusi	1972–3	138	17·6	21·7	46·4	50·0
	1973–4	91	7·1	8·1	12·1	14·3
Vengodu	1972–3	65	5·3	7·1	16·9	20·0
	1973–4	68	15·6	15·6	17·6	17·6
Vinayagapuram	1972–3	53	15·0	18·2	50·9	56·6
	1973–4	39	13·2	22·2	33·3	46·2
Amudur	1972–3	61	17·4	18·0	34·4	34·4
	1973–4	42	2·4	2·4	2·4	2·4
Randam	1972–3	55	25·0	30·6	38·2	47·3
	1973–4	52	26·5	29·0	55·8	59·6
Kalpattu	1972–3	69	2·0	18·1	2·9	39·1
	1973–4	102	1·3	10·7	2·0	32·4
Veerasambanur	1972–3	34	7·3	8·6	23·5	29·4
	1973–4	34	8·1	9·6	26·5	32·4
Meppathurai	1972–3	39	15·1	25·0	25·6	38·5
	1973–4	38	7·0	9·4	10·5	15·8
Vayalur	1972–3	39	11·8	25·9	20·5	46·2
	1973–4	24	11·2	12·6	16·6	24·3
All villages,	1972–3	545	13·4	18·5	29·5	39·3
excl. Dusi	1973–4	510	10·3	13·0	17·5	26·1

Source: As for Table 8.2.

canal) to cultivate HYVs on such land in 1972–3 and traditional varieties in 1973–4. This decision was apparently reached because of the quality of the soil, the poor drainage and lack of good water control (there were no pump-sets at all on pangu land), and the fear that, on the narrow plots of land, effective use of fertilisers would be difficult, fertiliser tending to wash away on to a neighbour's plot.

The low adoption rate in Kalpattu is explained by the fact that, although it has good water supply (all from wells), banana cultivation on a commercial scale is profitable and widely practised. The paddy grown is mainly for home consumption.

COMPARISON OF PERFORMANCE OF HYVS AND OTHER PADDY VARIETIES

Yield rates per hactare

The data in Table 8.6 on the average yield rates of HYVs and other paddy varieties in 1973—4 are based on the cultivator survey in phase 2 (146 paddy cultivators). Although the yield rates of the HYVs were about 45 per cent higher than those of the TVs in any season, they were nowhere near the yield rates quoted by research stations (of the order of 6000 kg or more of paddy per hectare), thus indicating that the research experience has not been replicated under actual farm conditions in this area. (Compare also yield rates of paddy: All India (1971—2), 1145 kg per hectare; Japan (1971), 5250 kg per hectare; Tamil Nadu (1971—2), 2010 kg per hectare — *Indian Agriculture in Brief*, 1973.)

Table 8.6   Average yield of paddy in kg per hectare 1973—4

Paddy varieties	Sornavari	Samba	Navarai	All seasons
HYVs	4,089	3,347	3,729	3,555
Others	2,877	2,292	2,597	2,459
All	2,931	2,525	2,939	2,676

Cultivators reported out-turn in bags of 75 kg of paddy each. A factor of 2/3 should be used to convert these figures to yields of milled rice.

The highest HYV yields obtained by any cultivator were 5655 kg of paddy per hectare in Sornavari, 5450 kg in Samba and 5859 kg in Navarai — all of IR.20. The variation in the yield rates between cultivators is examined in detail later in this chapter. The yield rates in the drier seasons (Sornavari and Navarai) were usually higher than those for Samba.

HYVs had higher average yield rates than other paddy varieties in all the sample villages, in all of the seasons (except in Kalpattu for the reasons given above). The highest average yield rates of paddy (HYVs and of all varieties) were in the villages which had an assured water supply: Vegamangalam, Vinayagapuram and Randam (ranked in order). The lowest average yield rates were in Vayalur which was the worst hit by the drought in 1973—4, where none of the twelve sample cultivators selected in phase 2 had cultivated in Sornavari. In Samba, although all the cultivators raised nurseries for traditional varieties, five had to abandon the cultivation and let cattle graze on the nurseries because of lack of water to continue with the cultivation. In Navarai only one among them cultivated paddy. The only other case of 'failed' paddy crops among the sample cultivators was reported by a cultivator growing Kullankar in Navarai in Randam village.

Risk in Growing HYVs: Variation in yield rates as compared to traditional varieties

A simple index of the risk in growing any variety of paddy is provided by the variation between yield rates obtained by individual farmers growing that variety, which for comparison between varieties is best measured by the coefficient of variation of the yield rates $\left(\dfrac{\sigma_x}{x} \times 100 \right)$. The higher the coefficient of variation of yield rates of any variety, the more 'risk-prone' its cultivation is likely to be.

Table 8.7 gives the means and coefficients of variation of yield rates per cultivator for some important varieties of traditional paddy and for IR.20, in one season or for all seasons combined (varieties cultivated by a sizeable sample).

Table 8.7　Variation in paddy yield rates between cultivators, 1973–4

	Paddy variety	Season	Sample size (n)	Mean yield rate (x̄) in kg hectare	Coefficient of variation of yield rate
TV	Kullankar	All seasons	72	2,571	35·0
	Kullankar	Sornavari	48	1,854	32·1
	Kichili Samba	Samba	95	2,346	31·7
	Sirumani	Samba	35	2,236	29·0
	Sitrai Kulli	All seasons	19	3,234	27·2
IV	Co.29	All seasons	14	2,875	16·9
HYV	IR.20	All seasons	20	3,462	36·1
	IR.20	Samba	12	3,119	36·8

The variation in yield rates of IR.20 appears to be only slightly higher than that of any of the TVs compared, indicating that from the standpoint of stability in yield rates it is not much more risk-prone than any of the latter. Note that the yield rates vary considerably between cultivators for all the varieties because of variation in the quality of the land, size of holding, the investment of inputs (including water, labour and management) and because of varying incidences of pest attacks.

The small sample sizes of HYV growers within villages does not permit a study of the stability of HYV yields between cultivators within each village.

Profitability

Table 8.8 shows the income per hectare, cost of cultivation per hectare and profitability in growing HYVs and other paddy varieties. The income was

Table 8.8   Profitability of cultivating HYVs and other paddy varieties (in rupees)

Item	Paddy varieties	Sornavari	Samba	Navarai	All seasons
Income per hectare	HYV	3,265	3,080	3,875	3,381
	other	2,124	2,028	2,485	2,122
Cost of cultivation per hectare	HYV	1,482	1,035	1,475	1,233
	other	1,220	771	1,030	902
Profitability index; returns per rupee spent (in rupees)	HYV	2·20	2·98	2·63	2·74
	other	1·74	2·63	2·41	2·35
Net income per hectare	HYV	1,783	2,045	2,400	2,148
	other	904	1,257	1,455	1,220
Increase in net income per hectare from HYVs (%)		97	63	65	76

estimated as the post-harvest farm-gate price of the grain produced. The value of by-products such as straw and husk were excluded. The cost of cultivation was estimated as the total paid-out costs for all inputs used – seed, manure, fertilisers, pesticides and seed treatment, hired labour (both human and animal) – and seasonal costs of electricity, water hire, fodder and maintenance of implements. The imputed value of own or family labour (human and animal), depreciation on farm implements, interest paid on farm loans and rents paid by tenants for leased-in land have not been considered. The index of profitability is measured as the ratio of the income from cultivation to the cost of cultivation (i.e. the returns per rupee spent), and is therefore a rough measure. However, it does give some idea of the comparative profitability of different varieties.

The returns from HYVs and the increased net income that a cultivator may earn from them, compared with TVs, remain substantial in every season despite the fact that the recommended doses of inputs in the optimum combinations are not being used (because of lack of water, fertilisers and cash) and despite the yields being much lower than potential (again, possibly because of insufficient inputs). The moot point, then, is whether the increased cost of cultivation of HYVs (of the order of 40 per cent) can be afforded by the smaller cultivators and whether the required credit for investing in these crops are easily available to them at reasonable interest rates. This is studied later in the chapter.

In comparing the profitability index between HYVs and other paddy varieties it should be noted that although, for reasons discussed above, both the numerators (values of output) and denominators (values of input) in these indices might be underestimated, the 'true' indices for HYVs are likely to be even higher than is apparent from Table 8.8. HYV adopters are usually bigger cultivators who can afford to sell more of their crop, and also to wait and sell at a time when prices are high. Hence the numerator of this index is likely to be underestimated for HYV adopters to a greater extent than for growers of traditional varieties. Also the contribution of family labour to the total labour input is lower for HYV cultivation (30 per cent), as compared to 36 per cent for cultivation of other paddy varieties, and this results in the denominator being underestimated to a lesser extent for HYV cultivators than for growers of TVs.

Marketing of Paddy and Prices of Different Varieties

Table 8.9 shows the proportion of growers who sell paddy, the proportion of paddy sold and the percentage sold by individual cultivators, by variety of paddy and season.

It is clear that in each season paddy is sold by a larger proportion of HYV growers than growers of other varieties and that a much larger percentage of the HYV paddy out-turn is sold, compared with other varieties. HYVs are apparently grown mainly for marketing. But we were told that most cultivators have now taken to consuming HYV varieties, especially IR.20; this was not earlier the case. The lower percentages sold in Navarai are explained partly by the fact that the survey ended soon after Navarai, and the complete sales percentages for the season's paddy were not available.

Figure 8.2 shows the price of different varieties of paddy during the survey period, in terms of prices prevailing in the village for the varieties available during those months. The dotted lines indicate periods for which no prices were available. In general the fine variety of rice for which Arcot is famous – Kichili Samba (GEB.24) – was quoted at much higher rates than the other, coarser traditional varieties and the HYVs – the prices of which were all within the same range in any month. But towards the latter half of the survey period, when prices of all varieties rose considerably, the rise was much steeper for the coarser varieties, including the HYVs; towards the end of the survey they were much closer to the price of Kichili Samba. It is possible that the lower prices for HYVs were a disincentive to cultivators and that the price rises consequent to the shortage of foodgrains – bringing them almost on par with the costlier varieties – would prompt more cultivators to grow HYVs in the year 1974–5. The constraints, of course, would be mainly availability of water and fertilisers.

Evidence from the survey has thus shown that in the study area the HYVs are more suited to the dry seasons, have higher yields per hectare, are possibly both as stable and more profitable than other paddy varieties, even though their prices do not compare with those of the favoured traditional varieties. These factors in favour of HYVs are particularly pronounced in villages which have an assured water supply the year-

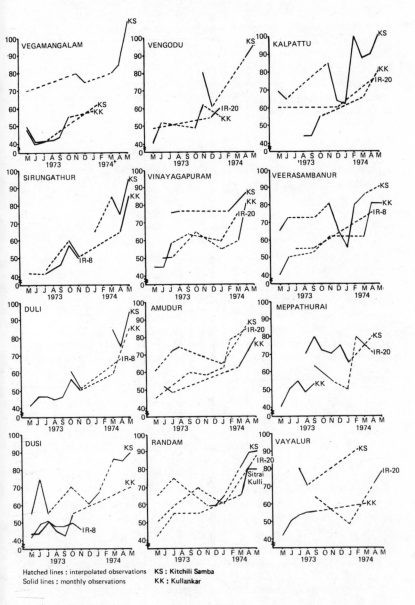

Fig. 8.2 *North Arcot: prices in rupees of different varieties of paddy in sample villages, 1973–4*

Table 8.9 Marketing of paddy, 1973–4

| Paddy variety | Sornavari | | | Samba | | | Navarai | | |
	Percentage selling	Proportion sold (%)	Range %	Percentage selling	Proportion sold (%)	Range (%)	Percentage selling	Proportion sold (%)	Range (%)
HYV	100	61	37–92	100	76	31–93	60	49	30–81
Other	45	31	22–85	55	34	11–91	28	16	17–91

round. Yet the proportions of cultivators adopting these varieties and of the areas under them, even in the better-endowed villages, are very low. Are the cultivators irrational in failing to adopt these new seeds or are there constraints that explain this lack of interest? The rest of this chapter is a study of individual farmers and the likely factors that influence their adoption of HYVs.

The evidence is in contrast to that from the survey area in Sri Lanka, where the picture is one of relatively low yields of HYVs and excessively high rates of adoption (see pp. 65–9).

Table 8.10   Percentage of HYV adopters and of HYV area, by operational holding size-classes, 1972–3

	Operational holding size-class in hectares						
	(≤0·4)	(>0·4, ≤1)	(>1, ≤2)	(>2, ≤3)	(>3, ≤4)	(>4)	Total
Percentage of HYV adopters	15	19	33	51	61	67	29
Percentage paddy area under HYVs	10	10	12	13	14	23	13
Percentage distribution of cultivators in these classes	21	29	33	8	4	4	100

ADOPTION OF HYVS AND FARMER CHARACTERISTICS

Operational Holding Size

The findings of many studies that adoption of HYVs is higher among cultivators with larger holdings is borne out by this study – as is evident from Table 8.10. The average size of the operational holding for HYV adopters was about 2 hectares as compared to 1 hectare for cultivators of other paddy. The percentage of HYV adopters increased from 15 per cent among those cultivating less than 0·4 hectare (1 acre) to 67 per cent among those cultivating more than 4 hectares and the proportion of area under HYV paddy increased from 10 to 23 per cent in the same classes. A study of these percentages, by village, showed a higher adoption by smaller cultivators possessing 1 hectare or less in those villages where water supply is reliable: Vegamangalam, Dusi, Vinayagapuram, Amudur and Randam, the percentages of adopters being 44, 26, 30, 24 and 10 per cent respectively. In the other villages the percentages were more or less negligible.

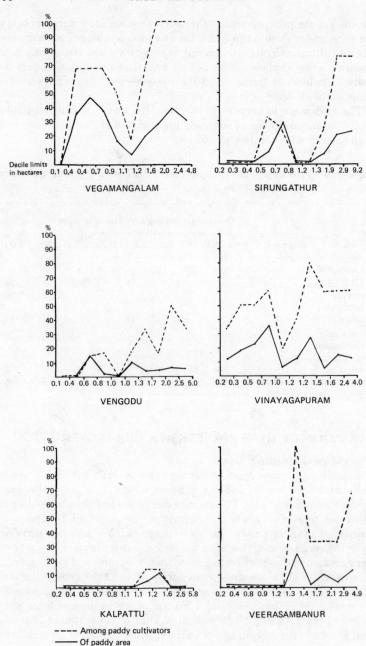

FIG. 8.3 *North Arcot: adoption of HYVs by deciles, 1972–3*

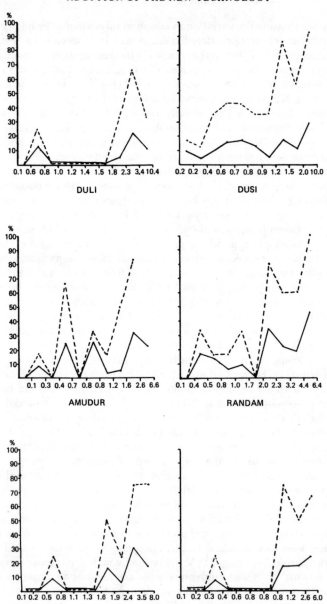

DULI

DUSI

AMUDUR

RANDAM

MEPPATHURAI

VAYALUR

In order to study the variation in adoption rates among the 83 per cent of cultivators whose operational holding size is 2 hectares or less, the cultivators in each village were arranged in increasing order of operational holding sizes and grouped as deciles. The proportion of area under HYV paddy for each of these deciles was calculated (Fig. 8.3). What is striking is the fact that, Kalpattu and Veerasambanur apart, one group of cultivators operating 2 hectares or less – usually around 0·4 to 1·0 hectares (1 to 2·5 acres) – with higher rates of adoption than those in the operation size-class immediately smaller or larger. (In Veerasambanur the zero adoption among those with less than 1 hectare and the steep increase after that was explained by the fact that only cultivators with more than 1 hectare had pump-sets. Among these, *all* those operating areas 1·2 to 1·4 hectares and all operating more than 3·6 hectares had pump-sets, whereas not all cultivators in the class operating 1·4 to 3·6 hectares had pump-sets. The relation between possession of pump-sets and adoption is discussed later. In Kalpattu adoption in all the groups was low, as explained earlier.)

The characteristics of this group of cultivators in comparison with the others was examined using the detailed data from the cultivator survey of phase 2; the results are presented in Table 8.11. Because of the small number of cultivators growing HYVs in each holding size-group the estimates may not be very precise, but the data confirm what was observed in Figure 8.3. The relative gains from cultivating HYV paddy, as compared to other paddy and measured by the increase in net income per hectare (income and costs as defined on pp. 104–5), appears to be highest for the 0·8 to 1·0 hectare group (which falls within the 0·4 to 1·0 hectare category identified as high adopters in Fig. 8.3); also, for the biggest farmers possessing more than 4 hectares. The first group achieved high yields for HYVs, as compared to the groups preceding it and following it, and hence earned high net income per hectare. They also spent more heavily on HYV cultivation – on a scale comparable to that of the largest cultivators. It is likely that this group of innovators are (i) small cultivators whose human and animal assets (family labour and own bullocks) are used most efficiently on the small holdings they possess as compared with those who have still smaller holdings and cannot afford to invest or risk HYV cultivation, or with those in the immediately higher size-class whose own labour and animals are insufficient to cultivate their holdings, who cannot afford to hire more labour or animals, and who therefore hesitate to adopt HYV cultivation which needs more intensive management; (ii) those cultivators who are anxious to improve their income by growing crops for the market, and hence are prepared to innovate whereas the smaller cultivators cannot do more than grow enough to subsist on, and those in the immediately higher size-class who do not have sufficient incentive to work harder to improve their earnings, and so perhaps turn to other easier to cultivate crops like groundnut to earn more cash (see p. 129).

Table 8.11 *Comparison of paddy cultivators in different operational holding size-classes, 1973–4*

Criterion	Operational holding size-groups in hectares							
	(≤0.4)	(>0·4, <0.8)	(≥0·8, ≤1)	(>1, ≤1.3)	(>1·3, ≤2)	(>2, ≤3)	(>3, ≤4)	(>4)
Percentage gross cultivated area under paddy	81	60	55	51	50	52	56	46
Percentage area irrigated	90	69	64	54	52	60	48	58
Percentage of cultivators possessing pump-sets	20	28	24	36	54	100	71	100
Intensity of cultivation (gross area cultivated per acre possessed)	1·36	1·32	1·17	1·34	1·26	1·30	1·39	1·14
Percentage paddy area under HYV among HYV adopters		100	43	22	27	48	26	20
Yield in kg per hectare — HYV paddy		2,224	3,632	2,984	3,540	2,808	3,614	4,203
Yield in kg per hectare — Other paddy	2,237	2,354	2,168	2,446	2,317	2,452	2,767	2,609
Income per hectare (Rs) — HYV paddy		1,546	3,282	2,613	3,107	2,427	3,325	4,313
Income per hectare (Rs) — Other paddy	1,838	1,954	1,867	2,250	1,934	2,060	2,366	2,260
Cultivation cost per hectare (Rs) — HYV paddy		946	1,292	956	1,319	773	1,262	1,277
Cultivation cost per hectare (Rs) — Other paddy	1,237	1,008	1,028	1,028	1,008	926	981	899
Returns per rupee spent (Rs) — HYV paddy		1·63	2·54	2·73	2·36	3·14	2·64	3·38
Returns per rupee spent (Rs) — Other paddy	1·49	1·94	1·82	2·19	1·92	2·22	2·41	2·51
Net income per hectare (Rs) — HYV paddy		600	1,990	1,657	1,788	1,654	2,063	3,036
Net income per hectare (Rs) — Other paddy	601	946	839	1,222	926	1,134	1,385	1,361
Percentage increase in net income per hectare from growing HYV paddy as compared to other paddy		−37	+137	+36	+93	+46	+49	+123
Sample size	20	25	22	24	26	13	7	9

Table 8.12   Agricultural credit availed of by paddy cultivators, by operational holding size-groups, (1973–4)

		Operational holding size-groups in hectares					
		(≤0.4)	(>0.4, ≤1)	(>1, ≤2)	(>2, ≤3)	(>3)	Total
Percentage of cultivators taking loans		20	55	46	46	56	47
Value of loan per hectare (Rs)	Among those taking loans	348	583	640	284	232	432
	Among all cultivators	62	333	296	124	126	215
Cultivation costs on all crops per hectare (Rs)		1,228	1,084	1,015	835	944	981
Percentage of cultivation costs met by loans	Among those taking loans	31	52	68	37	24	45
	Among all cultivators	5	31	29	15	13	22
Percentage contribution of co-operatives to total value of loans		21	10	28	45	62	32

Credit

Agricultural loans are utilised for all crops, and possibly for non-agricultural purposes also. Table 8.12 compares the credit taken up by paddy cultivators *vis-à-vis* their total costs of cultivation on all crops.

From Table 8.12, it can be seen that 47 per cent of cultivators take loans, in amount covering about 45 per cent of the cultivation costs of those taking them and 22 per cent of cultivation costs among all cultivators. About 32 per cent of the loans are from co-operatives. The inability of the cultivators in the smallest holding size-group (0·4 hectare or less) to avail themselves of credit to meet cultivation costs is evident from this table. The high costs per hectare incurred by these small cultivators arise because they grow mainly paddy (see Table 8.11), the average cost of cultivation of which is about 26 per cent higher than that of groundnut. Only 20 per cent of them take loans, representing a smaller amount per hectare as compared to the groups between 0·4 and 2·0 hectares and covering only 31 per cent of their cultivation costs (5 per cent if all cultivators in this group are included). Those with more than 2 hectares apparently invest cash from their own resources and use less credit. Whereas those cultivating more than 3 hectares receive 62 per cent of their credit from co-operatives, cultivators with 0·4 hectare or less obtain only 21 per cent of their loans from this source. The overall picture is therefore one of greater indebtedness among those possessing 0·4 to 2·0 hectares, and of insufficient credit available to the smallest cultivators even from the non-institutional sources such as moneylenders, traders, friends and relatives, on which they depend for the major part of their loans. HYV cultivators obtained 59 per cent of their credit from co-operatives whereas other paddy cultivators obtained only 25 per cent of their credit from this source. Non-availability of credit appears to be a constraint on adoption of HYVs, especially among smaller cultivators.

Age and Literacy

The age of the cultivator appeared to have no impact on adoption, the percentage of HYV adopters being respectively 13, 17, 16 and 14 per cent among paddy cultivators in the age groups 27 or less, 28–42, 43–57 and 55 and above.

On the other hand, literacy appeared to influence adoption, the percentage of adopters being 9 per cent among those with no education and 28 per cent among those with elementary or higher education. (64 per cent of the heads of all households were illiterate and 6 per cent could read and write but had no formal education. The proportion of literate workers in paddy-cultivating households was 36 per cent, which was higher than that in non-paddy-cultivator households (20 per cent) and in non-cultivator households (16 per cent).

Table 8.13   Percentage of HYV adopters, by tenure classes, 1972–3

Village	Only owners	Mainly owners	Mainly tenants	Only tenants
Vegamangalam	71	67	73	25
Dusi	39	50	50	58
Vengodu	17	21	0	0
Kalpattu	4	0	0	0
Meppathurai	31	0	33	0
Vayalur	22	0	100	0
All villages, excl. Dusi	31	13	46	14
Percentage distribution of cultivators in tenure classes				
All villages, excl. Dusi	83	7	4	5

Tenure

The majority of cultivators in the survey area (83 per cent) are owner-cultivators, 5 per cent are tenants (leasing-in all operated lands), 4 per cent are mainly tenants (cultivating smaller areas of own land than of leased-in land) and 7 per cent are mainly owners (cultivating greater areas of owned land than of leased-in land); thus 16 per cent of cultivators have leased-in part or all of their operated area.

Table 8.13 shows the percentage of cultivators adopting HYVs by tenancy in the six villages (where there is an appreciable proportion of tenants) and in all villages combined.

Table 8.14   Percentage of HYV adopters among scheduled castes and among other cultivators in different operational holding size-groups, all 11 villages (1972−3)

| | Operational holding size in hectares | | | | | | |
	$\geq 0{\cdot}4$	$> 0{\cdot}4, \leq 1$	$> 1, \leq 2$	$> 2, \leq 3$	$> 3, \leq 4$	> 4	Among all cultivators
Percentage distribution of cultivators by holding size							
Scheduled castes	33	28	31	4	3		100
Non-scheduled castes	17	28	33	9	5	7	100
Percentage of scheduled castes in total	28	16	16	9	12		17
Percentage of HYV adopters							
Scheduled castes	20	26	21	25	67		27
Non-scheduled castes	14	18	32	50	55	66	30

Adoption rates appear to be high among tenants, especially among the 'mainly tenants' of Vegamangalam. But that is a special case because most of them were cultivators who had leased-in pangu land and who grew HYVs in Navarai 1973 according to the common decision. In the other cases, except for Dusi, the sample sizes for tenants were too low to make these findings significant.

Scheduled Castes and Others

Table 8.14 shows the percentage of HYV paddy adopters among scheduled castes and non-scheduled castes in the eleven sample villages in the different operational holding size-classes. About 17 per cent of the cultivators in these villages belong to the scheduled castes. The table shows that there is a lower representation of the scheduled castes in the larger operational holding classes (greater than 2 hectares). It also shows that, although there does not seem to be much difference in adoption rates

between scheduled castes and others in all classes combined, the proportion of adopters among scheduled castes in each operational holding
size-class is higher than that among non-scheduled castes in that class
except in the 1 to 3 hectare group.

Irrigation

HYVs are grown both on wet land (irrigated by tanks and canals) and
garden land (dry land irrigated by wells) in all the three seasons, the
proportion being slightly higher in wet (55 per cent) than in garden land
(45 per cent). (The same is true of traditional varieties also.) The
proportion of gross paddy land under HYVs is 10 per cent both in wet and
in garden land; in wet land it is respectively 15, 7 and 15 per cent in the
Sornavari, Samba and Navarai seasons; in garden land, 8, 9 and 18 per
cent. Thus the proportion of land under HYVs in each of the dry seasons is
about twice that in Samba (compare above, pp. 98–9).

Pump-sets (44 per cent) and kavalais (bullock-drawn lifts) (7 per cent)
irrigated about half the gross wet paddy area, the rest being irrigated by
tanks and canals. Canals were used only in Vegamangalam and
Vinayagapuram. In garden land, pump-sets and kavalais fed respectively
69 and 31 per cent of the gross paddy area. Because of the extensive use of
pump-sets to supplement tank water in wet land also, the pump-set was the
major source of irrigation (irrigating 53 per cent of the land) in all types of
paddy land, followed by kavalai (19 per cent), tank (16 per cent) and canal
(10 per cent). Surprisingly, 72 per cent of paddy is irrigated by wells.

Most of the HYV paddy area (about 90 per cent) in both wet and
garden land in all the three seasons is irrigated by wells with pump-sets. Of
the area grown under traditional paddy varieties, 60 per cent is irrigated
using pump-sets in Sornavari and Navarai in both wet and garden land,
but in Samba – when the tanks are fed by the rains – tank water is the main
source of irrigation, irrigating a little over half the area under traditional
paddy in wet land.

There was considerable variation between villages in the percentage
possessing pump-sets (see Table 8.15), Randam having the largest
percentage (80) and Dusi the lowest (4). (The low percentage in Dusi is
explained by the fact that it has a reliable water supply from the huge
Mamandur tank.)

That having independent control over water (possessing pump-sets) is
an important factor in adoption is shown clearly in Tables 8.15 and 8.16.

Table 8.15 shows that the percentage of HYV adopters among pump-set
owners is almost three times higher than among cultivators without pump-
sets, though there is variation between villages. Again villages with assured
water supply (Vinayagapuram, Dusi, Vegamangalam, Amudur and
Randam) are those with high proportions of HYV adopters among those
without pump-sets.

A study of pump-set ownership and adoption of HYVs by operational

Table 8.15   HYV adopters among paddy cultivators with and without pump-sets, 1972–3

Village	Percentage of paddy cultivators possessing pump-sets	Percentage of HYV adopters among	
		paddy cultivators with pump-sets	paddy cultivators without pump-sets
Vegamangalam	56	91	26
Sirungathur	36	62	4
Duli	36	33	5
Dusi	4	83	45
Vengodu	29	37	9
Vinayagapuram	23	67	46
Amudur	30	61	23
Randam	76	43	23
Kalpattu	61	5	0
Veerasambanur	44	53	0
Meppathurai	31	67	7
Vayalur	21	47	4
All villages, excl. Dusi	43	48	15

holding size-groups is presented in Table 8.16. The proportion of paddy cultivators possessing pump-sets increased with increase in holding size. Lack of available credit for buying pump-sets might be the major reason for this. Among the smaller cultivators (with less than 1 hectare), the probability that a cultivator with a pump-set adopted HYVs was about thrice as high as for one without. The most interesting finding, however, is that the percentage of paddy area under HYVs among owners of pump-sets is as high among the smaller cultivators (with less than 1 hectare) as among the largest group (with more than 4 hectares), and that among those without pump-sets, the percentage area under HYVs is uniformly low (around 6 per cent) irrespective of the operational holding size-group.

Table 8.16 shows clearly that possession of a pump-set, which gives the cultivator independent access to and control over irrigation water, is the most important factor leading to adoption of HYVs. Small cultivators are at a disadvantage because of lack of capital and of loans to invest in pump-sets (see chapter 13).

Possession of Improved Implements

The traditional wooden plough was the most commonly used implement for ploughing. Among the 146 paddy cultivators in the phase 2 sample (excluding Dusi), only 16 per cent possessed Bose ploughs and only 10 per cent possessed iron ploughs – both improvements over the wooden plough. Three had both Bose ploughs and iron ploughs. The Bose ploughs were concentrated mainly in Vegamangalam and Vinayagapuram, the iron

Table 8.16 *Percentage of HYV adopters among paddy cultivators with and without pump-sets, by operational holding size-group*

		Operational holding size in hectares						
		≤0·4	>0·4, ≤1·0	>1·0, ≤2	>2, ≤3	>3, ≤4	≥4	All groups
Paddy cultivators with pump-sets	HYV adopters	36	38	44	53	67	67	48
	HYV area (%)	25	21	15	14	16	23	18
Paddy cultivators without pump-sets	HYV adopters	10	13	21	43	40		15
	HYV area (%)	5	5	7	7	6		6
All paddy cultivators	HYV adopters	15	19	33	51	61	67	29
	HYV area (%)	10	10	12	13	14	23	13.4
Proportion of paddy cultivators possessing pump-sets in operational holding size-groups		19	25	51	84	78	100	61

ploughs in Vegamangalam and Sirungathur. Two of the sample culti-vators had Burmese satterns (implement for trampling manure) and two had harvesters, one each in Vegamangalam and Sirungathur. Among those with Bose ploughs, 21 per cent were HYV adopters; among those with iron ploughs, 36 per cent were HYV adopters and among those with wooden ploughs only, 14 per cent were adopters.

None of the sample cultivators possessed a tractor. The number of privately owned tractors in the twelve sample villages totalled only three – one each in Vengodu, Kalpattu and Randam. The tractor was hired for paddy cultivation by four of the sample cultivators in Randam, all of whom were HYV adopters. In Amudur one cultivator used a tractor for groundnut cultivation only. (Compare the situation in Sri Lanka: see especially pp. 144–5 and 168–80.)

Adoption of Inputs

Table 8.17 shows the patterns of adoption of various inputs and the adoption of individual inputs or planting practices among HYV growers and TV growers of paddy in 1973–4. The packages of inputs listed are the most common ones only. For traditional varieties (TP, M) or (TP, M, F) seem to be the most popular input packages in each season. For HYVs, however, (TP, M, F) and (TP, M, F, P) appear to be the most popular packages in Sornavari and Navarai, whereas in Samba – the season prone to pest attacks–71 per cent of HYV growers adopt (TP, M, F, P).

Table 8.17   Percentage of adopters of various inputs in 1973–4 among HYV and other paddy growers

	Sornavari		Samba		Navarai	
	HYV	Other paddy	HYV	Other paddy	HYV	Other paddy
Input package adopted						
TP, M		40		27		27
TP, M, F	40	31	7	28	44	36
TP, M, P		2		3		22
TP, M, F, P	60	22	71	30	56	11
ST, TP, M, F, P			21			
Individual input adopted						
TP	100	98	100	88	100	98
M	100	97	100	96	100	100
F	100	57	100	64	100	51
P	60	23	93	40	63	35
ST			21	1		

Note: TP=transplanting, M=manure, F=chemical fertiliser, P=pesticides, ST=seed treatment.

Transplanting was generally adopted for all varieties of paddy. Broadcasting of seed was practised mainly on pangu land in Vegamangalam. In Dusi (not included in this table) a large number of TV growers broadcast the seed in Samba. The traditional fertiliser, organic manure, was used by almost all the cultivators for all varieties of paddy. Weedicides were not used at all. Flooding the plots with water, and hand-weeding, were the means generally used against weeds.

The use of the commonly adopted modern inputs (fertilisers and pesticides, particularly the former) is not limited to HYV growers. All HYV growers use fertilisers in all three seasons and the majority of HYV growers use pesticides, the proportion being the highest in Samba (93 per cent). The proportion of TV growers using fertilisers, though lesser than among HYV growers, is quite considerable – 57 per cent in Sornavari, 64 per cent in Samba and 51 per cent in Samba – indicating that the new inputs are being used for the traditional varieties also. The decline in use of fertilisers in Navarai is due to a scarcity at that time. Pesticides are, however, used by a much smaller proportion of TV growers – 23 per cent in Sornavari, 40 per cent in Samba and 35 per cent in Navarai.

Note that all the HYV growers used fertilisers in all the three seasons despite scarcity and high prices in the survey year. In Sornavari the prices shot up in the open market when supply was scarce and many cultivators had to pay exorbitant prices on the black market. Later, in June 1974, the government almost doubled the price of the fertiliser distributed through its agencies, because of the oil crisis.

Table 8.18   *Percentage of never-adopters (1972–3), de-adopters (1973–4) and non-adopters (1973–4) of HYV paddy among paddy cultivators by reasons given*

Reasons	1972–3 Farm survey		1973–4 Cultivator survey			
	Never-adopters	De-adopters	Non-adopters			
			Sornavari	Samba	Navarai	All seasons
1 Fertiliser problems: availability, cost, timeliness, distance of source, etc.			39	80	79	69
2 Pesticide problems: availability, cost, timeliness, distance of source, etc.			17	56	50	45
3 HYVs not profitable	4	15	42	50	29	44
4 Water problems: control, needs pump-set, insufficiency, etc.	27	23	19	34	29	29
5 Soil problems: needs testing, not suitable, etc.	12	15	14	38	15	27
6 Inadequate knowledge, lack of advice	4	2	12	35	13	24
7 Grain quality not satisfactory, unpalatable, etc.	1	6	14	18	23	17
8 Credit problems: lack of funds for inputs	36	32	15	17	23	16
9 Family members opposed	n.a.	n.a.	3	22	17	15
10 Not convinced about high yields of HYVs	4	2	10	18	4	12
11 Season not suitable because of pests	n.a.	n.a.	25	9		12
12 Tractors too expensive	n.a.	n.a.		12	4	7
13 Seed not available, price too high, etc.	1			10	4	6
14 Labour problems	n.a.	n.a.	2	8	6	6

Note: 'Never-adopters' were those who had never tried HYV paddy; 'de-adopters' were those who had tried HYV paddy before 1972—3 and not in 1972—3; 'non-adopters' were those not growing HYV paddy in 1973—4.

n.a. These reasons were not included in the check list for 1972—3.

OPINIONS OF CULTIVATORS: REASONS FOR NOT ADOPTING HYVS

Table 8.18 gives the distribution of 'never-adopters' (1972–3), 'de-adopters' (1972–3) and 'non-adopters' (1973–4) by the reasons they gave for not adopting or for stopping adoption of HYV seeds; the results are expressed as the proportion of respondents quoting the reasons listed. The reasons quoted have been grouped under broad heads in the table: the wording of the questions during the farm survey (1972–3) and the detailed survey of cultivators (1973–4) were slightly different. Investigator perceptions in open-ended questions like this cannot be ruled out. Yet it is interesting to note that 'credit problems' or lack of funds for inputs feature as the major reason for non-adoption and de-adoption in 1972–3, followed by water supply problems. In 1973–4 non-availability of fertilisers was the reason quoted most often, the proportion rising steeply from 39 per cent in Sornavari to 80 per cent in Samba and Navarai. Problems with pest attack and the availability of pesticides was quoted as the next important reason in 1973–4 Samba and Navarai. The unprofitability of HYVs was quoted by 15 per cent of the de-adopters in 1972–3, but by 42, 50 and 29 per cent of non-adopters in the three seasons of 1973–4. Unsuitability of soil appeared to be quoted fairly often, while non-availability of seed and labour were not given as important reasons. Some 32 per cent of all HYV adopters claimed to have grown less of other crops (29 per cent TV of paddy, 1 per cent of cholam, 1 per cent of banana in Kalpattu) as a result of changing over to HYV paddy. Few of the informants reported having heard of any adverse reports on fertilisers or pesticides, the percentages being less than 3 per cent and 2 per cent respectively.

CONCLUSIONS

The low rate of adoption of HYV paddy in the survey area is striking, although it must be noted that most of the 'traditional' varieties of paddy now commonly grown are 'improved' varieties developed by the agricultural research stations in Tamil Nadu. Farmers have adopted new varieties in the past, and would adopt them in the future also, if sufficient quantities of inputs – mainly water – are assured. They have sufficient knowledge of improved varieties and practices.

Transplanting and the use of manure are widespread. Fertilisers and pesticides are used widely for HYVs and by a substantial proportion of farmers for traditional varieties also. Seed treatment and use of tractors are limited in the survey area.

The high HYV yield rates (though low compared with potential), and their profitability as compared to traditional varieties, appear to favour HYV adoption. With the food scarcity and the rising price trend of HYVs (which, towards the end of the survey period, tended to compare well in price with the finest and costliest rice variety), the cultivator would seem to have more incentive to adopt in the near future.

Although adoption rates generally increase with operational holding size, an interesting finding was that small cultivators – particularly those possessing 0·4 to 1·0 hectares – have higher rates of adoption than cultivators with smaller acreages and those in the next higher size-group (1 to 2 hectares). In the survey area, possession of pump-sets emerges as the one factor leading to higher rates of adoption among all groups of cultivators, big and small; but the proportion of small cultivators who can afford pump-sets is much lower than that among the larger cultivators. Besides, increasing power-cuts and lowering of the water-table are placing constraints on those who have pump-sets.

Other constraints to adoption, especially on the realisation of potential yields, appear to be the scarcity and high price of fertilisers and the non-availability of credit, particularly to small cultivators. The much discussed scale-neutrality of the new technology is therefore belied by the greater access which the larger cultivators have to the crucial factors of production involved – cash, pump-sets and fertilisers.

Age of the cultivator, his tenure status and caste did not seem to influence adoption in this area, whereas literacy exerted a positive influence.

Seed-breeding priorities indicated for dry areas with poor and erratic rainfall are HYV paddy varieties suitable for the wet Samba season and also pest-resistant; also, water-sparing, short-duration varieties suitable for the dry seasons. In view of the severe water shortage prevalent during the period of survey, the erratic pattern of rainfall and the falling water-table, serious consideration needs to be given to shifting the cropping pattern away from paddy, which is water-demanding, to dry crops such as groundnut and pulses. Developing HYVs in these dry crops might well be a means of increasing food production and helping the small cultivator.

REFERENCES

Director of Statistics, Tamil Nadu (1969–70). *Season and Crop Reports*, 1969–70.

Directorate of Economics and Statistics, Ministry of Agriculture, Government of India (1973). *Indian Agriculture in Brief*, 12th edn, New Delhi.

Finance Department, Government of Tamil Nadu (1974). *Tamil Nadu – An Economic Appraisal*: part 2, Tables.

Rengarajan, V. (1975). 'Lacunae in Rural Statistics', *Financial Express*, 30, 31 Mar 1975.

Sen, S. R. (1967). 'Growth and Instability in Indian Agriculture', technical address at 20th Annual meeting of the Indian Society of Agricultural Statistics, Waltair, *Ind. J. Agric. Stat.*, 19, 1–30.

9 The Limitations of HYV Technology in North Arcot District: the View from a Village

John Harriss

CONTEXT: THE VILLAGE AND ITS SETTING

The village that we call 'Randam' lies on a plain some $3\frac{1}{2}$ miles south-east of the market town of Arni (pop. 39,000), to which it is linked by frequent bus services on the main road only half a mile away (for general village statistics see chapter 15). Proximity to the town helps to account for some important characteristics: early electrification and installation of pump-sets (in 1951); intensive use of organic manure of urban origin, which – farmers believe – is a significant factor in raising their yields above those in remoter villages; the involvement of villagers in town affairs and commerce, which appears to have made capital available for investment in agriculture and enables the villagers to be generally well-informed about price movements.

There is a tank, one of a series fed by an intermittent stream, with a capacity of three to four months; though during 1973–4 it did not fill up at all. A Revenue survey in 1951 records the acreage under command of the tank as 110·92, but since then this wet-land area has been supplemented marginally by the installation of electric pump-sets, while the potential paddy acreage has been substantially increased by pump-sets in the dry land, thus creating garden land (Table 9.1). Without supplementary well irrigation most of the wet land would only be capable of producing two crops in a year with better than average rainfall. Figure 9.1 shows the growth in the number of pump-sets. Almost half were installed between 1966 and 1971, when there was a widespread expansion of pump-sets throughout Chingleput and North and South Arcot Districts, which probably contributed more significantly than the introduction of HYVs to the increase in paddy production from these Districts (Mencher, 1974). Certainly the accounts of the karnam for Randam and two adjacent

Table 9.1   Land of Randam Revenue Village (in acres)

	According to Settlement Land Register, 1951	Actual land use classification
Dry land	561·44	385·56
Wet land	113·56	132·81
Poromboke	177·49	—
Garden land	n.a.	150·90
'Waste'	n.a.	173·23
Total	842·50	842·50

Notes: 'Wet land' and 'dry land' refer to the Revenue classifications of irrigated and unirrigated land. 'Garden land' refers to land irrigated from wells only. Some of it is 'high' potential, capable of carrying two paddy crops per year, and some of lower potential (two groundnut crops per year). 'Waste' refers to the village site, the area of the tank, channels, drains, paths.

villages show a marked expansion in paddy acreage from 1968 to 1972 (Table 9.2).

Madduma Bandara's research (see chapter 21) points to a secular decline in the groundwater level in North Arcot. In Randam the density of wells in the wet land, their depth (commonly 30−40 ft), and the extent to which they are now having to be deepened, together with the evident

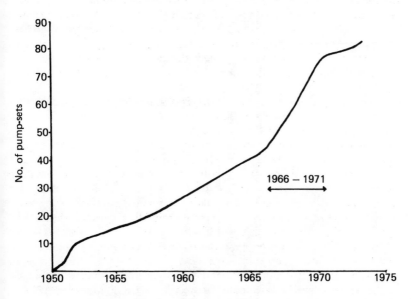

FIG. 9.1 *Numbers of pump-sets in Randam (total 83)*

Table 9.2   Changes in cropping pattern based on the Karnam's records for Randam plus two neighbouring villages

	1959–60	1960–1	1961–2	1962–3	1963–4	1964–5	1965–6	1966–7	1967–8	1968–9	1969–70	1970–1	1971–2	1972–3*
Paddy	566	589	810	794	653	850	757	652	808	910	1,032	1,235	1,380	600
Groundnut	547	530	504	545	594	492	509	560	823	920	758	936	685	723
Others	29	78	106	59	74	61	89	81	133	145	323	153	90	139
Total	1,142	1,197	1,420	1,398	1,321	1,403	1,355	1,293	1,764	1,975	2,113	2,324	2,155	1,462

*Different boundaries taken in 1972–3.

unreliability of tank water supply, suggest how precarious is the hydrological base of the very intensive system of cultivation – a situation further exacerbated by power cuts.

THE PATTERN OF AGRICULTURE

Intensive cultivation practices such as transplanting and heavy use of organic manures have a long history in the District (for example, Cox, 1895, pp. 258 ff.), and in Randam cultivation is even more intensive than in some other villages. Most farmers apply about 10 cartloads (4 or 5 tons) of manure per acre of wet land, using supplies from their own households and from Arni. Wealthier farmers also purchase urban 'compost' from the more distant centres of Vellore, Arcot and Ranipet, paying Rs150–160 per lorry load (increased to Rs240 by August 1974). Further, there are more than a dozen shepherds in Randam who receive payment from farmers for folding sheep in their fields overnight; and the four swineherds sell dung as well. The emphatic opinion of the farmers is that chemical fertilisers are much less effective alone than when used with organic manure.

The system of cultivation is one in which cattle play a central role, given religious recognition during the major 'pongal' festival in January. Most farmers own at least one bullock team, and there is a reserve of ploughmen in the Harijan colony who have their own teams. The fodder requirements of the animals impose constraints on cropping decisions, for example, one reason given for cultivating Sirumani in Samba is for fodder. The bran and oilcake left over after custom-processing of paddy and groundnut are retained by farmers for cattle-feed, and also purchased in Arni.

Wealthier farmers expressed keen interest in investing in tractors, which they would then hire out, but at present there is only one tractor owner. The two-wheel tractors so common in Sri Lanka have only just begun to appear in the Arni area, though their potential is the subject of keen discussion. There were indications in 1973 of increasing use of tractors for ploughing wet land, mainly by cultivators concerned over transplanting delays; until that year tractors had reportedly been used only for dry-land ploughing and for threshing (especially of HYVs, difficult to thresh by hand because of their short stems and tough rachis). Use of tractors for dry-land ploughing has given a further advantage to the bigger farmers, enabling them to cultivate larger areas at a time when there is heavy demand for plough cattle and to take maximum advantage of the few critical showers. Increased use of tractors may threaten livelihoods, and even the system of cultivation, so that quite apart from the oil crisis it seemed unfortunate that local extension officers should have expressed unquestioning belief in tractorisation as recently as January 1974.

Intensive hand-weeding and transplanting are normal practice, but depend on the availability of cheap labour, mostly supplied from the Harijan colony.

Most farmers talk of having used chemical fertilisers 'for about ten years', though only a handful follow extension recommendations, partly because some farmers believe that the recommendations are not right for their fields (and in a few cases results seem to justify this) and partly because of shortages and inability to pay for adequate quantities. The use of pesticides has begun with the advent of HYVs; chemical weedicides are known but not used.

Table 9.3   Cropping pattern, 1973−4 (in acres)

Sornavari		Samba		Navarai	
Paddy: local varieties					
Ottu Kichili	16	(Arcot) Kichili	103	Ottu Kichili	37
Kullankar	76	Sirumani	33	Kullankar	56
Chittirai Kuli	5	Kartigai Samba	12	Madangal Kar	15
HYVs		Mojanam	3	Chittirai Kuli	5
IR.20	22	Others	7	Co.29	18
Karuna	13				
Kanchi	2	IR.20	60	IR.8	28
		C.4	1·3	IR.20	15
		Vijaya	1·5	C.4	2
Total	134		221		176
HYVs 28 %		HYVs 28 %		HYVs 26 %	
Sugar cane	6		6		6
Groundnut (i)	83				101
(ii)			414		
Cholam, cumbu, ragi			63		
Fallow			56		

Notes:

1 Data refer to Randam village as defined in this chapter, not to the Revenue Village.

2 Groundnut (i) is grown on irrigated land in two seasons, the first of which overlaps between the periods of Sornavari and Samba, the second corresponding to an early Navarai. Groundnut (ii) is rain-fed groundnut. In both cases the groundnut is often inter-cropped with cholam and black, red and green grams.

3 'Others' under 'local varieties' in the Samba season includes mainly a crop which the cultivators intended to be IR.20. It turned out to be Co.29, which is not a suitable variety for the Samba season. The seed all came from one farmer, who insisted that he had confused the bags in his store.

4 Co.29 has been listed separately under Navarai, because it is not strictly a HYV. Cultivators in Randam usually refer to it as a 'local variety'. Like several other 'local varieties' it is an improved variety.

5 In comparing developments in Sri Lanka and Tamil Nadu it is worth bearing in mind that a variety such as Ottu Kichili compares closely with H.4 in Sri Lanka and, according to farmers' handbooks, has given yields of over 100 bu. per acre, equivalent to the performance of H.4 on research stations; yields of 80 bu. per acre were obtained in the village in 1973. 80 bu. per acre would be a good yield in Pahalagama with H.4 (see below, p. 150).

Cropping Pattern

The pattern of land use in Randam is shown in Table 9.3 and gives further evidence of the intensity of cultivation. The paddy acreage in Sornavari 1973 was probably rather greater than average because of the heavy rainfall of December 1972 (although even then the tank did not fill), while that in Navarai may have been below average because of the scanty monsoon in 1973–4. The acreage under HYVs in Navarai 1973–4 was only half that of Navarai 1972–3, a decline noted also in other villages in the sample survey (see above, pp. 95–6).

The importance of groundnut, usually intercropped even on irrigated land with grams and cholam, is revealed in Table 9.3, and indications of recent expansion of groundnut cultivation are provided by the karnam's accounts (Table 9.2) and the increase in value of dry land (Rs100 per acre about 1960, now Rs3000). Farmers who operate less than about two acres of wet land say that their chances of earning a cash income depend largely on the success of their groundnut cultivation (compare the interaction of paddy and chena cultivation in Sri Lanka, p. 145).

Table 9.4   *Distribution of land ownership among Randam farmers*

Size-category (acres)	No. of households	Percentage of total	Cumulated area (acres)	Percentage total of area	
Landless	123	44·2	0·00		62·6 per cent of house-
Less than 0·5	3	1·8	1·82	0·22	holds own 1·5 acres or
0·51–1·5	46	16·6	46·81	5·8	less, or 6 per cent of total area
1·51–2·5	19	6·8	38·20	4·5	83 per cent of house-
2·51–3·5	20	7·2	60·31	7·3	holds own less than 5
3·51–5·0	18	6·5	72·77	8·7	acres or 26·5 per cent of total area
5·01–7·5	16	5·8	95·60	11·6	15 per cent of house-
7·51–10	10	3·6	87·61	10·6	holds own between 5
10·01–12·5	3	1·1	32·68	3·96	and 20 acres, and con-
12·51–15	5	1·8	70·47	8·6	trol 50 per cent of the
15·01–20	7	2·5	129·29	15·7	area
20·01–25	2	0·7	42·28	5·1	the 2 per cent of
25·01–30	1	0·4	29·45	3·6	households owning
More than 30	3	1·1	118·21	14·3	more than 20 acres control 23 per cent of the area
Total	278	100	825·50	99·9	

Note: Of the 155 households owning some land, only 105 (38 per cent of all the households) have access to land on which some paddy may be grown.

THE DISTRIBUTION OF AGRICULTURAL RESOURCES

Table 9.4 shows the distribution of land ownership among the 278 households of the main village (excluding a hamlet at the main road, which is included in the Census definition of 'Randam'). Because there is little tenancy the distribution of operational holdings does not differ greatly from land ownership. Although land holding is quite heavily concentrated in the hands of a small number of men, even the largest holdings are of relatively modest size, and with two exceptions, all the big farmers themselves work on the land.

However, the agricultural value of land is considerably modified by access to water, and the small size of some holdings is compensated by the reliability of their wells. There is a significant relationship between the size of land holding and pump-set ownership. Only four of the 74 operators of more than one acre of irrigated land do not have wells and pump-sets (and they do have kavalai wells), while 11 of the 23 operators of less than an acre have no access to pump-sets. But this relationship disguises the different capacities of the wells.

THE PATTERN OF ADOPTION OF HYVS

Figure 9.2 and Tables 9.5 and 9.3 together illustrate the pattern of adoption of HYVs. About half the farmers have taken up HYVs since Navarai 1972–3, while the Samba season of 1973 saw the first participation of a majority of those who have adopted. In the main they have taken up IR.20 (in all three seasons) and to a lesser extent IR.8 (in Navarai), while Co.29 is still popular (see pp. 99–101).

Table 9.6 shows adoption of HYVs (and Co.29) in relation to land holding and to access to water. It seems clear from this table alone that

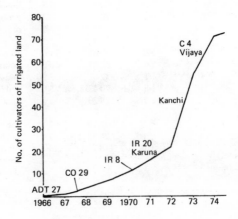

FIG. 9.2 *Adoption of new varieties in Randam*

these two factors account for a large part of the observed variation, as Mrs Chinnappa has found for the whole survey sample of cultivators (pp. 109–18). Among the 22 cultivators who operate land irrigable from

Table 9.5   Numbers of farmers who have tried particular HYVs at least once

ADT.27	5 (all have de-adopted)
Co.29	37
IR.8	38 (4 claim to have de-adopted)
IR.20	56 (1 claims to have de-adopted)
IR.5	2 (both de-adopted)
Karuna	6
Kanchi	2
C.4	2
Vijaya	1

5 farmers have tried Co.29 only; 20 have tried IR.20 only

Table 9.6   Adoption of HYVs by Randam farmers in relation to operational holding of paddy land and ownership of well and electric pump-set (EPS)

Operational holding size (acres)	Adopters with well and EPS	Adopters with no well or EPS	Non-adopters with well and EPS	Non-adopters with no well or EPS
Less than 1	7	5	5	6
1–1·99	17	1	12	2
2–2·99	9		1	1
3–3·99	8		2	
4–4·99	9		1	
5–7·5	5			
7·5–10				
10–12·5	1 ⎫ own 37%			
12·5–15	2 ⎬ of			
More than 15	4 ⎭ total			
Total	62	6	21	9

Notes:

1   In the category 'Less than 1 acre' with well, one of the 7 'adopters' has used Co.29 only. The five adopters in this class who do not have wells with pump-sets do have kavalais and three of them also hire water.
2   In the category '1 to 1·99' with well, two of the adopters have only marginal paddy land, and have only once experimented (with IR.20). Another two have used only Co.29. The one adopter who has no well or EPS has a well under construction and hires water at present.
3   In the category '2 to 2·99', one of the adopters has used Co.29 only.
4   In the category '3 to 3·99', one of the adopters has used Co.29 only.

pump-sets and yet who have not so far adopted HYVs, reasons for non-adoption include the following: the supply of water is scanty and unreliable, so groundnut is cropped; the cultivators are widows who operate their lands using the services of attached labourers; others are Untouchables, a majority of them also small tenant cultivators who are unable to raise sufficient money for fertilisers. In addition, a number of cultivators, who in terms of resource endowments might be expected to be innovators, are resistant to change (cf. below, pp. 135–8).

The process of adoption is evidently at an early stage. To what extent may the acreage under HYVs be expected to increase, given the environmental and structural constraints on the farmers, and their perceptions and attitudes?

LIMITATIONS ON THE ADOPTION OF HYVS

The crucial importance of water supplies has been sufficiently emphasised, but it has a surprising corollary, in view of the stress often placed in the literature on the potential of HYVs for multiple cropping because of their relatively short duration and insensitivity to photoperiodism. In Randam the available HYVs (IR.8 and IR.20) are relatively long-duration varieties, and are in that sense more water-demanding than most local varieties. Crop duration (in days) are:

Sirumani	160
IR.8	135–150
IR.20	130
Madangal Kar	120–130
Ottu Kichili	115–120
Kichili	120
Sornavari	100
Karuna (Co.33)	105
Kullankar	90

Kullankar is important in Sornavari and Navarai (both seasons in which the supply of water to the fields is hardly supplemented at all by rainfall) because it requires less water for a shorter period. Even in comparison with other varieties HYVs are not competitive in terms of water demand and duration, and the only variety which is competitive – Karuna – has not proved very successful in North Arcot.

Village water management practices also mean that HYVs require more water than the older varieties, even those of similar duration. Farmers believe that after transplanting HYVs there should be only a half-inch of water in the field, for about 15 days. Then, after the first weeding, 2 in. of water in the field is required until the second weeding, after 45 days. From then on, 3 in. of water is necessary, especially at the time of seed-setting (some poor IR.8 yields in Navarai 1972–3 were thought to result from insufficient water at this time). With local varieties, however, the usual pattern is for there to be 1–2 in. in the field throughout, after an initial dry period when the plants are very small (cf. Cox, 1895, p. 261).

The advantages of some of the older, local varieties have been further emphasised by the structure of the market. The keen interest which Randam farmers display in prices points to the inadequacy of analyses which attempt to divide Indian agriculture into 'commercial/capitalist' and 'feudal' sectors, at least when these categories are rigidly applied. Almost every farmer in a position to make the choice had considered cultivating groundnut instead of paddy because of the potentially higher profit (see Table 9.7). Similarly the low price of IR.8 in April and May 1973, in comparison with the price of Ottu Kichili and even the coarser Kars, caused general discussion of the profitability of IR.8. Even if the yield was higher, did the price justify the risk involved in cultivation? (cf. Mencher, 1974, p. 313).

However, the most important way in which relative prices influenced farmers' decisions was that the high price commanded by Kichili continued to make it the most attractive crop for Samba. This was true both for the largest, most commercially minded farmers and for the very small men, and all grew it almost entirely for the market. Even though a good Kichili yield would not produce much over 20 bags per acre, its price of around Rs75 per bag, against perhaps Rs50 for IR.20, together with the lower expenditure on inputs and risk of pest damage, obviously gave the former a considerably competitive edge (see Table 9.7). Another low-yield but high-quality variety called Minambur was actually introduced by a commercially minded farmer in 1973.

Subsequent events have rather changed the picture, however: as a result of inflation and foodgrains scarcities, prices of all varieties have risen steeply, and differentials have become less marked (see also chapter 24). Even so it is not likely that HYVs at present on offer will become very much more attractive to farmers, and certainly not in the Samba season. Different varieties are well adapted to the conditions of different seasons, and only IR.20 has been cultivated in all three. But IR.20 performed dismally in Samba 1973, when average yields were only about 25 bags per acre, in comparison with 20 bags or more with Kichili (and some Ottu Kichili yields of 25 bags per acre in Sornavari), and this seems to bear out the view of the most thoughtful farmers that there is no HYV well suited to the conditions of the Samba season – the only season when water supplies are generally assured – and that this may be because of the lesser amount of sunshine then, or because of the increased incidence of pest attacks in the humid conditions that prevail. The Extension Office in the Arni Panchayat Union persists in recommending IR.8 for all three seasons, but Randam farmers argue that experience has shown that IR.8 is only successful in Navarai. IR.8 is a more risky crop than IR.20, because it requires higher cash expenditure on fertilisers, and, according to the farmers, more careful management (e.g. in applying fertilisers at exactly the right time), whereas IR.20 is more flexible, more 'like a local variety'. Moreover, IR.8 is best cultivated in the season when there is greatest risk of loss at the end through lack of water. Altogether, it appears unlikely that the acreage under IR.8, though having the highest yield potential of the varieties currently available, will substantially increase. (All these points appear to apply in other villages also, cf. pp. 98–100.)

The constraints of water supply and of seasonal conditions are the most significant objective limitations on existing HYV technology, but they are strengthened in the farmers' view by constraints arising from soil conditions. The term 'seru' (meaning literally 'ooze', in Tamil) is used by Randam farmers to denote the mud, created by flooding and ploughing in paddy fields, that is essential for transplanted paddy (cf. Cox, 1895, p. 260). The term is also used to refer in general to the heavy grey-black soil found beneath the tank. The depth of seru which is created by ploughing varies on different soils and in different parts of the field. In the Samba season one reason for choosing Sirumani rather than Kichili, which commands a higher price on the market, is that it thrives on deep seru,

Table 9.7   Some Cultivation Accounts, Samba 1973 (A. L. Chandarasekaran)

IR.20: 1.50 acres

Kichili: 2.66 acres

Yield: 42½ bags (of 75 kg) (or 28 per acre)		*Yield*: 54½ bags (of 75 kg) (or 20 per acre)	
Kind costs: 4½ bags		*Kind costs:* 4½ bags	
Gross income: 38 × Rs 52.50 i.e. Rs 1995		*Gross income:* 50 × Rs 75, i.e. Rs 3750	
Cash costs:	Rs	*Cash costs*:	Rs
Labour	96		185
Draught cattle	24		23
Tractor hire	50		120
Materials	422		631
Tax	12		15
Electricity and pump-set maintenance	80		170
Total	684	Total	1144
Subsistence costs (imputed):		*Subsistence costs* (imputed):	
Payments to attached labourers	85		142
Maintenance of cattle	60		95
Manure	48		
Depreciation	20		30
Total	213	Total	267
Net income: Rs 1995−(684+213)		*Net income:* Rs 3750−(1144+267)	
=Rs 1098		=Rs 2339	
Per acre:			
Costs	598		530
Gross income	1330		1410
Net income	732		880

Groundnut, on garden land, 6 acres

Yield: 65 bags, 22 bags of kernels
    (cf. 112 bags before shelling in 1972)
Gross Income: 22× Rs 275   Rs 6050

Cash Costs:	*Rs*
Labour	556
Cattle	50
Materials	51
Tax	24
Power and set	210
Total	891

Subsistence costs: (imputed)	
Attached labourers	210
Cattle maintenance	150
Depreciation	65
Total	425

Net income: Rs 6050 − (891 + 425) = Rs 4734

Per Acre:	*R*⟍
Costs	219
Gross income	1008
Net income	789

Note: These accounts do not include interest payments, (subsistence) income from straw, nor the cost of providing meals for attached labourers; but the last-named cost can be shared out equally between crops, while the other two probably push the balance away from the HYVs. This is because the HYVs may require rather more credit while, according to the farmers, they produce less straw, and straw of lower quality than local varieties.

while Kichili does not. Similarly, Randam farmers do not like to cultivate HYVs on the deeper seru: IR.8 is thought to be much more sensitive in this respect than IR.20. Consistent with these views is the idea that HYVs are most likely to be successful if cultivated on garden land; and the suggestion that these IRRI varieties show a preference for well-drained soils because they were bred on such soils at the research station.

HYVS AND FARMER BEHAVIOUR

The limitations that have been discussed so far are, in general, 'objective' limitations. Admittedly they have been presented from the perspective of the farmers' perceptions; but the evidence of our survey data (see pp. 109–22 above) confirms their significance as obstacles to the more widespread adoption of the existing HYV technology, even if the farmers' understanding of them, perhaps with regard to soil conditions, does not turn out to be valid scientifically. There is evident need for 'feedback' from the farmers to research workers in plant-breeding and crop production.

There is a well-established body of local knowledge concerning cultivation – like that on the best times for planting the older varieties (cf.
Cox, 1895, p. 253) – and a new body of this quasi-experimental knowledge
is beginning to emerge for HYVs, as was demonstrated to me through an
earnest discussion on the optimum planting time for Karuna in Sornavari.
I found no evidence of the feedback of this kind of information into
scientific research.

If there are objective limitations arising from the combination of scarce
water supplies, seasonal conditions and soils which have tended to favour
the continued cultivation of older varieties (till recently anyway, also made
attractive by relative prices), there remain a variety of factors relating
more directly to the farmers themselves. It is manifestly true that 'No two
farmers are alike in their abilities', as some urged at the project seminar;
but such a view cannot serve as the ultimate in explanation of farmer
behaviour. In Randam regularities do emerge, some of them illustrated by
the way in which information on HYVs has been acquired.

The effectiveness of some extension activities in information dissemination appeared quite strong, for no less than 16 paddy cultivators said
that their initial knowledge of HYVs derived from an occasion 'when the
BDO (Block Development Officer) and the GS (Gram Sewak) came and
showed films in the school' in about 1971. Yet by that time a dozen farmers
had already cultivated IR.8 or had experimented earlier with ADT.27 and
Co.29 (Fig. 9.2). They did not appear to have influenced other farmers, for
though they tended to mention one another as the source of their original
knowledge, nobody else did. By contrast some of the more laggardly
adopters named members of the group who had been influenced by the
demonstration effort and by personal contacts with extension staff. Where
extension staff were mentioned, it was always when they had had some
personal, as opposed to 'professional' contact with the farmers.

In Randam then, there appears to have been a phase in the flow of
information preceding the 'two-step' pattern of dissemination hy-
pothesised by Lazarsfeld and others (cited by Danda and Danda, 1971):
the first step from formal extension sources to those called 'opinion leaders',
and the second from them to the average farmers. The 'leading cultivators'
who had innovated before 1971 are, with one notable exception, all well
endowed with resource assets, have rather large land holdings, and enjoy
especially good contacts with the bureaucracy. The members of this group
actively search out advice, in a manner which has also been observed in
Punjab (A. S. Kahlon, personal communication), and which might be
held to support Sharma's view that: 'If the Ford Foundation had not
exported the new technology to India, the new class of Indian kulaks
would sooner or later have imported it from wherever it was available'
(Sharma, 1973, p. 94) (though it must be noted that even the 'leading
cultivators' of Randam continue to cultivate the older varieties on large
parts of their acreages).

The importance of some ability to manipulate the bureaucracy on the part of those attempting to use the new technology has been emphasised by increasing fertiliser shortages. A black market in urea was already in being at least as early as Navarai 1972–3, when two of the 'leading cultivators' of Randam were reputed to have made large sums of money, but by late 1973, shortages of complex fertilisers were also noted. The black-market price for urea increased by nearly 50 per cent in December 1973: to obtain it at the controlled price it was necessary to purchase it through the Panchayat Union by means of a fertiliser card signed by the GS and the AEO (see p. 137). These officers were thus placed under a great deal of administrative pressure and subjected to temptations offered by some of the wealthier farmers. Even some of the wealthy took several days to obtain the necessary signatures, and some of the small cultivators did not succeed in obtaining controlled-price urea at all. For example, one cultivator of an acre of wet land preferred to buy urea at a higher price in the village, and be sure of applying it to his IR.20 on time, rather than risk seeking the necessary signatures, only to fail to obtain his fertiliser quickly enough.

A major point, here, is the emphasis that HYVs have placed on timely cultivation (as we might also suppose from their relatively long duration). Transplanting in particular must be finished on time, and delay in transplanting IR.20 seedlings in Samba – they were 60 days in the nursery – resulted in almost total loss for one farmer whose cultivation was subject to persistent and cumulative delays, largely because of his inability to pay labourers in advance. His holding is one of the largest in Randam, so we must not understand by the term 'big farmer' simply one who has a large holding – working capital and 'influence' are important criteria as well. The case also illustrates the importance of available cash; limited credit supply is a basic problem for many cultivators, constraining innovation. The credit problems of small cultivators are exacerbated by difficulties with the bureaucracy.

Small farmers are at a relative disadvantage, yet in Randam a feature of the pattern of adoption among cultivators has been that of relatively lower rates of adoption among those in an intermediate holding size-category. Some farmers with 3–5 acres of paddy land were 'laggards', and participants in the third phase of information dissemination. A similar pattern has been observed in other villages (see above, pp. 109–14). It may be that part of the explanation for this pattern lies in the relationship between the producer/consumer ratio in different households, and the resources available to them. As Mendras deduced for a similar pattern observed in the adoption of hybrid maize in south-west France (Mendras, 1970), farm families in the intermediate categories are in a relatively favourable position in terms of resources *per capita*, and to that extent have less incentive to innovate, while they lack sufficient productive capacity to make them into thoroughgoing commercial farmers. This was also the view put to me by an innovative farmer in Randam who operated less than an acre of paddy land, and who said of one of the bigger farmers: 'He doesn't *need* to use IR.8.'

In addition to objective limitations on the adoption of HYV technology there are, then, constraints relating to the resource availabilities of different farmers, which put small farmers at a consistent disadvantage. The economic objectives of different farm families, which probably relate to their consumer/producer resource positions, further influence the farmers' responses to the new technology.

CONCLUSION: THE FUTURE OF HYVS IN RANDAM

A majority of the farmers in Randam had at least experimented with HYVs by the end of 1973, but the cropping pattern shows that the new varieties had not yet come to occupy a dominant role in the village agriculture. The evidence put forward here suggests that, even under the conditions before the oil crisis, and given only the existing HYVs, all cultivators could be expected to continue to use some local varieties for at least part of the time. Even for the larger and wealthier cultivators who are most concerned with profits the HYVs constitute only part of the pack of possible choices. For a variety of reasons, including uncertain water supplies and soil conditions as well as fertiliser scarcities and the relative prices of HYVs and alternative crops, the cultivation of older varieties evidently remains rational even for the most profit-conscious. There is also the major problem of the lack of really suitable HYVs for the Samba season, the only time of year when the majority of farmers can be fairly sure of their water supplies. The limitations of the underground water that has evidently provided such a boost to agriculture in Randam are discussed by Madduma Bandara (chapter 21). Above all else, present fertiliser scarcities notwithstanding, water supplies constrain the further intensification of paddy cultivation in Randam, and the case of this village, advantageously placed in relation to roads and markets, with a population of industrious and generally well-informed farmers who apparently command between them quite large quantities of capital, illustrates the limitations of HYV technology as it exists at present.

It has been suggested by others that the research responsible for the present varieties has pursued genetic yield potential under high fertility conditions, to the exclusion of other considerations such as 'water-sparing', or 'sub-optimal fertility' (e.g. discussions at the ARTI–IDS seminar in Kandy April–May 1973; Robert Chambers and David Gibbon, personal communications October 1974), with the result that cultivators and areas already most favoured with regard to water resources in particular have been given a further relative advantage. This is not quite the same as the oft-heard comment that the Green Revolution can only be the instrument of 'growth with social justice' if it is linked with agrarian reforms. Nor does it necessarily contradict those who point out that HYV technology is scale-neutral, though it does argue that the technology favours some to the disadvantage of others. Though not necessarily attaching blame to technologists, or even technocrats, such criticism does point to an intrinsic limitation of the 'package' that is currently available, which makes it unlikely that the existing HYVs will displace the Kars and Kichili in Randam.

POSTSCRIPT: LATER TRENDS AND CHANGES IN RANDAM

The writer revisited Randam in May 1976. (He thanks Mr A. J. Smyth, Director, Land Resources Division, Ministry of Overseas Development, for making this visit possible and A. Kumanan for help in the field.)

Background: Years of Drought

There was a partial failure of the monsoons during the agricultural year 1973–4. In the following year Tamil Nadu experienced its worst drought since 1876, the year of the Great Famine. North Arcot suffered less acutely than most other Districts, but even so, the Navarai paddy acreage was halved and the crops withered on half the area that *was* planted. Prices of foodgrains rose very steeply, until halted by the good south-west monsoon of 1975: since October 1975 they have stabilised at a low level. As prices rose differentials between varieties were eroded: farmers in Randam received around Rs150 for a bag of paddy (75 kg), irrespective of variety, in mid-1975.

Government action included a ban from December 1974 on all wholesale trading in paddy and rice in a number of areas, including the study area in North Arcot. Paddy purchasing was thereafter undertaken in these areas only on behalf of the government by the Food Corporation of India, the State Civil Supplies Corporation, or the co-operatives. In May 1976, Randam farmers were selling their paddy to the Civil Supplies Corporation through agents, who were all bigger paddy traders able to pay the necessary Rs25,000 deposit to the Corporation. Other traders were still able to purchase paddy, but only for sale to the agents for Civil Supplies, and they could not store more than 50 bags of paddy at any one time. This regulation had existed before, but it appeared that it was now quite strictly enforced under the Emergency Regulations of the Government of India. According to the farmers, the prices then being offered were Rs65 per bag for first-quality varieties (including Kichili, Ottu Kichili, and IR.20); Rs60 for second-quality varieties (such as Karuna, Kanchi, Kannagi and ADT-31, a newly released HYV with a yield potential of 6 tonnes per acre); and Rs55 for third-quality varieties including IR.8 and Kars.

The Choice of Varieties

Given earlier misgivings on the suitability of the existing HYVs for North Arcot conditions, and also given the expected results of drought (namely, a major return to short-duration local varieties), it was at first surprising to hear Randam farmers talking of Kichili, Sirumani and the Kars as crops of the past. Checks with a number of farmers in all size-classes suggested that those with more reliable wells now generally grow IR.20 in Samba, Kanchi, Kannagi or IR.8 in Navarai, and Karuna in Sornavari season: although poorer farmers or those poorly supplied with groundwater continue to rely on Kullankar.

The explanation for this surge in the adoption of HYVs is consistent with the reasoning of our earlier work; though we may have misplaced our emphasis. The most important consideration is the equalisation of prices: now that Kichili and IR.20 command the same price, the latter, with its higher yield, gives a much higher return to the farmers. IR.20 is preferred to other HYVs in Samba because, as noted earlier, other varieties (especially IR.8) do very badly at that time. The drought also helped to make IR.20 more popular, because it proved itself then to be a particularly durable variety. The large-scale replacement of Kichili does suggest, however, that we may have overestimated the significance of soil and climate as constraints on the adoption of HYVs, especially in Samba; and underestimated the significance of price, given the strongly commercial orientation of Randam farmers. It was rather more surprising to hear of the success of Karuna in Sornavari, and of Kanchi and Karuna in Navarai, in view of the poor performance of Karuna in 1973–4 and of the earlier argument on the enduring advantages of the water-sparing, short-duration Kullankar. Those without access to reliable supplies of groundwater do indeed continue to rely upon Kullankar, but those with more reliable wells appear to have been persuaded by recent experience that the profits from HYVs do compensate for the additional risk involved, especially in Sornavari.

Explanation of the changing cropping pattern is complicated by the fact that in 1975–6 Randam was selected by the Madras Fertiliser Company as a fertiliser demonstration village. The Company has undertaken soil testing; held regular discussions (and it was encouraging to hear it said that the 'officers' had taken note of the farmers' ideas and experiences); assisted farmers to obtain crop loans from the Indian Bank; and sent an agricultural specialist to the village each week to assist the farmers. The programme in Randam has undoubtedly been successful. But farmers say that traditional varieties are still cultivated on relatively greater areas in other villages, though there too, Kichili has been substantially replaced in Samba by IR.20.

Other factors in the 'new look' of Randam's agriculture are the eased fertiliser and electricity supply situations; and it also seems that, with the deepening of many of the wells to about the maximum possible with the small suction pumps currently in use, a fairly stable water level may have been reached. Even during the drought, in Sornavari, about fifteen of the bigger farmers with deeper and more reliable wells were able to raise good crops, which gave them handsome returns. Only one new well has been brought into operation since early 1974, at the margin of the wet land. Power shortages became even more acute towards the end of 1974 than they had been in 1973, though even this appears not to have deterred the bigger Randam farmers from growing HYVs. By the beginning of 1976, however, power had become available for pump-sets for fourteen hours per day.

Drought and high fertiliser prices led to a declining offtake and to an accumulation of fertiliser stocks by the middle of 1975, against a national background of improving fertiliser production. In May 1976 farmers reported that private traders were selling fertilisers at lower prices than the co-operatives, and that there was no longer any black market. This changed situation reduced the risks of cultivating HYVs, for the acute shortage of early 1974 appeared to restrain many farmers from growing the new varieties in Navarai (see Table 12.3).

The Changing Organisation of Agriculture: Fears for Rural Livelihoods

Ploughing of dry land by tractor has become much more extensive, which can only have an adverse effect on the livelihoods of the ploughmen in the Harijan colony (from which at least one family had left since 1973–4). Tractor charges have evidently not increased. Mechanised threshing has also become quite common. In early 1974 there was only one mechanical thresher anywhere near Randam, whereas there are now about twelve of them and several farmers in the village wish to acquire them. The machines do not totally displace threshing labour, but do reduce labour requirements; and since this was an operation for which labourers received rather high kind wages – often contributing a substantial proportion of their rice requirements – livelihoods are bound to be adversely affected.

However, labourers' wages have increased since 1974. It was said that during the drought the daily wage paid to men went up to Rs4 and that to women to Rs2, roughly twice the rates paid in 1973–4; and that the rates now obtaining are Rs3 and Rs1.50 respectively, and Rs4 for a man and his plough. The increase, and then the reduction following the excellent monsoon of 1975–6, both appear to have come about without serious conflict, though in the opinion of one farmer the threat of a strike was enough to persuade farmers to pay higher wages.

But changes in the money market have adversely affected the poorest people and the smaller farmers. Under Emergency powers the government has made it impossible for anyone to foreclose on the debts of another for one year, and interest rates are evidently being much more strictly controlled by means of the wide and somewhat arbitrary powers of the police. Pawnbrokers and moneylenders were lending only to known and trusted clients in early 1976, while paddy traders of Arni, badly hit by the government take-over of their trade, had apparently stopped giving money loans at all. In Randam some big farmers had acted as intermediaries for client labourers and smaller farmers, obtaining loans from moneylenders on their behalf, and in the Harijan colony several men spoke of increased dependence upon village farmers. Although doubtless undertaken in the interests of the rural poor, the measures appeared to have enhanced the powers of the village élite.

REFERENCES

Cox, A. F. (1895). *North Arcot District Manual*, Madras, Government Press.

Danda, Ajit, K. and Danda, D. G. (1971). *Development and Change in Basudha: A West Bengal Village*, Hyderabad, National Institute of Community Development.

Mencher, Joan (1974). 'Conflicts and Contradictions in the Green Revolution: The Case of Tamilnadu', *Econ. Pol. Weekly*, Annual Number.

Mendras, H. (1970). *The Vanishing Peasant*, London and Cambridge, Mass., MIT Press.

Sharma, H. P. (1973). 'The Green Revolution in India: Prelude to a Red One?' in K. Gough, and H. P. Sharma (eds), *Imperialism and Revolution in South Asia*, New York, Monthly Rev. Pr.

10 Pahalagama: a Case Study of Agricultural Change in a Frontier Environment

John Harriss

The settlement that we call 'Pahalagama' lies on the right bank of the river Kirindi in Hambantota District of Sri Lanka, towards the tail-end of the area irrigated from Wirawila tank – the Kirindi Oya right bank scheme (KORB). It is not a 'village community' so much as an area of dispersed settlement, including 85 households, given a limited degree of unity because it surrounds a single yaya. Since it lies towards the tail-end of KORB, some of the existing paddy land did not come into the possession of the large and often absentee landowners who control most of the best lands under the major irrigation schemes of the District, but was cleared by encroachers who have now mostly acquired titles to their plots. Tail-end location also means that water supplies are uncertain; even in Maha, when there is almost invariably adequate water in the tank to irrigate the whole tract, the cultivators' supplies may be cut off at critical times because of illegal diversions upstream. Cultivation in the Yala season is always subject to substantial risk. There is no exploitation of groundwater, so Pahalagama cultivators do not have the independent water supply enjoyed by many in North Arcot District.

THE PATTERN OF AGRICULTURE

By comparison with other South Asian paddy regions, cultivation in Hambantota District is remarkably extensive; this is true in Pahalagama as well, though by comparison with farmers in other parts of the District the use of intensive practices such as transplanting and hand-weeding may be rather high (Table 10.1).

Organic manuring is virtually unknown in Hambantota, though cattle are grazed on the stubble after harvest. Cattle are rarely stall-fed and straw has little or no economic value, but less than 20 per cent of the cultivators in

Table 10.1   Cultivation practices

	Maha 1973–4 (Pahalagama)	Maha 1971–2 (Hambantota District)
	Percentage of cultivators	Percentage of cultivators
Transplanting	42	17
Transplanted in other seasons, and say they will again	35	
Have transplanted but believe method unsuitable	18	
Never transplanted	7	
Hand-weeding, plus weedicides	65	39
Reported use of hired labour for weeding	35	

Note: In the case of 'hand-weeding plus weedicides' most of the reported use of labour is of very casual family labour, generally not very intensive. It is mostly to remove etavarai and other weeds that have become a problem since intensive use of fertilisers began.

Sources: Pahalagama data based on survey of 43 of the 46 paddy cultivating households April–July 1974. Hambantota District data taken from ARTI (1974), Tables 5.xxi and 5.xxxiv.

Pahalagama burn the paddy straw in their fields. Pahalagama farmers, like those of the District and of the dry zone in general, are very heavily dependent on tractors for field preparation and threshing. This has been so in Pahalagama for fifteen years or more, and cattle and buffaloes are quite marginal to paddy production. In Maha 1973–4, only four of the 43 paddy-cultivating households used buffaloes for mudding. The use of ploughs has never been common: only six of the 43 farmers reported having used ploughs in the past. The marginal involvement of draught animals in the cultivation system is striking by comparison with North Arcot District. Kachcheri records show that shortages of draught animals were endemic in Hambantota District and exacerbated by outbreaks of rinderpest, so that there were drives to encourage the use of tractors during the Second World War and again in the 1950s, in order to improve the timeliness of cultivation so essential if the use of irrigation water is to be optimised. Tractors, both two- and four-wheel, have now become cheaper than buffaloes for field preparation, because the buffalo owners charge the same as the tractor owners, while it costs more to pay and feed the boys or men who drive the buffaloes than to feed one tractor driver.

Few of the cattle owners (and three men own upwards of 100 head each) take very much interest in their animals for much of the year, except for domestic cows whose milk is used in the production of curd for the market. These apart, cattle and buffalo graze in the jungle with little or no supervision. Bran left over after the custom-milling of paddy becomes the property of the millers and is sold by them (mainly for poultry feed in the Colombo area), rather than being fed to cattle.

The rather poor standard of field preparation on KORB may be traced to the use of tractors rather than animal-drawn ploughs. It is not uncommon to see fields so badly levelled that one part is depleted of water and another flooded. In this way, as in others (cf. Alles, 1967, p. 45), tractors seem to involve waste of water, as well as having a directly detrimental effect on productivity.

Alongside this 'extensive' system of paddy cultivation two-thirds of the paddy cultivators in Pahalagama, together with almost all of those who do not operate paddy lands, cultivate some 'high land', producing chillies as the main cash crop together with a variety of vegetables, maize and kurakkan. Not all the high-land plots are true chenas, if by that term shifting cultivation is implied: about half are semi-permanent, often fenced with barbed wire and mostly under cultivation for ten years or more. These plots are now used primarily for cultivating chillies for the market, and a more restricted range of vegetables than on the chenas; they are not as fertile as true chena, though only a few farmers (about half a dozen in Pahalagama) use fertilisers taken out of their paddy supplies, or obtained from paddy cultivators, on their plots. Perhaps the main reason for the existence of this semi-permanent high-land cultivation is precisely that the farmers also carry on paddy cultivation and that they are unwilling or unable to take on the labour of clearing chenas, while they would also find it difficult to guard crops at the distance from their homes necessary for true chena. The relationship between paddy cultivation and chena in Pahalagama appeared to be a complicated one (cf. chapter 7). Such competition as does exist is not the result of directly competing demands for labour over given periods, but arises because chena cultivation offers an alternative livelihood for those who would otherwise be landless labourers, and because it tends to draw off young men from participation in the family work-force in paddy cultivation. Chena cultivation is indeed bound up with an ideology of independence and of equality.

In addition to paddy and chena rather less than half the households have gardens (watte) where coconuts, plantains, areca-nuts and other water-demanding tree crops are grown. For a few households these are major supplementary sources of income, while for others, sale of curd provides part of the household income.

LAND TENURE AND THE SIZE OF PADDY FARMS

The very small units of paddy land that characterise much of the wet zone of Sri Lanka are absent here, and more of the small units are operated by owner-cultivators than by tenants. (Average size of owner-operated holdings is 2·2 acres, tenant holdings, 3·5 acres – see Table 10.2.) This is largely a reflection of colonisation: the smaller owner-operator units are those brought under cultivation by encroachment at the margins after the

Table 10.2   Distribution of holdings

Holding size (acres)	Tenants		Owners		Owner/Tenants	
	Population	Sample	Population	Sample	Population	Sample
Less than 1			1	0		
1–1·9	2		6	5		
2–2·9	2	2	7	6		
3–4·9	11	5	6	3	3	2
Over 5	2	2	3	3	3	2
Total Cultivators	17	(9)	23	(17)	6	(4)
Grand total 46						

Notes:

1   The two tenants recorded in the category 1–1·9 acres are nominal tenants only: they pay no rent to their mothers-in-law.

2   The sample columns show the number of cultivators in each category, not all in Pahalagama yaya, from whom apparently reliable statistical information was obtained on cultivation in Maha 1973–4. For certain purposes, such as innovation data – using material from a rather larger sample – a total of 36 was available. The data used in later sections gives a fair representation of the total population of paddy cultivators in the locality, as the table shows; although it is *not* a statistical sample.

disposal of most of the area in blocks of five acres or more. The Paddy Lands Registers of the cultivation committees under Wirawila show that only 15 operational units are less than one acre.

Tenant cultivators have acquired a degree of security since the Paddy Lands Act of 1958 (see above, pp. 17–18), although I know of a number of evictions at the time of the Act, and of several notorious instances since. Even though the Act laid down that the rent paid by tenants should be a quarter of the yield or 12 bu. per acre, whichever was less, only five out of 17 tenant-cultivators paid 12 bu. in Maha 1973–4; all the rest paid a quarter of the yield, which was in every case more than 12 bu.

Among the households of Pahalagama there are also three subtenants. Subtenancies are usually short-term affairs and come about when a cultivator has difficulties preventing him from operating his lands himself. Subtenants and share-croppers are not allowed to bear any of the costs of cultivation and must pay interest on them to the main tenant.

THE PATTERN OF ADOPTION OF IMPROVED VARIETIES OF PADDY

By Maha 1973–4, all the 46 paddy cultivators in Pahalagama had used H.4, and all referred their adoption of it to the early or middle 1960s (for rice varieties in Sri Lanka, see pp. 57–8). For nearly ten years H.4 has been cultivated extensively in Pahalagama in Maha, while some cultivators also reported having cultivated it in some Yala seasons – indicative of one of the problems of water management in KORB, for H.4 is a 4–4½ month variety and there is usually insufficient water in Wirawila to permit the cultivation of such long-term varieties throughout the command area in both seasons. H.4 has been cultivated by some farmers on KORB in Yala at the cost of disrupting the whole irrigation system.

However, until Yala 1974 a majority of farmers in Pahalagama – so far away from the tank and from 'influence' that H.4 cultivation in Yala must always have been risky – used traditional varieties such as Pachchai Perumal or Yakadavi, or the improved variety H.7, because they are of shorter duration than H.4 and thus involve less risk of loss towards the season's end. One cultivator only, having experimented with H.4 and other new varieties, decided to stick to traditional varieties in both seasons, because he believes that the soils on his lands are too 'kiule' (alkaline) to give him worthwhile yields with the newer varieties.

All the cultivators consider H.4 to be a very superior variety and say that it commanded higher prices than other varieties when there was a free market in paddy. There is a strong consumer preference for larger-grained 'red' varieties like H.4 as opposed to smaller-grained 'white' varieties such as BG.11-11.

Over half the cultivators (22 out of 36) had cultivated BG.11-11 at some time, though only nine grew it in 1973–4 (three of them with H.4 for their own consumption). Seven had experimented with the variety, and said that, results unsuccessful, they would not try it again. The other six cultivators had used BG.11-11 before, but four went back to H.4 for Maha 1973–4 and two switched over to BG.34-6. The reasons given for discontinuing BG.11-11 included consumer preference, and the unsuitability of the variety for kiule soils or for the rather sandy, well-drained soils at the higher margins of the yaya where most of the owner-operators have their lands. Analysis of the pattern of adoption of BG.11-11 in relation to ownership class and size of operational holdings does suggest that a rather higher proportion of the larger cultivators and tenant-cultivators have adopted BG.11-11. But the numbers involved are so small as to make positive conclusions impossible.

There is a record of successful experiment with other varieties in the past: IR.8 in particular might still be cultivated were it not that seeds are no longer available. A majority of the larger and more innovative cultivators buy seeds from the Agriculture Department rather than using their own stocks, which suggests that cultivators in Hambantota are rather dependent upon the availability of government seed-stocks, and certainly much more so than the farmers of North Arcot District. We might infer in turn that this is related to the much more restricted range of varieties now cultivated.

A demonstration of the potential of determined government action to influence farmers' decisions under the conditions of major irrigation (and another important contrast with North Arcot District) is provided by the case of BG.34-6 and BG.34-8. Until 1974, only three men had used BG.34-6 and one man BG.34-8, but in Yala 1974 the two varieties together covered almost the whole area cultivated by Pahalagama men (Only one farmer from the 46 paddy cultivating households did not use one of the two varieties, BG.34-6 being more popular than BG.34-8 because it is a 'red' variety). This dramatic development came about through a concerted effort made with the authority and personal involvement of the Government Agent, who ensured that sufficient seed was made available for the whole area. The decision to use the two varieties was taken at the Water Meeting for Yala: and the drive was part of a more general effort to improve the efficiency of water use on KORB. Some part of the success of the effort can be put down to the loss of the previous Yala crop.

The overall pattern of adoption of new varieties is uneven, the great success of H.4 not yet being matched by higher-yielding varieties – partly of course because of the very success and adaptability of H.4.

USE OF FERTILISER

Of the 30 cultivators asked about their use of fertiliser in Maha 1973–4, and about their knowledge of official fertiliser recommendations, none had followed the local advice as given by the Ministry of Agriculture and Lands (MOAL); and only one man knew the recommendations. He was a small gambāraya and the former president of a cultivation committee. Even the secretary of another cultivation committee who actually had the MOAL recommendations pinned on his wall turned out not to know their content. All but four of the 30 men believed that the same doses and applications are required for all varieties, whereas official advice clearly states different dosages for different varieties. A popular stereotype, held by rather more than half of the farmers, is that all varieties need 1 cwt per acre of each type of fertiliser (i.e. basal, urea as first top dressing, and mixture as second top dressing). Because most farmers think that the same amounts of fertilisers are required for both BG.11-11 and for H.4, differential input cost could not be a factor working against the adoption of BG.11-11.

Two of the 30 farmers used no fertiliser at all in 1973–4, in each case because of credit difficulties, while eight used no basal dressing – five of them because none was available at the co-operative at the time they required it. Otherwise a tendency to conformity with the norm of 1:1:1 was evident, though it results in considerable over-use of urea – on H.4 in particular, which according to official advice requires only ¼ cwt. When I mentioned this to the farmers, they all said that they had found that H.4 needed more fertiliser than the official advice suggested – though a number of them had earlier said that they believed that the official advice was 1 cwt of urea! Altogether, 60 per cent of the cultivators applied three doses of fertiliser (cf. 43 per cent of owner-cultivators and 63 per cent of tenants), under major irrigation conditions in the District during Maha (cf. ARTI, 1974, Table 5.xxxvi).

Fertiliser Use and Extension Advice
It is perhaps not surprising that there is confusion and ignorance among the farmers when official sources are at variance. The recommendations for Maha 1973–4 given to me by one Krushikarma Vyāpathi Sevak (KVS) were quite different from those in the widely distributed MOAL publications, and different again from the estimates of requirement per acre used for fertiliser targets.

It seems likely that apparently conflicting advice helps to account for the lack of respect sometimes shown by the farmers for the technical services of extension workers; although there must always be a risk of this when the ministry has to advise for large areas while the local staff have their own ideas based on experience. The lack of confidence in official extension advice was striking in Pahalagama, and altogether different from the views on extension of Randam farmers. Five cultivators recounted specific incidents which, they said, showed that the KVS and the Agricultural Instructors did not know what they were talking about, and occasions when higher officers had publicly criticised the KVSs for their ignorance.

ADOPTION OF IMPROVED CULTIVATION PRACTICES
Table 10.1 shows the extent of adoption of transplanting and the use of hired labour for hand-weeding. The first transplanting in Pahalagama was in about 1964, and now eight men say that they transplant every Maha; two, whose lands are nearer the tank, in Companiwatte, say that they also transplant in Yala. All the cultivators in Pahalagama however, say that it is rarely worthwhile to transplant in Yala when water supplies are uncertain, and I several times heard the statement: 'The Yala crop is just for food, the Maha crop is for market'. This attitude was reflected in their handling of the BG.34s in Yala 1974, for nearly half the farmers used little or no fertiliser. From what I saw of the harvest before I left at the beginning of August it seemed that yields were low (around 60 bu. per acre) although water supplies had been good. Amerasinghe (1972), in his studies of Minipe colonisation scheme has made similar observations. Local labour is now just about sufficient, and skilled enough to carry out all the transplanting in the yaya, whereas ten years ago most transplanting labour had to be brought in from outside.

Reasons given for not transplanting by those who had used the method, but not in Maha 1973–4, centred around the high cost. On contract, transplanting cost is Rs150 per acre (not met by co-operative credit allocated for the operation), and those farmers who recruited and supervised the labour themselves generally paid slightly more. They maintained that the extra effort and expense was worthwhile because a better job was done when they managed everything themselves. Eight men said that they had not been able to raise the money to pay for transplanting, because of debts and loss of income due to the missed Yala and the two rather poor Maha seasons which preceded it; another six cited difficulties with credit and in finding enough labour to complete operations on time. Timeliness is made difficult partly because delays often occur in field preparation (over 50 per cent of cultivators reported such delay in 1973–4: this is symptomatic of the heavy dependence on tractors, the services of which have become increasingly unreliable as the flow of new machinery has decreased and that of spares dried up almost completely as a result of the foreign exchange crisis).

THE DIFFERENT PATTERNS OF CULTIVATION OF OWNERS AND TENANTS

Examination of the characteristics of the adopters of transplanting and of the most recent and highest-yielding of the improved varieties suggests a broad difference between the cultivation patterns of owner-operators and tenant-cultivators. These patterns emerge from Tables 10.3 and 10.4, and perhaps most clearly from Fig. 10.1.

The whole population shows a bimodal distribution, reflecting the difference between operations on tenant fields and those on owner fields. Yields were higher on tenant fields and practices more intensive, although it must be remembered that tenant fields are generally more fertile, since the owner-operators are those who encroached at the margins, so that

Table 10.3   Variety and planting method

Variety	No. cultivating	Average yield (bu. per acre)	Trans- planted	Broad- cast	Combination
BG.34-6	3	73	1	2	
BG.11-11	5	102	3	1	1 row seeded
H.4	18	70	5	12	1
Traditional	3	44		3	
Mixed H.4/ BG.11-11	3	69	1	1	1

Table 10.4   Yield and land-holding type

Owners (20) (2 transplanted, 3 combination)	Average yield: 66 bu. per acre	Max. 93 (BG.11-11) Median 59·5 Mode 53 Min. 37 (Maha Menik)
Tenants (12) (8 transplanted)	Average yield: 89 bu. per acre	Max. 126 (BG.11-11) Median 88·7 Mode 93 Min. 49 (BG.34-6)

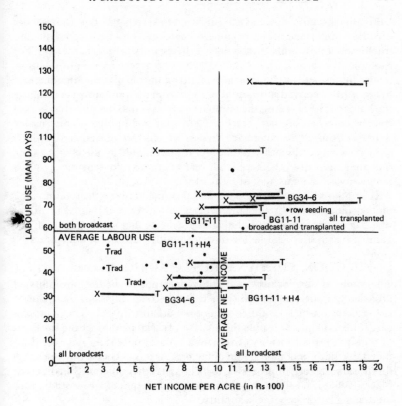

Fig. 10.1 *Labour utilisation and net income per acre*
T = tenant farmer; line T to X indicates difference in tenant's net income before
and after paying rent. The 'average' net income shown is based on tenants' net
income before paying rent. When variety is not indicated it was H.4

(quite apart from the slender statistical base) the material presented here
provides no basis for general judgements regarding the efficiency of tenant
as opposed to owner-cultivators.

If we allow for the fact that the 'average' income shown on the scatter
diagram is inflated because it is based on tenants' net incomes before rent,
then their real incomes per acre are not much higher than those of the
owners despite the fact that they used more intensive practices and
obtained higher yields per acre. Average family farm earnings per acre
among owners was Rs858; among tenants after rent payments, Rs908.
Without the use of intensive practices then, tenants' incomes per acre
would be lower than those of the owners, in spite of the higher fertility of
their lands. Perhaps one could thus argue in Toynbeean terms, that the
situation of the tenants gives them an incentive to intensify their

cultivation because 'they have to run faster to keep pace'. But what is more certainly important is the encouragement and provision of credit and tractor services by some landowners or their gambārayas (chapter 16). For example, the farmer who obtained 126 bu. per acre by dint of intensive labour inputs – so that his 'dot' goes right off the top of the scatter diagram in Fig. 10.1 – received substantial support from the gambāraya controlling the land that he operates, the gambārāya always making sure that he had the tractor when needed. Since the government supplies no alternative source of draught and there are 'strings' attached to official credit which deny it to some cultivators and render it unavailable to others at the time that they most need it, there is no real alternative to dependence upon gambārayas for many tenant cultivators.

It is impossible to draw a hard and fast line between decision-making and encouragement by the landowner/gambāraya; but there is no doubt that there are cases in Pahalagama where the involvement of the gambārayas is a crucial factor in determining patterns of cultivation.

CONCLUSION: THE DYNAMICS OF AGRICULTURE

The value of any locality case study does not lie in the possibility of abstracting from it statistically generalisable conclusions, for there can be few regions in which localities are not remarkably diverse. The point of a case study is to make possible the analysis of social processes from the focus of one quite small locality. Even then a case study does not reveal an inevitable pattern of interaction of factors, for it is of course quite possible for the same factors, or processes, to be linked rather differently in different places. What is possible, and the important function of a case study, is to analyse social processes as a totality.

We have seen that in Pahalagama adoption of new varieties has been influenced by such considerations as consumer preference; the farmers' ideas concerning the suitability of various varieties for the soils in their fields; the very success and adaptability of H.4; the reliability of water supply in different seasons; and government action (more significant in Pahalagama than where farmers have more independent control of water). Similar considerations, though perhaps more critically the availability of credit, have influenced use of fertilisers and intensive cultivation. All these factors apply elsewhere, though they do not necessarily result in the same patterns of adoption and of agricultural change, partly because they may manifest themselves differently, and partly because they must be considered in relation to basic processes, including principally, the stage of development of the farm family. The decisions made by individual cultivators will be heavily influenced not only by 'external' factors like water supply, but by such considerations as the availability of the family work-force in relation to consumption needs, and by both these considerations in relation to the resources of land and credit that are available. Different adoption studies appear to have emphasised different factors, but where family farming is concerned the different factors may simply be the manifestations of different patterns created by the same fundamental conditions. They have not, however, been analysed here, for it has seemed more important to draw attention to the overall structure within which all the farmers of Pahalagama, and Hambantota District, operate.

In the case of Pahalagama the pattern of adoption of new varieties and of intensive practices is causally linked with differences between tenants and owner-cultivators; these in turn involve differences in soil fertility and in access to crucial inputs (because it emerged that the availability of credit and draught from gambārayas could be a major factor). There is a correlation between the adoption of higher-yielding varieties, the use of intensive cultivation practices including increased use of labour, and higher yields. It is worthwhile drawing attention to this obvious fact because cultivation methods in Hambantota District are generally not intensive, and yields – even with improved varieties – are not high by comparison with other important paddy regions of South and South-East Asia. Improved varieties of paddy on their own, although increasing yield potential, do not in general add greatly to actual yields unless their adoption is accompanied by an overall improvement in cultivation practices; part of the success of H.4 may be attributed to its ability to give higher yields without substantial modifications in cultivation. But it seems clear that the potential of varieties like BG.11-11 will only be realised when a greater number of cultivators adopt more intensive practices. It is in this sense that there can be a kind over-adoption.

In Hambantota District the constraints on intensification are pre-eminently structural and grounded in the 'frontier' circumstances of the region, which we can see operating in Pahalagama. A historical perspective is important, and this is outlined in chapter 16 (cf. also Roberts, 1974, pp. 155–8). In summary, cultivation in Hambantota has persistently been constrained by shortages of labour, draught and credit, the former due specifically to its 'frontier' character (for less than a century ago much of the area was hardly populated at all). Population densities have been low in relation to cultivable land, and the cattle population was kept down by disease with the results in terms of mechanisation described above. The Boserup thesis concerning the positive relationship between population density and intensive agriculture is exemplified here (Boserup, 1965). In Pahalagama the working population has only very recently become adequate for all cultivators to use labour-intensive practices without recourse to costly import of labour from outside; and the availability of chena draws off labour from paddy so that there are no landless labourers, in the Indian sense. In this context the profitability of transplanting, for example, is not assured.

Extensive cultivation practices adapted to these conditions have their own inertia, which is also embedded in the agrarian power structure, itself deriving from the way in which the British elected to develop the lands of this frontier area by selling them off in large units to generally absentee owners thought to be 'indigenous capitalists' (misnomer though this was, cf. Herring, 1973). The poor tenant-cultivators, brought in from land-hungry Matara District to the west, remain substantially indebted to the land controllers. Today, as in the case of Pahalagama, the gambārayas have some power to influence patterns of agriculture. But that power depends in part on the indebtedness of some other cultivators, who may thereby be discouraged from attempting to intensify their cultivation. Extensive cultivation may also be bolstered by the gambāraya's control of draught power. Thus, there is a vicious circle involving population density, élitism, technology and environment which ultimately constrains paddy production in Hambantota, and which makes problematic there the recommendations of the ILO Mission to Sri Lanka (ILO, 1971) in regard to intensification of paddy cultivation.

REFERENCES

Agrarian Research and Training Institute, ARTI (1974). *The Agrarian Situation Relating to Paddy Cultivation: Hambantota District*, Colombo.

Alles, W. S. (1967). 'Soil and Water Conservation in the Dry Zone' in O. S. Peries (ed.), *The Development of Agriculture in the Dry Zone*, Colombo, Ceylon Association for the Advancement of Science.

Amerasinghe, N. (1972). 'The Impact of High Yielding Varieties of Rice in a Settlement Scheme in Ceylon', *Modern Ceylon Studies*, 3, 19–35.

Boserup, E. (1965). *The Conditions of Agricultural Growth*, London, Allen and Unwin.

Herring, R. (1973). 'The Forgotten 1953 Paddy Lands Act in Ceylon: Ideology, Capacity, Response', *Ceylon Studies Seminar*, 1974 Series, no. 1, Peradeniya.

International Labour Office, ILO (1971). *Matching Employment Opportunities and Expectations: A Programme of Action for Ceylon*, vol. i: *Report* and vol. ii: *Working Papers* (especially Paper 10), Geneva.

Roberts, M. (1974). 'Aspects of Ceylon's Agrarian Economy in the 19th Century' in *University of Ceylon History of Ceylon*, vol. iii, Colombo, Ceylon University Press, pp. 146–64.

11 Agricultural Extension: Myth, Reality and Challenge

Robert Chambers and B. W. E. Wickremanayake

Agricultural extension has generated a large literature for India (including the *Journal of Extension Education*; Roy *et al.*, 1968; Fliegel *et al.*, 1968; Hunter, 1970; Sinha (ed.), 1972; Heginbotham, 1973; Mook, 1974), and has also been studied in some of its aspects in Sri Lanka (Abeyratne, 1973; ARTI, 1974). Much of the concern has been with the diffusion of new technology in agriculture, with a tendency in India towards studies of the communication process. Our own selective study was concerned with comparing agricultural extension in North Arcot and SE. Sri Lanka; with considering to what extent, if any, the different levels of adoption of the new technology could be attributed to differences in extension; and with policy prescriptions that might flow from our research experience.

One of our main conclusions is that agricultural extension at the field level is both difficult to examine and easy to misperceive. (Space does not permit full criticism of our methods and their shortcomings, in so far as we are aware of them; but see above, pp. 50–1.) Surveys in which farmers are asked about extension contact are vulnerable to distortion; interviews with field staff are liable to founder on evasive and inaccurate responses; field investigators who become friendly with extension staff may report over-favourably on their performance; and what extension staff actually do may differ radically from their official instructions and from the initial ideas of researchers. We faced all these obstacles and gradually became aware how alarmingly easy it is to project preconceived interpretations on to ambiguous and poor information. That we have rejected much data and many of our early impressions may not necessarily mean that our findings and conclusions are soundly based, though we believe they are, and the reader is asked to exercise a healthy scepticism both in appraising what we report and suggest, and in examining and allowing for his own biases and possible misperceptions.

A central question is posed by the much higher levels of adoption of paddy HYVs in the study area in Sri Lanka than in the study area in India (see pp. 61–3 and pp. 93–7). It is important to ask, though exceedingly difficult to answer, whether – and if so to what extent – these contrasts in adoption can be explained by differences in extension staffing, in extension contact with farmers, in extension methods and in the content and value to farmers of the advice offered by extension staff.

STAFFING

North Arcot District is neither in the intensive agricultural development programme (IADP) nor in the intensive agricultural area programme and therefore has a normal staffing level for an Indian District. The Revenue District is divided into four Agricultural Divisions, each with a District Agricultural Officer (DAO). Responsible to him are a number of Deputy Agricultural Officers (Dep. AO), some of them in the blocks, one per block, and also some based more centrally and specialising (Dep. AO is the equivalent of Agricultural Extension Officer, AEO). In 1974 the DAO for Vellore Agricultural District had no less than 30 Deputy AOs; 12 in the blocks, 7 for HYV paddy and millets, 4 for plant protection, 3 for vegetables, and 1 each for horticulture, the cumbu crash programme, cotton, and pulses. At the block level the Block Development Officer (BDO) had administrative control of the Dep. AOs, while supervision in technical matters rested with the DAO. Typically a BDO had several specialised staff for fields other than agriculture, and for agriculture a depot assistant, a compost development inspector, two demonstration assistants (labourers) and 5 Gram Sevaks (VLWs) (agriculture). In addition there were 5 VLWs for general purposes.

In practice all 10 VLWs in a block did agricultural extension work, and according to Chakravarty and Arya (1974, p. 55) spent 80 per cent of their time on it. Using the Census counts of cultivators (Chockalingam, 1972, p. 3) and assuming 10 VLWs to each of the 38 blocks in the District, we have a ratio of VLWs to cultivators of 1:1342, equivalent to 1:1678 after allowing for only 80 per cent of VLWs' time being devoted to agriculture, say 1:1700 with rounding. There was roughly one VLW to every five villages (taking the 1971 Census definition of village).

Staff in Hambantota District were roughly comparable with those in North Arcot as follows:

North Arcot	Hambantota
District Agricultural Officer (DAO)	District Agricultural Extension Officer (DAEO)
Deputy Agricultural Officer (Dep. AO) or Agricultural Extension Officer (AEO)	Additional District Agricultural Extension Officer (Additional DAEO)
Agricultural Assistant (AA)	Agricultural Instructor (AI)
Gram Sevak/Village-level Worker (VLW)	Krushikarma Vyāpthi Sevak (KVS)

In 1973 the extension staff in Hambantota District was as follows (ARTI, 1974, p. 48):

Headquarters	Field	
DAEO	AIs	7
Additional DAEO	KVSs (in office)	7
AI (headquarters)	KVSs (in field)	46
AI (paddy)		
AI (plant protection)		

Comparing KVSs with VLWs, and estimating 25,000 paddy farmers and some 5000 high-land cultivators in Hambantota District who have no paddy, then the ratio of field KVSs to cultivators becomes 46 for 30,000 or 1:650, about two and a half times the density of 1:1700 for North Arcot.

At levels higher than that of the VLW and KVS, the density of staffing and degree of specialisation are harder to compare because Hambantota is one of 22 Districts serviced by staff from national headquarters. There was, however, a much higher ratio of specialised to unspecialised staff at the local level in North Arcot than in Hambantota.

FARMER CONTACT WITH EXTENSION STAFF

Survey studies support the belief that there are high levels of contact between extension workers and farmers. In India Roy *et al.* (1968, p. 64) found that for the year before the interview two-thirds of their farmer respondents implied that they had talked with the VLW. For Hambantota District a survey has reported that 62 per cent of farmers in a sample of 146 were visited by extension workers in the Yala season, and 79 per cent of respondents gave 'extension personnel visiting farmer' as a source from which they gained general agricultural information (ARTI, 1974, pp. 49, 53, 56). In concluding that 'the single information agency with the greatest impact on the farmer was the agricultural extension service through visits of its staff to farmsteads' (ibid., p. 50), the report of this survey supports a view which we believe to be a common but misleading myth generated by survey methodology.

The Indian survey (Roy *et al.*, 1968; Fliegel *et al.*, 1968) was subject to at least five biases: the Districts selected were unrepresentative, with an average staffing level much higher than that for India as a whole; in two-thirds of the Districts there were special programmes; the villages selected had abnormally high staff continuity; the sample was biased towards larger farmers; and the survey was two-stage, with the danger that the first stage influenced extension agent behaviour before the second stage when the contact question was asked. All these factors were liable to inflate the contact response, making it misleading for India as a whole.

The Hambantota survey (ARTI, 1974) was liable to exaggerate contact through at least three biases: the sample of farmers was drawn from a government crop-cutting survey in the course of which they were meant to be regularly visited by government staff, some of them agricultural extension workers; the interviews were arranged by extension staff, and the investigators were taken by extension staff to the farmers; and the holding sizes of farmers were above average.

The probability that these biases inflated reported contact between extension workers and farmers helps to explain why our own survey presents a sharply different impression.

In North Arcot a question was based on the instruction 'If the farmer has used any of the information services in the last year, fill in this block' and investigators were instructed to insert on the form VLW, AEO and BDO, to ensure that questions were asked about them. Taking the eleven villages in the sample proper, the results expressed as percentages of respondents were VLW 17 per cent, AEO 2 per cent, and BDO 1 per cent, contrasting with the two-thirds who implied contact with the VLW in the survey by Roy *et al.*

In the Hambantota survey, two questions were asked of the 192 cultivator respondents in the late stages of the survey: 'During the last two seasons, did any official of the extension service come to meet you?' and 'Did you go to meet the KVS/AI?' The results are presented in Table 11.1.

Table 11.1   Percentages of respondents recorded as reporting direct extension contact in Yala 1973 and Maha 1973–4

	Yes	No	No response	Total
Member of extension staff came to meet the cultivator	16	71	14	101
Cultivator went to meet KVS/AI	21	63	16	100

(One total does not sum to 100 because of rounding)

The gross contact in terms of numbers of cultivators who had one or the other form of contact is not known, since some cultivators may have replied positively to both questions. The 16 per cent of farmers who said they had been visited by extension workers during the previous Maha and Yala seasons contrasts with the 62 per cent of farmers reported in the ARTI survey as saying that they had been visited by extension workers during Yala alone.

Our findings are also subject to criticism for upward bias, including the probable distortion in all these surveys through deferential responses, with farmers feeling that they were expected to report contact, that it was prestigious to do so, or that it was prudent or right to give the impression that extension workers were diligent. Our conclusion is that our results also exaggerated contact and that survey methodology in general sustains a widespread myth of a high degree of direct contact between extension agents and farmers when in practice such contact is low.

One factor which might affect contact is distance and ease of travel. VLWs in North Arcot generally lived further from their villages (a mean of 4·8 miles, excluding Dusi) than KVSs in Hambantota lived from their cultivation committee areas (2·8 miles). For the eleven North Arcot villages, the estimated mean time for a round trip from house to office to village and back to house again was about 2 and a quarter hours, but much less for Hambantota. Not surprisingly, by far the highest contact was reported for Dusi, a very accessible large village near a major urban centre and with a resident VLW, as shown in Table 11.2.

Table 11.2   Percentage of cultivators who named VLW, AEO or BDO when asked if they had used any information service during the previous year

	Size of sample N	VLW	Percentage of N AEO	BDO
Dusi	139	57	16	10
Eleven sample villages, excl. Dusi	646	17	2	1

Investigators reported that five of the 11 villages were never visited by VLWs. These included one for which there was no VLW, and the only three villages to which the VLW had to use a bus. In Hambantota, the cultivation committee reporting the lowest contact with the KVS was precisely the one where he lived furthest away, a distance of 10 miles. Our general finding was that for most villages there was no clear relationship between distance and contact, except at the extremes – where they were very close (with high contact) or very distant (low contact).

EXTENSION METHODS AND CONTENT

To compare extension methods and content between North Arcot and Hambantota is difficult: it would require a far more detailed study than we could carry out, and during the year of the survey in Hambantota agricultural extension staff were diverted from what had previously been an almost exclusive concentration on paddy to an almost exclusive concentration on other high-land crops, making it impossible to examine at first hand either the method or content of extension for paddy. Two points of comparison of method and content between the two areas can, however, be made.

First, previous to our research Sri Lanka had a well-developed system of paddy extension through extension field trials, mini-kits, and production kits (Abeyratne, 1973 pp. 8–11). These were designed to facilitate trials of varieties to be undertaken in farmers' fields, so that they themselves could observe the performance of different varieties and themselves breed up seed of those that did well. Our best judgement is that this system contributed to the very rapid adoption of new varieties.

Secondly, the content of extension advice in Sri Lanka had probably been more in the interests of the farmers as perceived by them than was the case in India. In Sri Lanka substantial benefits to farmers accrued through the adoption of H.4, and then later the new HYVs, whereas there did not appear to have been equivalent benefits from adopting new varieties in India. A major factor in this was the much greater price differentials in India. In Sri Lanka there were never large differences in price for new varieties, but in North Arcot IR.8 had been known to sell for only just over half the price for Kichili Samba (GEB.24), so that very much higher yields were required from IR.8 to make it more profitable, particularly in view of its high-cost input requirements. Again, in North Arcot, the credibility of extension was undermined by the persistent advice, equally persistently (and rationally) rejected, that cultivators should grow IR.8 in Samba, for which it was unsuitable (see p. 99).

AGRICULTURAL EXTENSION AND THE ADOPTION OF HYVS

The much higher rates of adoption of new HYVs in Hambantota than in North Arcot might, then, be explained in terms of (i) Hambantota's higher ratio of low level staff to cultivators, (ii) shorter distances between homes and offices of low-level staff and farmers, (iii) resulting from (i) and (ii), perhaps somewhat higher levels of contact in Hambantota (comparing Tables 11.1 and 11.2, and ignoring Dusi as outside the sample proper), (iv) more effective extension methods, and (v) a content to extension which was more beneficial to farmers. Our judgement is that this last is by far the most important of these factors, an essential precondition for the effectiveness of all the others.

Explanations of adoption must, however, involve many other influences. Surveys have sometimes been simplistic in jumping from the characteristics of farmers who adopt to implying that those characteristics cause adoption. It is more useful to exploit the survey situation to find out why farmers themselves say they do or do not adopt. When we examine the reasons given by cultivators in the North Arcot and Hambantota surveys for not adopting HYVs (see pp. 122 and 146–9), it is not advice or knowledge but the supply of inputs, including water, which emerge as most critical in the eyes of farmers – fertiliser, pesticides and water in North Arcot, and seeds in Hambantota. Of these two constellations, that in North Arcot is probably more typical of South Asia since Hambantota District during the survey was liberally supplied with fertiliser as part of a special programme.

A further set of factors concern decision-making and water control. Adoption was high in three situations: where the water supply was reliable; where decisions were partly collective; and where there was some combination of these. Thus the four Indian villages with the highest proportion of paddy cultivators growing HYVs – Vegamangalam, Vinayagapuram, Dusi and Randam – were precisely those with the most reliable water supplies in their ayacuts. Vegamangalam had a perennial flow from its spring and the cultivation using that source was synchronised; Vinayagapuram had a communal channel which usually ensured a second crop for all cultivators in the ayacut; Dusi was the only village under a major irrigation tank and usually achieved two paddy crops a year; and Randam had the highest proportion of pump-sets to wells of any village in the survey. Moreover, no less than 90 per cent of the acreage under HYVs in the sample villages in North Arcot was irrigated from pump-sets. The other factor – the collectivity of decisions – applied mainly in Sri Lanka. On major and on some minor irrigation in Sri Lanka there was a tradition of agreeing on not only the dates of operations but also the durations of the paddy varieties to be planted. Much the same was true in India at Vegamangalam. In Sri Lanka this was exploited to secure adoption of new varieties. Thus the 'adoption' of BG.34-6 and BG.34-8 on Kirindi Oya right bank occurred through the dynamic leadership of the Government Agent, Hambantota, who persuaded cultivators at a meeting and then ensured the seed supply for the whole tract. In general, then, adoptions appear likely to be higher either when farmers control their individual water supplies (pump-sets in North Arcot) or where water control and decisions about which variety to grow are partly or entirely co-ordinated and collective.

We conclude, however, that agricultural extension even without major reforms may be useful through two activities. The first is the organisation of demonstrations. The evidence is strong (for example Roy *et al.*, 1968, pp. 68–9) that demonstrations are regarded by farmers as the most persuasive extension methods. In spreading a new variety rapidly, adequate and widespread trials and demonstrations may contribute significantly.

The second activity is the supply of inputs. Without seed, as cited by 32 per cent of the non-adopting farmers in the Sri Lanka sample, adoption of a variety is impossible. Without an adequate, timely and reasonably priced supply of fertilisers and pesticides, as cited by over two-thirds of the non-adopting farmers in India, adoption may not make economic sense. If extension staff and not the market determine access to and the allocation of inputs such as seed, fertiliser and pesticides, then extension staff have a very important role – and one which may become even more critical in the next few years in influencing the extent to which HYVs are grown and who grows them. A key question is whether staff can be induced to distribute access to these inputs to more smaller farmers rather than fewer larger farmers. The implications for complementarities and trade-offs between equity and production deserve careful analysis.

THE CHALLENGE: PROBLEMS

The evidence and arguments presented raise the well-worn questions of what extension staff at the lowest levels actually do and what they ought to do. We are often told that the VLW is, or ought to be, 'guide, philosopher and friend' to farmers. We are told, in India, that he does, or should, visit each village three to four times a month. We are told that he is, and ought not to be, badly educated, poorly motivated, idle, venal and ignorant. We are led to believe that his main activity is, or ought to be, visiting farmers in their fields and giving them advice. We are sometimes told that low-level staff are to blame for all that goes wrong. Thus Surinder Sud:

> . . . if most of the agricultural development schemes and crash pro-grammes have not yielded the expected results, it is due to the inefficiency of the base level implementation machinery, the extension service. (*Indian Express*, 25 July 1974)

All these views are part of the mythology of extension and all to some extent obscure the reality. This can be illustrated with examples of pressures which low-level extension staff face and their responses to them, especially concerning targets, reports and input supply.

Top-down targetry in agricultural administration has been criticised by Dandekar (1967), Hunter (1970), Heginbotham (1973) and Mook (1974) among others. The official rationale is presumably that staff will work harder and do what is required and programmes will succeed more if statistics derived from some senior imagination are disaggregated down the hierarchy with sufficient authority to induce those at the bottom to try, or try harder, to turn them into reality. The reality, as is well known, is made to exist on paper. In the words of one DAO to his AEOs, quoted by Mook: 'We have achieved all our targets. Do you understand? Make the necessary arrangements in your blocks' (1974, p. 143). The achievement of targets becomes 'largely a book-keeping affair' (ibid.). From the huge discrepancy between the project's North Arcot survey finding of 13 per cent of paddy area under HYVs in 1972–73 and the official figure for the same taluks in the same year of between 39 and 48 per cent (see above, p. 94), it is possible to gain some measure of the error resulting from this system. Moreover, it has bad effects on morale, honesty, and credibility with the public: morale because targets tend to be handed down without participation by junior staff, because they often relate to matters outside their control anyway (the weather and farmers' decisions) and because, as Mook points out, AEOs tend to keep the easiest targets for themselves and

hand on to VLWs the more difficult ones; honesty because of the pressure
to falsify and invent returns and connivance at this, all up the line; and
credibility because, to cite Mook again on the AEO, 'Members of the
public know that he is concerned about meeting his targets, and they
therefore tend to doubt his sincerity regarding the products and practices
which he peddles' (1974, pp. 141–2). While the system persists without
reform, the extension agent becomes discredited in his own eyes, in those of
his supervisors, and in those of the public.

A corollary of targetry is reporting. The number of reports required in
the two survey areas was startling. In North Arcot, according to our
information, a Deputy Agricultural Officer in a block was required to
submit 1 weekly, 3 fortnightly, 15 monthly, 1 quarterly and 1 half-yearly
report, a total of 316 a year. In Hambantota District, one Agricultural
Instructor was required to submit no less than 29 reports and returns a
month, or 348 a year. New reports are added but old ones are not stopped.
In Sri Lanka one effect of the creation of an extra ministry in Colombo was
to add to the reports required from the field. Moreover, as part of the food
war there was a flow of urgent demands for *ad hoc* information, demands to
the DAEO having often to be repeated to AIs and from them to KVSs who
then reported back to AIs who reported back to the DAEO. It would be an
over-statement to say that the food war became a paper war, but the food
war did add to the reports and information required from the field, did
increase the burden of paperwork on junior staff, did consume more paper,
ink and typewriter ribbon, and did perversely tie extension staff more than
ever to their offices. Often too, in such situations, much of the extra
information demanded is already available in other reports but senior
officials do not bother to find this out. This common failing is remediable.
Without reform the extension agent becomes a clerk.

When inputs are scarce and access to them is controlled by extension
staff it is not surprising that corruption should flourish. With the scarcities
to be anticipated in the next few years, the tendency may become more
marked. With scarcities, the introduction of rationing is a normal official
reflex. But one predictable cost is an income transfer of petty inducements
from farmer-customers to extension staff-suppliers. Barbara Harriss has
found that standard bribes given at the various stages of obtaining fertiliser
in North Arcot in August 1974 raised the price of a bag of urea to the
purchaser by between Rs20 and Rs35: one effect may be the emergence of
a new class of moneylender in the form of minor government officials (see
p. 265). Another may be to tie staff more firmly than ever to the stores.
offices and homes where these transactions take place, since it is only to be
expected that they will give these profitable activities a very high priority.
Without reform the extension agent becomes a storekeeper and money
lender.

In all these circumstances, it is not surprising that field visits are rare.
Staff may anyway be inclined to stay in their offices and wait for farmers to

come to them. The pattern of field visits reported by survey investigators for the North Arcot villages is indicative. Of the twelve villages, one had a resident VLW, was near a major town and on a main road, and received visits from the BDO and AEO. This was Dusi, purposively chosen and typical of those atypical villages which so often feature in surveys, especially when block staff are involved in the selection procedure. Of the remaining eleven villages, five were reportedly not visited by VLWs during the year. For all the remaining six, the pattern of visits was the same: the VLW saw village officials – the village president, the karnam, the munsiff – and some bigger landlords, landowners and, in one case, schoolteachers. Usually no fields were visited. The purpose of the visit was usually to obtain information and maintain reciprocal relationships with influential local people. Sometimes, too, extension agents had powerful political friends, which made it impossible for their superior officers to discipline them or post them. Without reform the extension agent is locked in with the local élite.

Other problems and difficulties could be added: the widespread falsification of diaries to show greater fieldwork than actual, to satisfy superiors and enable the claiming of full allowances; the special problem of AIs in Hambantota who felt that their counterparts in the wet zone had more time to study for promotion examinations and that they themselves would not be rewarded for hard work which left them less time and energy for study; the numbers of meetings which have to be attended; the priority of visits by superior officers and the time spent preparing for them; and last but not least, authoritarian management which communicates from the top downwards but discourages communication upwards of problems or of discordant information.

THE CHALLENGE: SOLUTIONS

To mitigate these problems and improve the performance of agricultural extension staff, seven measures can be suggested:

1   *Abandoning targetry* except where the achievement of the target is within the competence of the extension agent and where it can also be inspected. This would limit targets largely or entirely to physical actions with physical components, such as the issue of mini-kits, the preparation and holding of demonstrations, and the distribution of seeds.

2   *Rationalising reporting*, reducing the number and frequency of reports and eliminating duplication. This requires special skill, indeed brutality, for information often looks useful even when it is either misleading or unlikely to be used. Such rationalisation is also a time-consuming activity requiring care and courage.

3   *Appraising alternative systems for input supply* in situations of scarcity. It may be unrealistic to expect extension agents both to issue inputs and

to be active field advisers for farmers. It is also possible that in time of scarcity small farmers might have better access to inputs supplied through an open market than to inputs dispensed through systems of local patronage.

4 *A team approach to extension*, village by village, using methods which can reach all farmers. Sixteen farmers in Randam first heard of HYVs when extension staff visited the village with films (see p. 136). Such visits could begin with a period spent in the fields and listening to farmers' problems, and not only those of the larger and more influential farmers. Further, they would have the advantage of encouraging direct contact between staff and farmers and of providing an opportunity for feedback of farmers' problems and requests, jumping the bottom rungs in the hierarchy where they normally stick. They should also reduce the dangers of perpetuating bad advice such as inappropriate recommendations for basal fertiliser applications or for paddy varieties unsuited to particular soils or seasons.

5 *Concentration of effort on demonstrations* when there is something worth demonstrating. They have high credibility and are easy to supervise. There were rather few paddy demonstrations in either survey area.

6 *A sequence of carefully judged special programmes.* A continuous succession of initiatives, each superseding and burying its predecessors, is a characteristic of Indian administration and has had its critics. But it has advantages if used sensitively. Each new project or programme may in its early stages call forth special efforts and may work as intended in the short run before routines and evasions have begun to strangle effectiveness. But each time a new initiative is launched, there should be an appraisal of what earlier initiatives can be stopped so that extension staff are not presented with an impossible workload.

7 *A management approach to agricultural extension staff* (Chambers and Belshaw, 1973; Chambers, 1974). We know of no case, except perhaps Botswana, where – on any scale – agricultural extension has been tackled as a problem in the management of extension staff themselves, with a carefully designed training programme tied in with procedural reform. Yet the difficulties arising from targetry, from excessive reports, from corruption in the supply of inputs, from liaison with local élites, and from authoritarian management should lend themselves to such an approach. It is a task for civil servants and management specialists who have the imagination and courage to look from the outside and from below at the system as it actually operates. Reform has to be decided at the top but unless it is based on a realistic appreciation of conditions at the bottom, it is likely to fail. A successful reform would be a major breakthrough not only for South Asia but for other parts of the world also.

The above measures should improve the job design and performance of

166   GREEN REVOLUTION?

extension workers. But a crucial precondition for benefits from extension is
that the technology presented to farmers should be worth adopting, as all
too often it is not. Much evidence suggests that where innovations are
highly beneficial, they will be adopted rapidly, extension or no; and
conversely, that no amount of excellent communication can spread a poor
innovation. One immediately practical task for extension is to act as a
spearhead, making the adoption of good innovations faster and more
widespread than it would otherwise have been. But this should not obscure
the more difficult and longer-term task of improving the quality of the
innovations themselves through more effective feedback to research. This
is particularly difficult in an authoritarian, hierarchical organisation. The
greatest challenge to agricultural extension may well be so to reform the
style and procedures of management that a new upward flow of
information from farmers is generated to improve research and make the
technologies resulting from it more appropriate.

REFERENCES

Abeyratne, E. F. L. (1973). *The Extension of High Yielding Varieties*, paper to
    ARTI/IDS Seminar on the Social and Economic Consequences of the
    New Seeds, Colombo, mimeo.
ARTI, (1974). *The Agrarian Situation Relating to Paddy Cultivation in Five
    Selected Districts of Sri Lanka Part 1: Hambantota District*, Research Study
    Series no. 6, Agrarian Research and Training Institute, Colombo.
Chakravarty, T. K. and Arya, H. P. S. (1974). 'Village-Level Workers and
    Their Work: an Analysis of Job Structure in Different Contexts',
    Behavioural Science and Community Development, 8, 53–63.
Chambers, Robert and Belshaw, Deryke (1973). *Managing Rural Develop-
    ment: Lessons and Methods from Eastern Africa*, Discussion Paper no. 15,
    Institute of Development Studies, University of Sussex.
Chambers, Robert (1974). *Managing Rural Development: Ideas and Experience
    from East Africa*, Uppsala, Scandinavian Institute of African Studies.
Chockalingam, K. (1972). *Census of India 1971, Ser. 19, Tamil Nadu Part
    X–B, District Census Handbook, Village and Town-wise Primary Census
    Abstract, North Arcot vol. 1*, Madras.
Dandekar, V. M. (1967). Presidential Address to the Ind. Soc. Agric.
    Econ., *Ind. J. Agric. Econ.*, 22.
Fliegel, F. C., Roy, P., Sen, L. K. and Kivlin, J. E. (1968). *Agricultural
    Innovations in Indian Villages*, Hyderabad, National Institute of Com-
    munity Development.
Heginbotham, Stanley J. (1973). 'The Dynamics of Post-Colonial
    Bureaucracy: Culture, History and Ideology in Indian Administration',
    typescript, S. Asian Inst., New York, Columbia University (to be
    published as a book by Columbia University Press).
Hunter, G. (1970). *The Administration of Agricultural Development: Lessons*

from India, London, Oxford University Press.

Mook, B. (1974). *Value and Action in Indian Bureaucracy*, Discussion Paper no. 65, Institute of Development Studies, University of Sussex.

Roy, P., Fliegel, F. C., Kivlin, J. E. and Sen, L. K. (1968). *Agricultural Innovation among Indian Farmers*, Hyderabad, National Institute of Community Development.

Sinha, P. R. R. (ed.) (1972). *Studies in Extension Education*, Hyderabad, National Institute of Community Development.

12 Tractors, Profits and Debt in Hambantota District, Sri Lanka

Barbara Harriss

THE GREAT DEBATE

One technological transfer which has generated heated academic and political debate is that of mechanised traction. This controversy involves a number of disciplines, as may be seen from the following summary of the arguments with respect to Sri Lanka.

Tractors may break power bottlenecks 'in a tightly tuned system of multiple cropping' (ILO, 1971, p. 102). Tractors release grazing land for paddy or other crops. Tractors can dry-plough the non-friable reddish brown earths of the dry zone and thus conserve water (Panabokke, 1967, pp. 29, 33; Alles, 1967, p. 47). Tractors can release labour for alternative work and can relieve youths from the 'disagreeable tasks of tilling and puddling' (Carr, 1973, pp. 1–2). Tractors can thresh high-yielding grains normally resistant to shedding (Ahmed, 1974, p. 69).

The decision to tractorise far preceded the adoption of HYVs of paddy and was indeed made at a time when there may have been an acute shortage of labour (see below, pp. 153–4). From 1950, four-wheel tractors were imported at the rate of 8000 per decade and two-wheelers at 3500 per decade. According to Raj (1972, p. 332) an undervalued foreign exchange rate for tractors, spares and fuel helped to boost demand for tractors as substitutes for animal draught. At the same time as the planned rate of import doubled in 1970 (Ahmed, 1974, p. 69), so official policy on tractors changed in the light of evidence of their abuse.

Carr has found that 25 per cent of all tractors in the dry and intermediate zones were being used on commercial estates and not for paddy, in addition to which 40 per cent of all tractor time was for non-agricultural work (1973, p. 3). There is also growing evidence (reviewed in Duncan, 1974, pp. 1–5) that tractors do not significantly raise output. Widespread tractorisation has not changed the use of grazing land. Although 300,000 buffaloes may have been replaced by tractors there remain approximately 700,000, together with 1,700,000 cattle (Agricultural Census, 1974). Farmers and tractor owners persist in ploughing paddy land in a wet condition, thereby wasting, not conserving, water. Bottlenecks in hiring lead to untimely land preparation. Incorrect implements such as 'cultivators' create excessive quantities of ooze. Dry ploughing is not always correct either, and may create cloddy soil which necessitates further land preparation. Labour is displaced: for every acre ploughed by tractor, 8 man-days of labour is lost, for each acre threshed mechanically, 2 man-days (Ahmed, 1974, p. 67). Lastly, the undoubted appeal of tractors to educated youth does not lie in the agreeability of the work (it is dirtier than driving buffalo) but in the status-enhancement of machinery.

This chapter attempts to contribute to the debate over mechanisation by monitoring a neglected side of the agricultural economy – the economics of tractor ownership. Although outside the mainstream of debate this is no backwater, because of its relevance to the structure of government-sponsored loans to paddy cultivators. These loans are currently broken down as in Table 12.1.

Table 12.1   Co-operative loans for paddy cultivation, 1974

Operation	Maha 1973–4 (Rs per acre)	Yala 1974 (Rs per acre)	Increase: Yala over Maha (%)
Ploughing	70	90	28
Seed paddy	35	65	85
Fertiliser	65	85	31
Weedicides	50	65	30
Pesticides	100	130	30
Harvesting	50	50	0
Total	370	485	31

Source: Hambantota Multi-purpose Co-operative Society.

While allocations for the labour component remained static, the loan for ploughing increased relatively the least. The Paddy Lands Act of 1958 made provisions to regulate the 'charges made for the hire by paddy cultivators of implements and buffalo' (Kurukulasuriya, 1971, p. 163) yet the average tractor-hire rate in Hambantota District in 1974 was 1·75 times the quantity allotted for the Yala loan. Under the Agricultural Productivity Law (no. 2 of 1972), the government has power to requisition tractors in cases where rates are excessively high or tractors are 'inefficiently' used. Yet this had not been attempted in Hambantota District on the grounds that the increase in maintenance costs, in the costs of fuel, and in the general cost of living for both drivers and owners justified the rates charged.

In view of this situation the first part of this chapter examines the economics of ownership of two- and four-wheel tractors (hereafter 2WT and 4WT) and the second section considers the implications of the results for rural indebtedness.

THE SAMPLE AND ITS CONCENTRATION OF ASSETS

Hambantota District is remarkable in having 25 per cent of Sri Lanka's 2WTs and 10 per cent of the 4WTs. From a licensed 4WT population of 387, data for an 11 per cent sample of 42 were obtained. From an unknown population of 2WTs, data for 19 were assembled. These samples are non-random and comprise those owners of tractors who were caught by the random sampling procedure for a survey of Paddy Marketing Board (PMB) quota millers, private custom-millers, co-operative branch managers, licensed tractor agents and repairers, and private pesticide traders. The sample is biased towards those owners of tractors who have other businesses. Between them, the 30 owners also owned 12 PMB quota mills, 10 custom mills, 15 shops, 3 vans, 19 lorries, 5 pesticide and other businesses, 2 petrol sheds, 1 hotel and 3 tractor spares and repairs businesses. On average, each 4WT owner has 19 acres of paddy land and 23 acres of coconut; each 2WT owner has 6 acres of paddy and 3·5 acres of coconut or chena, while the median size of land holding in the District in 1973 was 4·5 acres (ARTI, 1974, p. viii). This bias in land and asset ownership will have little effect on the profitability of tractor ownership. Most farmers are not tractor owners (Ahmed, 1974, p. 70) and it is the owners who hire out tractors who create the market rate. The sample represents the latter type of owner.

Data

It cannot be assumed that informants gave accurate information. My computations use the figures they gave, but I suspect that many informants underestimated the number of acres a tractor ploughs per day and the number of days the tractor was used for ploughing, haulage, threshing and winnowing per season, in order to present underestimates of their gross income. On rates for operations, on the consumption of fuel and on the wages paid to drivers the data are probably accurate. But accounts of maintenance costs may have been exaggerated in order to over-estimate costs of operation. The net result of these under- and over-estimations is to underestimate net profit, in other words to flatten the gradient of the regression lines interpolated in Fig. 12.1.

PROFITABILITY

Net Profit and Private Profitability

Three points about net profits are immediately apparent from Table 12.2:
(i) the great absolute difference in net profit between the two technologies,

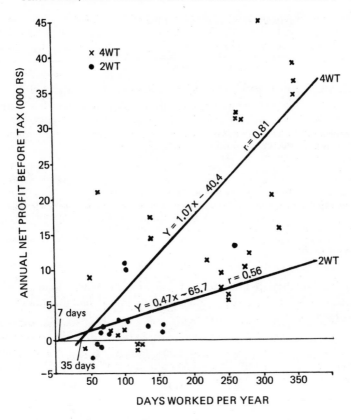

FIG. 12.1 *Operational intensity and profits*

(ii) the great internal variability in net profit, especially in the case of the 4WT sample, (iii) the large size of the mean and maximum profits earned by 4WTs. These points all require some explanation.

Relative Profitability of 2WTs and 4WTs

Annual net profit before income tax has been plotted against the total number of days worked at all operations (Fig. 12.1). The values of the 2WT sample, however, suffer from heterostochasticity – in the calculation of the regression line the extreme observations have disproportionate pull to the main, bunched observations. 2WTs, according to this trend line, make profits if used more than 7 days a year. 4WTs have to work longer – 38 days – before they make profits and 47 days before their absolute level of profits exceeds that of 2WTs. By 125 days, 4WTs make double the profit of 2WTs. Although in theory both traction technologies are almost equally versatile, the 2WT being unable only to thresh, the

Table 12.2   Summary of net profit and profitability

	Annual net profits before tax* (Rs)		Net profits per 8 hour working day (Rs)		Average annual rate of return on tractor new in 1974 (%)	
	4WT	2WT	4WT	2WT	4WT	2WT
Minimum	−1140	−1114	−18	−18		
Maximum	67,702	13,284	225	125	111	221
Mean	15,228	3,631	69	28·6	53	58
Median	12,500	1,500	50	37	37	37
Mode	7,500	1,500	110	15	37	37

* From total gross income have been subtracted maintenance costs (service, repairs, spares, labour and transport for spares), drivers' wages, fuel, depreciation at 7 per cent for 4WTs and 14 per cent for 2WTs, interest on capital at an official 10 per cent rate (though later calculations of average annual rates of return use an illegal 90 per cent rate), insurance and licence fees.

difference in absolute profit levels result from the latter's limited use for haulage, which reduces the average working year to half that of the 4WT (see Table 12.3).

Table 12.3   Average job mix and hours worked per year

	4WT		2WT	
	Hours	%	Hours	%
Ploughing	290	18	658	76
Haulage	926	58	98	11
Winnowing	111	7	108	13
Threshing	272	17	0	0
Total	1599	100	864	100

Internal Variability of Profits

Net profit is fairly strongly correlated with the number of days worked ($r^2 = +0.66$ for 4WTs and 0.31 for 2WTs). However, the explanation for profitability may also lie in some factor external to the number of days worked, such as the type and mix of jobs performed, the rates charged, and maintenance costs. Variation in job mix (averages of which are given in Table 12.3) is so great as to defy a meaningful summary.

Ploughing rates (April to June 1974) are the same per acre for 2WTs and 4WTs within Hambantota District. The average cash rate is Rs155 per acre. But rates vary from Rs110 to Rs175 in cash and Rs198 to Rs231 in kind (assuming the bushel is worth Rs33), i.e. they vary by 110 per cent. The factor market is highly imperfect. Cash rates vary, first, between irrigation tracts: Tissa averages Rs155 in cash while Ambalantota averages Rs137·15. Kind rates in Tissa, where owners were attempting to charge 8 bu. per acre prepared in late 1974, must be imputed at Rs264 per acre. Rates also vary according to the pattern of demand inter- and intra-seasons in relation to the spatial distribution of supply; the quality of the wet land and the proximity of the fields to the tractor owner's home on one scale and the position of the field within the yaya on another; maintenance costs (long waits for unavailable spares may be compensated for by high rates); and social and economic relations between the tractor owner and the cultivator of the field being prepared. The law of the jungle is unfortunately that of the yaya also. The takings of the tractor owner will be further enhanced if the paddy paid for ploughing is sold privately to be milled and ground for the up-country flour trade or for illegal sale locally; and recent rises in the guaranteed price for paddy disproportionately increase net profits for tractor owners. What is true for ploughing is true for the other aspects of traction. Threshing rates vary between Rs11 and Rs30 per heap, winnowing rates between Rs4 and Rs7·50 (tractors can thresh and winnow between 5 and 25 heaps per day depending on the supply of labour attending). Haulage rates vary between Rs80 including the price of diesel oil and Rs100 excluding fuel for the 4WTs; and between Rs30–40 per day for 2WTs. So it can be seen that the potential for variation in net profit from rates alone is very high.

Maintenance costs vary between 4 and 74 per cent of gross income, and while they bear no clear relation to age of tractor they are related to the job mix, since ploughing is much harder on a machine than is haulage. Of the fact that these costs have risen due to scarcities, unavailabilities and black-marketing there can be no doubt. Tractors other than the types presently imported by the Tractor Corporation are especially vulnerable to the black market. Political allegiance is often a barrier to obtaining spares. Many 'fast-moving' spares unavailable through the authorised agents are available round the corner with private repairers who charge, according to my informants, anything from 1·5 to 5 times the official price and presumably share the cuts. The unpredictability of demand for and supply of spares could be thought by the generous-minded to create a situation of uncertainty within the human environment sufficient to justify the high rates charged for jobs. With this and the possible data bias in mind it is perhaps surprising that average maintenance costs were as low as 21 per cent of gross income for the 4WT and 32 per cent for the 2WT.

The operation of a tractor can thus be a highly complex business: the type and age of tractor, mixture of jobs performed, rates charged, days worked and maintenance costs, all interact to make profitability highly variable.

Size of Profits and Average Annual Rate of Return

The fact remains that it is currently possible for the average 4WT (costing Rs35,000 now) to pay for itself within about two years, and the average 2WT (Rs6000) to pay for itself within eighteen months. These profits are 3 to 4 times higher than those said to have been made by youths with 2WTs under the special tractor programme in Hambantota District (MOAL, 1974, Table 7).

The average annual rate of return (AARR) on capital invested on a new 4WT is 53·5 per cent, and for a 2WT, 58 per cent. These are very high rates, though they are lower than those for moneylending, the obvious alternative use for such capital. If an illegally high interest rate on capital investment of 90 per cent were costed, representing the true opportunity cost of money in the informal economy, the AARR on a new 2WT is still 38 per cent, and on a 4WT 26 per cent. A potential tractor owner could currently raise a loan for a tractor from a commercial bank, using the tractor as security, at some 12·5 to 15 per cent interest. By using the tractor for its correct purpose his AARR has been calculated at some 55 to 60 per cent. But by not buying a tractor and by relending the amount of this loan his AARR would be anywhere from 62·5 to 150 per cent. Even the minimum rate exceeds the AARR for tractors, and the risk for moneylending is low! It is important also to realise that these profits are probably underestimates. The *potential* net profits for 200 days of ploughing (threshing), winnowing and haulage (generally acknowledged as a satisfactory level of work), using the regression lines in Fig. 12.1 is Rs17,500 for 4WTs and Rs5500 for 2WTs and net profit per day at current rates would be Rs87 for 4WTs and Rs30 for 2WTs. Moreover, the average 4WT owner in the sample owned 1·5 tractors, so that potential profits per owner at 200 days' use are about Rs26,500 which, if untaxed, would be over the Sri Lankan income ceiling.

There is only the crudest data with which to refute the suggestion that the increases in rates are due to inelastic supplies of tractors. Indices of the rates of change of demand for tractors never exceed indices of the rates of supply of tractors even when 20 per cent of the latter are assumed out of order. Ahmed also gives evidence to show that the use of tractors has not increased with the use of HYVs (1974, p. 65). If prices are rising because tractors are in increasingly scarce supply, then it is probably more because of a scarcity in supplies of spares than because of sharp increases in demand. It is more likely, given the historical concentration of economic assets (described by Herring, 1973 and by Dias and Wickremanayake, 1974 and evident in the description of the sample), that recent tractor rates reflect the operation of an oligopolistic market, and that non-tractor-owning farmers are in an extremely weak bargaining position.

It should now be possible to state an approximately 'reasonable' tractor hire to ensure 'reasonable' levels of profit to owners. What constitute reasonable profits is more a political question than an economic one, but if,

Table 12.4   Rates of change of some supply and demand parameters

Increase in cumulative no. of tractors supplied (%)		Indices of demand increase for tractors (%)	
All Island 1964–70			
2WT	630	Gross extent sown	118
4WT	170	Paddy production	153
Hambantota District 1972–4			
2WT	144	Gross extent sown	88
4WT	140	Paddy production	81
Assuming 20% of tractors redundant, Hambantota District			
2WT	114		
4WT	112		

Sources: MOAL; Sri Lanka State Tractor Corporation; Kachcheri file, Hambantota.

for instance, we take an average annual net profit of Rs12,500 for a 4WT as reasonable (near median for the sample and equivalent to the net profit from 5 to 6 acres of owner-operated paddy land at two crops a year), and if the machine works for 200 days a year, approximately the current average, mean net profits are 25 per cent in excess. The average ploughing rate should be Rs112·5 or 3·3 bu. (as opposed to the current 7 to 8 bu. in Tissa and 6 bu. elsewhere); haulage rate (Rs90) should be Rs70 excluding fuel; winnowing (Rs6) should be Rs4·5 per heap; and threshing (Rs20) should be Rs15 or under half a bushel per heap at the new rates. Such rates would bring a net profit of approximately Rs4300 to a 2WT owner at 200 days of operation, and about Rs2700 at current levels of use.

A 25 per cent reduction in rates might be brought about by the creation of much larger publicly owned tractor pools than at present exist. In North Arcot District, which has a rural population about 10 times that in Hambantota District, there are 790 4WTs and 4 2WTs. In the study area within North Arcot there are around 300 4WTs and no 2WTs. About 65 of these tractors are owned by the State government. Their rates are extremely low: Rs25 per acre prepared by ploughing twice. Free-market rates in August 1974 were Rs35 for two ploughings on a dry land, and Rs45 on a wet-land acre. Tractor owners admit that the 20 per cent of tractors owned by the government lower their own charges. In turn the Agriculture Department tractor unit runs its tractor pool at a loss, subsidising it from the high profits made from the private use of bulldozers and well-drilling equipment. For every two drivers there is one supervisor whose job it is to stop the illicit hiring out of tractors, and a simple device (with which it is apparently impossible to tamper) measures work-hours and monitors tractor operations. Drivers and mechanics are paid higher rates than in the private sector in order to encourage better-quality staff and service. A 20 per cent tractor pool in Hambantota District would consist of 180 4WTs and about 460 2WTs. The fact that there is no precise statistical proof of the price-lowering effect of the Indian tractor pool should not deter a decision to experiment and to re-create one in Hambantota. But most of the government-operated pool at Wirawila is out of action through lack of spares, and because of opposition by local tractor owners who may have exerted pressure to cannibalise the pool for spares for their own machines. The only effective competition between government-owned tractors and private enterprise is in the Hungama–Uda Walawe area, where low rates charged by the River Valleys Development Board do keep the charges of private tractor owners down to Rs110 per acre for ploughing. In this part of the District there are probably few, if any, gambārayas. It seems that the key problems of tractor pools are inadequate maintenance and supply of spares, together with the type and power of local competition. The social control necessary for the successful running of a tractor pool might be better achieved under the auspices of a politicised agricultural pro- ductivity committee than by a conventional government department.

It is by no means clear from the supply of machines and spares whether it is government policy to retain or jettison tractors for agricultural operations and haulage. And it is also by no means clear whether effective substitutes for mechanical traction exist (see pp. 387–8 for problems as- sociated with substituting for them in one locality), or whether these substitutes can be adapted to dry zone soils and to the requirements of major irrigation systems. If 2WTs and 4WTs are indeed to be maintained at current densities and levels of operation, then there seems to be a strong economic case for large tractor pools on the Indian pattern.

Use of Profits
Carr has interesting data on the use of profits from tractor ownership (1973, pp. 6–7). Since the acquisition of one or more tractors, the owners in her sample of dry zone tractors had also invested in an average of 6·3 acres of paddy land and had rented-in or resumed the cultivation of another 4·5 acres; they had actually doubled their command of paddy land, while the increase in land ownership of a control sample of non- owners of tractors had been negligible (1973, pp. 6–7). According to Duncan the ownership of tractors has caused a significant redistribution of land, income and wealth since tractor owners, formerly also buffalo owners, no longer require the tenants to act as intermediaries and manage their animals (1974, p. 7).

IMPLICATIONS FOR RURAL INDEBTEDNESS
The implications for the mass of tenant and owner-occupier cultivators who do not possess tractors are underlined by Fig. 12.2 which shows the way in which government supplies of credit for field preparation lag

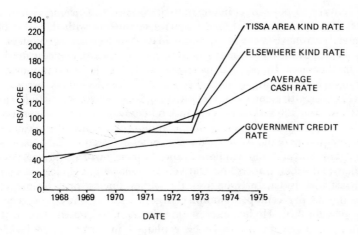

FIG. 12.2 *Rates for field preparation, Hambantota District*

behind the free-market charges. The imputed kind rate in the Tissa area for Maha 1974–5 was likely to be 8 bu. per acre, Rs264 at the new guaranteed prices. This will be 2·9 times the present government rate for ploughing, and – lest the criticism be made that the magnitude of payments in kind is irrelevant to the giving of a cash loan – the cash rate (increasingly paid in advance) will be 1·6 times the credit allowance for ploughing. But ploughing rates of this magnitude are likely to force even those farmers who do not default on co-operative loans to have recourse to the professional moneylenders.

> In the tractor owner who is invariably an affluent farmer the subsistence farmer has acquired a new oppressor. . . . A new feudalism of technology has grown up around tractor owners. The Paddy Lands Act notwithstanding, small holder subsistence farmers are slowly losing operational control of their paddy lots to the tractor owners (Jayaweera, 1973, p. 43)

Indeed, the tractor owner who ploughed for kind in the Tissa area in Yala 1974 was charging an interest rate of 80 per cent per annum. However, many urban tractor owners emphasise that they refuse to accept kind payments since this ties them to threshing the crop and since the opportunity costs of supervision and of time and labour in disposing of the paddy they get are excessive. Farmers are reputed to be borrowing from professional money lenders in order to pay urban tractor owners in cash. In this situation, and given the rise in guaranteed prices and the continuation of monopoly procurement, the annual interest rate in the Tissa area is now 164 per cent and elsewhere in the District it is 117 per cent.

Contrary to popular opinion, branch co-operative managers have a good idea of the informal credit market competing with them for the farmers' patronage (some even operate in it). Nineteen managers out of 25 supplied data on the dramatis personae of the informal credit market within their area. In the 19 areas there were 240 'major' sources of money (12 to each settlement). In total they lent out about Rs500,000 per season (Rs25,000 a settlement) at annual interest rates varying from 40 to 120 per cent cash and 120 to 170 per cent in kind equivalents. The interest on a season's lending in the sample alone amounts to Rs300,000. Probably about a quarter of these lenders have no other occupation: the remainder are 'gambārayas', 'big landlords' and 'tractor owners'. Private shop owners and urban traders are relatively insignificant as lenders, in sharp contrast with India. In India also, the highest interest rate encountered was the 36 per cent per annum charge by some – but by no means all – pawnbrokers. Higher interest rates in the unorganised than in the organised money market may be explained in terms of the lack of creditworthiness of the debtor; the elasticity of demand for funds coupled with an inelastic supply of them; the unpredictability of the repayment period; local monopolies and social relationships (Karkal, 1967, p. 81). In this case, however, the level of creditworthiness of those incurring debts over traction repayment may vary greatly. The nature of security – the paddy crop – together with its easy convertibility into liquid assets do not help to explain these exceptional rates. The urgency of demand for money for productive purposes at peak times may meet a blockage of supply, this type of lending being illegal. But some moneylenders are in a position to borrow from commercial banks, so that supply inelasticities are not to be presumed ubiquitous. The loaning of money does involve the risk of default, but all the evidence points to the fact that outright default is lower in the informal sector (2 per cent outright default rate over the years 1928–65 as far as can be gauged in India – Karkal, 1967, p. 27) than in the formal sector (46 per cent default rate on new agricultural loans – Central Bank, 1972, p. 23). The prestige of the informal lender (rather than his threats) and the absence of local alternatives assure high rates of repayment, even if, as Amunugama asserts (1964, p. 138), the process of debt collection is time-consuming. Since the activity is illegal there are few alternative investment channels, money lending and tractor-hiring being the most highly profitable, so it may be because of illegality that the rates are so high. There is no reason to suppose that, even given the restriction on alternative investments, the money is underutilised, since with two paddy seasons a year money will be invested in loans in a regular fashion. So evidence points again to local monopolies created by an extreme concentration of assets and power, a general shortage of money and the illegal nature of the activity as going some way to explain the high rates.

To put this commercial moneylending in its village context, interest-free friendly loaning may be around Rs12,000 per settlement (J. C. Harriss, personal communication, 1974) and co-operative society loans average Rs36,000 per settlement, while the average quantity outstanding is Rs47,000 per settlement (data from random sample of 25 branches in Hambantota District). The relative importance of each type of credit is confirmed by data from our sample survey of farmers. While 27 per cent of farmers borrowed from kith and kin and 60 per cent borrowed from co-operatives, 46 per cent borrowed from informal commercial lenders. (The total exceeds 100 per cent because of compound access to sources of money.) By such reckonings commercial and friendly loans approximately equal co-operative loans, and the very high interest rates on the first also reflect the inadequacy of the last. In Sri Lanka the infiltration of the formal money market into rural lending has not had the dampening effect on informal interest rates that has been generally the case in India.

When the government-sponsored credit rate lags behind the free market the non-defaulting farmer is forced back on to traditional sources, whose interest rates, for the reasons given earlier, together with the generous increase in the guaranteed prices for paddy, are rising seasonally.

IMPLICATIONS FOR POLICY

If profits are not to be 'reasonable' then somehow they have to be controlled. But there is no easy solution to the problem of excess profits made by many owners of tractors, and to the rural indebtedness it engenders, since if co-operative loans were to be raised till commensurate with current free-market rates the government would be held further to ransom by tractor owners who would in turn raise their rates. On the other hand if the government refuses to bow to the tractor owners, the farmers have to bow to moneylenders in their stead. Cash rates inevitably follow in the wake of kind rates, and co-operative credit trails in the wake of the cash rates. Some sort of compromise is necessary.

The field preparation component in the loan should be raised to about Rs115. It has been seen that cash rates for agricultural operations are about 25 per cent above what represents a 'reasonable' return at stated levels of operation, which in turn are likely to be fairly large understimates. The government could control the free market and lower cash rates by enlarging its tractor pools. Kind rates are excessively high (7 to 8 bu. instead of 3·3 to 3·5 bu.) and, unless the government finds some way of requiring kind payments to be commensurate with cash rates plus a quantity representing a 'reasonable' seasonal interest rate, there seems to be no solution to this problem.

If the policy of a return to buffalo technology is favoured by the government, it can be brought about only if buffalo rates are lower than those of tractors. At present tractor rates rise from west to east in the district, from Rs130 to Rs175 per acre. Buffalo rates rise much more steeply in the same direction from Rs90 per acre in the west to Rs200 at Tissa. If buffalo breeding or taming could be encouraged as an activity for small farmers in the Tissa area, rates could be lowered and animals made an increasingly attractive alternative. However, this is a gamble – incentives for which are currently lacking – and one in which farmers have neither historically nor of late shown any interest.

That profits taken by those who control the means of production are excessive in one matter, but the policies needed to reduce hiring-out rates are another very much more difficult matter. Moreover, if one were able to produce a solution to the problem of charges it would be in default of an attack on the underlying problem of the extreme concentration of productive assets. A multi-pronged strategy aiming to control the regional distribution and mobility of tractors and the type of ownership, as well as the rates charged for services rendered, is but a partial solution to the problems created by the recognition of extreme social and economic inequity.

Acknowledgements: I am grateful for their comments on the first version of this chapter to Dr S. W. R. de A. Samarasinghe of Department of Economics, Peradeniya, Dr M. J. Westlake of Department of Mathematics, Vidyodaya, and Mr D. Belshaw, University of East Anglia.

REFERENCES

Agrarian Research and Training Institute, ARTI (1974). *The Agrarian Situation relating to Paddy Production in Five Selected Districts of Sri Lanka*, part 1, Hambantota District, ARTI Research Study Series no. 6, Colombo.

Ahmed, I. (1974). 'Green Revolution with or without Tractors: The Case of Sri Lanka', *Marga*, 2, 64–74.

Alles, W. S. (1967). 'Soil and Water Conservation in the Dry Zone' in O. S. Peries, (ed.), *The Development of Agriculture in the Dry Zone*, Colombo, Ceylon Association for the Advancement of Science, pp. 9–58.

Amunugama, S. (1964). 'Rural Credit in Ceylon. Some Sociological Observations', *Ceylon J. Hist. Soc. Studies*, 7, 135–43.

Assistant Government Agent Hambantota (1922). Diary.

Carr, M. (1973). *Tractors in a Rural Economy: Some Social and Economic Aspects of the Introduction of Tractors into a Rural Economy: The Case of Ceylon*, University of Edinburgh, Appropriate Technology Conference, Paper RE/A-06, mimeo.

Central Bank of Ceylon (1972). *Survey of Defaults in the Repayment of Loans*, Colombo.

Dias, H. D. and Wickremanayake, B. W. E. (1974). *The Gambāraya System in Hambantota District*, Ceylon Studies Seminar Paper.

Duncan, A. (1974). *Farm Mechanisation in South Asia*, M.Sc thesis, Department of Agricultural Economics, University of Reading.

Herring, R. J. (1973). 'The Forgotten 1953 Paddy Lands Act in Ceylon',

Ceylon Studies Seminar, 1974 Series, Peradeniya.

International Labour Office, ILO (1971). *Matching Employment Opportunities and Expectations, a Programme of action for Ceylon*, Technical Papers, Geneva.

Jayaweera, C. N. (1973). 'Credit Support for High Yielding Varieties in Sri Lanka', *Marga*, 2, No. 2, 18–48.

Karkal, G. L. (1967). *Unorganised Money Markets in India*, Bombay, Lalvani.

Kurukulasuriya, G. (1971). *Co-operation, its Rise and Growth in Ceylon*, Colombo, Co-operative Federation of Ceylon.

Ministry of Agriculture and Lands, MOAL (1974). 'Two Wheel Tractors Programme in Hambantota and Amparai Districts', unpublished draft.

Panabokke, C. R. (1967). 'Soils and Land Use Patterns in Dry Zone Agriculture' in O. S. Peries (ed.), *The Development of Agriculture in the Dry Zone of Ceylon*, Colombo, Ceylon Association for the Advancement of Science, pp. 29–36.

Raj, K. N. (1972). 'Mechanisation of Agriculture in India and Sri Lanka (Ceylon)', *Internl. Labour Rev.*, 106, 315–34.

13 Rural Electrification and the Diffusion of Electric Water-Lifting Technology in North Arcot District, India

Barbara Harriss

EARLY HISTORY OF MECHANICALLY POWERED LIFT IRRIGATION

At the time of India's independence there were about half the present number of wells in North Arcot District. These were powered either by men or by bullocks. With the expansion of cultivated land in the 1950s, however, there was a considerable increase in the number of open wells. Madduma Bandara (Fig. 21.2) traces a first phase of well-digging innovation which culminated in the mid-1960s, to be followed by a much larger increase which continues to the present. It is tempting to relate the first phase of expansion to the use of diesel engines whose pattern of adoption closely parallels that of the digging of wells. Certainly the oil engine was economically and technologically superior to traditional irrigation practices (Table 13.1).

Table 13.1

Method	Cubic metres per rupee	Cubic metres per hour
Men (etram)	n.a.	52
Bullock (kavalai)	45–89	79
Oil engine	200–300	418

Source: Department of Agriculture, Government of Tamil Nadu, 1970, p. 308.

However, the proportion of all wells powered by oil engines was never more than 3 per cent, and from the late 1950s the oil engine was to a large extent de-adopted with the advent of the electric pump-set. The advantages of electric motors are their relatively long life, low maintenance costs, easy operation and dependability. Economically and technologically they are superior to all other forms of lift technology (Table 13.2).

Table 13.2

Method	Lift range (m)	Discharge m³/min	Cost of lifting one cubic metre by one metre (Rs)
Bullocks (kavalai)	8–12	5–8	0·009–0·029
Oil engine	4–8	18–29	0·01–0·02
Electric motor	6–12	45–54	{ 0·0015–0·002* 0·0056–0·0075†

* Subsidised – cost to farmer.
† Unsubsidised – cost to society.
Source: Department of Agriculture, Government of Tamil Nadu, 1970, p. 331.

Progress in rural electrification was restricted to less than 7 per cent of villages in 1957 when the Madras/Tamil Nadu Electricity Board took over from private electricity companies and started widespread implementation. The spread of pump-set retail outlets and maintenance facilities was not, however, planned by government but by many small private firms acting as agents for (now) six large and 60 small manufacturers in an increasingly competitive market. Farmers who decided to innovate had a free choice of type, firm and location, although whether or not a connection was allowed depends on rules about well density laid down by PWD.

Now 50 per cent, or 102,384, of North Arcot District's wells have electric pump-sets. This technology has been found to be a precondition for agricultural intensification (pp. 117–18) but its spread has been characterised by considerable inter-village variation (pp. 308–11). Moreover the adoption process has had serious ecological consequences (pp. 330–8). For these reasons a study of this innovation is justified.

THEORETICAL BACKGROUND
The process of diffusion of an electric water-lifting technology involves the planned spread of rural electrification and of farmers' electricity connections together with the unplanned spread of pump-set shops, of pump-set sales and of the adoption of the innovation through time and space by farmers. Apart from its practical relevance, the study of diffusion in a set of interlocking decision environments and under varying degrees of in-

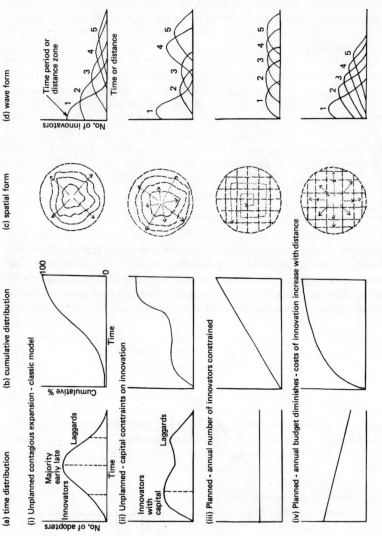

FIG. 13.1 *Models of innovation diffusion*

stitutional control has the intrinsic merit of permitting the testing of the current conceptualisation of diffusion and innovation adoption.

Briefly, 'innovation' is envisaged as a wave sweeping over a surface in different ways and impeded by various types of barrier. Much research has focused on the contagious expansion of an innovation from its heartland (Hagerstrand, 1967; Gould, 1969; Brown and Moore, 1971). This spread is often simulated stochastically using a gridded 'mean information field' of communication probabilities.

The temporal form of diffusion of an innovation throughout a bounded community is characterised by a bell-shaped distribution. In theory, in the initial stages of spread the probability of non-innovators coming into contact with innovators is slight; similarly at a late stage the probability of the reverse occurring is also slight; in between these stages the probability of an innovator contacting a non-innovator who will, on contact, innovate, rises then falls. Thus we have a bell-shaped time distribution of innovators, an S-shaped logistic cumulative distribution and an outward spatial spread. Morrill (1968) further hypothesises that with greater distance from an innovation centre the time-lag of adoption is greater, the ceiling of adoption lower and adoption is never complete. The normal model for diffusion and adoption is shown in Fig. 13.1 (i) a–d.

With reference to pump-sets in North Arcot District, we may hypothesise that, subject to lags, the diffusion of electrification, pump-set shops, pump-set sales and pump-set adoption will follow this model. We may also hypothesise that farmers acting rationally will minimise distance when they purchase pump-sets and that the adoption process will be conditioned by access to capital. My own fieldwork on pump-set sellers (33

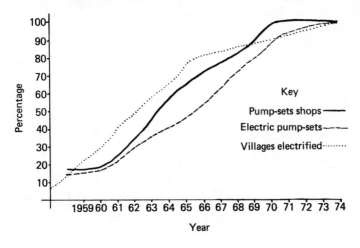

FIG. 13.2 *Diffusion of electric pump-sets, district level*
  Data sources: TNEB Administrative Reports, 1957–73; author's survey

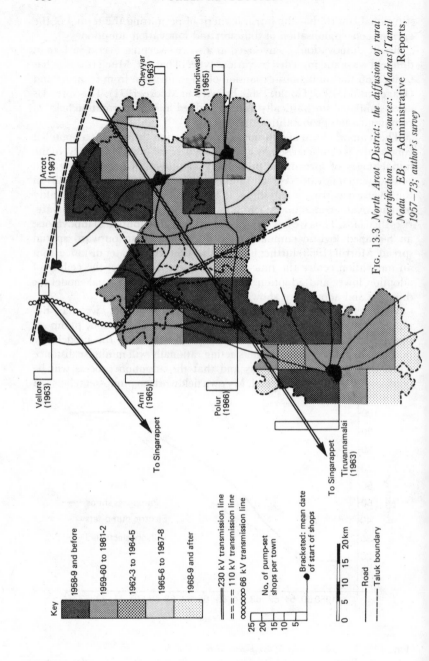

FIG. 13.3 *North Arcot District: the diffusion of rural electrification. Data sources: Madras/Tamil Nadu EB, Administrative Reports, 1957–73; author's survey*

Key

1958-9 and before

1959-60 to 1961-2

1962-3 to 1964-5

1965-6 to 1967-8

1968-9 and after

═══ 230 kV transmission line
= = = 110 kV transmission line
ooooo 66 kV transmission line

No. of pump-set shops per town

Bracketed: mean date of start of shops

0 5 10 15 20km

—— Road
- - - Taluk boundary

Cheyyar (1963)

Wandiwash (1965)

Arcot (1967)

Vellore (1963)

Arni (1965)

To Singarappet

Polur (1966)

Tiruvannamalai (1963)

To Singarappet

per cent of the 80 traders in the District) interdigitates with the phase 2 sample survey of farmers (44 per cent of whom owned or shared pump-sets) and with background data from Tamil Nadu Electricity Board, the State Land Development Bank and the Central Co-operative Bank, to provide perspectives on each part of this complex process.

RURAL ELECTRIFICATION

The provision of electricity is both an innovation in its own right and the bestowing on a village of a potential for further innovation. This process has been plotted in Fig. 13.2 where 'villages electrified' acts as a surrogate for an increase in potential innovators, and in potential land for innovation. While the cumulative adoption profile for villages takes a straight-line form, there is no reason to suppose that either the cumulative number of potential innovators or the cumulative acreage with innovation potential also increase in that form. They may both be S-shaped if the Electricity Board electrifies large villages first.

But the decision to electrify villages is a social decision with an opportunity cost. In rural electrification schemes in Tamil Nadu from 1967–72 the transmission-line losses rose from 16 per cent to at least 19 per cent (TNEB, 1973, p. 67). The cost to the Electricity Board of electrifying a village (averaging Rs35,300 in 1972) varies with its remoteness from a transmission line. So on a micro-scale does the cost to the Board of connecting a pump-set (from Rs5000 at 0·5 km to Rs9000 at 3 km) (Patel and Patel, 1969, p. 82). Electricity Boards will not electrify a village unless the annual revenue from electricity sold to it is expected to exceed 15 per cent of the capital costs of electrification. In North Arcot District at present, where 99 per cent of villages have electricity, the current annual return on past investment is 18 per cent, indicating the satisfactory profitability of electrification even among 'marginal' villages (from data in TNEB, 1973, pp. 173, 184).

Although distance variables affect the profitability of village electrification to the Electricity Board, they do not help explain the pattern of diffusion of 'potential', which is shown on Fig. 13.3. The diffusion surface of electrification is warped along a NE.–SW. axis. Two problems suggested by this map are, first, the form and location of the heartland from which this innovation spreads; secondly, the uncontagious nature of the expansion of electrification. Villages electrified early and late are juxtaposed in such a way as to suggest that infrastructural economies were not uppermost considerations for the Electricity Board.

The date of electrification does not seem to be related directly or obviously (i) to proximity to urban areas or to main roads, as public infrastructure is distributed elsewhere in the developing world (Blaikie, 1973, p. 84) (indeed in three taluks the reverse occurs: the rural fringes and remote hill villages were electrified before the areas closest to towns and main roads); (ii) to the main sections of the electricity grid, the heartland

strip being on approximately the line of the newest high-tension transmission line through the District; (iii) to density of paddy cultivation, the
ricebowl areas of Cheyyar and Wandiwash being electrified late while
remote villages in the Javadi hills of Polur taluk were electrified early.
Before nationalisation the largest villages may have been electrified earliest
irrespective of location. For example, in Cheyyar taluk the present average
population of villages electrified before 1957 is 1303, while for those
electrified after 1967 it is 685. However, over the whole time scale there is
no close relation between village size and date of electrification ($r^2 = 0.29$ in
Cheyyar taluk and 0.16 in Tiruvannamalai taluk). All this suggests that
the profitability of electrifying fields is great enough for other factors to
exert final influence on the form of spatial spread.

One explanation for the pattern, and one which is hard to verify, is that
it may result from a combination of all these factors but that most 'noise' is
caused by a further factor, that of the local political power structure. It is
striking that early electrified areas in rural Wandiwash for instance are
regions notorious for their inequity of holding size and their preponderance of 'big men' who might reasonably have been expected to
have had considerable interest in early electrification. Villages in the
mountains with little paddy land may also have been electrified for
sociopolitical reasons.

That the spread of electrification is not contagious and expansionary as
in the form simulated by Hagerstrand (1967) stands to reason if we
consider the rate of electrification shown in Fig. 13.4. The number of
villages that can be electrified is strictly determined by the annual budget,

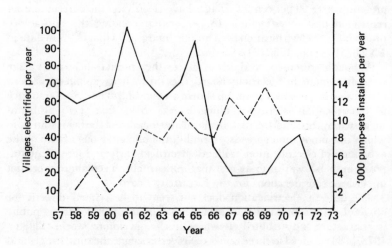

FIG. 13.4 *Planned installations*
Source: TNEB Administrative Reports

70 per cent of which is derived from borrowed funds, and by departmental allocations, for example, between village electrification and the provision of pump-set connections. The number of villages electrified annually fell after 1965, while the number of connections rose.

This has various theoretical implications. In cases where the spread of an innovation (here the potential for innovation) is constrained by an annual budget or a ceiling on the number of adopters per year, the time distribution and cumulative distributions are straight-line forms and the spread of the innovation may take a number of forms characterised by steep gradients in space, as in A–B in (iii)c of Fig. 13.1.

In cases where the capital costs of providing an innovation increase with distance and there is a budgetary ceiling, the number of villages electrified annually will decline over time as in Fig. 13.1 (iv), however attractive the innovation may be in private economic terms to the recipients. This most characterises the form of rural electrification in North Arcot District.

Thus the constraints imposed by planned innovation-spread radically alter the form taken by the process through space, time and society.

THE DIFFUSION OF PUMP-SET SHOPS

In Fig. 13.3 the urban diffusion of pump-set shops broadly corresponds with that of the rural trend surface of village electrification. There appears to be a four- to five-year lag between the modal date of start of rural electrification in the grid squares nearest each town and the mean starting date of shops retailing pump-sets. We must explain the time-lag between rural electrification and the creation of market potential on the one hand and the setting up of retailing outlets on the other in terms of the time necessary to overcome barriers to innovation, or the time taken to satisfy entry requirements to the trade.

1   There are no social barriers. The non-traditional nature of this agricultural input is reflected in the diversity of castes involved – there are nine. Agamudaiyans (the dominant land-owning and trading caste in the District) made up, however, a third of the pump-set retailers.

2   There appears to be a technical barrier to the trade; 65 per cent of entrepreneurs had 5–10 years of informal training in pump-set maintenance, assembly and repair literally on the shop-floor before starting their own businesses. All companies license their retailers to operate a guarantee and repair service so traders must satisfy certain levels of competence.

3   There is an economic barrier to entry to the trade in the form of the starting capital required to pay advance rent, install shop fittings, hire hands and buy stock. The minimum amount necessary to establish a business has increased from Rs500 in 1951 to Rs7000 in 1972. Most entrepreneurs made the decision to innovate several years before they were able to set up shop. Information about sales potential lay latent

for a period, while the entrepreneur saved, before manifesting itself physically.

The cumulative pattern of establishment of retail outlets shows a 'typical' S-curve characteristic of unplanned innovations (Fig. 13.1). Since village electrification is virtually complete there is no reason to assume that the process of entrepreneurial innovation is not complete also.

Sales Profiles

The cumulative sales profiles of pump-set retailing firms are given in Fig. 13.5. If the logistic cumulative curve reflects a bell-shaped distribution of the absolute number of adopters in time (as in Fig. 13.1), we may hypothesise that the individual sales patterns of firms should correspond to the same pattern. Only in the case of early innovators is this possibly so. The decline in sales of early starters is clearly caused by an increase in competition by the advent of the early majority. Through the early 1960s firms established themselves at an even rate while total sales increased exponentially. From the mid-1960s, however, expected sales were not matched by reality. The later a firm set up, the shorter the time-lag before it reached its maximum annual sales levels. The total level of sales has declined since 1970–71. Since then in Arni alone five shops (38 per cent of the maximum total) have stopped selling pump-sets altogether.

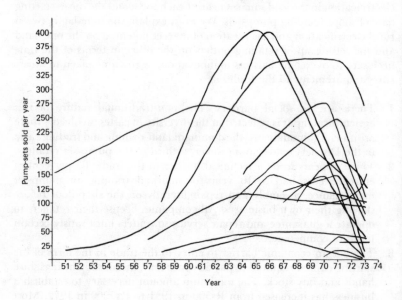

FIG. 13.5 *Sales profiles of sample traders in North Arcot District*
Source: author's survey

Thus an S-shaped logistic curve at aggregate level (total pump-set sales) in a situation where two variables are at work (date of start and number of pump-sets sold annually per shop) conceals a variety of actual sales profits. It is tempting to dismiss this pattern as characteristic of a bounded region reaching saturation point. This is untrue since about 50 per cent of North Arcot's wells remain to be energised. According to the perceptions of a number of entrepreneurs, demand is declining because of physical saturation only in a few areas. Other factors contributing to the general fall in sales include the independent decline in the number of government loans for pump-set installation and the contention that the region is reaching economic saturation, that farmers for whom pump-sets realised greatest returns innovated earliest leaving the wells of economically marginal laggards unenergised. The importance of loans in conditioning adoption, and the idea of economic saturation, will be returned to later. Government loans for pump-set installation did drop from 1400 in 1970–71 to 1000 in 1972–3 (State Land Development Bank, and Co-operative Central Bank, Vellore, 1974). At any rate the delivery system is now characterised by dropping sales and high rates of exit.

The response of the entrepreneur to what he perceives as saturation is characteristically varied. Where the sale of electric pump-sets was itself a diversification of a functionally unrelated line such as cloth or sweets, the entrepreneur reverts to the original commodity. Where the entrepreneur is technically trained, the rewinding and maintenance of pump-sets becomes the chief source of income. These firms are most likely to add oil engines to their functions. Presumably demand for oil sets emanates from the group of farmers for whom the greater capital and running costs of a diesel engine are compensated by greater net returns on a larger acreage of crops than that cultivated by farmers subject to electricity cuts.

For the majority of firms the reaction to saturation is to diversify: all enlarge the stock of spares; many add Bose or scratch ploughs, mill machinery and household wiring equipment; a few go in for fertiliser or cement. One additional problem is that the market for electrical and household wiring equipment is 'saturated' for precisely the same kinds of reasons as that for pump-sets. One can safely predict that new pump-set shops in North Arcot District are likely to be financial liabilities, and licences should be withheld.

'Rational' Sales Areas

In no settlement in the District have pump-set sellers a real spatial exclusivity. Several firms have maximum sales radii exceeding the entire district, and firms with large geographical sales areas may be located in very small central places (e.g. Chetpet, a village with a population of 5500) (Census, *District Handbook*, 1971). Reasons for such coverage are as below:

1 This extreme spatial competition may possibly be traced to the fact

that, if shop to village transport costs make up a negligible fraction of total purchase costs, the physical location of the retailing point is irrelevant to farmers in their purchasing decisions.

2   Other factors then come into play. Farmers act rationally if they buy most cheaply, so that one such factor is the price of the pump-set. This varies according to the horsepower of the motor required (determined by the average depth of water in the well in dry seasons and by the acreage for irrigation). It also varies according to the company. Each company has different production cost structures and different distributive margins, though the ceiling for the retail commission was fixed at the time of survey in 1973 at 25 per cent of retail price for electric sets and 35 per cent for diesel ones. Price variation is further accentuated by dealers' attitudes to commissions. In some towns, for example Arni, there has always been fierce price competition so that, although dealers are entitled to take 25 per cent commissions, they in fact take 5–10 per cent. In other towns, such as Tiruvannamalai, dealers take 20 per cent commissions. The commission taken by the dealer, and therefore the retail price level, depend also on whether he retails directly to the farmer or indirectly through an agent. The agent is a powerful intermediary: in all cases, if agents help farmers to purchase a pump-set, they – not the retailer – take the bulk of the commission (10–15 per cent). Lastly, the retail price level also depends on the volume of orders. If a whole village orders, according to one dealer the commission taken by him for services rendered will drop to 2 per cent gross. Thus, according to the degree of competition and the cost structures of companies, the prices of similar horsepower pump-sets and motors may vary greatly. Even though the economic market may be approximately perfect in the sense that no individual retailer has any personal influence on average market prices (Samuelson, 1967, p. 41), there is none the less no simple spatial behaviour.

3   Another factor which may do much to explain both seeming spatial irrationality on the part of farmers and overlapping sales areas of retailers is the quantity and terms of credit provided by retailers or purchasers. Credit is not related to sales volume. Nor is it related to starting capital or any other similar economic variable. The disbursement of credit depends on the attitude of the entrepreneur to one form of competition and one type of risk. It is a special part of service quality.

4   Quality and price are always correlated positively even though in the market for new pump-sets a minimum quality floor is established with universal post-sales service guarantees. That quality is an important aspect of retailing is evinced by the fact that 65 per cent of pump-set shops were local agents for more than one company and 15 per cent were agents for four companies. Large sales areas for individual firms can result both from brand exclusivity and also from the reverse. In other ways apart from brand ranges, retailers can be differentiated on

quality. Many actively canvass 'village leaders' in the wake of rural electrification and keep informal links with contacts in the Electricity Board. Others help to fill in farmers' forms for bank loans after the exquisite example of R. K. Narayan's *Financial Expert*. Yet others help with pump-set installation and connection and provide high-quality repair services. All the evidence points to the fact that the size of the area served is directly related to the quality of service.

5   Another factor which explains the overlapping of sales areas concerns the social geography of retailing. Even though there may be spatial overlap between towns as well as within towns, there is a considerable amount of mutual exclusivity in the information networks attached to each shop. All retailers pointed out that within their sales areas they had between one and fifteen 'special villages' where at least five and up to 100 of their pump-sets had been installed. Many dealers attribute spatially patchy demand to the perpetuation of sales patterns built up in former retail lines – a type of geographical inertia. Others specifically mention ties of friendship, ties through kin, through the entrepreneur's or employees' native places. In addition the location of agents (often selected for social reasons) may determine the sales areas.

6   Lastly, entrepreneurs reported that their sales areas have changed over time. This is understandable, given the nature of the process of demand. For many firms the sales radius for pump-sets simply expanded, took on a form determined by the factors discussed above, then contracted. For a minority the decline in demand has provoked an increase in the sales radius, not the reverse. This is characteristic of Tiruvannamalai, a major pump-set retailing centre attracting trade from a radius of 150 miles, and depends on the historical accident of early electrification in the hilly part of its hinterland, and on the emergence of a number of innovators. Here the radius of demand has expanded outwards, centring around the promotional activities of satellite agents at 10–30 miles distance who monitor a specified territory in search of market potential.

THE ADOPTION OF PUMP-SETS BY FARMERS: THE EFFECT OF DISTANCE

It is clear from Fig. 13.6 that the purchasing patterns of farmers are not straightforward, and that the overlap in marketing areas characteristic of retail shops is mirrored in the spatial patterns of farmers. Some 47 per cent of the innovating farmers did not buy from the nearest town, so that factors such as price, commissions, credit, quality, ties of caste, kin and friendship are together about as important as distance variables in explaining spatial patterns. The percentage of purchasers not choosing the nearest town varies between villages (Fig. 13.1). Sirungathur and Duli are very probably 100 per cent efficient because of the outstanding canvassing energy of one particular dealer there. The group which did not purchase

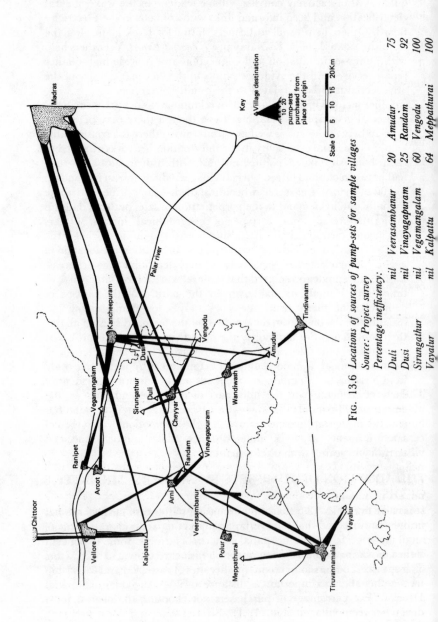

FIG. 13.6 *Locations of sources of pump-sets for sample villages*
Source: Project survey
Percentage inefficiency:

Duli	nil	Veerasambanur	nil	Amudur	20
Dusi	nil	Vinayagapuram	nil	Randam	25
Sirungathur	nil	Vegamangalam	nil	Vengodu	60
Vayalur	nil	Kalpattu	64	Meppathurai	100

Amudur 75
Randam 92
Vengodu 100
Meppathurai 100

from the closest town gave reasons for selecting their favoured location as follows:

Social %		Economic %		Administrative %		Other %	
Respondent knows or is related to dealer	24·0	Low price 24·0		Directed by Bank giving loan	5·2	No reason	5·2
Relative or friend of respondent knows/is related to dealer	9·0	Dealer canvassed/gave advice/ loaned money interest-free/arranged connection with Electricity Board	17·0				
Snowball effect of other farmer's choice	3·5	Easy repairs 3·5					
Knowledge of town	3·5	Quality	3·5				
Same caste as dealer	1·7						
	41·7		48·0				

These were not spur of the moment decisions. On average each farmer made four purposive visits to his chosen location. Only 3 per cent of farmers bought the pump-set unaccompanied, 27 per cent took relatives, 40 per cent took farmers from their village who already had pump-sets, or took village leaders and 24 per cent took electricians or pump-set repairers to help them with the innovation decision. One may conclude from this that purely social factors are as important as economic ones amongst the group not acting in a distance-minimising way. When in any case the price of a set is affected by any one or combinations of six factors reported earlier, farmers may act rationally by travelling longer than necessary distances.

Form of Diffusion and Innovation Adoption

The spatial diffusion of pump-sets is shown in terms of their density per hundred acres of land in each block (based on data supplied by the District Development Office) in Fig. 13.8. The diffusion surface depicted there does not correspond with those of rural electrification or of urban pump-set shops but slopes downwards from north to south and is warped about an axis running from Arcot to Chetpet. Some of the eastern blocks late to be electrified have greater densities of pump-sets than the early electrified western blocks.

Figure 13.7 plots for each village the time-lag and cumulative adoption patterns of 76 of the 161 farmers in phase 2 of the sample farm survey. Features needing explanation are first, the variable time-lag before adoption begins, secondly the stepped profiles of six of the 11 villages (less than half the villages exhibiting typical 'S' shapes) and thirdly the low adoption ceilings (below 55 per cent of the farmers in six of the 11 villages).

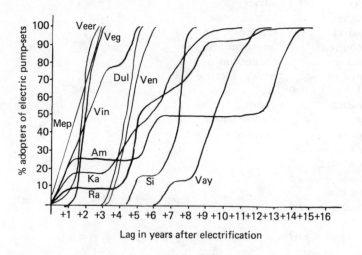

FIG. 13.7 *Adoption of electric pump-sets, sample villages*
Data source: Proj. ·t survey

EXPLANATIONS OF THE PROFILE FORMS

The Importance of Supply and Demand

In the context of the dual barrier of electric power and money the question of whether the innovation profile is determined by demand for, or supply of, the innovation (as postulated respectively by David, 1966 and Griliches, 1960) is fairly simple to resolve. At present, demand for pump-sets and the farmers' ability to finance the installation independently of government loans exceed the supply of connections. That demand for connections has increased at a greater rate than has supply is proved by the queue lengths for connections. Whereas in 1958 connection took under six months, by 1967 it took a year. According to *The Hindu* only 50 per cent of pump-sets bought in 1973 were installed by mid-1974, and by 1975 the backlog throughout the State exceeded 150,000 (Director of Agriculture, Tamil Nadu, personal communication). Overwhelmingly then, adoption is conditioned by the *supply* not of pump-sets so much as connections.

Information

Diffusion theory lays great stress on the idea of the gridded mean information field of communication probabilities. Communications intensity declines with distance from an innovation source (Gould, 1969, pp. 28–38). It is the lag of information spread which determines the process of learning manifested in innovation adoption (Brown and Moore, 1971, p. 124). The earliest innovators are the best informed: innovations which are hard to understand, or use, are adopted later than others (Found, 1971, pp. 145–6). Information about innovation diffuses primarily through the central place hierarchy (Misra, 1971, p. 3). In this case such types of explanation are irrelevant. Information on electric pump-sets in North Arcot was generally diffused by means of radio, formal agricultural extension, gossip and informal visual demonstration by 1957, when only 7 per cent of villages had electricity. Moreover, the technical problems associated with this new technology were resolved originally with the help of the Electricity Board and, universally now, with rural electricians and pump-set repairers. (There are 1440 helpers, 370 linemen and 720 wiremen now working for the Electricity Board alone in North Arcot District (District Electricity Board, Vellore).) These men may informally help to select, install and repair the machine. Many more operate full- or part-time in a freelance fashion. The lag between electrification and the beginning of adoption decreases through time and the gradient of the slope steepens, confirming that information is well diffused before the arrival of potential. It is the temporal and spatial allocation of resources by the Electricity Board and not the pattern of diffusion of the 'mean information field' which determines the adoption lag. As Blaikie notes, much literature has concerned itself with explaining the historical process of information diffusion rather than with that of innovations: 'It is only when diffusion variables are disentangled from economic variables which can often be shown to control them that their real lack of importance is revealed' (Blaikie, 1973, p. 102).

Profitability

Griliches (1960) has shown that the slope of the profile is determined by the profitability of the innovation; hybrid corn took longer to be adopted in States where it was more risky and therefore less profitable. It is not necessary to analyse social returns from well energisation, in spite of the fact that market prices for agricultural electricity are subsidised and therefore distort social profit (Lal, 1972, p. 14) since it is private profitability which motivates a farmer. The average capital costs of installation in Table 13.3 show the present advantages of electric pump-sets (rarely above 5 hp in this District) over diesel. Running costs for diesel sets are 50 per cent greater than for electric sets and the latter fetch 12 per cent more water for the same energy input than the former (Patel and Patel, 1969, pp. 100–106).

Table 13.3 Average installation costs borne by farmers (in rupees)

	Electric pump-set (3 hp)	(5 hp)	Diesel (5 hp)	Transport	Wiring	Building
1965	1200	1300	no data	30	70	250
1972	1950	2700	3000	30	300	800

The demand conditions for rice in India are such that average annual prices for paddy have never been depressed by increases in productivity and therefore in marketable surplus to the point that an innovation such as the pump-set ceases to become profitable. The only way by which this innovation's profitability is reduced is by the recent cuts in electricity which bode to become semi-permanent features of the agricultural economy, until Tamil Nadu has atomic energy in 1977. The large increase in diesel prices has not greatly changed the relative advantages of the two technologies though in August 1974 bigger farmers were investing in both, in order to minimise risk.

Risk
Griliches (ibid.) suggests that low adoption ceilings may be determined by the increased riskiness of innovation for laggard innovators. But in this case, assuming a successful well has already been dug, then the electrification greatly reduces risk of crop failure, increases cultivable acreage, enables more risky (water-, fertiliser- and pesticide-responsive) HYVs to be grown. The incremental social cost of installation is also far lower for latecomers than for early innovators because of the presence of electrical infrastructure and know-how.

Lumpiness of Capital Investment
The capital costs of installation not only prevent the experimentation or trial stages of adoption from occurring but also might be thought to deter small farmers from innovating at all in the absence of government loans for which (generally because of uncreditworthiness) they are ineligible (Lal, 1972, p. 137). First, however, a pump-set is not prohibitively lumpy for small farmers even though none borrowed from government sources. Of the innovating farmers with less than 2 acres, only 16 per cent borrowed any money to finance the purchase, all informally. The remainder used agricultural profits. Secondly, lumpiness can be reduced by sharing a pump-set, as was done by 25 per cent of innovating farmers with under 2 acres, although the acreage threshold to single pump-set ownership is under one acre. Thirdly, although the capital costs of adopting have increased through time, whether the innovation is lumpier in real cost terms is unknown. Also, if pump-set prices do not increase at more than the rate of increase of prices of agricultural produce from whose sale the pump-

set is financed, then the laggards are not penalised in real-cost terms. The source of investment capital are summarised in Table 13.4.

Table 13.4   Sources of investment capital for pump-sets

Source	Percentage of adopters
Profits from traditional varieties of paddy	33
Profits from groundnut cultivation	22
Government loans	12
Profits from bananas and turmeric	11
Loans from private sources (with interest)	10
Loans from pump-set retailers (no interest)	6
Miscellaneous	3
Profits from paddy trade	1
Profits from HYV paddy	1
Sale of land	1

Non-government sources of finance accounted for 88 per cent of capital sunk in pump-sets; profits from agriculture, 57 per cent. Loans from non-government sources were more important than loans from government sources.

Environmental Controls

A constraint on pump-set adoption is the level of the water-table, for evidence of the lowering of which see pp. 332–7. Maximum lift for a 3·5 horsepower electric motor is 27 feet. (Department of Agriculture, 1970, p. 310.) In North Arcot, motors can lift water to twice that height if installed deep in the well. Thus the low level of the water-table is not a complete barrier to innovation at least until dry, solid rock is reached but it raises pumping costs. It may, however, provide some explanation for the low adoption ceilings in some villages.

The PWD specifications for pump-set density are a more active limiting constraint. In a society where wells are sited by water-divining and where holdings are small and fragmented it is impossible to space wells evenly. A pump-set should not be given a connection if within 100 yards of another (Co-operative Central Bank, Vellore). In practice this has been known to have been circumvented. Farmers can also opt for diesel technology which does not require a connection. This may explain the small but steady demand for this inferior method of pumping. There do not seem to be severe environmental constraints upon adoption at present.

Since none of the six factors considered so far offers a convincing explanation of the variable time-lags, stepped profiles and variable adoption ceilings, it is necessary to consider one more:

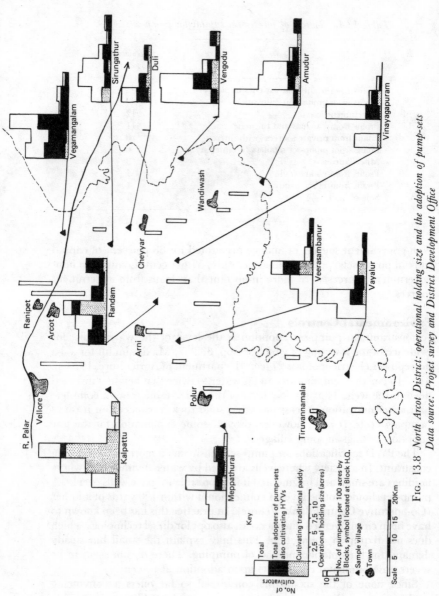

Fig. 13.8 *North Arcot District: operational holding size and the adoption of pump-sets*

Data source: *Project survey and District Development Office*

Holding Size (Fig. 13.8)

The question of the relation between operational holding size and pump-set adoption requires some reformulation in order to neutralise the effect of inter-village variation in the structure of land ownership brought out in the map, and in the date of electrification. This is best done by considering not just frequency of innovators in each size-group but percentage of total landowners who innovated in each size-group, against, not time, but the lag (in years after village electrification) with which each individual adoption took place. It is then apparent that, while 22 per cent of all owners of less than 2 acres have innovated, 90 per cent of those with more than 10 acres possess pump-sets. However, 100 per cent of those in the group 6–8 acres innovated. There is no correlation ($r^2 = 0.04$) between holding size and lag in adoption. Among innovators the lag in adoption after village electrification is least (2·5 years) for cultivators owning 4–6 acres and highest (6 years) in the groups immediately adjacent (2–4 acres and 6–8 acres), declining to 3·5 years at the size extremes.

It is therefore likely that it is owners of optimal acreages for pump-sets, utilising capacity most effectively, who innovate with least lag after electrification and those with sub-optimal holdings in relation to the irrigation potential of one energised well who tend to be laggards. The optimal acreage will vary according to horsepower, water-table depth and crop water requirements. It is fairly clear that, for the range of conditions in North Arcot, optimal acreages are within the group 5–8 acres. That the average holding size with one pump-set is now 5 acres and with two pump-sets 11·5 acres tends to confirm this. By itself the degree of concentration of land ownership in optimal acreage groups for one or two pump-sets would explain the stepped profiles and the variable time-lags, and also probably the low ceilings. If this is a reasonable explanation, the adoption ceilings are not absolutely fixed but rise slowly as and when sub-optimal laggards find opportunities to innovate. The possession of an energised well can safely be assumed to be a universal goal of all farmers.

CONCLUSIONS

The diffusion of an irrigation technology is a multiple process, the spatial congruity of parts of which is probably more accidental than controlled by distance variables. The cumulative adoption profiles of planned innovations take a straight line or concave form rather than the classic 'S'. More needs to be known about the spatial planning of cost-minimising diffusion patterns under situations of institutional control.

The process of pump-set adoption is only 50 per cent complete. But already in terms of the drain on connected load and on the underground water-table this technology shows signs of being over-adopted. For these reasons the Tamil Nadu government has halted further pump-set connections, though by 1977 atomically generated electricity will be abundant. In the mean time, agricultural productivity may be more greatly increased (not necessarily jeopardising welfare) if the 75 per cent subsidy on agricultural electricity is removed than if electricity is cut for 75 per cent of the time; for the latter policy effectively reduces the optimal acreage per set to 1·5 to 2 acres. If at the same time, control on the selling rates for water (at present 33 per cent of the purchaser's crop) could be exerted, conditions might be created where it was more privately economic and socially beneficial for a sub-optimal non-innovator to buy water from a sub-optimal innovator rather than innovate himself. Because most sub-optimal non-innovators are small farmers they are now disadvantaged as a group. Unless they can be made to share pump-sets (which only 4 per cent of innovators at present do), any encouragement for them to innovate will only help to create excess pumping capacity in the absence of a small-scale pumping technology (see pp. 394–5). Paradoxically they may be forced to innovate if water-levels sink to a point beyond which the kavalai can no longer operate.

REFERENCES

Blaikie, P. M. (1973). 'The Spatial Structure of Information Networks and Innovative Behaviour in the Ziz Valley, Southern Morocco', *Geogr. Annaler*, 55 B, 83–105.

Brown, I. A. and Moore, E. (1971). 'Diffusion Research in Geography: a Perspective' in C. Board, R. C. Chorley, and P. Haggett (eds), *Progress in Geography*, 1, 119–57.

David, P. (1966). 'The Mechanization of Reaping in the Ante Bellum Midwest' in H. Rosovsky (ed), *Industrialisation in Two Systems: Essays in Honour of Alexander Gershenkron*, New York, Wiley, pp. 3–28.

Department of Agriculture, Government of Tamil Nadu. (1970). *A Notebook of Agricultural Facts and Figures*, 7th edn., Madras.

Department of Census Operations, Government of Tamil Nadu (1971). *North Arcot District Handbook*, vol. ii, Madras.

Found, W. C. (1971). *A Theoretical Approach to Land Use Patterns*, London, Arnold.

Gould, P. (1969). 'Spatial Diffusion', *Ann. Assoc. Amer. Geogr.*, Resource Paper no. 4.

Griliches, Z. (1960). 'Hybrid Corn and the Economics of Innovation', *Science*, 275–80.

Hagerstrand, T. (1967). *Innovation Diffusion as a Spatial Process*, University of Chicago.

Lal, D. (1972). *Wells and Welfare*, OECD Development Centre, Cost Benefit Case Study no. 1, Paris.

Misra, R. P. (1971). *Growth Poles and Growth Centres in Urban and Regional Planning in India*, IDS Mysore Development Studies no. 2, Mysore.

Morrill, R. (1968). 'Waves of Spatial Diffusion', *J. Regional Sci.*, 8, 1–18.
Patel, S. M. and Patel, K. V. (1969). *Studies on Economics of Rural Electrification and Lift Irrigation*, Ahmedabad, Indian Institute of Management.
Samuelson, P. (1967). *Economics*, 7th edn., New York, McGraw-Hill.
Tamil Nadu State Electricity Board (TNEB), (1973). *Administration Report for the Year 1971–2*, Madras.

14 Impact of the Cultivation of High-Yielding Varieties of Paddy on Income and Employment

B. Nanjamma Chinnappa and W. P. T. Silva

Many studies have observed that the cultivation of HYVs has led to an increase in the income and employment of both cultivators and agricultural labourers – although the major benefits have gone to the former because of relatively large increases in their yields and net incomes compared with small increases in labour demand and wages to labourers – and hence to a greater disparity in incomes in rural areas (see, for example, Parthasarathy, 1971; UNRISD, 1971; Lele and Mellor, 1972; Mellor and Lele, 1973; Griffin, 1974). Wherever adoption of HYVs has led to increased mechanisation of operations and increased demand for family rather than hired labour, the benefits to the cultivators have been further enhanced to the disadvantage of labourers. Researchers have also observed an increasing tendency, especially after the advent of the HYVs, for wages to be paid in cash rather than kind, with an adverse effect on the incomes of labourers in times of inflation.

This chapter investigates some of these issues in the survey areas of North Arcot and Hambantota Districts. The basic relevant differences between the two areas are:

1 The high rate of adoption of HYVs in the Hambantota area as contrasted with the low rate in the North Arcot area.
2 The lower yield rates of the HYVs in Hambantota as compared to North Arcot.
3 The high degree of mechanisation of ploughing, levelling, threshing and winnowing in the former area as compared to the labour-intensive nature of these operations in the North Arcot area where mechanisation was negligible.

Whereas the study of the North Arcot survey area focuses attention on both the income and employment issues, that in the Hambantota area concentrates on the employment pattern since no paddy income data for that area were available at the time of writing.

NORTH ARCOT DISTRICT (BNC)

If widespread adoption of HYVs results in considerable changes in income and employment among agriculturists, it will also have an impact on non-agriculturists in rural areas, e.g. traders and craftsmen who depend on agriculturists as the major consumers of the goods and services they offer. But because of the low rate of adoption of HYVs in North Arcot (see pp. 93–7) its impact on the livelihoods of the non-agriculturists is as yet insignificant. This section therefore concentrates on *cultivators*, defined as those who operated their own or leased-in land, and *agricultural labourers* who hired out their services to cultivators.

The household was used as the basic unit of study since the total income earned by its members was usually pooled and shared among them. For a household with multiple sources of income, its major source of net income during the survey year was used to decide the group to which it belonged. The analysis was based on the data collected in the listing schedules in the first phase of the survey and in the cultivator and livelihood schedules in the second phase (see p. 39). Net income was calculated as the difference in value between the output of the enterprise (whether agricultural or non-agricultural) and the total costs paid out (see pp. 104–5). Income from hired labour was taken as the sum of cash wages and the imputed value of kind wages. Information on person-days employed was available for agricultural labour only. The discussion on employment and underemployment is therefore confined to agricultural labourers.

Characteristics of Cultivator, Agricultural Labour and Non-Agriculturist Households

Figure 14.1 disaggregates the households by ownership of land and by tenure status since 'land is the principal material basis of inequality' among rural households (Béteille, 1971). All percentages are of the total number of 2064 households in the eleven sample villages in 1972–3, as recorded in the listing schedules. Figure 14.1 also shows that 84·1 per cent of the households derived their major source of income from agriculture (49·3 per cent from cultivation and 34·8 per cent from agricultural labour); 66 per cent of all landless households were agricultural labour households. About 17 per cent of all households operating land, whether as owner-cultivators or as tenants, depended on agricultural labour as their major source of income, whereas 34 per cent of agricultural labour households had to depend on agricultural labour as their main source of livelihood in spite of possessing land.

The corresponding proportions from the detailed enquiry were very much the same: 81 per cent of villagers depended on agriculture as their major means of livelihood, 60 per cent of landless households were agricultural labour households, 20 per cent of cultivators depended on agricultural labour as their major source of income and 30 per cent of agricultural labour households possessed land.

Agricultural labour was therefore an important subsidiary means of livelihood for households possessing land, particularly among those with small holdings, as will be shown later in this chapter.

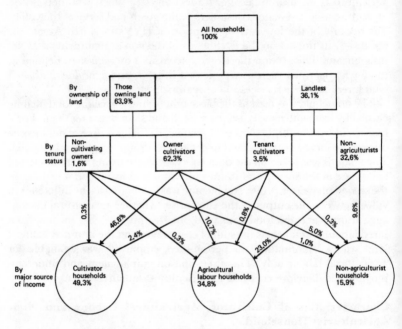

FIG. 14.1 *North Arcot District: Composition of households*

Impact on HYV Paddy Cultivation

The proportion of paddy cultivators growing HYVs in the study area (17 per cent) and the total paddy area under HYVs (10 per cent) were both low (Table 8.2). Given that our data refer to a single year, that the rate of adoption was low, and that the majority of adopters were the bigger and richer cultivators (Table 8.10), our findings may not be entirely applicable to a situation in which many more of the non-adopting cultivators (the majority of whom are medium and small cultivators) take to HYV cultivation. But the general trend of increased incomes and employment opportunities for cultivators and agricultural labourers, from HYV cultivation as observed in this study, is likely to be maintained, though the level or scale of increase may be different.

Impact on Income of Cultivators
The increased yield rate and profitability of HYVs as compared to other paddy varieties has been discussed in chapter 8 (pp. 103 and 104–6). The increase in net income per unit of land from cultivation of HYVs was of the order of 76 per cent. If the imputed costs of family labour are included in the cost of cultivation, the increase in net income is nearly 82 per cent – but that is because the proportion of family labour used is 25 per cent for HYVs whereas it is 35 per cent for TVs. (The term TV in this chapter refers to all non-HYVs and includes the IVs and TVs of chapter 7.) This again is due to the fact that most current HYV cultivators are those with bigger holdings who use less family labour. Such increases in net incomes, even when the yield rates of HYVs were far below potential, when the recommended package of inputs was not being applied in full, and when the market prices of HYVs were lower than those for TVs, suggests that substantial increases in incomes of cultivators are possible from the cultivation of HYVs. The scale-neutrality of the HYV technology will ensure similar increases in net incomes of all cultivators, big and small, provided they can afford the higher cultivation costs involved and provided that the necessary inputs are available to them at the right time, in adequate quantities and at reasonable prices (see pp. 119–21). The increase in income accruing to any individual cultivator will, of course, depend very much on the quality of his land, the inputs and cultivation practices he uses, and the market conditions when he sells the crop. An opinion enquiry among the sample cultivators gave responses for expected increases in net incomes from HYV cultivation varying from 20 to 300 per cent. Few of the cultivators believed that they would incur a loss or fail to equal previous net income.

Table 14.1 Number of person-days used per acre of HYV and TV paddy cultivation

Type of Labour	HYV			TV			Percentage change in demand for HYV cultivation		
	Male	Female	Total	Male	Female	Total	Male	Female	Total
Family, incl. exchange	27·9	7·5	35·4	28·1	9·5	37·6	− 1	−21	− 6
Attached	12·0		12·0	6·4		6·4	+88		+88
Hired, incl. contract.	25·4	50·3	75·7	21·4	40·6	62·0	+19	+24	+22
Total	65·1	57·8	123·1	55·8	50·1	106·0	+17	+15	+16

Impact on Employment of Cultivators

Table 14.1 shows that there was no increase in the demand for labour from the cultivator's family. In fact, family labour employed per unit of land in HYV cultivation was less, by 6 per cent, than in TV cultivation in spite of an overall increase of 16 per cent in labour demand for HYV cultivation. This might be due once again to the HYV cultivators being mainly the bigger cultivators who use less family labour. Also, even among smaller cultivators, hired labour is the major component of the labour used in the most labour-intensive operations (pulling seedlings, transplanting, weeding, harvesting and threshing), which together account for about 60 per cent of the total labour in paddy cultivation, which need to be completed within a short period of time, and which create the major increases in labour demand for HYV cultivation. At present, all available family labour among smaller cultivators is utilised fully before they hire labour, and hence there is little scope for further employment among their family members unless there is further spread of HYV cultivation in all seasons (cf. pp. 98–100). But even so, for the reasons stated, the increase in demand for hired·labour will be much higher than that for family labour.

Table 14.2 shows that the operations for which a major or substantial part of the labour used was from the cultivator's family were ploughing, manuring, fertiliser application, pesticide application, irrigation and miscellaneous operations (including sowing, and repairing bunds). Among these operations, an increased participation of family labour for HYV cultivation of 2·6 man-days, or an increase of 33 per cent, was observed only in ploughing. That, and an increase of 57 per cent in family labour used in transplanting (0·8 woman-days) – although in an operation where the proportion of family labour used is low (15 per cent) – supports the earlier statement that all available family labour is utilised fully before hired labour is employed.

Impact on Employment of Agricultural Labourers

As far as agricultural labourers are concerned, their incomes are closely related to their employment in agriculture. The increase in demand for hired labour from cultivation of HYV paddy as compared to TV paddy was 22 per cent and that for non-family labour (attached plus hired) was 28 per cent (see Table 14.1): that for hired female labour (24 per cent) was higher than for hired male labour (19 per cent), although, if attached labour is included, the increase for non-family male labour was 34 per cent. In absolute terms every acre that went over to HYVs from TVs of paddy generated an additional demand for 17·1 person-days (9·4 man- and 7·7 woman-days) of all types of labour. The increase in demand for non-family labour was 19·3 person-days (9·6 man- and 9·7 woman-days). Although this increase is likely to be met to a greater extent by family labour if HYV adoption spreads to smaller cultivators it will mean an overall additional

Table 14.2   *Analysis of person-days spent in different operations for cultivation of HYVs and TVs of paddy*

Agricultural operation	Percentage of person-days spent in the operation		Percentage family labour used		Percentage female labour used		Additional person-days for HYV over TV per acre		
	HYV	TV	HYV	TV	HYV	TV	Family	Non-family (hired+ attached)	Total
Ploughing	18	18	49	41	0	0	+2·6	− 0·2	+ 2·4
Manuring	2	3	68	67	22	26	−0·2	− 0·3	− 0·5
Fertiliser application	0·5	0·4	43	67	0	3	0	+ 0·1	+ 0·1
Pulling seedlings	4	4	13	22	17	21	−0·3	+ 1·2	+ 0·9
Transplanting	15	15	12	9	100	98	+0·8	+ 1·7	+ 2·5
Weeding	12	12	8	16	100	97	−0·9	+ 2·4	+ 1·5
Pesticide application	0·2	0·1	56	77	0	2	0	+ 0·2	+ 0·2
Harvesting and threshing*	32	28	10	20	57	60	−1·8	+11·9	+10·1
Irrigation†	13	15	69	78	0	1	−1·1	+ 1·7	+ 0·6
Other	3	4	69	88	29	55	−1·8	+ 0·6	− 1·2
Total	100	100	29	35	47	47	−2·2	+19·3	+17·1
Male	53	53	43	50			−0·2	+ 9·6	+ 9·4
Female	47	47	13	19			−2·0	+ 9·7	+ 7·7

* The labour required for harvesting and threshing could not be separated in many cases and hence they are lumped together.
† The non-family labour used for irrigation consisted almost entirely of attached labour. Irrigation involves switching the pump-set on, waiting for electricity, or operating the kavalai.

demand for hired labour since the increase is mainly for the labour-intensive operations for which a major portion of the labour used is hired. The very high increase in demand for attached·labourers for HYV cultivation (which accounts for about 10 per cent of the total labour used in paddy cultivation) is due to the fact that they were used mainly by the bigger cultivators who formed the majority of HYV adopters. Table 14.2 shows that the operation creating the highest increase in demand for non-family labour for HYV paddy cultivation was harvesting and threshing (an additional 11·9 person-days per acre). The increase was only 1·2 days for pulling seedlings, 1·7 days for transplanting, 2·4 days for weeding and 1·7 days for irrigation.

An opinion enquiry from the sampled cultivators on comparative demand for labour between HYVs and TVs showed that most of them believed that more labour was required in pulling HYV seedlings because they were shorter; although some believed this to be counterbalanced by the larger number of seedlings in TV nurseries (where a higher seed rate was normally used). Moreover, only one weeding was needed for TVs compared with at least two for HYVs, which also needed decidedly more labour in the application of fertiliser and pesticides. However, since the total number of man-days spent on these was small, they had very little impact on the overall increase in demand. HYV threshing was more labour-demanding because the shorter stems made the operation difficult. Opinion generally was that the labour requirements for ploughing, transplanting and harvesting were roughly equivalent for HYVs and TVs. Thus the overall increase of 16 per cent in total labour required (or 28 per cent in non-family labour required) although useful, is not sufficient to relieve the considerable underemployment among agricultural labourers in the area.

Impact on Income of Agricultural Labourers
Although there was not much difference in the wages paid for individual operations as between HYVs and TVs (this is to be expected in a labour-surplus area) the average wage rate for HYV operations (about Rs2·18 per person-day including wages in cash and in kind) appeared to be about 20 per cent higher than that for TVs (about Rs1·81 per day), while the total wages paid per unit of land for HYVs was about 33 per cent higher than that for TVs. This was due mainly to the increase in employment of hired labour for HYV harvesting and threshing: these were the best-paid operations, not only because of the value of the wages (on average about Rs4 per person-day) but also because the whole wage was paid in kind as paddy. About 68 per cent of all wages for labour in paddy cultivation was paid in kind in the study area (whether for HYVs or TVs). In times of inflation and rising food prices, such payment is very welcome to poor agricultural labourers; if it continues, increased adoption of HYVs will thus mean some increase in food supply to agricultural labourers.

The 33 per cent increase in wages earned from HYV cultivation by agricultural labourers compared poorly with the increase of nearly 76 per cent in net income earned by cultivators. Since the output per person-day for HYVs was 25 per cent higher than that for TVs (see Table 14.4) and since labour costs for both HYV and TV cultivation accounted for only 30 per cent of the total cost of cultivation, it is clear that the absolute increase in wages earned by the agricultural labourer does not compare with the increase in net income gained by the cultivator (Table 14.3).

In interpreting Table 14.3, it should be noted that whereas the increase in net income of Rs928 per hectare went to the single cultivator family which possessed the land, the increase in wages of Rs93 was shared between the agricultural labourers working on it. Also, members of

Table 14.3   *Average net incomes earned by cultivators and agricultural labourers per hectare of paddy land*

	HYV	TV	Increase from HYV cultivation	
	(Rs)	(Rs)	(Rs)	(%)
Average income earned by cultivators				
Gross income	3,381	2,122	1,259	59
Cost of cultivation	1,233	902	331	37
Net income (i.e. return to cultivator's family labour, land and capital)	2,148	1,220	928	76
Average wages earned by agricultural labourers (i.e. return to agricultural labour)	371	278	93	33

cultivator families often worked as agricultural labourers on other farms; and not all agricultural labourers' households were landless (see above, pp. 205–6).

In absolute terms, the difference in increased earnings is more striking. An average cultivator household has 1·5 hectares of land and grows paddy on about 1 hectare of it. Its net income from paddy therefore increases from Rs1220 to Rs2148 – i.e. by Rs928 – if it switches from TVs to HYVs. The average landless agricultural labourer household has an income of Rs836, and the increase in its income because of HYV cultivation is Rs276, which is 30 per cent of the increase earned by the average cultivator household. Table 14.3 shows, further, that the average wages paid to agricultural labourers expressed as a percentage of the average net income earned by cultivators decreased from 23 per cent in TV cultivation to 17 per cent in HYV cultivation. If the wages paid to agricultural labourers for HYV cultivation were to be slightly more than doubled, it would result in an equal sharing of the increased net income earned from HYV cultivation between cultivators and agricultural labourers. For if the wages paid to agricultural labourers for HYV paddy are increased by a factor of 2·12, to Rs786 per hectare, the cost of cultivation increases to Rs1649 and the net income to cultivators is reduced to Rs1732, so that the increase in net income of the cultivator from HYV cultivation as compared to TV cultivation is Rs512 – a decrease from 76 to 42 per cent in increased returns – whereas the increase in wages earned by agricultural labourers from HYV cultivation as compared to TV cultivation is Rs508, an increase from 33 to 183 per cent in enhanced wages.

The social, economic and practical implications of a policy that would ensure both a much higher rate of adoption of HYVs by paddy cultivators and an equal sharing of the resulting increased profits (by enforced doubling of the wage rates paid to agricultural labourers) are bound to be complicated. It might result in disincentives to HYV cultivation under conditions of limited availability of water and fertilisers, and a worsening of the social relations between cultivators and agricultural labourers (see pp. 235–42), the result possibly being increased mechanisation, to the detriment of agricultural labourers.

Seasonal Variation

More labour per unit of paddy land cultivated was used for both HYVs and TVs in Sornavari than in Navarai, and in Navarai than in Samba. Additional effort appeared to be required for ploughing, transplanting, harvesting, threshing and irrigation in the drier seasons. However, because of the smaller areas cultivated in these, the total number of person-days employed in paddy cultivation in Sornavari and Navarai was about 40 per cent and 34 per cent respectively of that in Samba. The percentages for non-family person-days was very similar to that for total person-days.

Table 14.4 shows that the output of HYV paddy per unit of labour employed was 20 per cent higher than that of TV paddy in Sornavari and Samba, 35 per cent in Navarai, and 25 per cent in all seasons combined, a result of the higher yield capabilities of the HYVs and the efficacy of the inputs used in their cultivation. (That the productivity of land is also higher for HYVs than TVs by about 45 per cent has been shown in chapter 8.)

Table 14.4   Output of paddy in kg per person-day

Paddy varieties	Yield in kg per person-day			
	Sornavari	Samba	Navarai	All seasons
HYV	10·5	11·5	12·3	11·6
TV	8·8	9·6	9·1	9·3

Traditionally, multiple cropping – at least double cropping – seems to have been quite popular in this area and the pump-set innovation in the 1960s appears to have increased that tendency. Because of the low rate of adoption of HYVs, it is difficult to assess the impact of HYVs on multiple cropping. Besides, as described in chapter 8, none of the HYVs could compare with the 'short duration' of the traditional Kullankar variety that was widely grown in the dry seasons, so that HYVs were no more 'amenable' to multiple cropping than were the TVs. Among the sampled cultivators, as many as 45 per cent grew some crop in all the three seasons and 56 per cent grew some crop in two or more seasons. Among paddy cultivators, 34 per cent grew paddy in all the three seasons and 58 per cent grew paddy in two or more seasons. Only 4 per cent of HYV paddy-growers grew HYVs in all three seasons and only 17 per cent grew them in two or more seasons. The highest proportion of double and multiple

croppers were in the villages of Vinayagapuram, Amudur, Randam and
Kalpattu.

Table 14.5   Agricultural labour employed in the months of
1973–4, expressed as a percentage of the labour
employed in September 1973

Jan	Feb	Mar	Apr	May	June	July	Aug	Sept	Oct	Nov	Dec
98	82	63	42	59	58	62	80	100	76	68	68

Table 14.5 shows the labour employed in each month in all the sample
villages expressed as a percentage of the labour employed in September,
the month with maximum employment. Figure 14.2 shows the number of
person-days employed in agricultural labour (in paddy and other crops)
among the sample households surveyed for the livelihood schedule, by
months for each village. In all the villages, April, May and June were the
deficit months, with only about half the demand for agricultural labour
that occurred in the peak periods. March and July, as well as November
and December, were also lean months to a lesser extent. The leanest deficit
period coincided with the hottest months of this year, those between the
Navarai and Sornavari seasons when the tanks were quite dry. November
and December were in the middle of the long Samba season when
transplanting was complete and harvesting not yet begun. Because of the
seasons overlapping in all the villages (except in Vayalur where there was
little cultivation in Sornavari because of the drought), the peak periods
August to October and January to February coincided with the start and
finish of the Samba season when harvesting of the earlier Sornavari crop
and field preparations for the following Sornavari crop were also in
progress.

    Figure 14.2 shows the severity of underemployment of agricultural
labourers in the lean seasons. The maximum fluctuation between months
in the agricultural labour employed was in the villages of Randam and
Kalpattu – the villages with maximum labour demand (see chapter 20 on
inter-village variation and chapters 9 and 15 on Randam) – where there
was a high percentage of multiple cropping. The demand for labour for the
cultivation of non-paddy crops such as banana and groundnut increased
the peak in Kalpattu and Randam respectively.

Hired Labour from outside the Village
Cultivators found it difficult to apportion the person-days used in an
agricultural operation between hired labour from within the villages and
that from outside, because the labour used often had components of both
kinds. The survey data showed that about 11 per cent of the hired labour

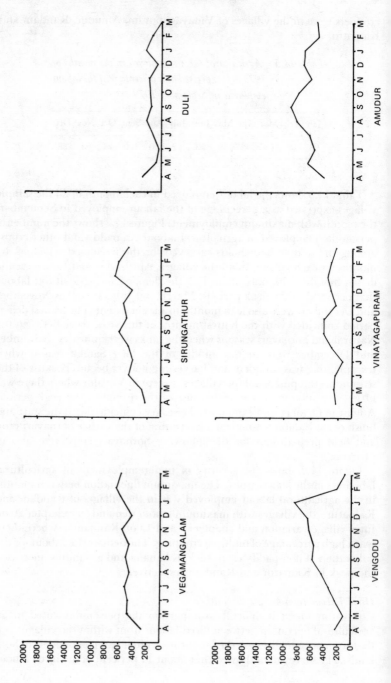

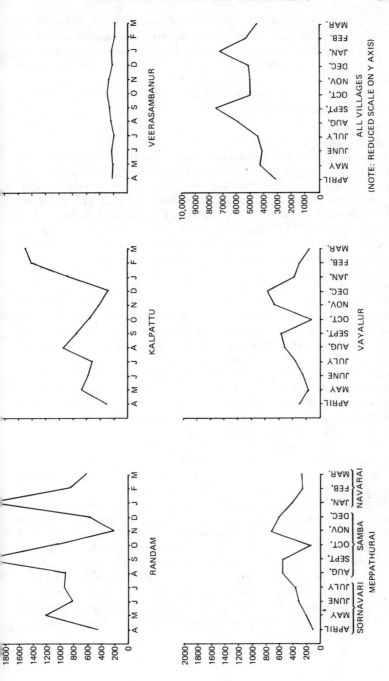

FIG. 14.2 *Number of person-days of agricultural labour among sample households, 1973–4*

and 9 per cent of the female hired labour in Sornavari was from outside the village. In Samba the proportion of male hired labour from outside the villages was negligible, and it was about 5 per cent for female labour. In Navarai there was hardly any hired labour from outside the sample villages. The operations for which labour from outside the villages were utilised were the peak operations of ploughing, transplanting, weeding, harvesting and threshing.

Conclusions

The analysis shows that the major benefits from HYV cultivation in the study area have gone to the cultivators and that, although agricultural labourers have also benefited from the increased employment opportunities, their gains were not as high as those of cultivators. The net income earned by cultivators from HYV cultivation was 76 per cent higher than that earned from TV cultivation. There appeared to be no increase in demand for family labour for HYV cultivation since the major increase was for the peak period operations, especially for harvesting and threshing, when even the smaller cultivators had to employ hired labourers. On the other hand the increase of 28 per cent in the demand for non-family labour for HYV cultivation (with hardly any increase in wage rates) helped to increase the income of agricultural labourers by 33 per cent, since the increase was mainly for harvesting and threshing which were the best-paid jobs. The increase in demand for agricultural labour for HYVs was not sufficient to meet the underemployment in the area. Further spread of HYVs in the remaining 90 per cent of the paddy area and in all seasons (but especially in the major Samba season) would improve the lot of cultivators and agricultural labourers, but the gap between their incomes would then increase. Better utilisation of inputs, and more cultivation in all the seasons, would lead to greater employment opportunities for agricultural labourers throughout the year. Increase in the wage rates would also help to increase their incomes: doubling the current wage rates would lead to an equal share of the increased profits from HYV cultivation between the cultivators and the hired labourers working on the land.

It must be noted that this study (except for the section on seasonal variation) is confined to paddy, which covers about 50 per cent of the gross cultivated area. About 40 per cent of the area is under groundnut, and agricultural labourers are employed in its cultivation also. An acre of groundnut gives a net income to the cultivator which is 65 per cent of that from an acre of paddy, whereas the agricultural labourers working on it earn wages that are 60 per cent of that which they would have earned from paddy. Thus paddy is a more profitable crop to both cultivators and agricultural labourers except where lack of water necessitates the cultivation of dry crops like groundnut.

AGRICULTURAL EMPLOYMENT IN HAMBANTOTA DISTRICT, SRI LANKA (WPTS)

One of the significant changes in paddy cultivation in the Hambantota District within the last decade has been the rapid spread of improved varieties of paddy (see pp. 61–3 above). In Maha 1973–4 the area under improved varieties amounted to 96 per cent of the total area cultivated in the District. Of this, 17 per cent was under 'old' improved varieties and the rest under 'new' improved varieties (see pp. 57–8). These new varieties require proper management at all stages of cultivation; hence their adoption has been accompanied by the spread of certain improved cultural practices such as weed control, plant protection and the use of fertiliser. Farmers have varied considerably in the combination of practices adopted (see pp. 61–5).

A priori, each of these practices generates a demand for extra labour. Furthermore, higher yields mean more work at harvest time. The amount of labour required per acre for the cultivation of HYVs is thus generally considered to be greater than that for traditional varieties. Shaw has pointed out that: 'With the exception of one study of the rice variety ADT-27 in Thanjavur District, Madras State, where most farmers used tractors for land preparation, the consensus of the material is that introduction of the new varieties does require the use of considerably more labor' (1970). This has been confirmed by Amerasinghe in his study of the impact of HYVs on a settlement scheme in Sri Lanka: 'The adoption of HYV rice has not only been capital intensive but also labour intensive. The labour requirements between the ante- and post-HYV periods have changed from 51·34 to 68·44 man-days which indicates a 31·3 per cent increase in labour use' (1972). A similar increase has also taken place in North Arcot (see pp. 208–10).

Whether the high level of adoption of HYVs in the Hambantota District has in fact led to new employment opportunities is difficult to ascertain. (The word 'employment' in the rest of this chapter means labour for hire; that is, it excludes labour by the cultivator or his family on his or their own holding.) On the one hand the absence of any previous studies on labour utilisation in the District prevents a comparison of the present patterns with those for the pre-HYV period; on the other hand the very high proportion of adopting farmers eliminates the possibility of meaningful comparison between adopters and non-adopters in terms of labour use for different field operations. However, from the present patterns of employment, a number of useful conclusions can be reached.

The data for the analysis is derived from two sources: (i) the household schedule administered to the total sample of 1112 households in the early stages of the survey, and (ii) the livelihood schedule administered every month to a selected number of cultivators and non-cultivators in the sample. It has not yet been possible, however, to process all the resultant data on labour utilisation and employment in paddy cultivation. What is

Table 14.6   Cultivator households in Hambantota District, by type of labour utilisation for different field operations

Operation	Total no. of paddy cultivator households	No. of households reporting operation	Percentage of households			
			using only family labour	using only hired labour	using family and hired labour	using other types of labour
Nursery	676	100	40·0	7·0	52·0	1·0
Ploughing	676	634	15·3	8·4	75·4	0·9
Levelling	676	635	14·5	9·1	75·3	1·1
Bunding	676	638	14·6	7·2	76·6	1·6
Sowing	676	616	23·4	6·5	66·7	3·4
Transplanting	676	114	9·6	17·5	71·9	1·0
Weeding	676	568	41·5	14·5	44·0	
Manuring	676	42	88·0		12·0	
Application of fertiliser	676	519	72·4	6·7	20·9	
Application of pesticides	676	604	42·2	21·3	36·5	
Harvesting	676	625	10·6	6·9	79·0	3·5
Threshing	676	620	19·2	11·6	65·4	3·8
Winnowing	676	621	28·3	9·5	58·2	4·0

presented here represents only the preliminary findings; hence the observations are necessarily only tentative.

The relative importance of family and hired labour in the different field operations can be seen from Table 14.6.

The figures show that manuring and fertiliser application are the only operations for which a high proportion of farmers rely exclusively on family labour. Exclusive use of hired labour is not very important, perhaps, except in transplanting, weeding and the application of pesticides, but the majority rely on a combination of family and hired labour for most operations. Hired labour in some form or other is used for all field operations, the proportion being quite high in the case of pre-planting and planting, and in harvest and post-harvest operations. If farmers use more hired labour today than they did when cultivating traditional varieties, a substantial number of people among the gainfully employed population would depend on employment as labourers in paddy fields: but the available information does not reveal such dependence.

Table 14.7 shows that, among cultivator households, nearly 70 per cent of the gainfully employed were farmers, i.e. owner-cultivators. Moreover, if we take the non-farmer population among the cultivator households, the proportion of persons whose major source of income was from agricultural employment was only 13–17 per cent lower in each case than the proportion engaged in non-agricultural occupations. Even among non-

Table 14.7 *Major occupations of the gainfully employed population*

Type of household	Total gainfully employed	Farmers (%)	Among sample households	
			Agricultural labourers (%)	Non-agricultural workers (%)
Paddy cultivators	1,204	68·7	12·9	18·4
Other cultivators	227	69·6	13·7	16·7
Paddy cultivators with holdings outside CC	30	60·0	16·6	23·4
Non-cultivators	437	3·0	32·3	64·7

cultivators, the proportion depending on agricultural labour as the major source of employment was less than one-third. By way of contrast, in the survey area in North Arcot, 42 per cent of the gainfully employed reported agricultural labour as their major occupation. Only 15 per cent were in non-agricultural occupations (see above, p. 205). The available data do not permit us to say whether the proportion of people whose main income is from paddy employment has increased since the introduction of HYVs. If there has been such an increase, the numbers today still represent only a relatively small proportion of the gainfully employed.

The demand for hired labour is also met by people who are part-time workers in agriculture. These include: (i) some cultivators who were able to take time off from their own agricultural operations, (ii) some non-cultivators who also had a major occupation other than agricultural labour, and (iii) members of some cultivator and non-cultivator households who had no major income-earning occupation, e.g. housewives (Table 14.8).

The figures show that the part-time agricultural labour force amounted to nearly 300 persons. Once again, we cannot say whether this represents a large increase over the pre-HYV period. It has been pointed out that in so far as the use of HYVs has been associated with an increase in the area transplanted (although a trend towards increased transplanting is not necessarily correlated with HYVs), there has been a considerable increase in the demand for female casual labour in Pahalagama (John Harriss, personal communication). However, even today the number of persons among cultivator and non-cultivator households with part-time employment in agriculture represents only 16 per cent of the gainfully employed population as shown in column 1, Table 14.8, and 28 per cent of those with subsidiary occupations. Furthermore, even among other members of households who reported a subsidiary occupation, less than 25 per cent found paid employment in agriculture.

The people who rely on agricultural employment either as a major source of income or as a subsidiary source do not find employment only in

Table 14.8 Occupational patterns of persons with subsidiary occupations

	Persons with subsidiary occupations	Agricultural labour (%)	Cultivators (%)	Non-agricultural labour (%)	Other occupations (%)	Family help (%)	Housewives (%)
Cultivator households	460	36·3	12·4	11·9	19·6	16·5	3·3
Non-cultivator households	123	18·7	33·3	10·6	17·1	7·3	13·0
Household members	490	22·3	0·4	0·4	1·42	75·5	
Total (nos)	1,073	299	100	70	118	455	31

Table 14.9 Employment in paddy, by type of operation

	Total employed	Ploughing and bunding (%)	Transplanting (%)	Weeding (%)	Application of pesticide and fertiliser (%)	Harvesting (%)	Threshing (%)	Transplanting (%)
Paddy cultivators and members of households	41	39·0	21·0	19·7	7·3	46·3	19·5	9·7
Non-cultivators and members of households	52	48·0	30·7	13·4	5·7	71·1	25·0	3·8

paddy. Chena cultivation has become increasingly profitable in recent years (see p. 85) and this has induced many cultivators to rely on some form of hired labour for operations such as clearing and weeding. Of the 111 cultivators and non-cultivators interviewed at monthly intervals, 46 reported an income from agricultural employment. Of these, 15 per cent depended only on chena and another 59 per cent on both paddy and chena. Likewise, of the 66 members of cultivator and non-cultivator households who also reported an income from agricultural employment, 17 per cent had depended only on chena and 47 per cent on both chena and paddy. Thus, of the 112 persons who had reported an income from agricultural employment, only 33 per cent depended exclusively on paddy.

It may be argued that the high proportion of cultivators and members of their households relying on chena employment does not necessarily reflect the lack of employment opportunities in paddy cultivation. Even if there is a heavy demand for hired labour, especially during land preparation, harvesting and threshing, they may not be in a position to take advantage of all such opportunities because of a clash with their own operations. On the other hand they are in a much better position to make use of employment opportunities in chenas because, there, much of the demand for hired labour occurs during the slack seasons in paddy (see pp. 86–91). Non-cultivators and members of their households, however, do not have to face any such constraints. Yet it is apparent from Table 14.8 that, as a major occupation, agricultural labour provides employment to only 32·3 per cent of the gainfully employed among non-cultivators and, from Table 14.8, that part-time agricultural employment is even less important to this group. Had there been a heavy demand for hired labour in paddy it seems certain that the proportion of individuals depending on paddy employment would be higher than today.

The present levels of agricultural employment among cultivators and non-cultivators and members of their households thus do not seem to match the demand that should be generated by the large proportion of farmers using hired labour. This seemingly paradoxical situation may arise from a number of causes. First, paddy cultivation in the Hambantota District is not labour-intensive (see pp. 143–5). Machinery is used for ploughing, levelling, application of weedicides and pesticides, threshing and winnowing; and the proportion of farmers using mechanised equipment varied from 35 per cent in the case of winnowing to 68 per cent in the case of ploughing. Most of the equipment for these operations is not owned by the cultivators but by landlords and merchants, and therefore the use of hired labour becomes inevitable. However, the number of people finding employment in this way is not very high, partly because the number of people needed to handle the equipment is very small and also because the operation, being mechanised, is usually completed within a relatively short space of time. A part of the demand for hired labour is presumably met by

imports from other areas (see p. 154). Secondly, it is likely that many
farmers use hired labour only for operations that have to be completed
within a limited period of time. For example, the time available for land
preparation from the first issue of water to the time of sowing is said to be
30–40 days (ARTI, 1974). Farmers therefore have no choice but to rely on
some hired labour if they are to complete on time such operations as
ploughing, levelling, bunding, harvesting, threshing and winnowing. The
use of machinery no doubt assists in achieving this objective, but there are
certain operations such as bunding and harvesting in which machinery is
not used. Furthermore, even in operations in which machinery is used, a
certain amount of manual work is inevitable. The demand for hired labour
in 'rush' operations means that more people find employment in land
preparation and harvesting operations than in such other operations as
weeding and the application of fertiliser and pesticides. This is clear from
Table 14.9 which gives the number of people among cultivator and non-
cultivator households who reported agricultural employment.

Table 14.10   Number of days employed in paddy cultivation

	Total reporting	10 days and below (%)	11–20 (%)	21–30 (%)	31–40 (%)	41–50 (%)	51–60 (%)	Over 60 days (%)
Paddy cultivators	15	26·7	40·0	20·0		13·3		
Members of paddy-cultivators' households	25	36·0	24·0	20·0	12·0	4·0	4·0	
Non-cultivators	23	26·1	13·1	18·7	8·7	4·3	4·3	34·8
Members of non-cultivators' households	29	31·1	20·7	10·3	13·8	10·3	6·9	6·9

Not only is the proportion of agricultural labourers low but the length of
time in which they have been employed has also been relatively low (Table
14.10). The figures show that a very high proportion of paddy cultivators
and members of their households worked for less than 30 days away from
their own holdings during Yala 1973 and Maha 1973–4. This is to be
expected because much of the demand for hired labour obviously comes at
peak periods when both cultivators and members of their families are
occupied with their own work. Non-cultivators however, are free of such
constraints. Many of them are engaged in the cultivation of their own
chenas or find employment in others' chenas, but, since chena operations
do not usually clash with paddy operations, they are free to make use of all

employment opportunities in paddy. It is significant therefore that, despite this flexibility, nearly 50 per cent of the non-cultivators and members of their families had worked for less than 30 days during both seasons.

Because the periods of employment have been short, the receipts from paddy employment have been rather low. Of the cultivators working away from their own holdings, none had received an income of over Rs400. Furthermore, 75 per cent had received less than Rs200 for both seasons. On the other hand the higher proportion of non-cultivators working for relatively longer periods of time has been reflected in a wider range of incomes received. Some 18 per cent reported an income between Rs600 and Rs1000 and 8 per cent between Rs400 and Rs600. Nevertheless, it is noteworthy that nearly 60 per cent had received less than Rs200.

Besides agricultural employment, both cultivators and non-cultivators rely on two other sources of income: (i) crafts, services and business enterprises, and (ii) high-land agriculture. Of the cultivators who had reported paddy employment, 60 per cent had an income from crafts, etc. and high-land agriculture combined, 25 per cent from high-land agriculture alone and 15 per cent from crafts, etc. alone. Similarly, among the non-cultivators, 44 per cent had an income from high-land agriculture, 20 per cent from high-land agriculture and crafts, etc., 12 per cent from high-land agriculture and other employment, 12 per cent from other employment and 3 per cent from crafts, etc. Only 8 per cent had depended exclusively on the income from paddy employment. How significant is the income from paddy employment in relation to the income from these sources?

It can be seen from Table 14.11 that 81 per cent of the cultivators and 65 per cent of the non-cultivators have received a major part of their income from sources other than paddy employment, especially highland agriculture. It is likely that the limited opportunities for employment in paddy cultivation have encouraged such people to depend on other sources of income. On the other hand, as John Harriss has pointed out, if people can make do on chena cultivation and employment of other kinds, they may prefer not to work on paddy fields for others; and when they do it is often to oblige friends, allies and patrons more than because of purely economic motivation (see p. 249).

Table 14.11   Income from paddy employment as a proportion of income from other sources

	Total reporting	Percentage of persons reporting an income			
		below 25	25–50	51–75	over 75
Paddy cultivators	16	69·0	12·0	19·0	
Non-cultivators	29	39·0	26·0	26·0	9·0

In short, present employment patterns do not suggest that the demand for hired labour has increased substantially since the introduction of HYVs. The proportion of people finding employment in paddy cultivation is relatively low: had there been a marked increase in demand it seems clear that this would have manifested itself in higher levels of agricultural employment. Furthermore, much of the demand for hired labour appears to have come not from new technology but from operations that have traditionally been heavy consumers of labour, i.e. land preparation, transplanting, harvesting and threshing. Land preparation has to be done regardless of the variety sown, hence the use of hired labour is related more to the size of holding and the availability of family labour than to anything else. Transplanting provides employment mainly to women and in any case it is not a practice that has been widely adopted. This leaves harvesting and threshing, which like land preparation, have to be completed within a short period of time. It is possible that the high proportion of people finding employment in these two operations, notwithstanding mechanisation, points to more employment opportunities arising out of higher yields from HYVs. But on the other hand it is equally likely that it is simply a reflection of the farmers' desire to complete the operation on time. Finally, the income from paddy employment has accounted for only a small proportion of the off-paddy income of the majority of the cultivators and the income of non-cultivators.

REFERENCES

Amerasinghe, N. (1972). 'The Impact of High Yielding Varieties of Rice on a Settlement Scheme in Ceylon', *Modern Ceylon Studies*, 3, 19–35.

Agrarian Research and Training Institute, ARTI (1974). *The Agrarian Situation relating to Paddy Cultivation in Five Selected Districts of Sri Lanka*: part 1, Hambantota District, Research Study Series no. 6, Colombo.

Béteille, A. (1971). 'Agrarian Relations in Tanjore District, South India' in UNRISD, op. cit.

Griffin, K. (1974). *The Political Economy of Agrarian Change: An Essay on The Green Revolution*, London, Macmillan.

Lele, Uma J. and Mellor, J. W. (1972). 'Jobs, Poverty and the "Green Revolution" ', *International Affairs*, 48, 20–32.

Mellor, J. W. and Lele, U. J. (1973) 'Growth Linkages of the New Foodgrain Technology', *Ind. J. Agric. Econ.*, 1973, 36–55.

Parthasarthy, G.(1971). *The Green Revolution and the Weaker Section*, Bombay, Thacker.

Shaw, R. D.'A. (1970). *The Employment Implications of the Green Revolution*, Washington, DC, Overseas Development Council, mimeo.

United Nations Research Institute for Social Development (UNRISD) (1971). *A Study of the Social and Economic Implications of the Large-Scale Introduction of High-Yielding Varieties of Foodgrain*, Report no. 71.6, Geneva.

15 Implications of Changes in Agriculture for Social Relationships at the Village Level: the Case of Randam

John Harriss

It has been widely supposed that the cash inputs required for the successful adoption of the new technology, together with the enhanced profitability of cereal cultivation, will substantially increase the level of commercialisation in South Asian agriculture; accelerate the incorporation of villages into regional and national market networks; create or further expand a capitalist sector in agriculture; and further increase economic differentiation. The most important social implications of these processes are thought to be that, whereas in the past employment was offered within a traditional set of social relations involving a range of obligations and sanctions, it will come to depend on the cash nexus; that, in place of vertical alliances with landowners and bigger farmers, the labourers and small farmers will seek security in horizontal alliances with other members of their own group, or with outside political authorities; in other words, that increasing 'proletarianisation' will take place.

All the elements in this schema have been observed (see many papers in the *Economic and Political Weekly*, some of them commented on by Byres, 1972); but expectations deriving from different theories of modernisation have also played a part in interpretations of some of the relevant data (see above, pp. 34–6). Here I present a study of the social consequences of change in agriculture in one locality; for one case, well studied, may contribute more to understanding of problems of this kind than a host of statistical generalisations, especially if these are used to demonstrate the working out in practice of some previously conceived 'grand theory' (cf. above, pp. 35–6).

I shall consider evidence for changes in patterns of interaction consequent upon decisions to innovate in agriculture, and then examine the dialectical relationship between ideas and action. I shall inevitably be concerned with other factors which may also be contributing to change, such as political forces outside the arena of the village.

THE BACKGROUND: SOME FEATURES OF RANDAM

An account of the location, agricultural economy and distribution of land holding in Randam appears in chapter 9, and it only remains to add some comments on social organisation in the village. Twelve castes are represented among the 278 households. There are no Brahmins, and the dominant caste is that of the Agamudaiyan Mudaliars, among whose 78 households only one is dependent upon agricultural labour. The other major land-holding community is that of the Yadhavas (or Idaiyans), who together with the Mudaliars make up nearly half the population. The largest single community however, is that of the Paraiyans, untouchables, about a quarter of whom own some land, though it is nearly all dry land. Also in the cheri (untouchable hamlet) are several Muslim households, earning a living from shopkeeping and as tinkers; two households of Chakkilis (leatherworkers); and some Velluva Pantarams who are hereditary astrologers and priests to the Paraiyans. Most of them have a little dry land, but all the families have members working away in the big cities. All these cheri communities, except the Muslims, are scheduled castes.

There are four households of Acharis, carpenters and blacksmiths who still make and repair agricultural implements for which they are paid in kind at harvest times; as are the two dhobis, the temple priest (a Naydu), the thoddi (see p. 351), and the three barbers who come to Randam from neighbouring villages. All these service castes, and the Paraiyans, continue to perform their ritual offices: the dhobi to perform sacrifices, the Velluvans to blow the conch at funerals, the barbers to act as funeral priests. In addition there are small communities of Naydus (two subcastes), Odda Chettys (traditional earthworkers and brickmakers, and swineherds), and the interesting Jangamma Pantarams who are astrologers, country doctors and professional beggars. None of them has much land and most are landless.

The temples of the village and a number of festivals give symbolic expression to the unity of the village, which is also seen in the attempts which are made to resolve even serious disputes within the village.

Randam retains many of the characteristics of the 'traditional' Indian village even though its cultivators are already largely 'incorporated' into the wider economy, certainly in terms of their dependence upon the market (cf. chapter 9).

CHANGES IN THE ORGANISATION OF PRODUCTION

The introduction of HYVs has not in itself changed the system of agricultural production very radically: farmers cultivated paddy before in much the same way, although they did not use so many inputs purchased from the town. However, the use of electric pump-sets has had a substantial impact on Randam's agriculture by increasing the likelihood of multiple cropping in the old wet land and by effectively increasing the amount of wet land available. Tractors are attractive to many of the farmers because of their contribution to timely cultivation; because they make the cultivation of larger areas of dry land possible; and because they make threshing, particularly of HYVs, easier and quicker. Tractors are also attractive at the moment because of the profits which the farmers think they can make by hiring them out, and as a status symbol (cf. chapter 12).

The labour requirements of the traditional water-lifting devices were considerable. I was told that to irrigate one acre by means of an etram required the labour of three men for nearly a whole day; and to do the same job with a kavalai that of one man and a bullock team for a day. By 1973, only one farmer was cultivating paddy by means of kavalai irrigation alone and there were no etrams (several other cultivators used kavalais to supplement water obtained from other wells with pump-sets or from the drainage water in the tank). The farmer in question cultivated only one-third of an acre in Sornavari but even that needed his kavalai for two hours almost every morning and evening throughout the growing period of the crop. So, before the introduction of pump-sets the bigger farmers in particular needed more attached labourers than now, mainly to lift water, while several men in the cheri told me that they had had much more secure employment at that time. If only 50 acres were irrigated by means of kavalais, that still means some 40 labourers to do irrigation work, even if we allow for a contribution from family members. This is over and above the requirements of other operations, for which Randam farmers, between them, still employ 37 attached labourers, mainly from among the Paraiyans with a few Velluvans and Jangammas.

However, although the installation of large numbers of pump-sets has evidently caused a decline in the availability of work on this semi-permanent basis, for the farmers now mostly manage the flow of water from the pumps themselves, the increase in paddy acreage associated with the pump-sets has increased the overall demand for labour in other operations. The majority opinion among the landless labourers was that there is more work available now than ten years ago, though equally there was widespread concern about the increasing use of tractors. It is too early to say what the effect of tractorisation will be (and the likelihood of a very rapid increase in the use of tractors has probably diminished in the past year); but despite the possible contribution of tractors to overall labour demand because of a slight increase in the acreage of dry land under cultivation, and the occasional possibility of an additional paddy crop being fitted in, it seems likely that the demand for *male* labour will decrease. Already the pump-set revolution in Randam has led to a much greater increase in the availability of work for women than for men, because the most labour-intensive operations in paddy cultivation (transplanting, weeding and harvesting) are carried out mainly by women, who also do as much manuring work as men and contribute to threshing. Men are mainly employed in field preparation (ploughing and mammoti work), in plucking seedlings in the nursery (an average of about 2 man-days per acre, compared with 20 woman-days for transplanting) and in threshing. A number of cultivators – those who can afford several plough teams and have a number of sons – can do almost all their own ploughing without calling in labourers, and the need for men for hand-beating at threshing time has decreased with the increasing use of tractors.

The introduction of HYVs has probably exacerbated the imbalance in demand for male and female labour. Several farmers thought that the use of HYVs had probably increased their overall demand for labour, particularly in weeding. However, they required rather less female labour for transplanting because of the wider spacing of HYV plants; and they thought it possible that less labour would sometimes be required to harvest HYVs, because of their sturdy stance. Table 15.1 summarises data from 25 cultivators who are representative of the total spectrum of farmers in Randam, and whose operations I followed very closely (there are in all 86 observations of different cultivation operations). It appears that rather less female labour is indeed required for transplanting HYVs, but that more such labour is required for weeding (though the Sornavari figure is inflated by one man's exceptionally high demand), and in harvesting and threshing (where, when a tractor is used, women can do the supporting work as well as men). Rather more male labour is used in plucking seedlings in the nursery (perhaps because of their small size), but less is used in threshing. Overall requirements for male labour are roughly constant, or might even be reduced (if we take the Samba figures), but the demand for female labour is increased. Since there is no evidence to suggest that the introduction of HYVs has increased the demand for attached labour, we can assume that the level of demand for padials remains constant as between HYVs and local varieties, so that it appears that the introduction of HYVs has increased the tendency towards imbalance noted earlier on the basis of more qualitative evidence.

The real disparity in the demand for male and female labour is nothing like so marked as Table 15.1 suggests, because more than 30 men are employed as padials; and, as Figs. 15.1 and 15.2 show, more women than men are available for employment in agricultural labour. The disparities in supply and demand for male and female labour are also comparable, although for several months of the year the demand for female labour is absolutely greater than that for male casual and attached labour combined; while it also appears that the demand for female labour approaches or exceeds supply more markedly than the demand for male labour. These last trends are compensated to some extent by the availability of well-digging work for men, although almost as many women as men are employed. The 'imbalance' is not so much a matter of absolute

Table 15.1 *Casual labour demand in the cultivation of HYVs and of local varieties, 1973–4*

	No. of observations	Preparation of main field (m)	Transplanting (m)	(f)	Weeding (f)	Transport and spreading of manures (m)	(f)	Harvesting (f)	Threshing (m)	(f)	Total (m)	(f)	Combined
HYVs													
Sornavari	5	12	4	21	23·5	2	1·5	23·5	7·5	4	25·5	75·5	101
Samba	15	10	2·5	18	16	0·5	1·5	22·5	6·5	4	19·5	62	81·5
Navarai	7	4	2	16	11	1	1	23	5	3	12	54	66
Local													
Sornavari	22	8·5	2	24	13	1	0·5	20	10	2	21·5	59·5	81
Samba	22	10·5	2	20	16	1	1·5	20	9·5	1·5	23	59	82
Navarai	15	4·5	1	17	7·5	0·25	0·25	16	5	1	11	42	52·5
Average for HYVs		8·5	3	18	17·5	1+	1	23	6+	3·5	19	63	82
Average for local		8	1·5	20	12	0·5+	0·5+	18·5	8	1·5	18	53	71

Note: The table shows the number of man-days of *casual* labour required per acre for each operation; it does not include family labour or attached labour. Harvesting is also carried out by a few men so that the fact that only the female labour is shown does introduce a very slight bias; when averaged out, the male labour in harvesting would amount to less than half a man-day per acre. Requirements of casual labour for operations other than those shown, such as nursery preparation, haulage and application of fertilisers and chemicals, are slight.

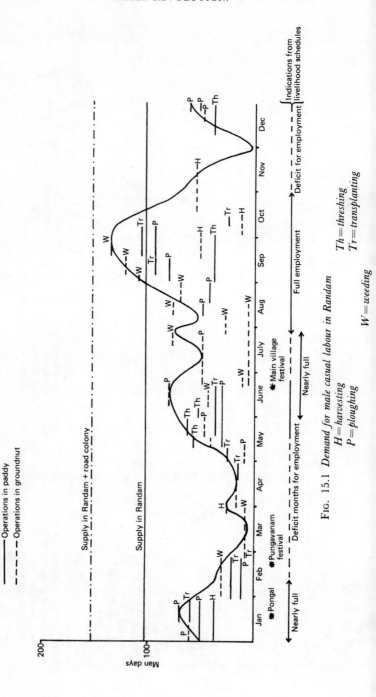

Fig. 15.1 *Demand for male casual labour in Randam*

H = harvesting

P = ploughing

Th = threshing

Tr = transplanting

W = weeding

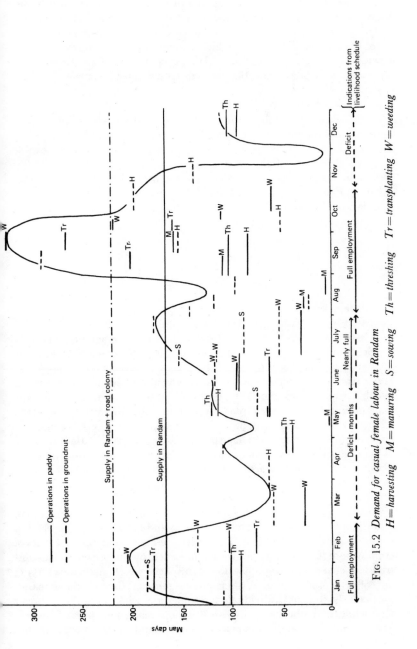

FIG. 15.2 *Demand for casual female labour in Randam*

H = harvesting   M = manuring   S = sowing   Th = threshing   Tr = transplanting   W = weeding

disparities as of trends. About 100 men have to seek employment as casual daily labourers, rather than being employed on a semi-permanent basis. More of them would have found secure employment but for the introduction of large numbers of pump-sets, while there would be rather more casual employment available to them but for the introduction of tractors. Further, the adoption of HYVs has increased the demand for female labour while leaving that for male labour constant or even reduced.

DEMOGRAPHIC CHANGES

It is difficult to be certain of the exactness of a comparison of the Census figures for 'Randam' of 1961 and 1971, because it is not absolutely clear that the same entities are described in the two years, and it seems possible that the definition of the scheduled castes has changed as well. But although I suspect that a simple comparison of the 1961 and 1971 figures inflates the trends, I have little doubt that between 1961 and 1971 the caste population of Randam increased by 20—25 per cent while the scheduled caste population decreased by 15—20 per cent:

	1961	1971
Total population	1353	1446
Caste	810	1015
Scheduled caste	543	431

The depression of the scheduled caste population of Randam is further indicated by the rather small size of scheduled caste households:

| Caste | 5·3 individuals per average household |
| Scheduled caste | 3·9 individuals per average household |

The small households of the scheduled castes are associated with poverty, and a tendency to export people, notably young males; for although it is possible that higher mortality or lower fertility rates enter into the explanation of the observed trends, it is unlikely that they can account for a 15 per cent decrease in population over a decade. (This argument is confirmed by comparison of age-specific sex ratios and child/adult ratios, as between caste and scheduled caste populations.) A substantial minority of the men in the cheri who do not have access to land work or have worked in Vellore, Madras or Bangalore (for employment opportunities for Harijans in Arni are limited: very few silk mills will employ Harijans or Velluvans; they are largely excluded from work in the paddy mandi and in retail shops, except in fruit and vegetables; and there is only one band of coolies made up by Harijans). That there are not enough opportunities of employment in the cities is indicated, however, by the presence of a semi-transient element in the population of the cheri, which made the carrying out of a census and of further surveys among the scheduled castes particularly difficult. Individuals and sometimes whole families disappear for a while, and others may appear. Relations may come to stay for weeks at a time, not only at times of peak labour demand. If these people are not exactly rural transients, as Epstein has used the term (1973 in a seminar at Kandy), some of them are at least semi-transient.

The explanation for the demographic trends in the recent history of Randam involves a variety of factors. In both caste village and cheri there is a marked tendency for members of families which have no stake in land to seek employment outside. And in Randam the scheduled castes have been steadily losing control of land. Now, of the 300-odd acres of paddy land operated by Randam farmers only 35 acres is operated by 22 Paraiyans, with 1 Muslim and 2 Velluvans; and of that area, less than 2 acres is in the old wet land under the tank. Yet four hours of the 48-hour cycle 'karai' system – the old way of dividing up scarce irrigation water, in theory at least – belong to 'Sittan Paraiyan', because Sittan's lineage formerly owned 15 or 20 acres of wet land. Sittan's family is thought to have obtained the land by taking over unclaimed poromboke at the edge of the irrigated area, and this probably took place during the last quarter of the nineteenth century when the population of Randam increased very considerably and at a rate indicating substantial immigration. Comparison of the 'pariah' population as it is shown in the 1871 Census with that of the other villages in our sample shows that Randam had an unusually high proportion of Untouchables at that time, while the indications of the occupation data in the same Census suggest that one or two of them were cultivators even then. More recently the Paraiyans have become indebted at different times to one of the Mudaliar lineages in particular, and have gradually forfeited control of almost all their land. In general, and in contrast to some other villages like Vegamangalam in our sample, the story of Randam's Harijans is one of declining fortunes.

After the very rapid population expansion of the late nineteenth century it seems that up until the end of the 1940s rather steady population growth was maintained, probably by a combination of increasing labour intensity and investment in agriculture, using funds obtained from outside sources. There were carters and traders in Randam, and for a long time at least one family of public works contractors. But it seems that despite such investment and the intensification of cultivation the carrying capacity of the village economy had become saturated by about 1951, and that the pump-sets that were installed in the 1950s, and the increasing use of urban manures from about the same time, only enabled the population to be maintained at a little over the 1941 level. In 1961 the scheduled castes still made up 40 per cent of the population, but their share had dropped to 30 per cent by 1971. Perhaps it is only a coincidence that Sittan's family gave up its last pieces of land to the Agamudaiyans in 1961, but it does seem that the scheduled caste people have steadily lost out in the increasingly precarious saturated economy of Randam because they have lost their stake in the land, partly for want of the same kind of stake in the town economy that the caste people have enjoyed. Certainly they have lost their land to urban money. The increase in the caste population appears to have been supported since 1961 by the augmented carrying capacity made possible through the rapid expansion of pump-sets. (Though local report has it that even this increase has been possible only at the expense of living standards.) Meanwhile, the demand for male labour has not increased despite the intensification of agricultural production, so that some members of the scheduled caste population have had to seek work outside Randam, because their original rather large 'share' in the population has had to be supported on a declining share of the resources available.

CHANGES IN THE EXTERNAL RELATIONS OF THE VILLAGE
There has been a significant increase in the dependence of Randam cultivators upon inputs which can only be purchased outside the village, a development linked with the introduction of HYVs, through which most farmers have been brought into increased contact with the bureaucracy and with the trading community in the town. Within the village, the smaller farmers have come to rely to some extent on the pull of bigger men as brokers – in persuading the directors of the Land Mortgage Bank to sanction a loan, for example, or more directly for supplies of fertiliser (cf. above p. 137); and until they began using HYVs none of the cultivators of Randam needed to go to the Panchayat Union or to merchants for pesticides (though none of these trends must be exaggerated). Moreover, the fact that there are important scarcities of inputs does appear to have created objective conditions in which we might expect patron–client ties to be reinforced if we accept, as Wolf suggests, 'that such ties would prove especially functional in situations where the formal institutional structure of society is weak and unable to deliver a sufficiently steady supply of goods and services, especially to the terminal levels of the social order. Under such conditions there would be customers for the social insurance offered by potential patrons, while the formation of a body of clients would increase the ability of patrons to influence institutional operations' (Wolf, 1966, p. 17). The latter part of Wolf's statement is true at the village level in the sense that the position of Panchayat President in Randam is seen as a profitable niche in which it is worthwhile investing because of the pickings to be made from work done in the village under contract, and because of the pull that office as President can provide in the urban–regional sphere of operations. To become President in Randam, until the last election, required only the building up and maintenance of rather general support, but the last election was hotly contested and both candidates built up retinues of clients.

But it is also to the advantage of men like the fertiliser dealers and paddy merchants of Arni to maintain retinues of clients, because there is such strong competition in business and because it is part of the status game of the town (and that in turn, partly bound up with town politics). The increasing importance of the connections obtaining directly between some farmers and traders in the town may exercise a pull which conflicts with the strengthening of intra-village ties just suggested. In Randam, although 'traditional' forms of organisation like the ur panchayat and the jajmani relations between farmers and service castes continue to exist, there is a strong tendency for the big men to occupy themselves less with the affairs of the village and more with the affairs of the town. The Panchayat President is building himself a house in town and mentions his important business connections (like a directorship in a Mortgage Bank) and his wish to ensure good education for his children, as reasons for this; three brothers who form something of a family corporation and who together operate more than 10 per cent of the total area cultivated by Randam farmers were rarely mentioned as leaders and took little interest in village activities such as the major festivals. All the same they are still potential Presidential candidates because of their prestige, though village affairs seem to be increasingly dominated by a kind of second-division élite – as I saw in the constitution of an ur panchayat during my stay in Randam.

So there are several tendencies involved, not all working in the same direction. However, on balance it seems likely that, although the introduction of HYVs and the succeeding conditions of scarcity may strengthen patron–client relationships within the village, at least as strong a trend will be towards increased orientation outside the village – for the small farmers will also develop direct links with traders and urban political and bureaucratic authorities (cf. Epstein, 1973; her account of the possible future of Dalena is along somewhat similar lines).

RELATIONS BETWEEN FARMERS AND LABOURERS: RELATIONS BETWEEN HARIJANS AND CASTE PEOPLE

Not all farmers are caste people and not all labourers are Harijans. Categories like 'farmer' and 'labourer' refer to different relationships to the ownership of the means of production and to different roles in the division of labour, whereas categories such as 'Mudaliar' and 'Paraiyan' refer to the ideology of caste and to the way that the ideology is worked out in social interaction. I use the two sets of categories and put them alongside one another in this way to emphasise that analysis of 'class relationships' and of 'caste relationships' should not be exclusive. Although it may be true that much Indian sociology has been idealistically biased and that 'the sociology of interests' has been neglected – as Béteille for example, maintains – I believe with him that 'A comprehensive sociology of India must give their proper place to both values and interests, for it is the dialectical relation between these two which gives to human societies their distinctive qualities' (Béteille, 1969, p. 18). It is in this vein that Béteille has pursued his studies of agrarian social structure in India. He argues for example, that the relationships between caste ('values') and the agrarian hierarchy ('interests') can be studied on two levels. On a superficial level there is an empirical association between the grades or layers of the two systems, for large landowners are generally high-caste, and members of the lowest castes landless labourers, while sometimes the correspondences can be worked out in quite minute detail. At a deeper level: 'The caste system contributes to the persistence of . . . inequalities by providing the values and norms . . . appropriate to the agrarian hierarchy . . . although different in principle, agrarian relations were often expressed in the idiom of caste' (Béteille, 1972, p. 25). He goes on to account for some changes in agrarian social structure in India in terms of increasing inconsistency between what he calls 'the existential order', of the agrarian structure and the 'normative order', of caste; and he emphasises that the relationship between the orders is a two-way process. Such emphasis should be the cornerstone of analysis of 'social change' in Randam.

The kind of hereditary relations between Peasant farmer families and Untouchable labourer families that obtained in Epstein's 'Wangala' (1967) and which guaranteed the labourers a minimum subsistence while permitting the cultivators to profit greatly from the relationship in good years, have not existed within living memory in Randam. None the less, rather similar relationships do exist between farmers and labourers, principally between Agamudaiyan Mudaliars and Paraiyans. It has recently been pointed out by Meillassoux that Indian sociologists have confused the kinds of relations of clientship that existed between skilled artisans and some service castes on the one hand, and landowners on the other, in which clients through the patron profit from the exploitation of the labouring classes 'with all forms of protection or paternalism, whatever their actual content, including relations of exploitation' (Epstein, 1973, p. 102). This is an important distinction, but bearing its terms in mind we can still say that the kinds of relations that exist between farmers and labourers in Randam remain predominantly personal, and continue to involve obligations of mutuality. Work relationships are exploitive, but not yet depersonalised. They still often have the kind of moral quality which characterise patron–client relationships according to James C. Scott's view of them (Scott, 1972). Scott suggests that we should look at the relations between landed élites and agricultural labourers in the framework of exchange theory, and he argues that when the two partners in a relationship do not exchange equivalent goods and services, but there is none the less an important element of reciprocity in their relations the status of the dominant partner in the exchange may be legitimated as that of a 'patron'. It follows that 'there are thresholds in the balance which produce sharp changes in legitimacy'. Such a threshold was crossed in England in the early nineteenth century according to E. P. Thompson's view of *The Making of the English Working Class*, which includes 'The classic exploitive relationship of the Industrial Revolution . . . depersonalised in the sense that no lingering obligations of mutuality – of paternalism or deference, of the interests of "the Trade" – are admitted . . .[so that] . . . Antagonism is accepted as intrinsic to the relations of production' (Thompson, 1968, p. 222).

Close personal relations between farmers and labourers are seen most clearly in Randam in the case of those who serve as 'attached labourers' (padials), but in practice many 'casual labourers' are almost invariably to be found working for the same farmers, so that there is a kind of 'informal' attachment as well. In both cases the relationship is often mediated by credit, and the status of the labourers is comparable with that of bond servants, like the Dublas in the Hali system of South Gujarat recently described by Breman (1974). On the farmers' side, one frequently hears expression of a sense of obligation towards regular employees – it is for example, kadamai (duty) for a farmer to help his regulars with their wedding expenses, to make gifts on such occasions and to help with medical expenses. For a Mudaliar farmer not to give in these circumstances would detract from his mānam (honour – or perhaps dignity) because he would lose respect (matippu). On the labourers' side, there are parallel expressions of loyalty and it is not uncommon for the labourers to take the part of their masters in disputes, even against their own caste fellows. Demonstrations of deference on the part of the labourers are the essential transitive component of the individual farmer's status.

There is then a range of values surrounding the labourer–employer relationship, but these do not in themselves explain the persistence of the prevailingly personal quality of work relations. In part, explanation lies in the pattern of demand for labour through the year, which is illustrated in Figs. 15.1 and 15.2. The diagrams show that the conjunction of labour demands for groundnut and paddy cultivation creates a situation of fairly acute labour demand which presses against and even exceeds supply for several months of the year. The persistent labour difficulties of one of the biggest farmers in the village were mentioned above (p. 137), and put down to his inability to pay labourers in advance; while the heavy demand for labour in the Samba season was one factor leading some farmers to stick to local varieties in that season. In short, it is to the advantage of the cultivators to have a retinue of dependent labourers. I found, for example, that one of the cultivators whose operations I followed closely paid less to his ploughman than other farmers, even during the very busy time in August and September (Rs2 rather than Rs2·50 or 3). He explained that he gave regular employment to the men in question so that they would work for him at a lower rate. But he added, disingenuously, that he also gave them credit whenever they needed it, and that they all happened to be in debt to him at the time.

The suggestion of labour demand exceeding supply fits oddly with the decrease in the scheduled caste population which supplies the great majority of agricultural labourers. The resolution of this contradiction lies in the uneven pattern of the demand for labour through the year, and in the imbalance discussed earlier; while it must also be remembered that Randam started out with an unusually high proportion of scheduled castes, who had some land. The imbalance in the demand for male as

opposed to female labour also confuses the apparently logical consequences of the further use of tractors in releasing farmers from
dependence on labourers, because the tractor substitutes unequally for
male and female labour. It is probably easier for wheat farmers in Punjab
to substitute tractors for labour, and thus to become mechanised capitalist
farmers employing a small full-time labour force, than it is for paddy
cultivators in Tamil Nadu, because of the heavy demand of the paddy crop
for female labour particularly in transplanting and weeding. Transplanting could be mechanised and weeding done, as in Sri Lanka, with chemical
weedicides, but both would be more expensive at present than female
labour. The consequences of the oil crisis make it even less likely that
labour in these operations will soon be substituted, so that future labour
demand will probably maintain a sufficient balance in the needs of farmers
for labourers, and of labourers for farmers, for social relationships of interdependence to survive. Again, however, it is possible to see continuing
imbalance upsetting the prediction and threatening the harmony of the
system.

However, the future development of labour relations in Randam
involves further considerations, for the social relations of production are
interwoven with caste relationships. It is not just that the labourers'
awareness of themselves in opposition to the farmers is still in terms of caste,
but that the Mudaliar or Yadhava farmers depend on the Paraiyans and
Velluvans as the dhobi, the barber and the temple priest for a variety of
functions which have to do mainly with the maintenance of purity. They
depend on the Paraiyans for the disposal of dead cattle, and both Paraiyans
and Velluvans as well as barbers have functions in death ceremonies and
on the burial ground. The services of the Paraiyans as drummers will be
essential to the Mudaliars and Yadhavas for as long as customary religious
observances are important to them. The interdependence of castes is
expressed in various ways on religious occasions, and the generalised
dependence of lower upon higher castes in the kind of 'giving' which takes
place. At Pongal the Mudaliar families (even some rather poor families)
give cooked food to Harijans and to some Velluvans; and they are also
given the kuzh (ragi gruel) which is offered to the goddess Panjalammal at
the major village festival. Similar 'giving' takes place on important
religious occasions within the family, like weddings and the anniversaries
of parents' deaths, while the 'paternal' attitude of the Mudaliars and
leading Yadhavas towards the Paraiyan community is also shown in
remarks like 'Our Harijans wouldn't do anything like that' – with reference
to an incident of theft; and, in case I have over-emphasised the benevolent
aspect of the relationship, the harsh treatment that I saw them mete out to
the Paraiyans on two occasions. Special caste functions, and the ritual in
which they are expressed, are indicative of the special nature of the
relationships that obtain between groups of people, who also share class
relations, in Hindu society. Patronage itself has particular connotations in

India arising from the exigencies of Hindu religious ideology.

Dumont in his classic work on the caste system (1966) has argued that Hindu thinking is fundamentally hierarchical, in contrast to that of the West where an ideology of equality has been prevalent for the last two hundred years or so. He acknowledges an intellectual debt to De Tocqueville and refers to a passage from *Democracy in America* for an evocation of the 'hierarchised interdependence' of some societies: 'As in aristocratic communities all the citizens occupy fixed positions one above the other, the result is that each of them always sees a man above himself whose patronage is necessary to him and below him another man whose co-operation he may claim' (quoted in Dumont, 1970, p. 18). The orthodox, brahminical interpretation of Hindu belief can be understood as an ideological legitimation of such hierarchical social organisation, in terms of ideas about degrees of religious purity. Certain aspects of the division of labour in Indian society (no matter whether it is absolutely unique to India or not) arose from a concern with degrees of purity and with the separation of the 'relatively pure' from the 'less pure'. The relatively pure depended on the relatively impure to maintain their purity by the performance of certain services (like those mentioned earlier), and the relatively impure depended on those above themselves for the performance of important ritual offices. While the system as a whole may have broken down, or at least come under increasing stress, the attitude of separation and concern with purity remain strong in a small town like Arni as well as in the village. It is the sacred authority for hierarchical thinking and for emphasis on separation that has imparted a particular character to agrarian social relations in India, and even to labour relations. Religion itself requires patronal attitudes and imparts a moral quality to the relationships of production.

An important qualification to these assertions, which also affects the relations between farmers and labourers, concerns the attitudes of the Paraiyans. For if they share the religious beliefs of the higher castes, then logically they should accept the inequalities inherent in their lot as 'natural' (rather than 'legitimate' which implies that alternatives are actively considered: a useful distinction suggested to me by Ronald Herring). We can be fairly confident that acceptance of inequalities as 'natural' has never existed except in the ideal model; but that positive rejection of the ideas that account for them has substantially gained strength in the recent period. (This is part of Béteille's model of the shift from a 'harmonic' to a 'disharmonic' system; Béteille, 1974, chapter 8.) Kathleen Gough writes of the Harijans of a village in Thanjavur: 'Whatever they may have believed in the past, Thanjavur ADs in general denied the orthodox Hindu theory – so reassuring to high-caste landlords – that the performance of duty in a past life determines one's wealth and caste status in this one' (Gough, 1973, p. 234). Acceptance of the orthodox theory was not common among the Paraiyans of Randam

either, and the acquiescence of the majority with the existing order, and
the cynical resignation with which they view things like their 'participation' in the village Panchayat, cannot be said to derive from their
religious beliefs. Where caste ideology seems to be more significant is in
contributing to the dependence of the Mudaliars and the other higher
castes on lower-caste people, over and above need for their labour services.
The farmers have an interest in the welfare of the low-caste labourers
because they do hold orthodox beliefs. If they do not meet their obligations
to the low castes then they are denying the beliefs that legitimate their
status. I cannot agree with Wood when he asserts that 'control over the
principal means of production render the ritual, caste aspects of the
hierarchical patron–client system superfluous' (1973, p. 68); though
neither am I trying to assert the priority of the system of values over
ownership of the means of production.

Further, there is no absolute conformity to one system of norms and
values. All farmers do not try to maintain dependants, and a number of
them change their padials regularly – once a year, or perhaps every
season – because, they said, a permanently employed man would quickly
become lazy and take advantage. Similarly, not all landless labourers seek
an attachment to a particular farmer, for in spite of the security and side
benefits that attachment offers they resent the element of servitude that it
entails. Some men prize their independence, while some farmers do not
appear to value 'merit' very highly. Two of the most enterprising farmers
in Randam might well be described as rationalists, and have very little to
do with customary religious observances. They do not give to the Untouchables at Pongal or on other occasions, though they are still respected
because of their prestige (antasthu) as successful and wealthy cultivators,
because of the strength of their personalities, and because they do look after
their own servants and their families very well indeed. Their attitudes to
labourers are well described as paternalistic, because although they have
less interest than other farmers in the maintenance of labourers for reasons
other than those connected with production, they evidently retain a keen
concern for the welfare of their own particular men. To refer back to the
distinction suggested by Meillassoux, the more the farmer–labourer
relationship is stripped of its other connotations the more obviously
paternalistic it may become.

There are therefore a range of factors influencing the form and content
of production relations in Randam, which are not completely uniform.
Indeed, the opposition between a system of personal relationships
involving mutual obligations and sanctions, and a depersonalised system
dependent entirely upon the cash nexus, seems to be inherent and not to be
related to particular historical stages: though, of course, production
relations have probably never remained entirely depersonalised for long.
As Thompson shows, a new paternalism had to be developed in early
nineteenth-century England (Thompson 1968, pp. 222–3). But the

question remains, albeit rephrased slightly: is it likely that the 'depersonalised' pattern will come to dominate, that the social relations of
production will cease to be embedded within a complex structure in which
caste relationships have some determining effect? Is it likely that labourers
will cease to be aware of themselves mainly in terms of caste?

None of the changes that have so far taken place in the system of
production in Randam have absolutely eliminated the benefits to be
derived by farmers from paternalistic relationships with some labourers, so
that although the social structure of the village as a whole might be seen as
having moved even further away from the model of hierarchised
interdependence, there are still important vertical alliances cutting across
class relationships. There is evidence from other villages in North Arcot
which suggests that this may be generally true. (In chapter 20 we show that
there appears to be both a greater likelihood of semi-permanent labour
relations, and of higher wages, in those villages in which production is most
continuous. This, in turn, is likely to be the result of the adoption of pump-
set technology, so improving the reliability of water supplies.) On the
labourers' side, in a context of imbalance, and when rather little work is
available for part of the year in spite of heavy demand at other times, it
seems at least as likely that conflicts among the labourers will be
exacerbated as that they will become united in their class interest. As
Wood says of Bihar: 'It is the landless labourers who are competing for the
opportunity to work and who are consequently divided amongst
themselves' (Wood, 1973, p. 56). In Randam the landless labourers are
divided among themselves anyway, along caste and kinship lines (ethno-
graphic evidence from Randam tends to support those writers who have
suggested that the social organisation of the lower castes may be more
complex than that of the higher castes).

Comparison with an area in which conflicts on class lines have occurred
is informative. In the eastern taluks of the Old Delta in Thanjavur, for
example, explanation of class conflict includes the acute peak of labour
demand created by the particular ecological conditions of paddy cultivation, and altogether different in character from the peaks in North Arcot
District, where the use of groundwater gives individual farmers a flexibility
denied to the Thanjavur cultivators; the resentment generated through the
replacement of kind payments by cash in an inflationary situation; and the
fact that 'The economic and cultural unity of the Harijan agricultural
workers in the eastern taluks . . . has made it particularly easy for them to
be *organised into a class* (my italics) for the purpose of political action'
(Béteille, 1974, p. 167). Béteille goes on to observe, 'I would like to
insist . . . that these conditions are unusual rather than general for rural
India as a whole.' They do not obtain in North Arcot District, where peak
labour demand reinforces personal labourer – employer relations rather
than the reverse (for in the parts of Thanjavur in question there is such an
acute shortage of labour at the time of change-over between the two main

cultivation seasons as to require an army of labourers to be imported from outside. Landowners 'play off' migrant and resident labourers against one another).

Béteille writes of the agricultural workers in Thanjavur having been 'organised into a class'; and the political mobilisation of labourers along class lines seems generally unlikely in the absence of strong leadership and political organisation. In North Arcot the work of organisation is made especially difficult because of the deep entrenchment of DMK populism; while latterly the ADMK, which the *Economic and Political Weekly* (29 June 1974) describes as having done 'a most important job in shifting the major part of the DMK mass to the left', appears to have mopped up potential Communist support. Partly because important personalities commanding vast popular followings are involved, and partly because of the populist character of the parties' platforms, both the DMK and the ADMK tend to unite some farmers and labourers in Randam, in spite of their opposed 'class' interests.

Béteille also makes the point that caste *may* reinforce the unity of agricultural workers as a class. Again, in a village like Randam, the pressures are if anything working in the opposite direction, for the influence of the DMK is responsible in some measure for reducing some of the more obvious restrictions on the behaviour of low-caste people, by comparison with some of the neighbouring villages. In Randam Harijans may walk in shoes or ride cycles in the caste streets, and they are allowed to drink out of the same glasses as the caste people in the teashop. The general toning down of the more marked forms of caste differentiation may be another factor tending to reduce the likelihood of political mobilisation along class lines.

Conclusions: The Differentiation of the Peasantry

Neither conditions in Randam, nor according to Béteille in most of South India, are such as to make it likely that class-consciousness will emerge in the manner suggested by some commentators – an idea much beloved also by certain Indian intellectuals. There has indeed been a great deal of misinformed discussion of this problem, and as Foster-Carter says, 'These days it is not a question . . . of a class developing "naturally" because of its position in production relations, a certain consciousness . . .' (Foster-Carter, 1974, p. 90).

However that is not the end of the story, for recent developments in agriculture have undoubtedly increased economic differentiation among the peasantry. Other chapters document the structural disadvantages of the small farmers which mean that, even though they may have adopted the new technology, they have not been able to benefit by it to the same extent as the larger farmers and landowners. Some of the social implications of this have been considered here in the context of the external relations of the village. The new technology has reinforced the small farmers' needs for patronage (their brokers may be big farmers or traders), while the big farmers, because of their own growing involvement in urban activities have come increasingly to share relations with millers and traders in the towns. As the village élite of large farmers comes to participate more and more in a regional trader–farmer élite, so a new group of village leaders is emerging.

Another process of differentiation is taking place at the bottom of the pile. We saw that, although there are labour shortages in Randam which keep paternalism alive, there has been a tendency for the agricultural economy to shed male labour, so that the stability of the system of hierarchised interdependence has been associated with zero growth of the labouring population. While the urban economy has so far been able to provide some employment for surplus men, and sometimes to support the emigration of whole families, it is likely that the class of rural transients will substantially increase in the future, thus constituting a kind of rural lumpenproletariat in distinction to labourers in more secure employment. (Epstein, 1973, describes a distinction of this kind between AKs and migrant Vodda labourers in Wangala.)

If agricultural development is concerned with rural livelihoods as well as with increasing production (as I believe it should be), then it is a matter for great concern that in a village like Randam, even though there has been intensification of activity in agriculture, the agricultural economy of the village has not been able to support the natural expansion of a large section of the population. Some of the more modest claims for the new technology have suggested that it provides a breathing space. In Randam it seems hardly to have done even that, because of the economic structure into which it has been introduced and which it serves to reinforce.

APPENDIX: CONSTRUCTION OF THE LABOUR DEMAND PROFILES (FIGS. 15.1 AND 15.2)

(i)   The profiles show the demand for *casual* daily labour only and do not include family labour or attached labour. Similarly the lines indicating the level of labour supply include only the casual labourers available, excluding padials. Both the capacity of the casual labour force in the main village, and that in the main village plus the colony at the main road, are shown. My observation suggests that the capacity of the main village alone represents the best approximation to the real labour force: the labourers in the road colony mostly work for farmers outside Randam.

(ii)   I have had to assume that 'Randam' is a closed system in terms of the supply of and demand for labour; and believe that the errors are more or less self-cancelling.

(iii) The estimates of labour demand that have been used are those found in Table 15.1, worked out for acreages according to the actual cropping pattern in 1973–4 (given in Table 9.3). Estimates of labour demand in groundnut cultivation are based on statistics obtained from 22 cultivators.

(iv)   The demand for a particular operation has been spread equally over the number of days available for the completion of that operation. The period has sometimes been conpressed slightly where there are long 'tails' at either end: this seems justified since demand is not spread evenly, but tends to bunch around crucial times. The profile is then worked out by cumulation.

(v)   The 25 (in the case of paddy) and 22 (in the case of groundnut) cultivators from whom the basic data was obtained represent only a small sample of 155 cultivators in the main village, which was my universe of study. It is not a random sample, although I started with a stratified random sample of 25 per cent of the total cultivator population. I found that it was quite impossible for me to keep a sufficiently careful track of the activities of 40 cultivators, and further that a number of the cultivators selected were such difficult informants as to make me very dubious of the value of the data obtained from them. In their place, I substituted cultivators from whom I found that I could obtain reliable information and who closely approximated to the defaulters in terms of operational holding, family size, and caste. Thus, I achieved a sample representative of the whole spectrum of Randam farmers, despite the sacrifice of strict 'randomness' in the interests of accuracy of data.

(vi)   The figure used for some of the big farmers in the preparation of Table 15.1 represents the average of what happened in a number of discrete cultivation operations, although in the same season. The same farmer in the same season, and for the same crop can sometimes be seen to have used very different amounts of labour on different units of his total holding; and for this reason it would be misleading to use figures pertaining to only one unit of the holding. The variations are linked to factors such as additional ploughings required on certain types of land, additional labour required where field preparation is carried out by mammoti; variations in labour used for manuring, dependent upon the location of the field and the source of the manure; differences in amount of labour used in weeding according to incidence of weeds and sometimes also because of farmers' cash problems; whether a tractor was used for field preparation and/or threshing. These are over and above the variations from season to season that are apparent from Table 15.1.

(vii)   Inspection of the data does not show any very systematic variation in the use of casual labour in relation to holding size, although the bigger farmers tend to use more casual labour for operations like weeding, transplanting and threshing. In part, this is because some of them are prepared to pay more for additional weedings; in part it reflects their need at certain times to get jobs done quickly, whereas a smaller farmer may be able to do the same job with family labour by taking longer over it. Size of family and ownership of bullock teams also appear to be important sources of variation.

REFERENCES

Béteille, A. (1969). 'Politics of Non-Antagonistic Strata', *Contributions to Indian Sociology*, New Series, 3, 17–31.

Béteille, A. (1972). *Inequality and Social Change*, Delhi, Oxford University Press.

Béteille, A. (1974). *Studies in Agrarian Social Structure*, Delhi, Oxford University Press.

Breman, J. (1974). *Patronage and Exploitation, Changing Agrarian Social Relations in South Gujarat, India*, Berkeley, University of California Press.

Byres, T. J. (1972). 'The Dialectic of India's Green Revolution', *S. Asian Rev.*, 5, 99–116.

Dumont, L. (1966). *Homo Hierarchicus*, Paris, Gallimard English Translation: London, Weidenfeld & Nicolson, 1970.

Epstein, Scarlett (1967). 'Productive Efficiency and Customary Systems of Rewards in Rural South India' in R. Firth (ed.), *Themes in Economic Anthropology*, London, Tavistock Publications.

Epstein, Scarlett (1973). *South India: Yesterday, Today and Tomorrow*, London, Macmillan.

Foster-Carter, A. (1974). 'Neo-Marxist Approaches to Development and Underdevelopment', in E. De Kadt and G. Williams, (eds), *Sociology and Development*, London, Tavistock Publications.

Gough, Kathleen (1973). 'Harijans in Thanjavur' in Kathleen Gough and H. P. Sharma (eds), *Imperialism and Revolution in South Asia*, New York, Monthly Rev. Pr.

Meillassoux, C. (1973). 'Are there castes in India?' *Econ. and Soc.*, 3, 89–111.

Scott, J. C. (1972). 'The Erosion of Patron–Client Bonds and Social Change in Rural SE. Asia', *J. Asian Studies*, 32, 5–37.

Thompson, E. P. (1968). *The Making of the English Working Class*, Harmondsworth, Penguin Books.

Wolf, E. (1966). 'Kinship, Friendship and Patron–Client Relations in Complex Societies', in M. Banton (ed.), *The Social Anthropology of Complex Societies*, London, Tavistock Publications.

Wood, G. (1973). *The Process of Differentiation among the Peasantry in Desipur, Bihar, North India*, IDS Discussion Paper no. 24, University of Sussex.

16 Social Implications of Changes in Agriculture in Hambantota District

John Harriss

In December 1953, the Government Agent for Hambantota reported on the working of the Paddy Lands Act of that year:

> Two propaganda meetings for the purpose of seeking the co-operation of landowners and a peculiar creature which exists only in the Hambantota District known as 'gambārayas' . . . held at Tissa and Ambalantota. Both meetings were rather stormy and have only served to accentuate the gulf between the 'haves' and the 'have-nots'. . . .
> (*Monthly Reports*, 1953)

The 'peculiar creature' of this report is still at the heart of the distinctive agrarian social structure of Hambantota District. The report implies that the gambārayas and landowners stand opposed to measures intended to improve the lot of the 'have-nots'. Twenty years later the problems of social and economic change in Hambantota still hinge around the status of the gambārayas. However, to a long series of legislative attacks directed at their power – such as the Paddy Lands Acts of 1953 and 1958 – have recently been added certain consequences of agricultural development. This chapter will be concerned mainly with these consequences, but it is necessary also to give some account of the impact of recent political developments, and first, to outline the social history of the District.

THE ORIGINS AND ROLE OF THE GAMBĀRAYAS

A century ago that part of Hambantota District which lies in the Dry Zone was very sparsely populated indeed, but it knew remarkable population increases after about 1880 (46·5 and 48·5 per cent respectively between the

Census years 1881–91 and 1891–1901, cf. Roberts 1974, p. 155) as a result of the restoration of ancient irrigation works on the Kirindi and Walawe rivers. The lands under these major schemes were sold off in large units to owners who were often absentees, businessmen and lawyers of Colombo, Galle and Matara; or to local government officials and traders (see *Administration Reports for Hambantota District*; and Herring, 1973). Such men frequently operated their lands with the assistance of intermediaries, who became known as 'gambārayas'. The term originally meant 'village guardian', but cultivation rules for the Kirindi scheme drawn up in the early part of this century represent it as meaning 'one who manages land for others'. By the 1930s and possibly earlier, the name might also be used for a buffalo owner, and it now means simply 'a wealthy man', though it is not used with reference to traders and rice-millers who are more likely to be called 'mudalalis'. The term seems always to have been used to refer to those whose wealth rests on the control of agricultural inputs.

The status of the actual cultivators of the land, who were mostly brought in from the adjacent densely populated regions of Giruwa Pattu West and Matara District, is clearly shown in the suggestion of C. F. S. Jayawick-reme, the registered owner of 496 acres on the left bank of Kirindi and a resident of Kegalle, that among the cultivation rules should be one stating: 'Every cultivator when leaving a manager shall possess a memo signed by such manager showing whether he is and if so in what amount indebted' and another to the effect that 'The manager may dismiss any cultivator found guilty of negligence' (in a letter written in 1916, Hambantota Kachcheri Records, File E293). Again, in February 1934 the Assistant Government Agent noted in his diary: 'There is no doubt that the ordinary goiya generally finishes his paddy cultivation in debt to the landlord and at the last has very little to show for his labour, though he has been fed in the meantime' and even in the late 1940s we find an AGA referring to the cultivators as 'thralls to the gambārayas' (*Monthly Reports*, 1947).

The power of the gambārayas (landowners and/or managers) was based on their control not just of the land but of other essential inputs (seed paddy, draught and credit), the significance of whose control was heightened by the need for timely cultivation under the major schemes if two crops were to be obtained during one year. Very high interest rates have always been quite usual (they are now often 120 per cent per annum); while the shortages of draught animals which led to much official encouragement for the use of tractors more than twenty years ago have been replaced by the dependence of ordinary cultivators upon the tractor owners (see chapter 12).

A distinctive characteristic of this élite was that its power was secured upwards rather than being founded on the command of allegiances and respect in the community, or even upon the control of land. Although control of land was one important component of élite status, that status did not arise from it, but rather the reverse: control of land followed from élite

status. Whether the gambārayas were managers or landowners they were
not usually residents of rural areas, and they acquired control of land
because of wealth or access to power, arising generally from trade or a
position in government service. Land then formed the basis of a control of a
wider kind involving command of credit and ownership of draught,
though there were also men who entered the élite by means of ownership of
draught animals. Land, cash and draught were all components in the
appropriation of economic surplus and the domination of the goiyas. This
does not mean to say that some of the gambārayas were not respected. I
heard one of the tenant farmers in Pahalagama, for example, refer to the
gambāraya who controls his land as being 'like mother and father' to him.
But the records in the Kachcheri, and the life histories of some of the men of
Pahalagama, show that the extent of the control that some gambārayas
exercised over the lives of their tenants was such as to deny that element of
reciprocity in a relationship of dependence that characterises
patron–client relationships (cf. chapter 15; and Scott, 1972).

OTHER FEATURES OF SOCIAL ORGANISATION IN HAMBANTOTA

As we might expect, with the absence of an internally generated social
hierarchy, at the local level a tone of egality and of individualism co-exists
with the external gambārayal élite. One looks hard and long for a purāna
village such as those described by Leach (1961) and Yalman(1967), and
even an old settlement like Magama on the left bank of Kirindi (marked on
Robert Knox's map of Ceylon) has a population of recent immigrants from
the western areas of out-migration. Gambārayal power was such that
whole settlements were sometimes evicted, as happened at Rotawala and
Jansagama on the right bank of the Walawe river in the early 1950s, when
the managership changed hands. In an area of such recent and rather
unstable settlement it is not surprising to find that village communities
defined by the ties and reciprocities of kinship and marriage, and by
common interests in village lands, have not developed.

Kinship links within a locality like that of Pahalagama usually represent
the mobilisation of rather distant connections that have more to do with
place of origin than with 'real' kinship ties. Marriage alliances are almost
entirely with villages in the western places of origin, and rarely involve
close cross-cousins, or any clearly definable relationship at all. Marriage is
indeed rather informal, even haphazard (but cf. Yalman, 1967, e.g.
p. 134), and there are at least five cases of cross-caste marriage. Common
interest in land hardly exists at all, both because most of the land does not
belong to those who cultivate it, and because residential neighbours or
'kinsmen' do not necessarily have their lands in the same yaya.

Above all, it has been the existence of more cultivable land for
colonisation that has limited the emergence of a sense of 'moral
community' bound up with differential rights in a particular tract of

agricultural land. This is suggested by the ideas expressed about inheritance, which include the view that it is 'customary' for the youngest son to inherit the property because it is to be expected that older sons will have established themselves in some 'new' land, probably with their fathers' assistance. In several cases in Pahalagama, elder sons have encroached in one of the two major areas that draw water illegally from the Kirindi Oya right bank (KORB) scheme, while other sons have moved right away from the neighbourhood. Others, less fortunate, have established themselves on high land alone.

In this context a rather individualistic style of life has developed, and there is a strongly egalitarian ethos which is consistent with the character and importance of chena cultivation, and possibly reflected in the importance of the idea of 'jealousy' in daily life (see chapter 23, pp. 374–5). Some of the more articulate young men of Pahalagama say: 'Our chenas make us independent, free': and it is true that, because of the chenas, nobody is absolutely landless; while men who operate no paddy land of their own and sometimes work as labourers commonly lend money to the paddy farmers, albeit in small sums – effectively they use the proceeds of their chenas to purchase cheap rice, for the paddy farmers repay the loans in kind after harvest. The chenas also enable young men to carry on their own agricultural enterprises independently of their fathers (with the consequences for family labour participation noted in chapter 10, p. 145), while the building of a new house on chena in semi-permanent cultivation is invariably associated with marriage. There is no tradition of 'joint family' land management in Pahalagama, or in Hambantota District in general.

Until the recent past there has been a general lack of marked economic and social differentiation within small localities in dry zone Hambantota, while leadership is still very informal, and ideas about 'status' and 'respect' confused. Yalman's description of a village not far away in Uva applies very well also to settlements like those on KORB:

> Slash-and-burn cultivation was part of the economic foundation of the community . . . this tends to emphasise the separation and independence of the nuclear family and it is essentially only the energy and power of the man in the household that limits the amount of land that can be cultivated. It is a way of life that gives a distinctly egalitarian tone to the entire community. In the general similarity of economic background such caste differences as are delineated stand out as clear and lasting rents in the social fabric. . . . (Yalman, 1967, p. 237)

'Rents in the social fabric' are expressed in Pahalagama in the kind of battle for territory that is going on in the high land. The Goigama caste are numerically inferior to the Karava and are much less 'united' as a group, but two of them have cleared much larger areas of high land than they can

possibly cultivate because, they say, they must 'hold the Karava off'.
'Caste' in Pahalagama is a phenomenon different from 'caste' in Tamil
Nadu, for in Pahalagama there is no caste *system*. There are no hierarchised
social relationships, but instead the simple opposition of blocs—or
expressions of difference. Of particular significance for agrarian social
relationships is the fact that there is no large class of landless labourers who
are distinguished also by caste and whose economic condition is to some
extent sanctioned by religion. Those who work as labourers in the paddy
fields are members of the same castes as the cultivators.

CHANGES IN PROGRESS

Political and administrative opposition to gambārayal power has quite a
long history. In the 1940s Agricultural Improvement Co-operative
Societies were formed with the idea of releasing ordinary cultivators from
financial dependence upon the land controllers, and in 1953 the Paddy
Lands Act was designed to limit some of the exploitation inherent in the
gambāraya system, in the interests of greater productivity. The GA
expressed his fear that 'the Bill is likely to be sabotaged by the landowners'
(*Monthly Reports*, 1953), and the Act finally proved to be quite unworkable,
as Herring has described (1973).

The Paddy Lands Act of 1958 was more effective, though it has not
prevented some evictions of registered tenants (Pahalagama men among
them), or had much success in limiting rents. The Act laid down that no
tenant should pay more than a quarter of the yield, or 12 bushels per acre
whichever was less; but only five of the 17 tenant cultivators in my sample
paid a rent as low as 12 bushels in Maha 1973—4. The remainder, who paid
a quarter of their yields, are all registered tenants and all are aware of their
legal rights (which were affirmed afresh in the Agricultural Lands Law of
1972), but they maintain that usually the yield is so low that a quarter is
less than 12 bushels, or more frequently explain their behaviour in terms of
'friendship' and 'respect' for the landowner. In some cases there was
evidence of genuine warmth between the parties, but in others 'friendship'
seemed to mean rather a relationship of dependence and indebtedness on
the part of the cultivator, and a few of the tenants were very cynical about
the 'help' that the land controllers give.

In spite of these limitations cultivators in Pahalagama speak of the
'gambāraya kirame' (gambāraya system) as a thing of the past, since the
system whereby the landowners or their managers invariably supplied all
inputs which had to be repaid with interest is no longer so prevalent.

The present government of Sri Lanka has enacted a number of radical
laws affecting agrarian affairs. However, the Land Reform Law of 1972
has had little effect on KORB, or in the District as a whole, because very
few have registered holdings in excess of the prescribed 25-acre ceiling on
paddy land. This does not mean to say that there are no real operational
holdings of much greater size, but they are divided up in terms of registered

ownership. On KORB, only one cultivation committee area has been much affected by the Law, and there it is rumoured that the landowner voluntarily surrendered his lands but secured registrations in his own name and in those of his two sisters for 25 acres each, and of a further 25 acres for the gambāraya, so that only about 42 acres of the worst land will be left for redistribution. The case illustrates some of the weaknesses of the Law, which has done little to change the structure of paddy cultivation in Sri Lanka (see also Sanderatne, 1972).

It is too early as yet to gauge the impact of the Agricultural Productivity Law of 1972, for the agricultural productivity committees which it set up have hardly begun to operate. Attendance at one meeting of the committee in which Pahalagama is concerned suggested that its affairs would be dominated by the president, not so much because of his power as because of the apparent lack of interest on the part of the other committee members.

Of greater significance than all these legal and administrative developments, and the rhetoric of national politicians, is evidence of a degree of consciousness of their common interests among the poorer cultivators. An agricultural labourers' and tenants' union has recently been formed by a group of young men who have eschewed large public meetings in favour of a slow and careful building up of a network of activists, and who have been careful to avoid infiltration by gambārayas (unlike another union set up recently in the same area which works through large public meetings and is represented in localities by the former cultivation committee officers). The union has already had some success in protecting tenant farmers, as in the case of one of the farmers of Pahalagama:

K. D. P. is a registered tenant who has been obtaining good yields for several years, and in Maha 1973–4 he sent word to the gambāraya that the Govimandala Sewaka (the administrative secretary of the cultivation committee) had said that he needed only to pay 12 bushels, and that he intended to exercise his right. The secretary had, I believe, just succeeded to the office and as a result of a feud in the gambāraya's family was for the first time a member of a cultivation committee executive that was opposed to the gambāraya. When K. D. P. sent for him to come to the threshing floor to take the rent the gambāraya did nothing, and so K. D. P. set off home with the entire produce, acting on the advice of the secretary. On the way the gambāraya arrived with the police and arrested him and took his paddy into custody. He was bailed out of jail by his brother, and then, calling upon the help of the secretary of the newly formed union went to the MP.

The MP charged the Inspector of Police with unlawful arrest, and in an enquiry conducted by the Commissioner of Agrarian Services the gambāraya was ordered to return K. D. P.'s paddy with the exception of the rent of only 12 bushels. According to K. D. P. the local MP wanted

to take further action against the gambāraya, but had been approached
by the powerful landowner, who had persuaded him to let things lie.
The secretary of the union, however, told me that K. D. P. preferred not
to charge the gambāraya, because he is still afraid of him.

This case aptly illustrates several new features of the agrarian scene in
Hambantota District: that rising yields have given tenants a greater
interest in the legal provisions that have existed for over fifteen years, the
traditional rent of a quarter of the yield now usually being substantially
more than 12 bushels; and that the balance of political power has changed,
and even that the way in which politics works has begun to change.
Traditional political allegiances are breaking down in Pahalagama;
landowner–tenant relations are the subject of public debate both in the
MP's speeches – like those of the summer of 1974 when he began to advise
cultivators to pay only 8 bushels of rent per acre, or even no rent at
all – and in keen boutique gossip which even includes talk of 'imperialist
economic structures' among some of the young men.

However, it is important not to over-estimate the significance of these
trends. For one thing, they have so far been directed at the land controllers,
and as we have seen, control of land is only one component of the
domination exercised by the élite. Control of draught and credit remain
relatively inviolate, and it is quite possible for a gambāraya even to support
agitation against rents and yet to retain his power. The introduction of
improved varieties of paddy has served to emphasise the significance for
wealth and power of the control of draught and credit, because of the
enhanced need for timeliness. But the new varieties also seem likely,
certainly in the longer term, to contribute significantly to the
diversification of the élite, and at the same time to contribute to greater
degrees of social inequality within localities.

The ARTI Hambantota survey and cultivation data collected in
Pahalagama indicate that the introduction of improved varieties has
increased the profitability of paddy cultivation, as indeed we might
surmise from their success in substantially replacing traditional varieties.
There is some connection between the greater profitability of paddy
cultivation and the emergence of a kind of second-division élite in a locality
like that of Pahalagama, although the investment patterns of the four men
concerned also illustrate the continuing significance of control of draught,
for between them they own two four-wheel tractors and four two-wheelers,
while one still owns a large buffalo herd. Two of these men started out in
the late 1950s as nothing more than small tenant cultivators, and though
their wealth is now dependent upon their other activities, without
cultivation incomes they would neither of them have been able to start
these other enterprises (moneylending, and for one, a rice mill). Of the
others, one is only a chena cultivator, who 'made it' on the chilli boom of
1973 – when chilli prices shot up astronomically following a government

ban on imports – while the fourth man started out as a buffalo owner.

The workings of the credit market in Pahalagama also suggest the possibility that higher incomes from paddy cultivation may have increased the independence of the ordinary cultivators, or at least released them from the former abject state of dependence described in some of the documents cited earlier. Members of the 'second-division élite' were those most frequently named as sources of credit among the 85 households studied, but there was a great deal of very generalised borrowing among them, on what they call a 'kaymatu' ('hand loan'/exchange) basis – short-term borrowing of small sums without interest payments. It seemed from the data that I was able to obtain – and my stay in Pahalagama was too short for me to be very confident of the reliability and completeness of the information – that a larger volume of credit had been raised from among the 85 households than from outside, although the outside sources that were named had usually supplied larger individual sums. In addition to this suggestion of the development of a degree of financial independence, we may infer that the expansion of co-operative credit has had some effect in limiting the power of the old élite. Certainly in one case a big gambāraya had gone to the lengths of becoming a co-operative manager, in order to neutralise the potential of co-operative credit for reducing his profits.

But the same trends which seem to be bringing about greater dispersion of power may also result in more marked differentiation within the society of a locality like that of Pahalagama. Some demonstration of this trend is evident in the careers of the local élite, made up by men of modest means in comparison with some of the big gambārayas who tend to be concentrated around Tissamaharama, but men who are intimately involved in local society. Moreover, it is possible that further reductions in the rents paid by tenant farmers will increase the disparities both among them, and between them and owner-operators. Data for Pahalagama show that it is only rent payments which keep down the tenants' level of profit close to the owner-operators'. In the circumstances of the 'traditional' gambāraya system, if sources such as the AGAs' diaries can be relied upon, the cultivators were usually left with almost nothing at all, and there can have been little difference between them and chena cultivators in terms of livelihood. The increasing freedom of the paddy cultivators from dependence upon gambārayas has already been responsible for the appearance of greater disparities between some paddy cultivators and chena cultivators, though the recently improved profitability of chena cultivation has done something to redress the balance.

CONCLUSION

The implications of the introduction of improved varieties have to be considered together with the impact of legislative and political changes, which began a process of breaking down the power structure of the old gambāraya system of Hambantota District, in which power was acquired not so much by control of land as by prior access to wealth or influence outside the agriculture of the District. The system still survives to the extent that control of critical agricultural resources remains the key to power and wealth. But the external linkages of the system are no longer so important and it is based more closely upon the District itself. Contemporary political developments seem likely to further the demise of the significance of control of land *per se*, and of the 'peculiar creatures' mentioned by the AGA in 1947. The enhanced profitability of paddy cultivation seems to have contributed to the emergence of a lower-level élite, more firmly grounded in local society and probably weakening the power of those who control draught and credit, by a process of dispersion to which the provision of increased amounts of institutional credit has also made a contribution. Increased control of the rents paid by tenants will contribute to it substantially as well. Although there are strong elements of continuity, the kind of 'abject dependence' that characterised agrarian social relations in Hambantota, probably until the middle or late 1950s, has gone, but the same process is resulting in greater degrees of differentiation within local society.

Acknowledgements: The fieldwork upon which this chapter is based could not have been carried out without the help and companionship of Jayantha Wickremanayake.

For permission to use records listed under Primary Sources I am most grateful to Mr Justin Abeygunasekere, the Government Agent in Hambantota until July 1974; and to members of his staff for their assistance.

REFERENCES

Primary Sources
The *Diaries* of the Assistant Government Agents (AGA,) of Hambantota District, from 1920 to 1942.
Monthly Reports of the AGA's from 1942 onwards.
Files in Series 'E' (Irrigation) in the Hambantota Kachcheri Records Room.

Secondary Sources
Herring, R. (1973). *The Forgotten 1953 Paddy Lands Act in Ceylon: Ideology, Capacity, Response*, Ceylon Studies Seminar, 1974 Series, no. 1, Peradeniya.
Leach, E. R. (1961). *Pul Eliya: a Village in Ceylon* (Cambridge, Cambridge University Press).
Roberts, M. (1974). 'Aspects of Ceylon's Agrarian Economy in the 19th Century', *History of Ceylon*, vol. iii, Colombo, Ceylon University Press.
Sanderatne, N. (1972). 'Sri Lanka's New Land Reform', *S. Asian Rev.*, 6, 7–19.

Scott, J. C. (1972). 'The Erosion of Patron–Client Bonds and Social Change in Rural South East Asia', *J. Asian Studies*, 32, 5–37.

Yalman, N. (1967). *Under the Bo Tree*, Berkeley, University of California Press.

17 Marketing Scarce Chemical Inputs: an International Comparison

Barbara Harriss

India cannot avoid importing 40 to 45 per cent of its fertiliser requirements and being affected by increases in world market prices and by world shortages. Table 17.1 demonstrates the growing gap in Tamil Nadu between supply and demand, while Table 17.2 shows that North Arcot District of recent years has taken a diminishing proportion of the State consumption, except for potash.

Sri Lanka imports virtually all its fertiliser and is even more vulnerable than India to world market conditions. Hambantota District in 1973–4 was the site of a special project on fertiliser distribution and management training run by Co-operative Management Services: adequate supply for quadrupling of demand was assured (Co-operative Management Services, 1974, pp. 39–42). It was only in Yala 1974 that this inflated demand met with problems of supply. Hambantota District has thus not met with the same degree of fertiliser shortage as North Arcot. It has, however, faced more severe shortages of agrochemicals, world market prices of which doubled in 1973–4 and again in 1974–5, while the foreign-exchange allocation remained static. The Petroleum Corporation of Sri Lanka now imports 44 per cent of Sri Lanka's agrochemicals, eight private firms

Table 17.1   Fertiliser Distribution in Tamil Nadu (in tonnes of N)

Year	Requirements (A)	Receipts			A − B
		Pool	Non-pool	Total (B)	
1971–72	190,000	52,000	151,000	203,000	+ 13,000
1972–73	284,000	108,191	74,729	182,920	− 101,080
1973–74	305,000	96,256	93,831	180,087	− 124,913

Source: Revenue Department, Food Commission.

Table 17.2 Fertiliser consumption (tonnes)

Year	Tamil Nadu (TN)			North Arcot District					
	N	P	K	N	Percentage of TN	P	Percentage of TN	K	Percentage of TN
1972–3	179,252	52,890	47,653	13,147	7·3	4,270	8	4,677	9·8
1971–2	not available								
1970–71	172,847	72,590	51,182	15,324	8·8	5,735	7·9	3,940	7·6
Percentage change 1972–3 over 1970–71	+3·6	−37	−7·4	−16		−34		+18	
1969–70	147,873	41,597	32,883	16,876	11·4	4,789	11·5	1,150	3·4
1968–9	104,072	23,109	28,050	9,974	9·5	1,414	6·1	502	1·7

Source: FAI *Fertiliser Marketing News*, August 1972 and November 1973.

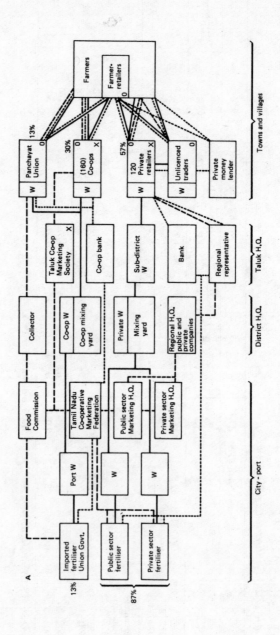

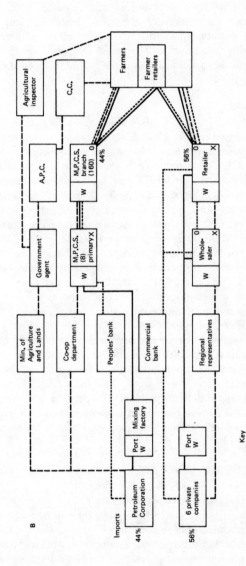

FIG. 17.1 *Formal marketing systems*
A. *Fertiliser in Tamil Nadu*
B. *Agrochemicals in Sri Lanka*

Key

—— Physical distribution system
–– – Information system
–·–·– Money system
X Commissions
0 Points most susceptible to corruption and illegalities
W Warehouse or store

sharing the residue. It was in 1973–4 that scarcities of both fertiliser and agrochemicals really began to bite (see chapter 24).

It is important to reassess the role of inputs delivery systems in supplying scarce chemicals in agronomically correct and socially equitable fashion. This chapter describes existing marketing structures, distortions which arise from shortages in commodites, and the likely effects of some prescriptive remedies. Most attention will be paid to Indian fertiliser marketing and Sri Lankan agrochemicals supply. For methods of data collection see above, pp. 47–50.

MARKETING SYSTEMS

Distribution channels for the physical goods, money and information in both countries are summarised in Fig. 17.1. A system where these three components are reasonably similar in organisational terms is most likely to have the co-ordination and flexibility necessary to the efficient allocation of scarce inputs. The delivery system for fertiliser in Tamil Nadu does not have such congruence. It has developed in a complex fashion to cope with the distribution of privately and publicly manufactured, as well as imported fertiliser by co-operatives as well as by private retailers. Until 1972 it was farmers rather than fertilisers who were scarce, so that the evolving distribution system became highly competitive. Private dealers slashed commissions to undercut co-operatives and sold on credit at low or zero interest rates. While supply exceeded demand, this system was very efficient, but in the reverse situation is subject to distortions.

By contrast the Sri Lankan inputs marketing systems are physically less complex. However, fertiliser and weedicides estimates are supplied by Agricultural Instructors, while requirements and targets are planned by paddy farmers and aggregated by cultivation committees (and increasingly by agricultural productivity committees). Information is then funnelled through the Government Agent to the Ministry of Agriculture and Lands. But the physical delivery system is operated by other government departments – Agrarian Services, the co-operatives, and the Petroleum Corporation. There is, therefore, disco-ordination in information and in spatial coverage.

EFFECTS OF INPUTS SCARCITY

The Information and Decision-making System

In a free-market situation it is price which conveys information about demand to suppliers and about supply to consumers. In both study areas price for both types of chemical inputs is strictly controlled within all types of delivery system; information about quantity, quality and timing of supply is conveyed by special intermediaries. When supplies are scarce the roles of such intermediaries change. At the rural end of the information channel in India, the dealer or co-operative manager is a key intermediary who has to predict both demand and delivery time. In the past the latter has been constant, and the nature of demand at the farm level has been the more difficult to predict. Now, however, public and private companies formerly queuing for the farmers' demand are now themselves faced with lengthening queues of dealers and of farmers. Average waiting time for the receipt of goods ordered by retailers increased from 5 hours to 7 days in 1971 to 10–30 days in 1973.

Great emphasis has been placed on the private retail dealer as an entrepreneur (see for instance Broehl, 1973), but one result of fertiliser scarcity is to deprive him of managerial responsibility, since decision-making for the allocation of scarce supplies is centralised. There is considerable variation in the allocation policies of the distributing systems, government and private. Imported fertiliser is distributed on the orders of the Collector equally to every co-operative. Non-pool fertiliser is distributed to co-operatives on the basis of the area served, the intensity of HYV cultivation and their repayment performance. Private companies may allocate in proportion to past orders or sales; proportionally to sales but with priority to larger dealers; equally between dealers; taluk by taluk according to the availability of suppliers; and proportionally to past sales within each taluk. In cases of equal sharing, whether in public or private sectors, decision-makers, often with relatively little experience, form certain assumptions which may not be correct: that all retailing units cover the same area, that they have similar acreages of HYVs and the same irrigation potential, and – if fertiliser is sold on credit – the same repayment capacity. The result is a patchy distribution among innovative farmers, and the encouragement of resale of fertiliser from less innovative areas. In cases of allocation by area, timeliness and equity of coverage may be forfeited because productive agricultural areas are not always served by towns with the best retailing facilities. Clearly, allocations proportional to past performance have greatest equity.

All distributing agencies, private or public, have co-ordinating personnel at District level. In the past they acted as funnels for information, canvassed new dealers, set up networks, gave extension advice, monitored a buffer stock and allocated from it to those dealers or co-operatives who ordered small loads. The centralisation of decision-making has brought about a shift in the power structure of marketing systems adverse to the regional representatives, who have exchanged an information and promotional role for a vigilant and supervisory one.

As centralisation of decision-making proceeds, information about fertiliser requirements may become cumulatively distorted. In 1973 in North Arcot, part of the increase in demand may have been related to orders appearing to fall on deaf ears, so that more and more orders were placed with other companies, and demand appeared to rocket. Subsequent allocations based on such a pattern of orders would be distorted.

In Sri Lanka the supply of information on agrochemical requirements becomes increasingly irrelevant to the planning of imports, since demand so greatly exceeds supply. Estimates of weedicide demand based on aggregations of Agricultural Inspectors' figures derived from data on acreage and crop requirements have been found to be underestimates of demand as measured by sales and the stated needs of co-operative branches. Indeed the imports of weedicides may be only one-sixteenth of what is necessary. Pesticide requirements cannot be predicted in time, space or quantity. The Petroleum Corporation allocates to co-operative wholesale depots proportionally to past sales and on a first-come, first-served basis. Allocation from the depot to the branch is subject to considerable variation, equally between branches (encouraging lateral transfers), proportionately to acreage, or proportionately to forseeable demand, according to season or on a first-come, first-served basis. From branches to farmers, allocation is generally on the latter basis, though farmers at the front of queues are increasingly amassing stocks of weedicides and pesticides to resell later at black-market prices. Private companies allocate on the basis of past performance; in turn retailers diversify their sources in efforts to maximise stocks. At the same time, companies are forced by rigid quotas to reduce the ranges of brands, thereby reducing the range of chemicals on the Island.

In both countries the roles of retailers are rendered passive, allocation decisions are centralised, and information about requirements becomes distorted.

Effects on the Physical Delivery System

Since commissions on fertiliser sales are low (2–5 per cent) and since few companies sell a full range, dealers ordinarily license themselves with several distributing companies in their attempts to maximise the quantity and range of stock and to minimise uncertainties of supply. When supply exceeds demand, companies are in a weak position to retaliate but in scarcity situations may offer single-licence dealers preferential treatment, achieving the reverse of the multiple-licence stratagem. Private dealers also react to shortages by buying from private dealers in other regions where the agricultural seasons are differently timed. If dealers in seasonally surplus regions are selling fertiliser bought legitimately from companies then this reflects bad planning by those companies. On the other hand these dealers may be selling fertiliser that has been provided in an untimely fashion by co-operatives and resold by farmers who need cash; another example of cumulative distortion. Opportunist small-scale retailers dealing entirely with resold, black-market fertiliser emerge. In mid-1974 some of this informal trade was stifled when the Tamil Nadu government made all movement of fertiliser District-specific, requiring a permit. But it was estimated in August 1974 that up to 20 per cent of urea sold to North Arcot still evaded supervision at District boundaries.

In times of scarcity the mutually exclusive public and private agrochemicals marketing systems in Sri Lanka also become irregular. Co-operative wholesalers and branches start to trade in scarce commodities between themselves and to purchase illicitly from private stores. Co-operative agrochemicals issued on credit may also be resold by farmers to private traders attempting to diversify their sources, as in India. Trading patterns then become complex and re-ordering may distort the picture of demand.

Between March 1973 and August 1974, freight rates trebled in India, affecting the geography of fertiliser distribution. Freight for complex and mixtures ('poor man's' fertiliser) are borne by the private distributing companies: it is tempting, therefore, to favour areas nearest major stores. Remote dealers are penalised and their profit margins reduced.

Because of transport difficulties, about half the managers in Hamban-tota District try to keep a large buffer stock of agrochemicals in case of emergency, which locks up capital; while the other half keep a small buffer and rely on quick service from the co-operative wholesaler, running a risk of delay. In fact co-operative wholesale depots themselves tend to keep small buffers, relying on speedy service from the Petrochemicals Corpor-ation. This would be an efficient strategy if transport scarcities did not hinder speedy supply to any pest-stricken region. In mid-1974, whatever the buffer strategy, stocks of both pesticide and weedicide in most co-operative branches were 25–31 per cent of demand and the waiting time for orders had trebled. Waiting times of two weeks or more mean that pesticides may arrive too late. In private trade the proportions of maximum and minimum stock levels to total annual turnover averaged respectively 50 and 14 per cent but varied greatly from 8–160 per cent for the former and 3·6–30 per cent for the latter. Average waiting time for orders increased from seven days in 1972–3 to 39 days by July 1974, and there is a tendency to hoard.

In North Arcot, by contrast, stock levels throughout the system are reduced. Rising bank rates and rising prices are a disincentive to long-term stocking. A low stock level is a rational strategy where demand is predictable, the waiting time for replenishment is short, and lorries are not scarce. Because of its proximity to the Madras depots and because farmers generally place advance orders, North Arcot District is less affected by low stock levels than Thanjavur District or Hambantota District of Sri Lanka.

Effects on the Money System

In the past, private companies have allowed dealers substantial credit. As fertiliser has become scarce, credit sales have been abolished. Increased waiting times also lock up working capital, the time-cost of whose retrieval is not to be underestimated. Moreover, the most vulnerable dealers are those whose annual turnover is smallest. In turn, dealers withdraw credit facilities and the small farmer is increasingly dependent upon co-operatives.

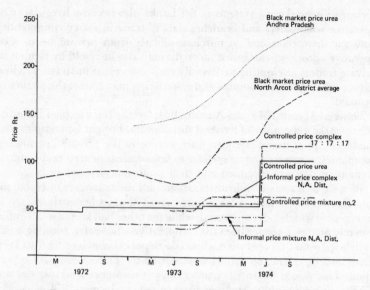

Fig. 17.2 *Fertiliser: Prices per 50kg bag, North Arcot District*

Abuses proliferate in the pricing system which, from strict control, bursts into informal duality. The broad outlines of formal and informal price movements are shown in Fig. 17.2. Before the oil crisis the black market was never more than about 30 to 40 per cent above controlled market prices; with the crisis this quickly rose to 150 per cent of the controlled price; after it, when the controlled price was doubled, the black-market price settled to about its pre-crisis relationship. Until mid-1973, complex and mixed fertilisers were resold by farmers at 'white-market' rates, some Rs2–5 below controlled prices. Towards the end of 1973 all mixed fertiliser was dragged by prospective scarcity on to the black market, one characteristic of which is its great temporal and spatial variation. A contour map of black-market prices would show peaks in urban areas and a trend surface inclining upwards to the State border between Tamil Nadu and Andhra.

The black market in Hambantota is not so highly developed. Many private traders and farmers participate in it, but at present the co-operatives are able to restrain prices. By August 1974 the trend surface of black-market prices was, as in North Arcot, highest in urban areas and lowest in rural areas where the co-operatives were still in a position to compete.

In North Arcot for most of 1974 urea was rationed out to farmers by permit, of which it was not difficult to procure more than one. These permits caused great delays, increased the likelihood of untimeliness and therefore resale, and opened up opportunities for preferential treatment.

At one stage, dealers – disinclined to sell fractions of 50 kg bags – penalised at least 30 per cent of the District's farmers who cultivate less than 2 acres.

Excessive profits were reaped at first by private retailers. Even with squeezed margins after May – June 1974, they continue to enjoy untaxable profits. But more recently the form of profiteering has changed and some of those in a position to control the permit system have taken advantage of it. It is in the interests of private traders to encourage government inefficiency since if urea stocks are unsold for more than 21 days they may legally be sold to anyone. The farmers' interests are the reverse, while small farmers have an interest in encouraging allocation by co-operatives. In theory an official with decision-making power may be given speed and sloth money at the same time by competing interest groups. Some of the profits are invested in moneylending, so that minor government officials may be emerging as moneylenders, while traditional sources of credit are closing up.

From the farmers' view point the cost of speeding a permit is indistinguishable from that of the black market; and a farmer whose time is precious may rationally prefer the latter. That black-market prices, increasing misallocation of inputs, and unpredictability of timing have a deleterious effect on agriculture need not be stressed. The effects of scarcities depend on the wealth and/or power of individual cultivators. In both countries the richest farmers search for correct brands of fertilisers and pesticides at private shops. They have an extra advantage in their creditworthiness. Poor farmers use nothing. By late July this reaction had wrecked Yala yields over several remote yayas in Hambantota District. In the case of weedicides, scarcities may force small farmers to use family labour, while larger farmers, baulking at the costs of labour for weeding, may buy weedicides whatever the price.

Significance of these Effects

Strong parallel reactions in both Districts to scarcities in the chemical inputs delivery systems may be observed. Since short supplies may occur for the next three or four years, measures are needed to minimise their antisocial effects. In Hambantota the main reaction has been to explore the potential of local alternatives and substitutes in line with a political will for self-sufficiency (see pp. 386–92). In North Arcot, since traditional inputs are already extensively utilised, organisational solutions are needed. Many of the complex problems that result from fertiliser scarcities in a mixed distribution system stem from the increasing unpredictability of the rate of servicing and length of the queue. The solution lies in the identification of the best possible compromise involving controllable factors. For distributing agencies quantity, type and timeliness are not controllable, but the length of the queue of retailers may be: all private companies are refusing to appoint new dealers. However, it is doubtful whether this counterbalances the generation of intermediaries engaged in

illegitimate trade. What is needed in every network is a weeding-out of
retailing points with poor past performances. As a first stage they might be
forbidden to sell urea, and later all types of fertiliser. The financial position
of most smaller dealers has weakened. In two-tier wholesaler–retailer
systems the retailers' licences should be cancelled; in one-tier systems the
smaller, more rural dealers should be withdrawn. Since rural dealers
almost invariably have alternative means of livelihood this would not
cause great hardship to dealers, or to farmers, who are prepared to travel
up to 20 miles for fertiliser. A geographically centralised system would
be much easier to police and might reduce the social costs of distribution.
Companies and dealers would have lower total transport costs and the
farmers' increased transport costs might be offset by a reduction in bribery
and/or black-marketing. To a certain extent the co-operatives have
already effected this kind of change. Village co-operatives, which in April
1973 superseded the Panchayat unions for the sale of imported fertiliser,
are ordering directly through Madras headquarters. If the scarcities grow
more acute, the co-operative system should consider centralisation to taluk
headquarters. A reduction in intermediaries would reduce opportunities
for corruption. What is certain is that, as the small farmer grows more
vulnerable, the co-operatives' role in supplying inputs becomes more
important.

The percentage gross margins allowed to dealers or retailer co-
operatives which cover handling, sale and overhead costs might be raised
to keep pace with increases in rents, labour charges and freight rates: this
might reduce the incentive to the black market.

Finally, it is necessary to step up the money rewards for those who expose
corrupt practices, as well as the penalties for black marketeers. A
movement verification office has been created in Madras and authority for
District-level vigilance is vested in the Agriculture Department (block
offices), Revenue Department and police. This intensification of vigilance
personnel is none too early. Until mid-1974 the black market was
impossible to police. With 160 co-operatives and over 150 formally
licensed dealers in the seven taluks of the study area, the total number of
people engaged *inter alia* in vigilance operations amounted to 15:13 from
the District Civil Supplies Office and the police and 2 from the District Co-
operative Society. Two charges had been made in eighteen months.
Increased vigilance has reduced the possibility of black-marketing, and in
some areas honest and able block-level officials are allocating fertiliser
efficiently. But until farmers themselves refuse to participate in the black
market or to be intimidated little progress can be achieved. Farmers in
Randam in August 1974 expressed great cynicism about current systems of
fertiliser distribution, but a complete absence of desire to reform them.
Through the media, attempts might be made to reverse present attitudes
where ties of patronage, politics or caste supersede public interest. This
may seem Utopian, but there is some recent evidence from prosecutions of

malpractising businessmen that this change in attitude is happening in urban areas.

REFERENCES

Broehl, W. G. (1973). 'The Fertilizer Distributor as Change Agent'. *Econ. Pol. Weekly, Rev. Agric.*, 8, 52, A. 157–63.
Co-operative Management Services (1974). *The Hambantota Story*, Colombo.
Fertiliser Association of India, FAI (1973). 'Strategy for Fertilizer Use under Limited Availability', *Fertilizer Marketing News*, 4, No. 11, 7–10.

18 Besieging the Free Market: the Effects of the Paddy-Rice Levy

Barbara Harriss

One of the welfare measures which the Indian economy is able to sustain is the public distribution system for essential commodities by means of which wheat, rice and sugar and often kerosene are bought and sold at fixed rates, sometimes involving a government subsidy. The levy in paddy and rice has been an integral part of this system in Tamil Nadu since the abandonment of monopoly procurement and total rationing in January 1970: it is a percentage of the marketed surplus varying temporally and spatially from zero to 50 per cent compulsorily taken as either paddy or rice, and bought at a standard All India price, fixed and periodically revised by the Agricultural Prices Commission. Both the State-run Civil Supplies Corporation and the Central Food Corporation of India act as purchasing agents for within-State distribution and for contributions to inter-State trade. The consumers of levy rice within Tamil Nadu in 1973 were the 'vulnerable sectors' in the urban areas of Madras, Coimbatore and Madurai and rural people in the highly deficit District of Kanyakumari, defined as those earning under Rs300 per month (raised in late 1974 to Rs1000 per month) and therefore not liable to income tax. For the percentage of marketable surplus levied and procurement prices see Tables 18.1 and 18·2.

Partly to police the implementation of the levy, partly to control supplies of rice to Districts highly in deficit and/or bordering the deficit State of Kerala, no rice may be traded between Districts, and in some cases taluks, without a 'no objection' certificate from the taluk supply office at the receiving end and a 'movement permit' from that of the surplus market.

It is the purpose of this chapter to describe ways in which the levy and the associated movement restrictions control and distort the behaviour of the free market in paddy and rice and the choice of milling technology, using data from North Arcot, a surplus District.

Table 18.1   Levy percentages in North Arcot District

Year	Date	Percentage of marketable surplus
1970	8 January to 6 August	15
1970–1	December to 5 October	15
1971–2	15 December to 5 October	25
	12 April to 12 July	15
1973	18 January to 25 May	20
	26 May to 3 August	25
1974	4 December to 22 April	25
	23 April to 11 June	15

Table 18.2   Levy prices per quintal (in rupees)

Item	Quality							
	Superfine		Fine		Medium		Coarse	
	1972–3	1974	1972–3	1974	1972–3	1974	1972–3	1974
Paddy	58	78	56	75	53	70	49	66
Transport plus incidentals	1	2	1	2	1	2	1	2
Total	59	80	57	77	54	72	50	68
Rice (boiled at 68 per cent out-turn)	86·77	121·2	83·82	116·6	79·41	105	73·53	100
Handling	0·75	6·7	0·75	6·7	0·75	6·7	0·75	6·7
Hulling	1·5		1·5		1·5		1·5	
Gunny	2	2	2	2	2	2	2	2
Total	91·02	129·9	88·07	125·5	83·66	119·6	77·78	108·7

Source: Commissioner of Civil Supplies, 26 July 1973, August, 1974.

Invariably the levy results in a loss for the trader who pays it. Coarse paddy on the free market exceeded Rs50 per quintal (the 1973 procurement price) on average by Rs18. The difference is greater for rice. A trader who bought coarse paddy at Rs51 per 75 kg bag had to bear the costs of weighing, loading and unloading the levy paddy and part of the transport costs to government godowns. His loss in August 1973 was Rs19 per quintal or Rs14 per bag. In 1974 the average levy loss rose from Rs26 to Rs100 per quintal for fine rice and from Rs17 to Rs59 for coarse paddy. The loss made on the levy is therefore hoisted on to non-levy bags. Thus from the moment a levy is imposed, the free market's price levels are determined partly by levy losses. The magnitude of the hoist will vary

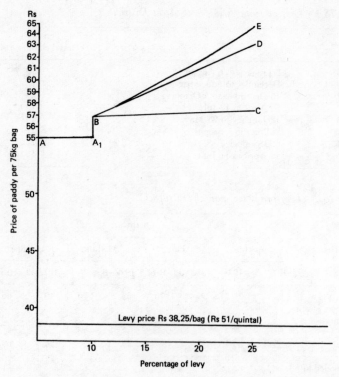

FIG. 18.1 *Hypothetical example to show various possible market reactions to increase in levy percentages, assuming one variety of paddy and no changes in supply and demand*

> A-A_1 = *free market level*
>
> A_1-B = *initial price hoist on 90% (non-levy) trade is response to 10% levy at rate shown in diagram*
>
> B-C = *loss made on levy bags averaged out as price hoist on non-levy bags assuming traders base each successive hoist on original free market price*
>
> B-D = *case where traders add original levy loss averaged out over non-levy bags using each successive price level as base*
>
> B-E = *case where traders calculate successive levy losses based on successive price levels and add averaged-out hoist to each preceding level*

according to the levy percentage and the price paid for paddy or for rice and for transport. The government classifies paddy and rice into four sorts, while on the market there are not only those varieties listed in Table 18.3 but probably three times more (to all of which prices are sensitive); this encourages traders to pay in the cheapest variety in any 'sort'. Thus for fine and superfine varieties traders will not pay in highly priced Kichili if they can pay in IR.20; nor for medium and coarse varieties in Kar if they can pay in IR.8. So the public distribution system contains relatively more HYVs than the 'free' market. Evidence of this response was obtained for only two procurement points (Table 18.3).

However, while in 1974 the percentage difference between free-market and government rates increased from 23 per cent in January to 87 per cent in June because of unprecedentedly high increases on the free market as a result of poor harvests, the actual price ranges between superfine and coarse varieties were reduced (see Table 18.4) so that HYVs become more relatively profitable and no longer obvious choices for levy payment.

Table 18.3   Percentage of levy by variety, 1972–3

Variety	Type	Arni	Vellore
Kichili	(1)	0·9	
ADT.27	(2)	3·9	10·57
IR.20	(2)	6·1	0·5
Sirumani	(1)	0·03	12·5
IR.8	(3)	83·4	40·5
Co.25	(2)	0·4	0·4
Rosekar	(4)	4·8	23·4
Co.29	(3)	0·004	10·8
		100	100
		(1,311 rice tonnes)	(140 rice tonnes)

Source: Department of Civil Supplies, Vellore.

Table 18.4   Price trends in North Arcot District – average difference between finest and coarsest varieties (in rupees per quintal)

	Paddy		Rice	
	1973	1974	1973	1974
Producers' markets				
Arni	36	20	83	38
Polur	47	21	86	42
Tiruvannamalai	29	26	65	63
Secondary markets				
Arcot	46	45	79	46
Vellore	48	27	66	50

Prices are for June in each year.
Data source: GoTN Department of Statistics, Market Intelligence Division

A Rs14 loss on a 25 per cent levy will therefore give rise to a Rs5 per bag compensatory hoist on the free market. Each time the levy percentage is raised, the free-market price rises. The nature of this rise, however, is not straightforward. The trader who lost Rs14 per bag was typical in raising his non-levy bags by Rs8, not Rs5. It is important to try to explain this behaviour.

First, wholesale traders may attempt opportunistically to maximise their share of the distributive margin (and therefore add antisocially to inflationary forces). Secondly, reactions may be conditioned by perceptions of the base-level by which they gauge their levy loss. A hypothetical example illustrated in Fig. 18.1 may help to clarify this point. If the levy is at 10 per cent the free-market price before levy is Rs55 per 75 kg bag and the government's procurement price is Rs51 per quintal, i.e. Rs38·25 per 75 kg bag; the loss on the levy is Rs16·75 and therefore the first free-market hoist will be Rs1·86. The free-market price will rise by this amount to Rs56·86 (assuming no change in supply and demand). When the levy is raised to 15 per cent the free-market hoist will rise further. If traders use the original yardstick of loss, and base each successive hoist on the original free-market level, the hoist will be Rs1·97 and the free-market price Rs56·97. At a 20 per cent levy the hoist will be Rs2·09 and the free-market price Rs57·09, and at 25 per cent Rs2·23 and Rs58·23 respectively. This price reaction is A-A₁ to B-C in Fig. 18.1. However, if traders perceive each successive price level as a starting point to which they add the averaged-out levy losses at different percentages, the free-market prices will be Rs58·83 at 15 per cent, Rs60·92 at 20 per cent and Rs63·15 at 25 per

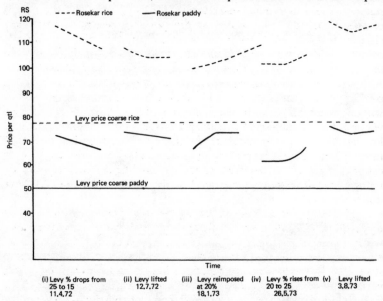

FIG. 18.2 *Actual price behaviour, Rosekar paddy and rice in Vellore market in response to changes in levy*

cent. This is A-A$_1$ to B-D in Fig. 18.1. If traders perceive the loss made by levy sales as set against each successive free-market level rather than against the original truly free-market level, at 15 per cent the loss will appear as Rs18·61, the hoist as Rs2·18 and the free-market level as Rs59·04; at 20 per cent, Rs20·79, Rs2·59 and Rs61·64 respectively; and at 25 per cent, Rs23·38, Rs3·11 and Rs64·76 respectively. This is represented by A-A$_1$ to B-E. Which of these potential explanations is correct can only be determined by very careful analysis of pricing behaviour. Figure 18.2 is a first attempt at this, showing the reactions in the principal rice market of North Arcot District to changes in levy. Paddy graphs are for a period of three weeks beginning one week before the levy change and rice graphs are from the date of change, since there is a time-lag of up to one week in the processing of rice from paddy.

The reactions are clear in all cases in spite of the possible effects of other factors. One such factor is the response of prices to supplies. The January 1973 price reaction to reimposition of the levy at the time of post-Samba harvest arrivals to market is a rise of Rs7 in paddy and Rs10 in rice when prices should, in the normal course of events, drop.

A second such factor is the relationship between the levy and the price elasticity of supply for paddy-rice, which is quite high (Harriss, 1977) and acts informally and illegitimately to cushion the effects of the levy. In the markets of surplus areas, prices for paddy and rice at times of levy are low relative to those in terminal markets since the levy is paid only at the point of export and the hoist added at the point of receipt. Under these circumstances landlords and levy evaders are usually tempted to smuggle surpluses into these terminal markets to reap excess profits. They will also find acceptable selling prices at below reigning 'free' market rates. Although such individual consignments are rarely large (rice is taken in rickshaws (2–3 bags), by head or bicycle load or on the top of buses with or without connivance and bribery), the cumulative effect of an increased volume of trade transacted at possible lower than 'free' market rates is to lower prices in the terminal markets. The reverse occurs when the levy is lifted. Terminal market prices drop; there is no longer a price incentive to counteract the risk of detection or the costs of bribery; and supplies are reduced so that the price slumps less heavily than it would otherwise have done.

A third factor affecting the reaction of the 'free' market to changes in the levy is that such changes are not always very predictable, whereas a trader wishes continuously to predict future market conditions. If traders in an exporting town anticipate a rise in the levy percentage they will attempt to stock IR.8 to reduce loss. Traders from importing towns will buy other varieties in order to maximise purchases before a further price hoist on the free market. If traders in an exporting town anticipate a lowering of the levy percentage they will tend to sell all rice varieties, while buyers may hold back, awaiting greater sales at lower prices. If such speculations prove to be correct, then uncertainties created by levy changes increase free-market price fluctuations.

These three muddying factors act in different ways so that the precise influence of any one of them at any one time would be hard to determine. It is thus not very easy to relate the graph of actual market reactions (Fig. 18.2) to the three reaction simulations in Fig. 18.1. Given the difference in vertical scales between the graphs, resemblance would appear to be greater between reactions (iii) and (iv) in Fig. 18.2 and A-A_1 to B-E simulation in Fig. 18.1. If this is correct as an interpretation of traders' reactions to the levy, they are not acting opportunistically but are misperceiving the basis of levy losses; but none the less contributing to inflationary forces in the economy.

However, although this has been considered in greatest detail it is not the only effect of the levy on the structure of the residual market. It also affects the geography of prices and the relative location of markets within the foodgrains distribution system. It is only wholesale prices in secondary and terminal markets which are notably affected by changes in the levy; and in general, rice prices in these markets react more strongly than paddy prices. Responses to levy changes are most exaggerated in Arcot and Vellore and least marked in the primary producer markets of Tiruvan-namalai, Arni and Polur. That they are marked at all in the primary markets is a sign of market imperfection. If we disregard market type and location the price hoist for high-quality varieties is less than that for coarse ones.

The practical effect of movement restrictions on the free market is to generate a black market, since quotas to deficit areas never exceed demand there. In any one market town in a surplus District three sets of prices may be ruling: (i) levy prices which vary neither temporally nor spatially and only slightly in response to quality (as in Table 18.2), (ii) 'free' or residual market prices which do vary spatially and temporally, and also vary in response to quality and to adulteration, to supply and demand and to the character and possible future changes in the levy and the black market, and (iii) black-market prices, which vary potentially with every sale lot and depend on the nature of demand perceived by particular visiting traders from officially cordoned-off deficit areas. Such transactions may potentially divert trade from both the free market and the levy, but maximum effect is felt on free-market prices.

Finally, government policy on foodgrains also affects technological choices and capacity utilisation in public-sector mills. The levy can be paid in paddy or in rice. The choice as to the form of payment is often, though not always, left to the discretion of the miller or trader. As is seen in Fig. 18.2 less loss is made by paying in paddy than in rice, but only 18 per cent of the traders did this. Statements given by Civil Supplies officials on the extent to which traders may use their discretion have conflicted. They may be forced to pay in rice so that the government may avoid making direct losses on the Modern Rice Mill (MRM) now supposed to be milling the levy and examined in detail in chapter 19. But if traders pay in rice the hoist is greater than it need be if they paid in paddy, so consumer rice prices on the 'free' market rise more than strictly necessary. If the MRM were to mill more levy paddy its running costs would fall, but it would not make a profit. This means that its operation has to be subsidised from profits earned by other trading enterprises within the Civil Supplies Corporation which now owns it. Moreover, the amortisation of repayments on the initial loans from the National Co-operative Development Corporation are a further subsidy. This capital has come on the one hand from profits from the sale of commodities within the public distributive system whose prices could otherwise be reduced, or on the other hand from bank loans (which have an opportunity cost) and from general taxation. It is not known whether or not such 'subsidies' amount to less than the excessive hoist in the foodgrains market caused by levy payments in rice, and whether by extension, social costs would be reduced by increasing supplies of levy paddy to the MRM.

In conclusion, it is by now obvious that in a dual (or treble) market for foodgrains it is the free or residual market that is most distorted and that it is here that the price movements are most uncertain. The government, in investing in a large-capacity milling technology when public procurement at low rates often de-stabilises cropping-pattern decisions, enhances the risks attached to the operation of this technology. The system of levy and movement restrictions is subsidised not by farmers or traders, nor by the government, but by consumers in the income group unentitled to rice at Fair Price Shops. These people comprise the tax-paying groups in urban areas but make up a large proportion of rural areas where coverage of the vulnerable sector is most incomplete.

Given the fact that the urban vulnerable are for practicality's sake more vulnerable than the rural vulnerable, the Fair Price system must continue as a welfare measure. This being so, the 'free' market most continue to be distorted. A reduction of the difference between procurement prices fixed by the government and true free-market prices would reduce the *magnitude* of distortions described earlier which affect more consumers than the number served by the FPS system. Further, to impose the levy permanently and not alter its percentage would reduce some of the *types* of distortions which result from traders' inflationary reactions to changes, and from speculative stocking.

REFERENCE

Harriss, B. (1977). *Paddy and Rice Marketing in Northern Tamil Nadu: Studies in Surplus, Market Efficiency, Technology and Livelihoods*, Madras, Sangam.

19 Paddy-Milling: Problems in Policy and the Choice of Technology

Barbara Harriss

To most people progress has become synonymous with imitation of Western models but where we have followed models from the industrial society and have been insensitive to our own circumstances the results have not been happy. The time has come for us to think deeply about the kind of progress we want. (Indira Gandhi at inauguration of the National Committee on Environmental Planning and Co-ordination, Delhi, April 1972)

INTRODUCTION

In 1963 the Ford Foundation, in the wake of their important blueprint of a modernised agricultural production technology (Ford Foundation, 1959), moved their attention to the technologies of the foodgrains distribution system, anticipating problems of processing future surpluses. They found that marketable surpluses of food grains were of low quality, as were storage facilities, and that hulling technology was antiquated; and they advocated a comprehensive updating of the system (Faulkner *et al.*, 1963). In 1970 the Rice Milling Industry (Regulation and Licensing) Amendment Rules prescribed that all traditional mills should be replaced by newer technologies (NCDC, 1975, p. 12). These rules have been a notable failure: in the face of difficulties imposed by government policy the obsolescent technology continues to diffuse through the South Asian countryside.

North Arcot and Hambantota Districts are no exception: there are currently 1700 huller mills in the former and 155 in the latter. The huller is a cast-iron or steel cylindrical roller revolving round a horizontal axis inside a sheath-casing. It can double-mill an average of 0·75 tonnes of paddy per hour. It was imported to India about fifty years ago and has been manufactured there for about as long. The antiquated paddy-processing technology involves much more than milling. Paddy is dried on cement floors using the heat of the sun and the labour of women who skilfully turn the paddy at regular intervals in order to prevent it from becoming over-heated and cracking. In North Arcot District roughly half the paddy marketed and much of the paddy consumed by producers is parboiled. This does not make the rice smell, as did traditional lengthy cold-soaking methods, and during the process the proteins, vitamins and oil are absorbed from the bran layer of the grain into the starchy endosperm. This renders the rice far more nutritious than if it is milled 'raw'. Parboiled rice in North Arcot District is, however, an inferior good. In Hambantota District no rice is parboiled and this sort of rice is again inferior. This is not so all over Sri Lanka: in the wet zone parboiled rice is preferred to raw rice. (For Parboiling see Glossary.)

The technology introduced to replace the huller is the Modern Rice Mill (MRM), a semi-automated factory consisting of mechanical hand-ling and conveying equipment and oil-fired driers, cleaners, bulk silo storage, mechanised parboiling equipment and a 2–4 tonne per hour (tph) mill of a rubber-roll type with paddy and by-product separators and polishers. These mills were developed in Japan, Germany and the US; 17 of the 33 built in India are in Tamil Nadu and one 2 tph mill is at Cheyyar in North Arcot District. Two 3 tph mills are shortly to be operational on the Uda Walawe scheme in southern Sri Lanka, one at Kachchigala within our study area. Many of the components of the MRM may be adopted in isolation. There are paddy driers in operation in Thanjavur District, for instance; and 37 rubber-roller sheller mills with paddy separators and cone polishers milling on contract to the parastatal Paddy Marketing Board in Hambantota District. In that District there is also an under-runner disc sheller mill of large capacity using horizontally revolving and abrasive grinding stones to remove the silica-rich paddy husk. Thus in the two study areas there are four main types of technology being used to mill paddy (Harriss, 1974a).

This chapter will confine itself to the two technological extremes, looking at the operational economics of milling–trading enterprises in Cheyyar taluk. A comparative social cost–benefit analysis is not given here, for we are dealing with a *fait accompli*. The effects of policy decisions on capacity utilisation and on profitability will be examined, using 1973 data. We will look at the adoption rationale of the MRM in North Arcot in order to derive lessons applicable to the MRMs under construction in Sri Lanka.

MARKETING POLICY AND RICE MILLS TECHNOLOGY

Cheyyar Modern Rice Mill was built on a 6 acre site in 1970 and is of 2 tph capacity. It was intended as a link in an expanded hierarchy of co-operatives which would have dealt in the marketing of agricultural commodities as well as the supply of inputs. This system has developed in a

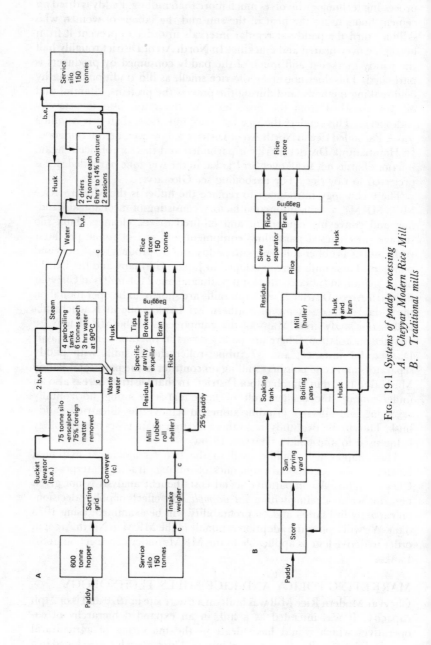

Fig. 19.1 *Systems of paddy processing*
A. *Cheyyar Modern Rice Mill*
B. *Traditional mills*

spatially patchy way throughout the State and the Co-operative Marketing Societies relinquished control of their 13 MRMs in 1972 to the newly formed Civil Supplies Corporation. This corporation's job is *inter alia* to purchase the levy described in chapter 18. Cheyyar Taluk Marketing Society is the only co-operative society in North Arcot District which markets paddy, buying 56 tonnes in 1972–3, none of which was in fact milled at the MRM (it was sold as paddy to other co-operatives in Tamil Nadu).

The distribution system for which the MRM was built differs from that prevailing at present; for had the co-operatives expanded as a paddy marketing system, the reticulation of godowns supplying the mill would have been far better developed. Civil Supplies godowns are situated in all taluk headquarters, have a total capacity of 12,000 tonnes, and are considerably underutilised. Levy paddy compulsorily purchased by the Civil Supplies Corporation is either surrendered at the mill by the private traders or brought by lorry contractors from these godowns to Cheyyar. The MRM itself can store 600 tonnes. Rice is then sent to Vellore and to Madras to be sold at controlled rates in Fair Price Shops to families whose income is less than Rs300 per month. The component processing units of the modern and the traditional technologies are summarised in Fig. 19.1.

There are 132 huller mills in Cheyyar taluk, 17 in Cheyyar itself, around which is a halo of low density. In the depths of the taluk, hullers are fairly evenly spread at 1 huller per 732 hectares (Fig. 19.2). Some mills are 'coolie mills' hulling, not marketable surplus, but paddy for on-farm and in-village consumption. Other mills have between one and five totikaran, traders who buy paddy, have a standing arrangement with one or several mills for hulling paddy, themselves pay the coolie work-force, and sell rice at a short or a long distance. Some millers are themselves traders. Some of these hullers also mill levy paddy on contract to the Civil Supplies Corporation and in direct technological competition with the MRM because the corporation's fixed milling margins are derived from periodic (inadequate) surveys of the operating costs of the huller technology.

COST STRUCTURES OF MILLING ENTERPRISES IN TWO TECHNOLOGIES

Capital Costs
While the National Co-operative Development Corporation advanced 62 per cent of the capital for the first MRM at Tiruvarur in Thanjavur District in 1964, it supplied all of Cheyyar's in 1970. A loan of Rs1·087m. was awarded on estimated construction costs and a further Rs 0·19m. from general funds to cover initial overspending (these have a 5 per cent interest rate and a long-term repayment period). None of the original loan was repaid by the Taluk Marketing Society, nor has the Civil Supplies Corporation finalised negotiations either for the transfer of mills from the

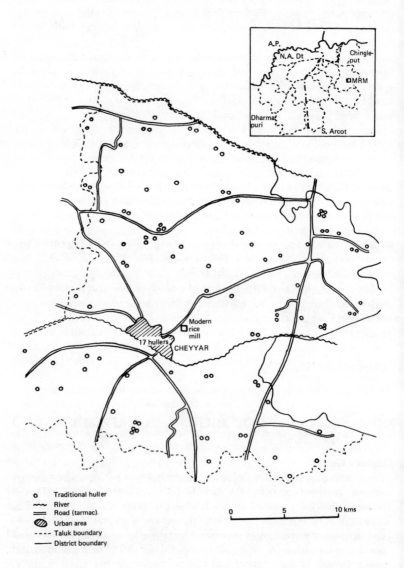

co-operative sector or for loan repayments to NCDC. The structure of capital costs shows a good deal of difference from those of the equivalent 2 tph MRM analysed by Lele (1971, p. 3). Not only is the total cost at

Table 19.1 Capital costs of 2 tph Modern Rice Mills (in rupees)

	Cheyyar, Tamil Nadu	Memari, West Bengal
Land	9,124	195,000
Buildings	437,773	39,300
Mill warehouse		1,810
Permanent warehouse		180,000
Electrical installations	95,908	
Mill equipment/Machinery	648,123	323,480
Total	1,190,928	739,620

Cheyyar 60 per cent more than at Memari, within a gap of four years, but also bearing in mind the extremely low cost of land at Cheyyar (a barren tract above a tank) the cost of buildings and machinery has doubled within four to five years (see Table 19.1).

By contrast the capital costs of huller mills in the private sector constructed in Cheyyar taluk in the last 20 years average Rs30,000, 2 per cent of the costs of MRM. If the MRM were to operate at engineering capacity, the capital costs per tonne of paddy milled would be Rs90·22 as against Rs8·23 for a huller. If it operated at effective capacity, they would be Rs99·24 and Rs21·56 respectively. The MRM's capital costs per tonne are between 5 and 11 times greater than the huller's.

Operating Costs

(i) *Fixed Costs*
Comparison of the two technologies is made difficult by problems of definition. According to Lele (1971, p. 14), fixed costs include the salaries of permanent employees, taxes and licences, establishment costs and depreciation. Establishment costs include telephone, travel, postage and stationery at MRM which do not vary very much with the tonnage milled. These items happen to be negligible in the sub-sample of huller mills, but are not fixed costs (except for telephone rental and annual account books) in this sector. Similarly while machine maintenance is considered a fixed cost in MRMs, including as it does the biannual cleaning of silos, it has both fixed and variable components in the traditional sector. Fixed costs of maintenance include the biannual overhaul of the electric motor, cleaning and greasing the huller parts and rewinding the electric motor every ten years. All other maintenance costs are variable: plates have to be replaced

every 30 bags milled and cost Rs45, the hulling cylinder (Rs28) per 200 bags and the shaft and rings per 500 bags (Rs75), although few traditional millers would maintain their machines with the scrupulousness that this implies. Depreciation on the MRM is accounted at 5 per cent for buildings and 10 per cent for machinery. In the traditional sector depreciation is nil: in fact, in the current climate of inflation most millers claim that they can sell their hullers at a price equal to or greater than the price at which they were bought. There is no part of a huller which cannot be and is not replaced. Many millers make their hullers entirely from spare parts. In this way there is a conceptual fusion between 'depreciation' and 'running costs'. It is commonly thought that any depreciation on buildings (and there is little evidence of this) is more than amply compensated for by appreciation on land. Depreciation is therefore not included in the accounting for the traditional sector.

Table 19.2   Average fixed and variable milling costs – huller sector, Cheyyar taluk

Fixed costs per year (Rs)		Variable costs per 75 kg of paddy (Rs)		
Salaries	2,186	Coolie wages:	loading	0·10
Taxes	50		unloading	0·10
Licences	150		parboiling and	
Maintenance	262		drying	0·42
			hulling	
Total	2,648		bagging	0·10
			husk removal	0·02
			miscellaneous	0·03
		Electricity		0·50
		Maintenance		0·76

Average turnover=610 tonnes per year. Average effective capacity=1391 tonnes. Average engineering capacity=3645 tonnes.

Fixed costs in the traditional sector vary greatly (see Table 19.2) but average Rs11·14 per tonne, whereas in MRM for prevailing turnover they are Rs50·27 per tonne (Table 19.3). Fixed-cost curves (Fig. 19.3) show a much greater marginal reduction in fixed costs with turnover in the traditional sector than in the modern sector. If approved policy were to be the minimisation of milling costs, then traditional mills should be encouraged to hull more than 500 tonnes per year.

(ii)   *Variable Costs*
These include wages for coolie work on loading and unloading and for parboiling and drying, bagging, stitching and carrying. They also include storage costs if any, fuel and power, and some maintenance and establishment costs. The cost of the gunny bag is a variable cost, as is that of transport involved in supplying the mill. Transport data are not available for MRM and are unreliable for the sample of hullers, so are not included.

Table 19.3   Fixed and variable costs – MRM Cheyyar, 1973

Fixed costs per year (Rs)		Variable costs per tonne paddy (Rs)	
Salaries of permanent staff	88,200	Coolie labour loading	1·50
Depreciation on buildings (5%)	21,888	Coolie labour unloading	1·50
Depreciation on machinery (10%)	64,812	Coolie/loading/labour bran	1·50
Land Revenue tax	30	bagging and stitching	2·50
Licence fees	500	2 months' storage	3·00
Machine maintenance	4,187	Husk	3·00
Telephone	1,800	Electricity	6·66
Administration expenses	3,600	Furnace oil	11·70
	185,067	Gunny	2·00
Less			
Subsidy for managerial staff	13,333		
Subsidy for grading staff	833		
Subsidy for grading equipment	2,500		
	16,666		
Total	168,401		

Total processing costs at 3350 tonnes per year turnover = Rs82·12 per tonne of paddy.

Transport costs have been simulated in a later section (p. 293) and in practice increase the variable costs of MRM to a greater extent than in the traditional sector. In the latter, variable costs for milling average Rs21·33 per tonne of paddy and, for boiling, Rs10·40 (see Table 19.2). The Civil Supplies sector estimates costs at Rs22·5 per tonne for hulling and Rs7·5 for boiling, and allows Rs10 per tonne of paddy for 'transport and incidentals', 'incidentals' covering fixed costs. So while in the private sector the average total cost of processing is Rs42·87 per tonne, the State government allows Rs40 per tonne (Civil Supplies Commission District Office, Vellore, 1973). The difference, at least Rs3 given that transport costs are omitted, is made up in practice by hoisting the price of free-market rice (chapter 18); but the loss is one of the reasons why traditional millers are not easily persuaded to mill for the government. On the same basis, MRM variable costs are Rs28·36 per tonne of paddy, which compares very favourably with public-sector allowances for milling margins.

In view of the oil crisis and the power shortages in Tamil Nadu an additional cost might be added: the consumption of non-human energy per tonne milled, at late 1973 prices Rs6·9 per tonne for the huller, contrasting very favourably with Rs18·89 for the MRM. This does not include the tendentious issue of transport costs; these represent energy in the form of diesel oil, the use of which a wise government would seek to minimise.

(iii)   *Total Costs*

The average total cost of processing since the time when the mill began

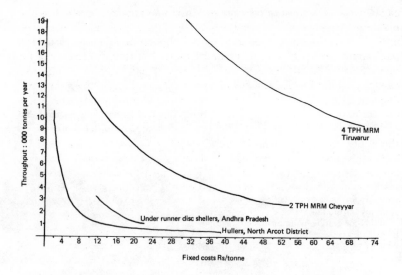

FIG. 19.3 *Fixed cost curves for MRM, URD shellers and hullers*

operations (4000 tonnes of paddy per year) is Rs71·06 per tonne which represents a loss per tonne of Rs31. At 1972–3 government rates for milling, the MRM would have to work at 14,517 tonnes per year in order to break even. This is greater than its engineering capacity so that over and above the MRM's un-repaid loan for its capital costs, it must at present be sustaining subsidies at the rate of Rs31 per tonne.

Capacity Utilisation

When capacity utilisation is low, fixed costs rise relative to variable costs. Total milling costs increase and may further widen the milling margins determined by technology and by the type of competition (Lele, 1970, pp. 14–18). Since 1972 Cheyyar MRM has milled about 3500 tonnes of paddy per annum (Tamil Nadu Civil Supplies Corporation, 1974). This is 25 per cent of its engineering capacity, defined by the production manager at 2 tph × 20 hours a day × 330 days a year, or 13,200 tonnes. By comparison the first MRM, the 4 tph model at Tiruvarur, was operating in 1972–3 at an 'average capacity utilisation' of 34 per cent.

Engineering capacity in the traditional huller sector may be defined as 'highest number of working days maintained in a year' (Lele, 1970, p. 17). From conversations with millers this is equivalent to maximum bags per hour × 18 hours per day × 300 days per year. Traditional mills work at from 3 to 34·5 per cent capacity and average 14·3 per cent. They are therefore using their capacity less efficiently than the public-sector mills, even though these too are underutilised. However, instead of engineering capacity we can use the concept of 'effective capacity', defined as the maximum number of days and the number of hours per day for which the miller is now prepared to operate the mill, given an adequate supply of paddy and electricity and an adequate market (if this is necessary to his operations). On this basis the MRM uses 28 per cent of its effective capacity while the traditional mills use between 7 and 88 per cent and average 40 per cent of effective capacity. Now the traditional sector works out as more, not less, efficient than the MRM, where low quantities of paddy supplied by the government are a major cause of high fixed costs. In the public sector, problems of supply, quality and polish alone hold up milling. Electricity is not denied MRMs in times of power cuts in the way it is withheld from the private sector. While supply of paddy may also stop traditional mills from being better utilised, the entrepreneurial attitude of the miller is another factor to be taken into account. Since fixed costs are relatively lower and free-market prices higher than in the public sector, a private miller can earn profits at a low rate of capacity utilisation while the MRM is said to break even at 20 tonnes per day at 4 per cent polish (50 per cent capacity) or 24 tonnes per day at 6 per cent polish (60 per cent). Many millers admit to having purchased a mill as a status symbol and to running it (profitably) as a sideline. However, it is obvious that before the MRM was built there was enormous excess capacity in engineering terms in the traditional sector in Cheyyar taluk. The MRM has increased the amount of this excess capacity and may thereby have widened margins.

Some Technological Caveats

In calculating the variable costs of the MRM it was assumed that milling conditions were those for which the technology was originally developed. If we relax these assumptions, the MRM's variable costs will rise and some problems in the transference of technology within Asia will be revealed.

1   The percentage polish at which hullers operate is higher than that for which the MRM has been deliberately designed. The polish which maximises nutritious elements (proteins and vitamins which lie closest to the husk) is 4 per cent. But rice with a 4 per cent polish is heavily coloured and is unacceptable to most of the public. In the absence of any forecast of a change in preference, MRMs are forced to increase the polish from 4 to 6 per cent. This reduces throughput, and therefore capacity, by 25 per cent which would therefore adversely affect the total cost calculations. At 4 per cent polish, out-turn of rice from paddy is theoretically 72 per cent by weight. At 6 per cent it is 68 per cent, robbing the MRM of its technological advantage over hullers. At 7 per cent polish, 25 per cent of the paddy has to be recycled for rehulling while at 4 per cent only 12 per cent of paddy has to embark on a potentially infinite journey of recycling. Low throughput also arises because of blockages in the silos and conveying machinery and because

the paddy cleaners may have a lower capacity than the mills (NCDC, 1975, p. 30).

2   The Japanese machinery was designed for a standard type of paddy, which is impossible to achieve in India, although there is less range in variety within the paddy taken as a levy than in the free market since levy paddy is usually the coarsest available (see p. 270 and Somasundaram, 1973, p. 28). The effect of variety in paddy inputs is again felt in throughput and therefore capacity. While small round ADT.27 grains can be milled in a 2 tph mill at 2·5 tph and Kichili at 2 tph, IR.8 with its large grain, yields rice at under 2 tph and raw IR.20 at 1 tph. Large losses have been experienced by mixing varieties in silos (NCDC, 1975, p. 75).

3   The MRM was designed to mill parboiled paddy and not raw paddy. Much of the paddy at Cheyyar is being milled raw, possibly to cut down on variable costs of parboiling. Raw milling reduces throughput by up to 50 per cent and also generates the problem of husk disposal, which will raise variable costs.

4   In India a bag of Kichili may contain some IR.20 plus some grit and sand. If it contains Kichili alone it is likely that the quality within the bag will vary. Variable grain sizes put strains on the milling machinery and additional grading units have to be added, increasing capital costs.

5   So far we have considered the hulling process alone. It is State government policy to calculate milling margins on a break-even basis: a miller's profit comes from the by-products. In the traditional technology 75 kg of paddy gives 45 kg of head rice, 5 kg broken rice and 25 kg of bran and husk. Broken rice is usually sold at two-thirds free-market rates; husk is generally used as a parboiling fuel (imputed at Rs3 per tonne); bran with 5 to 12 per cent oil content (CANTOR ATAC, 1972, p. 58) is usually sold at Rs5·5−7·0 per 50 kg raw and Rs2·5−4·0 boiled. However, one of the main arguments in favour of MRM technology is that paddy can be made to yield 4 per cent by weight of high-quality bran which contains 20−25 per cent oil sold for solvent extraction at between Rs450 and Rs700 per tonne: 100 tonnes of paddy result in 1 tonne of oil which sold at Rs3000 in 1972 but at Rs1400 in 1975 (NCDC, 1975, p. 98) in the free market. An income of Rs4·5−7·0 per tonne of paddy does not considerably reduce the losses made at 25 per cent capacity utilisation. The 13 MRMs supply a solvent extraction plant at Tiruvarur MRM in Thanjavur District. Clearly, unless the economic structure of this factory unit is examined (which is outside the scope of this chapter), there is no way of assessing the true profitability of the MRM at Cheyyar. The MRM may work at a loss while the bran-oil factory working at full capacity and supplied by other mills may work at a compensating profit. The take-over by Civil Supplies Corporation in 1972 of the MRM-bran oil system from the more autonomous co-operatives ought to help to centralise and

possibly streamline the logistics of supply to the factory, since enzymes quickly destabilise the bran and render it useless for oil extraction (NCDC, 1975, p. 98).

INCREASING PROFITABILITY: POLICY CAVEATS

The relationships between government policy, technology and capacity utilisation are often overlooked. If the MRM operated entirely in the free market the milling margin for coarse parboiled rice in Cheyyar in 1973 – assuming a 68 per cent out-turn – would approximate Rs110 per tonne and require a turnover of 2062 tonnes per annum to break even. There is no doubt that operation in the free market would prove profitable to the mill and ultimately to the NCDC whose capital loan has to be repaid. But such operation cannot be contemplated because of the intensive procurement policy of central and State governments to which the MRM system is now harnessed. In any case the profitability of milling in the free market would be less than the above figures suggest if the levy system were to be abolished, since wholesale rice prices are at present artificially hoisted to cover the loss made by traders on the levy paddy.

In addition free-market operation requires trading skills (pricing quality, managing large supplies) which management may not have. Nor does the Cheyyar mill have the six months' storage capacity necessary for such operations (Faulkner et al., 1963, p. 23). Another solution to the problem of financial losses is exemplified by MRM at Raipur in Madhya Pradesh which sells 60 per cent of its rice at a loss to the Indian government but is allowed to sell the remainder at a partially compensating profit on the free market. The few successful mills in the small co-operative sector make profits by operations of this kind and by small-scale custom-hulling (which caters to the bulk of rural households) (NCDC, 1975, pp. 15–54): the smallest consignment millable by an MRM is to be reckoned in tonnes, not basketfuls, so that the MRM is technologically inappropriate for such enterprises.

Problems of management mean that a fixed-pricing environment is essential, yet the fixed prices are determined by the operational economics of hullers, with which the MRM cannot presently compete.

Given that the mill operates entirely in the public sector, ways of reducing fixed and variable costs may be found. The major item of expenditure within fixed costs is on staff. If the complement of permanent staff were reduced this would weaken the employment-generating propensity of the mill. Similarly the major item of variable cost expenditure is that of drying the paddy using furnace oil at Rs11·70 per tonne (Rs14·1 in November 1973). In the traditional sector, drying costs are unlikely ever to exceed Rs3 per tonne. Cheyyar site has 6 acres, of which 2·5 are covered by buildings. The costs of constructing, maintaining and operating a drying yard large enough for half an average day's hulling should be investigated for the eight months of the year when sun-drying is no problem. It has been suggested to me by several millers that the capital costs of such a drying yard (about 10×60 yards) would be in the region of Rs10,000–15,000, and that it would generate employment for more than 12 women coolies. Increased throughput would reduce fixed costs per tonne. The proportion of North Arcot District's levy paid in paddy and milled at Cheyyar MRM could be increased, especially as the loss made on levy paddy is less than the loss made by traders on levy rice (see p. 269) and as the levy presently paid in paddy is only 18 per cent of the total. Increasing it would, however, also increase average transport costs.

Adoption Rationale

(i) Out-turn

An important argument for the modernisation of the rice milling industry is that the quality and out-turn of rice and the quality of bran will be improved (IIM, 1969, p. 13, 83–7). Income from such improvements has been calculated to result in high rates of return to capital invested, provided mills are operated at capacity. Since we have already considered bran and the problem of polish it is only necessary here to summarise the lengthy debate about the out-turn rates of various technologies (Harriss, 1974a, pp. 3–15). The operational out-turn of MRM has been closer to 64 per cent by weight than the 72 per cent claimed for it (NCDC, 1975, p. 30). Out-turn varies according to the varieties milled, being especially low when varieties show great internal variation or are mixed, and according to quality. Both these variables may in turn be an indirect function of government policy in cases where low purchase prices give producers no incentive to achieve the standards which would be *de rigueur* if they sold on a free market sensitive to quality along a price continuum. Out-turn also varies according to whether paddy is parboiled or milled raw. While there is a strong contrast in out-turns of raw riceheads between the huller and the rubber-roll sheller, there is very little contrast if the paddy is parboiled (Gupta, 1974, p. 37). Parboiling in North Arcot is carried out using a local adaptation of the Mysore hot-soak method (IIM, 1969, p. 44) and product quality on the free market is high. In practice low-capacity utilisation, mixed paddy supplies, raw milling and fixed price margins in the MRM sector suggest that both the physical out-turn and the rates of return are higher in the traditional sector.

(ii) Climatic

It is not entirely coincidental that more than half the MRMs in Tamil Nadu are in Thanjavur for it is there that the main justification for this technology holds true. The traditional technology depends upon the sun for drying both boiled and raw paddy from the 20–27 per cent moisture content at which it is harvested to 14–16 per cent prior to milling. The Kuruvai harvest in Thanjavur takes place in the imminent presence of cyclonic depressions from the north-east monsoon. Harvests in Japan, which exported the technology, are similarly threatened. In Thanjavur, the traditional, small Kuruvai harvest was immediately exported in a 'wet' condition to regions where it could be dried and stored or milled. Those millers who use the Kalam (drying yard) in Thanjavur during this period are liable to make losses since the process of drying under a cloudy sky, and therefore in lower temperatures, takes longer, squalls are unpredictable, and drying paddy takes time to remove. Here policy has once more interacted with technology, for the fixing of trading cordons round Thanjavur District at a time when the spread of double cropping with HYVs has greatly enlarged the wet season harvest has made the adoption *in situ* of costly oil-fired mechanical driers essential.

The MRM package is 'monsoon-neutral' with its built-in oil- or husk-fired mechanical drying unit and, on this risk-minimising account, is attractive. But not all Districts share Thanjavur's agricultural calendar and in the eight surplus-rice taluks in North Arcot District the Sornavari paddy crop, the only crop whose harvest is at all jeopardised by monsoons, is spread over only 3·5 per cent of the total land area (Tamil Nadu State Department of Agriculture data, 1973).

The climatic argument is not as important a rationale for the MRM in North Arcot as in Thanjavur, and in any case actual monthwise statements of tonnage milled for both Cheyyar and Tiruvarur show the same inverse relationship with rainfall as do mills in the traditional sector. The quoting of the Thanjavur case as a universal adoption rationale (e.g. IIM, 1969, pp. 44–8; NCDC, 1975, pp. 95, 120, 139) is another example of generalising from an exception (see p. 35 above).

(iii) *Locational*

The original site selected in North Arcot District for an MRM was at Arcot, the traditional paddy-milling and marketing centre for the District with about 10 per cent of its working population employed in this industry (Tamil Nadu Census, 1971). But Cheyyar Taluk Marketing Society put forward a site at Puliarambakkam Village, 3 miles north-east of the taluk head quarters on the Kanchipuram Road leading out of the District (see Fig. 19.2). This site was approved on the grounds of its being south of the productive 150,000 acres of land watered from Mamandur tank, and of the taluk having a 'large percentage of pump-sets', although the main pump-set belt in North Arcot would appear to be a tract of land from Kaveripakkam to Thurinjapuram, skirting Cheyyar on a north-east to south-west tangent. As far as agricultural productivity is concerned, Cheyyar is now the most intensive paddy-producing taluk in the District, having a notably large Navarai crop and an average paddy land use intensity of 60 (where a maximum would be 300). It also has the most seasonally consistent adoption of IR.8 and its derivatives (although Arcot taluk has the highest level of adoption in Samba, and Arni in Navarai).

Table 19.4   Production data for study area, North Arcot District, 1972–3

	Taluks					
	Arcot	Arni	Cheyyar	Polur	Thiruvan-namalai	Wandi-wash
Total area (ha.)	56,276	41,056	84,188	159,448	94,248	93,929
Total irrigated area (ha.)	2,890	9,528	21,593	22,414	19,630	17,923
Samba						
Percentage land in IR.8 etc.	17	8	12	16	8	13
Percentage land in other HYVs	9	4	6·3	8	4·6	7
Percentage land in TVs	11	8	13	10	10	13
Total (%)	37	20	31	34	22·6	33
Area (ha.)	20,794	8,200	26,102	54,196	21,289	30,987
Total production (tonnes)	68,620	27,060	86,136	178,846	70,253	102,257
Navarai						
Percentage land in IR.8 etc.	5	9·5	8·8	6	6	7
Percentage land in other HYVs	2	5	5·2	3·5	3	4·2
Percentage land in TVs	3·3	6·2	6·1	6	6	4·8
Total (%)	10·3	20·2	20·1	15·5	15	16·8
Area (ha.)	5,788·6	8,302	16,924	24,645	14,145	15,775
Total production (tonnes)	19,102·3	27,399	55,849	8,132·5	46,678	52,057
Sornavari						
Percentage land in IR.8 etc.	0·2	nil	4·5	2·8	4·1	nil
Percentage land in other HYVs	0·21		2·5	1·4	2·1	
Percentage land in TVs	0·1		2·5	2·0	3·0	
Total (%)	0·41		9·5	6·2	9·2	
Area (ha.)	2,248		7,999	9,882	8,666	
Total production (tonnes)	741·8		26,396	32,610	28,597	
Marketable surplus at 40 per cent						
Samba (tonnes)	27,440	10,800	34,440	71,520	28,080	40,880
Navarai (tonnes)	7,640	10,920	22,320	32,520	18,640	20,800
Sornavari (tonnes)	280		10,520	13,040	11,440	
Total	35,360	21,720	67,280	117,080	58,160	61,680
Grand total	361,280 tonnes					

Sources: Tamil Nadu Census 1971 for area data; Tamil Nadu State Department of Agriculture for land use data.

Notes:

Production: official yields for the District given by the Department of Agriculture for 1972–3 were Samba, 5000 kg per hectare for IR.8 etc., 3500 kg per hectare for other HYVs, 2500 kg per hectare traditional varieties; Navarai, 5200, 3500, 1300 kg per hectare respectively; Sornavari, 5200, 3500, 1400 respectively.

Project pilot survey gave yields for Samba 1972–3 as 4192 kg per hectare for IR.8 and 2377 kg per hectare, traditional varieties. The average yield according to official statistics was 3250 (Samba), 3300 (Navarai), 3366 (Sornavari); survey yield was 3284 kg. The average of the averages was taken for the basis of calculations, i.e. 3·3 tonnes per hectare.
Marketable surplus: average marketable surplus from the project survey was 40 per cent; in the absence of any other data this figure has been used.

The location decision was made however before IR.8 and its derivatives were introduced into North Arcot, so this fact was unknown.

If well placed within Cheyyar taluk (although five of the six tarmac approach routes converge on the congested urban area itself) and well placed in terms of local productivity, the MRM is very highly skewed in relation to the District as a whole. Had the mill been intended to function in an unzoned free market this would not have mattered, since similar quality land and similar agrarian systems exist in Chingleput District to the east. It has in practice never milled paddy from outside the District. An eccentric location and an administrative brick-wall to the east distends its paddy catchment area, already artificially enlarged because it mills a maximum of only 18 per cent of the region's levy, itself rarely more than 20 per cent of exported marketed surplus. This function of policy results in transport costs greater than minimum.

Three simulations are described below to show the spatial coverage of the MRM under different economic and physical assumptions. The total seasonal production and marketable surplus for the study area have been calculated using the available data from the Census, the Tamil Nadu Department of Agriculture and our pilot survey (Table 19.4) and cross-checked against District Supply Office totals of levy procurement. There is a 9 per cent discrepancy which is acceptable for calculations but indicative of the margins of error between two types of official information.

(a) If Cheyyar MRM operates at effective capacity (i.e. 12,000 tonnes per year in the absence of any other mills; and assuming three harvests a year at current land use intensities, and a network of supply godowns sufficient to store up to four months' paddy), the radius of a circular area commanded by the mill is $\sqrt{\dfrac{A}{\pi}}$ where A is the area of land generating 4000 tonnes of marketable surplus, varying with the season. In Samba, when the paddy crop occupies 31 per cent of Cheyyar taluk, there is 0·41 tonnes of marketable surplus per hectare (calculations presented in Table 19.4), the command-area radius is 5·6 km. In Navarai the corresponding figures are 20 per cent, 0·264 tonnes per hectare, and 7 km; and in Sornavari 9·5 per cent, 0·125 tonnes per hectare, and 10 km. These radii all encroach on the urban area of Cheyyar so would be slightly longer in practice.

(b) Working at effective capacity, again in the absence of competition but with the supply from an average levy of 20 per cent of marketable surplus, the Samba radius is 12·4 km, the Navarai 15·5 km, and the Sornavari 22 km. In every case the command circle hits the district boundary to the east of the mill, and the circle would have to be very considerably distorted in Sornavari to account for the urban area and the District boundary; also the huller mills, being small and scattered, are far more accessible not merely to private traders but also to the Civil Supplies collecting points.

(c)   The third simulation supposes that the MRM works at effective capacity and competes with trading – milling enterprises working at their average annual trading turnover. Of the 60 per cent of the sub-sample which have trading enterprises, an average of 70 per cent of their turnover and therefore 28 per cent of their effective capacity is being used for trading (exactly on a par with MRM). Average turnover of these mills is 648 tonnes and trading turnover 478·8 tonnes paddy. This latter is the marketable surplus of 262·7 hectares and comprises 56 per cent of the total marketable surplus of Cheyyar taluk. There is enough surplus therefore for the MRM to work at effective capacity.

An iterative procedure for calculation season by season of the radius for this simulation has to be followed:

$$r_1 = \frac{\sqrt{(60\% \ M \times A^1) + A}}{\pi}$$

to

$$r_j = \frac{\sqrt{(60\% \ M(j-1) \times A^1) + A}}{\pi}$$

where r = radius of command area of MRM at effective capacity (calculated in the first simulation)

r_1 = radius of command area of MRM plus command areas of mills within radius r

M = no. of huller mills within r

M_1 = no. of huller mills within r_1

A = Command area of MRM

A^1 = Area of land generating 33 per cent of annual traded through-put of huller mills at land use intensity of season 1

The process stops when $M_j = M_{(j-1)}$

Go to next season.

The procedure adopted in these simulations is geographically over-simplified since no account is taken of the shape consequences of the District boundary or of Cheyyar, nor of the distorting effect of the road network (which works to the disadvantage of MRM and focuses on Cheyyar, whose 17 mills probably have a combined effective capacity of 2·5 times that of the MRM); nor of the fact that the proportion of marketable surplus milled by huller technology varies inversely with distance from towns.

However, using these simplifying assumptions, after three iterations, the radius of supply for Samba would be 8·2 km, that for Navarai after five iterations would be 12·3 km. But for Sornavari after two iterations the radius exceeds that of the whole taluk. It is impossible to supply MRM after Sornavari. If extra Samba and Navarai supplies were stockpiled for Sornavari operations, this would further increase the radius of supply and the iterations. It might then prove extremely difficult to operate the mill at capacity in a free-market situation, existing mills running at existing average throughputs.

The average transport costs to supply the mill from the circular command area are derived as follows:

$$\text{Average distance} = \int_0^R \frac{2\pi r \times r dr}{\pi R^2} = \tfrac{2}{3} R$$

Average transport costs are therefore $\tfrac{2}{3}RC$, where R is the radius and C the per unit transport costs. If transport costs are Rs0·40 per tonne kilometre then the average transport costs for MRM in the first simulation are Rs2 per tonne and in the second Rs4·40 per tonne comparing with Rs0·25 per tonne for the huller. This fact may explain why the government apparently prefers to mill the levy using scattered hullers, since milled rice loses 50 per cent by volume and 30–35 per cent by weight. Total social transport costs are therefore greatly lowered.

(iv) *Employment*

A concept to which much lip-service is devoted by government is the employment effects of the new technologies. Lele (1971, p. 7) reports the employment generated by the 4 tph mill of Thanjavur Co-operative Marketing Federation at Tiruvarur as 326 and is concerned that this number adds significantly to the fixed costs per unit of output, which in turn affects its competitive position, especially when the mill is working at well below capacity, however defined.

The employment effect of the MRM at Cheyyar is far less than at Tiruvarur, 35 salaried staff and approximately 25 daily coolies (see Table 19.5) being involved. Lest this mill be criticised as aberrantly over-capitalised it must be noted that Lele's figure of 326 includes the total complement of labour at Tiruvarur Co-operative Marketing Federation, while those salaried workers connected with the mill itself, the paddy and rice division, and R and D number 121, 75 of whom are in the MRM. This is more directly comparable with Cheyyar.

Traditional, standard Number One hullers are manned by an owner (plus his family or two partners (rarely three)) and a number of 'technical staff' trained in the mills who drive and repair the huller and supervise the boiling and drying of paddy (skilled operations). This number ranges from one to six, an average of three, regardless of turnover. On average their salaries amount to a total of Rs2200 per mill per year, i.e. 70 per cent of fixed costs.

Table 19.5　Civil Supplies Corporation staff at MRM Cheyyar

Administrative		Engineering	
1	Junior accountant	1	Production engineer
1	Typist	2	Shift engineers
2	Peons	7	Operators
1	Junior assistant	1	Fitter
	Godown:	2	Boiler attendants
1	Keeper		Technical staff:
1	Accounts clerk	2	Technical assistants
1	Store clerk	3	Mill technical
2	Shift clerks		assistants
		1	Technical maistry

Source:　Tamil Nadu Civil Supplies Corporation, Nov 1973.

The Cheyyar MRM has an administrative complement of eight, doing work done by the traditional mill owner. Its engineering and technical sections, comparable with the salaried employees of a traditional mill, number 19, eight of whom are of higher formal technical calibre than ever found in the traditional sector. The godown section gives work to five people.

In Lele's view the high contribution of staff to fixed costs affects MRM's competitive position with regard to traditional mills. In fact Cheyyar's MRM's ratio between staff salaries and total fixed costs is 47 per cent, which is 22 per cent lower than in traditional mills, as one might expect from a highly capital-intensive technology housed in purpose-built buildings. With regard to coolie and unskilled casual labour (though it is strictly incorrect to call even coolie labour unskilled), there is a great difference in employment generation between MRM and traditional mills. The average mill with a turnover of 610 tonnes per annum has a gang of about ten casual or semi-permanent coolies, mainly women, attached to it, who earn between Rs3 and Rs5 per day according to the piece rates in Table 19.3. Carrying work is done by male casual workers according to both its and their availability.

Cheyyar MRM has on an average day about 25 coolies, mostly men, but they are mainly used for loading, unloading, bagging and humping. The coolie requirements of the traditional labour-intensive boiling and drying process in the MRM is nil.

It is worthwhile to look at employment multiplication in relation to turnover. Studying employment in relation to 'capacity' as does Lele (1971, p. 6) is unrealistic unless mills are being run at engineering or effective capacity and we have already seen how far from actuality that is, and what great variation in capacity utilisation there is in the huller sector.

In the private traditional sector 400 tonnes of paddy milled per year generates one owner, 180 tonnes generates a salaried employee and 41·5 tonnes a coolie. In the MRM, the question of owners is irrelevant, 418 tonnes is generating a highly qualified employee, 124 tonnes generates a semi-skilled employee and 134 tonnes a coolie. This does not include clerks in the Madras headquarters dealing with trade, nor does it include the District Supply Office network, since the personnel all deal in other commodities as well as paddy and rice, and data to assess their relative involvement in one mill are lacking.

(a) In terms of throughput, MRM has the same employment-generating capacity as the traditional sector for all types of labour, except coolies. Running at effective capacity it would, however, be about four times less generative in the salaried sector than the traditional mills running at 1972 rates, and ten times less generative of coolies.

(b) In spatial terms, as MRM requires an average radius of 7·5 km to operate at effective capacity and as there are 28 huller mills within this radius, it would put 332 people out of work. It is six times less employment-generative than the traditional system in this particular area.

(c) In cost terms, the capital costs of MRM could have built 50 small mills which would have generated 70 owners, 150 salaried employees and 500 coolies, 720 people in all. In these terms, MRM is twelve times less employment-generative.

(v) *Management and Policy*

Although MRM creates employment for skilled manpower rather than for ordinary landless rural people, the type of trained engineer required is scarce in India (IIM, 1969, p. 18). Moreover, engineering skills – though essential for management of an MRM – do not help with the management of storage, the logistics of supplying a mill, and free-market purchasing operations, at which millers in the traditional sector 'qualified in neither rice processing technology nor in general education' (Gupta *et al.*, 1970, p. 105) are in fact skilled. Storage at the MRM is sufficient for only two and a half weeks of operation at capacity and two months at present rates. Already, however, there are accomodation difficulties at Cheyyar Mill (Civil Supplies, 1973). A decentralised feeder system of stores exists but is not managed either from or for the mill. In any case, were the feeder stores to supply the mill more actively, transport and handling costs would be raised.

LESSONS FOR THE SRI LANKAN MILLS

Lessons from this study of the operation of the MRM technology are that the mill cannot operate at a profit using fixed milling margins determined by a traditional technology except at engineering capacity, if at all. The quality of rice produced is more a function of difficulties with the institutional control of paddy quality and price than of the technology. The management of supplies is difficult. Higher transport costs are involved in supplying a given quantity to an MRM than to a series of small mills. The MRM has to be accepted as being far less generative of livelihoods for ordinary people than are traditional technologies.

The lack of institutional control of the logistics of supply which have so hindered the efficient operation of MRMs in India may not be such a difficulty in Sri Lanka, where the Paddy Marketing Board has monopoly powers of purchase and supervises storage, transport and milling of paddy throughout the Island. No evaluation has been made of the MRMs in process of construction on the Uda Walawe scheme to the immediate north of Hambantota District. In 1971 the River Valleys Development Board in charge of the scheme, aided by the Paddy Marketing Board, made the decision to adopt MRM technology in order to process paddy grown under the scheme, apparently on the grounds that it minimised rice losses and generated skilled employment. Two identical 3–3·5 tonne per hour rice mill complexes were planned, each to operate at 5000 hours per annum and therefore to mill, 17,500 tonnes of paddy. Two 3 acre sites, Moraketiya and Kachchigala, both centrally located in what is planned to be paddy land, have been selected and construction has been in progress since early 1972.

In 1973–4 some 16,200 acres of the Uda Walawe scheme were under paddy in the Maha season and 11,067 acres in Yala. Average yields were 67 bu. per acre in Maha and 62 in Yala. Government paddy purchases in those two seasons totalled 855,000 bu., or 18,269 tons. This paddy is being milled in conventional rubber-roll sheller mills which the MRMs will soon replace. There are also over 50 huller or huller–sheller mills milling for private consumption within the area of the scheme. What the government at present collects is sufficient only for one mill working at capacity. The original plans for Uda Walawe envisaged 50,000 acres under paddy. Water shortages have, however, necessitated frequent revisions of plan and the current target is 35,000 acres. If this paddy acreage for both Maha and Yala seasons remains at present yield levels, total paddy production will be 2,170,000 bu. in Yala and 2,345,000 bu. in Maha. If (as in Yala 1973) marketed surplus is 80 per cent of production, a total of 96,494 tons of paddy will be the responsibility of the Paddy Marketing Board or the RVDB to mill. This would keep 5·5 MRMs of the size under construction operating at capacity. Provided these assumptions are ultimately fulfilled, there will be no problems of supply for these mills. At present levels, however, both mills would be working at 52 per cent of installed capacity.

Similar but necessarily tentative calculations using present paddy–rice margins derived from the operational economics of the modernised rubber-roll sheller mills on contract to the Paddy Marketing Board suggest that unless the mills work at around 90 per cent of engineering capacity they will not break even. Moreover, small changes in variables such as the out-turn of rice and bran, the paddy–rice price margins, and the price of bran alter profitability considerably (Harriss, 1974b, pp. 3–6). It is therefore important that the Paddy Marketing Board organises storage and supply systems sufficient to allow the mills to work at a level unprecedented in South and South-East Asia.

For two identical seasons each year, storage space will be needed to provide each mill with six months' supply of paddy, i.e. 8750 tons. In fact at Moraketiya there are two conventional bag stores with a combined capacity of 100,000 bu. (2136 tons), and the MRM will have 1000 tons of silo storage. This is plainly insufficient for the mill to operate at capacity. The RVDB intends to construct 'smaller paddy stores all over the project area, though locations are as yet undecided'. Dispersed small stores will be unnecessary break-of-bulk points. For the efficient supply of an MRM, storage has to be centralised.

Finally, with regard to livelihoods the labour schedules supplied by the Japanese contractor suggest that increased capitalisation is taking place with the MRM technology. They allow for one skilled operator per 1848 tons and one unskilled employee per 342 tons. On the basis of throughput, then (admittedly a crude criterion of evaluation but used in the absence of better data), the MRMs in Sri Lanka are to be 4·5 times less generative of skilled labour and 2·5 times less generative of unskilled labour than is the Cheyyar mill.

SUMMARY AND CONCLUSIONS

The relative efficiency of utilisation by the two technologies of the three factors of production are summarised in Table 19.6.

To return to the quotation at the beginning of the chapter, a rice-milling technology developed for milling large quantities of clean and varietally homogeneous paddy cannot be transferred even within Asia to an area of mixed varieties, albeit technically high-yielding, without deleterious consequences to milling quality and out-turn. Moreover, within India a technology suitable for a District such as Thanjavur with a high level of public control over marketing and with wet-season harvests, is not necessarily suitable for a District such as North Arcot with a low level of public control over marketing and a very small wet-season harvest, with which existing technologies can cope.

Government policies have been shown to exacerbate operational difficulties with this new technology. There are few ways in which policy might be used creatively, and these may be contradictory. If the mill lacks the technological flexibility to process many varieties, in succession or

Table 19.6   Summary of factor utilisation by two milling technologies in North Arcot District

Factor	Efficiency criterion	MRM	Average traditional huller
Capital	Capital costs	Rs1,190,928	Rs30,000
	Fixed costs per tonne 1972–3	Rs50·29	Rs11·14
	Variable costs, boiling and hulling	Rs28·36	Rs31·73
	Engineering capacity utilisation	25 per cent	14 per cent
	Effective capacity utilisation	28 per cent	40 per cent
Labour	'Managerial' (salaried: MRM)	8	1·4
	Salaried	27	3
	Coolies	25	10
	Turnover per manager	418 tonnes	400 tonnes
	per employee	124	180
	per coolie	134	42
Land	Area required to supply mill at effective capacity:		
	Samba	9,756 hectares	397 hectares
	Navarai	15,152 hectares	830 hectares
	Sornavari	32,000 hectares	1,660 hectares
Consumption of non-human energy per tonne milled		Rs18·89	Rs6·9

mixed, then governments might try to ensure that levy paddy is a non-shattering parboiled variety such as IR.8, or ideally ADT.27 since this most nearly approximates to the quality of Japanese paddy. The fact that currently popular HYVs are difficult to mill highlights the neglect by seed-breeders of this aspect of rice production. We have seen that the best way of ensuring good quality is to trade on the free market, but that managerially this is not possible; it is also counter to government ideology and would raise prices in the public distribution system. The next-best alternative would be for government to offer procurement prices nearer those of the free market with distinct premia for quality on a par with free-market practices. This would also raise prices at the retail end; but it is simply not possible to purchase high-quality grain from either producers or traders at low prices. Government could increase capacity utilisation in the mill by insisting that the levy is sold as paddy and not as at present in the form of rice. This would reduce the level of subsidy to the mill. The level of subsidy within the whole system might, however, be reduced by allowing or encouraging private-sector huller mills to operate at throughputs exceeding 500 tonnes per year (since great economies of scales are enjoyed) and by neglecting the MRM completely.

Lastly, in the face of these problems of gigantism, it would be worthwhile to explore the economics of developing modern mini-mills using the rubber-roll technology (assuming current problems with the quality of rubber used can be solved: NCDC, 1975, p. 68) perhaps along the lines of the small-scale co-operative milling, drying and storage centres being created in Indonesia (Timmer, 1974; Tainsh and Hawkey, 1975). Appraisals of the economics of the MRM should take into account the technological problems discussed as well as the problems of operating at low capacity within fixed margins. It also seems that some overhaul of public-sector decision-making in this sphere would be in order.

Acknowledgements: Thanks are due to Mr J. P. Narayan for help with miller interviews; to the Civil Supplies Corporation, Madras, and the production manager, Cheyyar Modern Rice Mill, Tamil Nadu; and to the assistant general manager and the administrative secretary, River Valleys Development Board, Embilipitiya, Sri Lanka, for much of the raw data and for permission to visit the sites in both countries. I am grateful to Mrs B. N. Chinnappa, Dr U. J. Lele and Dr Robert Chambers for their criticism of an earlier draft.

REFERENCES

CANTOR ATAC (1972). *Tamil Nadu Nutrition Project: A Survey of Food Processing Industries in Tamil Nadu by the Operations Research Group, Baroda.*

Civil Supplies Department, North Arcot District (1973). *Report for the Committee of Estimates, Government of Tamil Nadu*, Vellore, mimeo.

Faulkner, M. D., Reed, G. W. and Brown, D. D. (1963). *Report to the Government of India on Increasing Milling Outturn of Rice from Paddy*, New Delhi, mimeo.

Ford Foundation (1959). *Report on India's Food Crisis and Steps to Meet it*, New Delhi, Ministry of Food and Agriculture.

Gupta, V. K. (1974). *Study Report on the Paddy Marketing Board's Areas of Organisational Concern and Change*, Colombo, Paddy Marketing Board.

Gupta, V. K., Gopalswamy, T. P. and Mathur, D. P. (1970). *Under-utilisation in Sheller Rice Mills*, Ahmedabad, Indian Institute of Management.

Harriss, B. (1974a). *A 'Which' Guide to Appropriate Rice Milling Technologies*, Centre of S. Asian Studies, University of Cambridge, Seminar on Agrarian Change in Rice-growing Areas of Tamil Nadu and Sri Lanka, mimeo (to appear in *Tropical Science*).

Harriss, B. (1974b). *An Attempt to Pre-evaluate the Operational Economics of Three ton per hour Modern Rice Mills on the Uda Walawe Scheme in Sri Lanka*, ibid.

Indian Institute of Management, IIM (1969). *Modernisation in Rice Processing Industry*, Ahmedabad.

Lele, U. J. (1970). *Modernisation of the Rice Milling Industry: Lessons from Past Performance*, Ithaca, New York, Cornell University Press.

Lele, U. J. (1971). *The Modern Rice Mill in India: a case study in agricultural marketing*, Occasional Paper no. 29, Department of Agriculture, Cornell University.

National Co-operative Development Corporation (1975). *Papers of the All-India Conference on Co-operative Rice Milling Industry*, New Delhi.

Somasundaram, T. (1973). 'Green Revolution – Paddy – Rice Utility', *Sci. and Eng.*, 26, 27–8.

Tainsh, J. A. R. and Hawkey, R. (1975). *Paddy Marketing in Indonesia*, Economist Intelligence Unit Marketing Meetings, no. 3, London, mimeo.

Timmer, C. P. (1974). *Choice of Technique in Rice Milling on Java*, Agricultural Development Council Research and Training Network reprint, New York.

20 Comparing Twelve South Indian Villages: in Search of Practical Theory

Robert Chambers and John Harriss

> There are no theories generating models of change and development at village level which are theoretically persuasive and amenable to policy implementation. (Irma Adelman and George Dalton: Dalton 1971, p. 493)

Recent dissatisfaction with urban-biased macro-planning of rural development has called forth a variety of responses. Among them a common concern is to relate planning at national or regional levels more closely to village needs and conditions. It is not so much a question of adapting programmes and methods of implementation to local circumstances (important as that is) as of reformulating approaches to rural development planning on the basis of improved understanding of economic and social processes, in their interaction at village level. Some very detailed studies of one or two villages, mainly by anthropologists, have given profound and valuable insights, but they do not constitute the kind of general theory referred to by Adelman and Dalton, and which has been the concern of the village studies programme at the Institute of Development Studies (Lipton and Moore, 1972). One approach to the building of such a theory is through the questions: Why are villages so different? And what of it so far as policy is concerned? The possible absurdity of the first question is reduced by the practical significance of the second.

Many village differences are related to regional contrasts; but this was not so in our study area in North Arcot, which was selected for its homogeneity (pp. 7–13), yet which still exposed us to substantial inter-village variation. Indeed, it was exposure to the twelve villages surveyed by the project which drew us to the important general question of whether comparison of villages can help us to isolate critical dynamic factors in village-level development, and so to generate theory with practical implications for policies at higher levels.

DATA AND METHODS

Accounts of the method of selection of the twelve villages, and of the characteristics of the region in which they lie are to be found in chapters 1 and 5. Our main data fall under seven heads:

- 1 Between us, several visits to each village with several interviews on each occasion, sometimes with the benefit of colleagues, and often assisted by survey investigators familiar with the villages.
- 2 Reports and answers to supplementary questions by the survey investigators. This includes much of the labour and wage data and information on land prices.
- 3 Data from the survey, mainly the household listing, the farm survey, and to a lesser extent the cultivation schedule survey.
- 4 The Resettlement Registers, usually dating from the 1910s, with base-line information on land areas, irrigation, cropping patterns, and other economic and social matters.
- 5 Volumes of the Census of India from 1871 to 1971.
- 6 Statistical information from village karnams, including acreages and crops by year and sometimes by season.
- 7 Village maps, updated by investigators.

Major difficulties arise over the definition of 'village'. Only Kalpattu, of the twelve, is not a nucleated settlement, but the villages as defined by the Census, which supplied the list from which the sampling frame was constructed, include various types of social units. Our sample includes these cases:

> The 'village' has a physically separate settlement for scheduled castes, either contiguous with the caste village (Randam, Vegaman-galam, Duli) or apart from it (Kalpattu, Veerasambanur, etc.).
> The 'village' does not include the scheduled caste settlement that supplies much of its labour (Dusi).
> The 'village' contains a scheduled caste settlement which is not regarded as part of the village and which supplies labour to another village. In the case of Sirungathur, the Melandai Colony, which serves another village, lies within the Sirungathur boundary but was not enumerated with any village in the 1971 Census.

It is obvious both from this variety and from our observations that some villages are labour-surplus and others labour-deficit, and that discussion of man/land ratios becomes tenuous if one naïvely takes the Census population and the Revenue area of a village.

A second difficulty is the extent to which villages are interpenetrated by ownership of land, wells and pump-sets. Except for Randam, it has been difficult to obtain reliable information about land owned by villagers outside; though ownership by outsiders of land within the villages is more dependably known. Thus we have found that no less than 54 per cent of the land in both Meppathurai and Sirungathur is owned by outsiders, although none of the other villages approach these proportions; over half the pump-sets in Sirungathur, and nearly half the pump-sets in Meppathurai are similarly outside-owned.

These problems of reliability of data and of definition are so serious that the ratios given in this chapter should be treated with great caution. Our partial solution is to accept the Revenue definition of the village, to accept sceptically the various records and other information that are available, and to try to bear the many necessary reservations in mind when arriving at judgements. To avoid painful longwindedness, however, we will not repeat continuously these caveats or our own misgivings.

Had a comparative study of the villages as villages been intended from the beginning, we would have collected additional information and collected it differently. As it is, much of the argument which follows is based on impressions and upon evidence of rather low reliability. Moreover, we are unable to 'prove' in any strict sense the validity of the main lines of thought. But through our field experience and through scanning much more data than can be presented here a set of interpretations, which is by no means the set with which we started out, appears to hang together, and – as we shall finally see – raises policy issues. Although, therefore, we cannot be sure that we are right, it does seem worthwhile to present the main outlines of the framework, which seems to fit the facts as we perceive them.

APPROACHES TO COMPARATIVE STUDY OF VILLAGE-LEVEL DEVELOPMENT

Comparative analysis involves an exercise in classification. Yet as many typologies of villages are possible as there are dimensions or scales against which villages can be assessed. The challenge in searching for a typology is to choose scales or dimensions which are both powerful in making sense of other factors and useful in seeing what might be done to improve rural livelihoods; so that the important result should be not so much the categories that are produced as the principles of classification. It would be easy to be carried away by the fascination of trying to describe villages in terms of neat types, but we must expect to find many intermediate cases. What is important is not that we should be able to say 'This is A, that is B' but rather that we should understand the principal reasons for variations between villages, because it is probable that those reasons will tell us much about the critical variables in rural development.

One possible approach to the problem of classification would be to use numerical techniques with the power of handling masses of diverse data regarding a large number of dimensions, which is what Adelman and Dalton have attempted in their study, 'A Factor Analysis of Modernisation in Village India' (1971). But as they are careful to point out 'Factor analysis does not allow us to attribute cause and effect', so that the regularities defined by the analysis still have to be interpreted. While we are conscious of the potential of quantitative techniques, we have preferred so far to proceed by postulating causal relationships, and testing their explanatory power. Our approach to theory building is to test simplifying models which set relative weights to different factors; and we have found it useful to distinguish factors which appear to be mainly causal and those which appear to be mainly derivative. The mainly causal factors which we shall consider here are as listed below:

location
resources and population
the nature of the production process

while mainly derivative factors include:

demographic trends
farming practices such as adoption of HYVs
some aspects of social relationships such as the existence and strength
   of patron–client relationships
wages

LOCATION AND ACCESS
In the early stages of our investigations we were inclined to attribute importance to location in relation to towns and communications as being likely to exercise causal influence on access to resources such as capital and political influence. But we found it to be of limited explanatory power, as a comparison of Randam on the one hand, and Duli and Sirungathur on the other, goes to show.

The physical access to a town enjoyed by Randam has been exploited successfully by some men of the village both in commerce and in politics. A kind of self-generating process has been set in motion: proximity to the town – Arni – has meant that village residents have been able to combine agriculture with participation in trade; the village has come to have a stake in the town, and this ensures that some men in the village enjoy favourable access to political resources and influence which may guarantee a higher degree of access to scarce inputs like fertiliser and credit. Yet physical proximity in itself is no guarantee that the members of a village will enjoy such access, or that the emergence of significant leaders or entrepreneurs will be encouraged. Duli is closer to Cheyyar than Randam is to Arni, and Sirungathur is almost as close. Yet, so far as we could see, in neither

Sirungathur nor Duli are there significant individuals like those of Randam who enjoy some power within the local region; and cultivators in the two villages are unable to obtain credit in the town to the same extent as Randam farmers. Several factors are involved in explanation of this evident contrast.

First, there is the different nature of Arni and Cheyyar as towns. The former is an old-established market town with important paddy and groundnut markets. The markets of Cheyyar are less important, and much of its recent growth has been thrust upon it by the location of facilities like a government Arts College. Secondly, the most numerous agricultural castes of Duli and Sirungathur are Gownders, but only one Gownder is believed to be operating a paddy business in Cheyyar. By contrast the dominant caste in Randam – the Agamudaiyan Mudaliars – are one of a group of related castes found very widely in Tamil Nadu, often in eminent positions, who are agriculturalists and traders, businessmen and professionals. In Arni they are perhaps the leading group of businessmen. The Agamudaiyans of Randam are extensively connected with the traders in the town, and their ties of kinship and caste are unquestionably helpful to them. By contrast, the Gownders of North Arcot, although also members of a large group of related castes found over a wide area, are a rather depressed community mainly of poor farmers and labourers, though some caste members have established themselves in business. There seems some justification, then, in concluding that location alone influences access much less than village – urban caste connections.

The survey villages provide other examples of the limited value of location as a factor. The two most outstanding are Kalpattu and Vinayagapuram. Kalpattu is not on a tarmac road or near an urban centre, yet it has the highest land values, the highest wages and the most intensive agriculture of any village. Vinayagapuram is remote yet has a high cropping index on irrigated land and a high literacy rate. It is arguable that these two villages, like all those in the sample, are not really remote in an All India sense. Still, the point holds that, within this sample, location on its own is a weak predictor of other characteristics and not a reliable proxy for access or urban links.

POPULATION AND RESOURCES

The relationship between resources and population is *a priori* an obvious mainly causal factor, with population changes as a prime dynamic. The relationship has for long been a preoccupation in rural India, and even in the 1910s the Resettlement Registers all calculated ratios of population to cultivable land. It has, indeed, been the time-series population statistics for these twelve villages (Table 20.1 and Fig. 20.1) which have been as intriguing and provocative as any of the data unearthed. Unfortunately we have no birth rate or mortality data: it would be surprising if these did not differ between villages, with perhaps higher mortality rates in the remoter

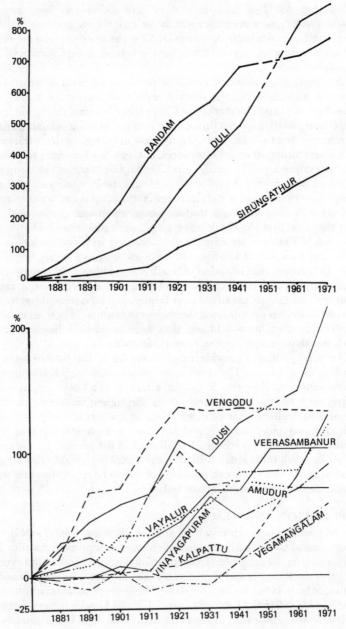

FIG. 20.1 *Demographic trends showing growth from 1871 (not including Randam, Duli and Sirungathur, which cannot be shown on this scale)*

Table 20.1 *Village populations from Census sources*

Village	1871	1881	1891	1901	1911	1921	1931	1941	1951	1961	1971	Percentage change	
												1961–71	1911–71
Vegamangalam	691	647	631	711	601	648	638	771	886	974	1,028	+ 5·5	+ 71
Sirungathur	209	n.a.	233	273	297	429	514	609	n.a.	862	980	+11·4	+230
Duli	45	52	72	94	115	179	233	274	367	423	450	+ 6·4	+291
Dusi	762	n.a.	1,090	1,196	1,266	1,593	1,491	1,701	1,808	1,896	2,398	+26·5	+ 89
Vengodu	457	530	769	775	947	1,080	1,068	1,078	811	1,069	1,061	− 0·7	+ 12
Vinayagapuram	n.a.	n.a.	460	499	482	613	760	678	844	780	784	+ 0·5	+ 63
Amudur	493	627	655	596	816	989	857	870	831	841	934	+11·1	+ 14
Randam	163	253	376	560	799	995	1,098	1,292	1,329	1,353	1,446	+ 6·9	+ 81
Kalpattu	831	816	478	1,047	875	894	972	950	1,177	1,495	1,942	+29·9	+122
Veerasambanur	266	284	320	272	˙346	380	451	447	n.a.	543	540	− 0·6	+ 56
Meppathurai	261	n.a.	353	438	465	441	473	478	525	759	804	+ 5·9	+ 73
Vayalur	285	n.a.	314	380	384	418	457	525	468	535	634	+18·5	+ 65

Source: Census of India, 1871–1971.

Note:

To the best of our knowledge and belief these figures are reasonably accurate and comparable. Various checks, including comparison of the stated surface area of villages at different censal dates, have been carried out.

The 1961 and 1971 figures provided some complicated puzzles which leave a higher degree of doubt about the accuracy of the inter-censal increase in the cases of Sirungathur and Vayalur than in the case of other villages. The Sirungathur 1971 figure is an adjustment after including an estimate for the Melandai Colony which was almost certainly not counted in 1971.

Checks have been made where possible and appropriate with karnam's famine register censuses, school censuses, and the project's household listing. Nevertheless it is possible, indeed even likely, that this table contains one or more substantial undetected and undetectable errors.

and smaller villages. If, however, we make the heroic assumption that birth and death rates were equal or nearly so, we are left with startling contrasts between the implied migration histories of the different villages. Some of the changes have been of such magnitude as to make it certain that migration has been involved.

Relating population to what we advisedly call 'resources' (rather than land, in order to take account of differing soils and more particularly irrigation systems) is bedevilled by the differences between the endowments of the different villages both at any one time and over time. At any one time, in terms of pressure of population on resources, it is difficult to compare one acre of dry land with one acre of wet land, or one acre irrigated by a pump-set with one acre irrigated with a kavalai; to compare the reliability of one tank with another; or to compare the soils and other cultural conditions between villages. Over time, changes in the technology and scale of exploitation introduce a complication. Water is land-augmenting. As more wells are dug, so more labour is employed in cultivation and very likely for more of the year. As the rather modest water extractions of the kavalai are replaced by those of the pump-set, so larger acreages are irrigated: labour is released from kavalai but is demanded for the increased acreage now cultivated. Again, as water extractions become heavy in some villages (notably Randam and Vayalur, where this problem has become serious) so the water-table drops and smaller acreages may be cultivated. This is far from being a complete catalogue of problems, but it should be enough to show that what is required is either inspired and informed guesswork about population pressure on resources, or careful and detailed calculations which are at present beyond our means.

The very rough order-of-magnitude solution which we have adopted is to take the proportion of population to acres reported cropped. These are purportedly the gross acreages for the whole year of three seasons. For eleven of the villages we have ratios for a year in the 1910s, and also for a recent year (Table 20.2).

Fitting together population changes, resources and their exploitation, we can postulate the following patterns of change and village types:

(i) Population growth supported through extending the exploitation of resources: Duli, Meppathurai and Kalpattu.

Duli's population has grown steadily. There has been little scope for well-digging because of a 20 ft impervious layer of kaolin which underlies the village area. The acreage cultivated has apparently depended upon careful husbanding of tank water, progressive raising of the tank bund, and more extensive cultivation of the dry land of the village into which there has been room to expand.

Meppathurai has also had a frontier of dry land on to which to expand. The number of wells used for irrigation increased from 65 in 1919 to 148 in 1974, but a substantial proportion of these are owned by people outside the

Table 20.2 Population, cropped areas and wells

Village	Resettlement				1971 population	Mean acres cropped 1970–1 and 1971–2	Population: cropped acreage	Wells used for irrigation at time of resettlement	Wells used for irrigation 1974	Number of pump-sets 1974
	Year	Population	Gross cropped acreage*	Population: cropped acreage						
Vegamangalam	1913–14	610	501(132)	1·2	1,028	775	1·3	n.a.	45	38
Sirungathur	1913–14	323	495(31)	0·7	980	645	1·5	60	130	51
Duli	1913–14	128	205(10)	0·6	450	473(1971–2)	1·0	nil	12	9
Dusi	1913–14	1331	1,242(590)	1·1	2,398	1,315·5	1·8	3	26	23
Vengodu	1915–16	1000	850(91)	1·2	1,061	950·5	1·1	74	80	39
Vinayagapuram	1915–16	534	846(251)	0·6	784	604(1971–2)	1·3	112	124	26
Amudur	1915–16	885	462(119)	1·9	934	360(1971–2)	2·6	72	90	56
Randam		n.a.	n.a.	n.a.	1,446			n.a.	73	63
Kalpattu	1914–15	881	742(186)	1·2	1,942	915·5	2·1	73	173	116
Veerasambanur	1914–15	356	513(139)	0·7	540	551·5	1·0	n.a.	89	38
Meppathurai	1919–20	446	528(93)	0·8	804	1,233·5	0·7	65	148	57
Vayalur	1919–20	411	312(80)	1·3	634	394	1·6	35	85	34

* Figures in parentheses are double-cropped acreages.

village. (Meppathurai's statistics are complicated more than usually by definitional problems.)

Kalpattu has no tank and relies entirely on wells. Population growth has been sustained through the extension of wells into new areas, the total used for irrigation rising from 73 in 1914 to 173 in 1974. The rapid adoption of pump-sets in the 1960s quickly increased the intensity of cultivation.

(ii)   Village saturated, with a population stabilised through death and emigration: Amudur and Vengodu.

From 1911 to 1971 the populations of Amudur and Vengodu grew by only 14 and 12 per cent respectively. From 1915 to 1974 the number of wells used for irrigation rose only by 25 and 8 per cent respectively. Our interpretation is that these two villages had by 1911 reached a saturated condition which could only be sustained by high death rates and emigration, and that no subsequent development of resources has been able to accommodate a substantial additional population, with the exception of the 1960s in Amudur when the electrification of pump-sets may have helped to generate additional employment.

(iii)   Village saturated agriculturally and holding population with outside or other employment: Dusi, Sirungathur.

Dusi has two economies: irrigated agriculture which is dependent on labour from neighbouring colonies outside the village, and outworker industries for Kanchipuram (silk weaving and beedi (cigar) making). Sirungathur has a large scheduled caste population, many of whom seek work outside the village. It has something of the character of a labour dormitory.

(iv)   Village holding part of its population increase through greater labour-intensity: Vinayagapuram, Vegamangalam.

In Vinayagapuram the number of wells used for irrigation has only increased from 112 in 1915 to 124 in 1974 and the percentage of pump-sets to wells is low, only 20 per cent of wells having pump-sets (the lowest of all villages). The ratio of population to cropped acre has increased from 0·6 persons per acre in 1915 to 1·3 in 1974 (the largest proportionate increase of any village except Sirungathur). There appears to have been a high degree of sub-division and fragmentation which partly accounts for the very high proportion of cultivator to non-cultivator households (88 per cent cultivators). The village appears to be locked in with labour-intensive technology and an irrigation system which permits two reliable crops per annum but which offers low returns to capital-intensive innovation in the form of pump-sets. Innovation rather takes the form of new cultivation practices such as the adoption of HYVs.

Vegamangalam reached a high degree of occupational differentiation in the nineteenth century. Increasing population pressure has been associated with shifts from broadcasting to transplanting, and the colonisation of dry land with wells has expanded the cropped acreage, and so population, more or less evenly during the past half century.

We have discussed here only some of the clearer cases. In practice, as with many typologies, one finds intermediate cases, and the various influences (population pressure, cultivating new land, putting down new wells, emigration, providing a labour pool for outside employment, increased labour-intensity of operations) which are postulated as dominant in one case are nevertheless quite likely to be operating, if less evidently, in another. However, the concept of saturation for any given level of exploitation and technology does seem useful, and to have practical as well as analytical implications.

THE NATURE OF THE PRODUCTION PROCESS

Examination of the population and resource data, however, still leaves puzzles. Why is it, for example, that Kalpattu's population grew by 30 per cent between 1961 and 1971, giving it now a ratio of population to cropped land of more than 2 persons per acre? Why is it that the scheduled caste population of some villages diminished during the period, while that of caste people rose? Why is it that Vinayagapuram has succeeded in holding more of its (presumed) population increase than, say Vengodu, but without increasing its cropped acreage?

The answers to such conundra can be to a large degree supplied by an examination of the production process. This can be seen as a continuum from, at one pole, quasi-industrial continuous production, and, at the other, highly seasonal production. Regarded from this point of view we can at once separate out the villages as follows:

Quasi-industrial (fairly continuous irrigation and labour demand throughout the year)	Kalpattu	very reliable wells
	Dusi	major irrigation, two crops a year
	Vegamangalam	perennial irrigation from spring
	Vinayagapuram	two crops a year from tank and river channel
	Randam	86 per cent of wells have pump-sets
Seasonal-cum-industrial	Amudur	combinations of small tanks, wells, and some pump-sets, with water supplies of varying reliability and depth
	Vengodu	
	Veerasambanur	
	Vayalur	
	Meppathurai	
	Sirungathur	
Seasonal	Duli	wells negligible – reliance on one crop a year from small tank

Considered together, the degree of population saturation and of 'industrial' or seasonal employment take us a long way in understanding factors like migration, wage rates, land values, and some social relationships. Kalpattu and Dusi stand alone as villages which may be regarded as 'industrial' and as perhaps having a non-seasonal labour deficit, or at least a continuous non-seasonal capacity to absorb and support additional population. Kalpattu's rush into pump-sets in the 1960s and its highly intensive and commercialised agriculture created a labour demand which forced wages up to urban levels (Rs4 a day) and induced in-migration of labour, some of which shows up in the increase in scheduled caste population inter-censally (more than doubling from 1961 to 1971) and in the pronounced male/female imbalance (1·2:1). Kalpattu does have cultivation seasons but the demand for labour is continuous throughout most of the year. It cannot be surprising that Kalpattu's population rose by 30 per cent inter-censally. Dusi's population rise of 27 per cent over the same period cannot with any confidence be attributed to agriculture, but is probably associated with the outworker cottage industries for Kanchipuram and the growth of the informal sector in the large extra-urban village. From the point of view of supporting population, both these villages can be seen to have been successful in accommodating and supporting what was probably net immigration during the 1960s.

In contrast, the other three industrial villages appear to suffer from labour saturation. Their inter-censal population growth rates were 6 per cent for Vegamangalam, 1 per cent for Vinayagapuram and 7 per cent for Randam. There is some evidence that the widespread introduction of pump-sets in a village increases the total labour demand and spreads it more evenly over the year. In both Randam and Vegamangalam, where electricity arrived early (in 1951 and 1955 respectively), this effect may have operated and been absorbed in the 1960s. More recent evidence suggests that it is after taking up the 'slack' created by pump-sets, that the scheduled castes decline in numbers most, being forced to emigrate from the new situation of saturation (see chapter 15 for Randam). The seasonal emigration of landless labourers is a well-known feature of North Arcot, but it is perhaps unexpected that a village like Randam was so saturated that migration would have been forced on them so shortly after cultivation had become much more 'industrial' (but see pp. 232–4 above).

In the seasonal-cum-industrial villages there is some evidence that, with the coming of pump-sets, there has been a temporary capacity to hold more of the rising population. A very rough indication can be found in Table 20.3. It is precisely the three villages that were last to receive electricity which had the lowest population increases intercensally, and there is some evidence from the project survey that Veerasambanur's capacity to retain its population has increased since the rapid installation of pump-sets there.

The typology which emerges if we combine production process and

Table 20.3 Year of installation of electricity; with population growth and percentage of wells electrified

Year of installation of electricity	Village	Percentage inter-censal population growth 1961–71	Percentage of irrigation wells with electric pump-sets (1974)
1951	Randam	7	86
1955	Vegamangalam	6	84
1958	Amudur	11	60
1960–61	Vayalur	(19)	38
1961	Meppathurai	6	36
1962	Kalpattu	30	60
1965	Sirungathur	(11)	39
1966	Vinayagapuram	1	20
1968–9	Vengodu	−1	(45)
1971	Veerasambanur	−1	43

Duli and Dusi are not included since pump-sets are insignificant for them; parentheses indicate especially doubtful figures.

population pressure as the principles of classification can be summarised as follows:

Industrial (not saturated)   Kalpattu, perhaps Dusi
Industrial (saturated)   Randam, Vegamangalam, Vinayagapuram
Seasonal-cum-industrial   Amudur, Meppathurai, Sirungathur, Vayalur, Veerasambanur, Vengodu
Seasonal   Duli

The classification 'saturated/not saturated' is difficult to apply to seasonal-cum-industrial and to seasonal villages, though we can be fairly sure that Vengodu is saturated.

We must now determine whether this analysis helps us in understanding other aspects of variation between villages – whether indeed these classificatory principles are dynamic factors in village-level development.

THE POPULATION – PRODUCTION PROCESS DYNAMIC IN RELATION TO CULTIVATION PRACTICES

Reference to the statistics on the percentage of cultivators who have adopted HYVs, the percentage of paddy acreage occupied by HYVs, and average yields, as in chapter 8, confirms that the 'industrial' villages show evidence of more intensive cultivation practices. The highest rates of adoption of the new varieties and the highest yields are in Vegamangalam, Randam and Vinayagapuram. They are also quite high in Kalpattu, even though paddy cultivation is a subsidiary and largely subsistence activity there, because of the importance of commercial banana and turmeric cultivation. The pattern is somewhat disturbed by the evidence of rather low rates of adoption and of low yields in Dusi, especially when compared with the high yields (though low rates of adoption) obtaining in Sirungathur, and the high rates of adoption (though low yields) obtaining in Vayalur. Individual factors enter into the explanation of such divergent trends, but they do not detract from the utility of our production process approach in accounting for the overall picture.

LABOUR RELATIONS AND RURAL LIVELIHOODS IN RELATION TO PRODUCTION PROCESS

There is some correspondence between production process and population density, and the proportion of landless households – as we might expect from our general argument on the production process continuum. Thus:

Quasi-industrial	Dusi Kalpattu Randam Vegamangalam Vinayagapuram	on average 37 per cent of households landless; 43 per cent if Vinayagapuram (involuted) excluded
Villages in which there has been room for expansion	Duli Meppathurai	on average 28 per cent of households landless
Seasonal production process (with recent pump-set based expansion)	Vayalur Amudur Veerasambanur ?Sirungathur	on average 32 per cent of households landless

(for basic data see Table 20.4)

High wage rates in particular, and the employment of attached labourers to a lesser extent, show a positive relationship with continuous production process, rather than with indications of the inequality of land holding which it seemed might be another important correlate (see below). The 'quasi-industrial' group includes the four villages with the highest wage rates (Tables 20.4 and 20.5), with Vinayagapuram appearing as a 'rogue' with rather low rates probably because of its 'involuted' character of sub-division and fragmentation.

Other factors, outside the population – production process dynamic may however exercise an important influence upon labour relations. Attitudes to employment as attached labour vary among landless labourers (pp. 235–42), but the numbers of attached labourers in a village depends in part upon the need of the landless labourers for the security that

Table 20.4 The distribution of land ownership and labour relations

Inequality of land holding (1)	Village	Percentage of households landless (2)	Percentage of total land owned by the top 10 per cent of households (3)	Man cropped land ratio in 1971 in rank order 1 = high 12 = low (4)	Scheduled castes as percentage of population (5)	Samba wage rates ranked 1 = high 10 = low (cf. Table 22.5) (6)	Meals given to labourers (7)	Whether many employed as attached labourers
high ↓	Randam	48	60	n.d.	30	4	Yes	Yes, padials not kuttalis
	Vayalur	34	52	4	19	6	Limited	Limited – not liked
	Sirungathur	37	50	5	64	7	Limited	Insufficient opportunities
	Vengodu	45	45	8	18	10	Limited	Few
	Amudur	24	50	1	35	9	Yes	Only young men
	Kalpattu	40	38	2	8	1	Yes	Increasing numbers
	Meppathurai	27	40	11	32	5	Yes	None
	Veerasambanur	33	33	9	41	8	No	Yes, but insufficient opportunities
↓ low	Duli	28	35	9	17	11	Yes	None
	Vinayagapuram	16	40	6	18	12	Yes	Some kuttalis, not padials
Tenancy important	Dusi	48	n.c.	3	4	1	Yes	n.d.
	Vegamangalam	35	n.c.	6	52	3	No	Few – not liked by labourers

Sources: Columns 1, 2 and 3 – survey data, column 4 – Table 20.2, column 5 – 1971 Census, corrected, column 6 – survey investigators, column 7 – personal visits to villages and survey investigators.

Notes: n.c. = not calculated, n.d. = no data.

We have distinguished the two villages (Dusi and Vegamangalam) in which there are appreciable numbers of tenant cultivators, and then ranked the remainder in order of decreasing 'inequality' in the distribution of land amongst the members of the village communities, as this was shown up by the different shapes of Lorenz curves.

The shape of the curves is heavily influenced by the proportion of landless households, so we have also tried to take into account the degree of concentration of land ownership among those households which do hold some land. Some indication is given by the percentage of the total land owned by the members of each village which is held by the top 10 per cent of households.

attachment offers. However, our limited evidence suggests that what is most important is rather the need of cultivators for a permanently attached labour force. It is striking that the two villages in which attached employment seems to be most common – Kalpattu and Randam – are the two villages in which we found indications of labour shortages at different times of the year (cf. pp. 226–32). In Vegamangalam in particular, farmers told us that they would like to employ attached labourers but that the labourers, mostly Harijans, did not like to do such work. In Vegamangalam the scheduled castes are numerically dominant, and have substantial land holdings. Only 32 per cent of scheduled caste households are landless, in comparison with 35 per cent for the village as a whole; and only the few scheduled caste households of Duli, in what has been an expansion situation, own more land per head than the Harijans of Vegamangalam. The Panchayat President is a Harijan. It is hardly surprising therefore that the Harijans of Vegamangalam have been more assertive than elsewhere and do not as a rule like to work as attached labourers – much as the Vellala Mudaliars with their aversion to physical labour in cultivation would apparently like to employ more padials.

Something of the same trend applies also in Vayalur. There the 'Kshatriyas' said that until about 1940 hereditary ties existed between themselves and particular Harijan labourer families. They believed that these relations had broken down because large numbers of men from the Colony went into the army during the war, and the Harijans had subsequently become 'uppity', evidently valuing their independence more than the possible security of employment as attached labour. However, another consideration in the case of Vayalur is that more highly paid agricultural employment is available outside the village; while both there and in Vegamangalam reports of labour shortages appeared to have more to do with the rather tense relations between caste farmers and Harijan labourers than with any absolute shortage of numbers. Both villages appeared to have an odd pattern of labour relations, in which casual labourers very often came from outside, while inside labourers themselves went to work in outside villages: outside labourers who came in were fed as well as receiving payments, while locals were not. In three other villages – Vengodu, Sirungathur and Veerasambanur – we found little evidence of labour coming in from outside, and the limited provision of food to labourers appeared to be linked more directly to the existence of an absolute labour surplus. In all three, big farmers employ padials. In Sirungathur we encountered Harijan landless labourers who were pre-pared to work as padials, but for whom such work was not available.

Meppathurai and Duli stand out as villages in which there are no attached labourers, but in which meals are provided to labourers and in which wage rates are next on the scale to the most 'industrial' villages. These characteristics seem consistent with their 'expansionist' character. The demand for labour is evidently such as to keep the rather small proportion of landless households fairly well employed, and this fact and their land holdings mean that scheduled caste labourers are not prepared to work as attached labourers. Neither the Gownders of Duli nor the Yadhavas of Meppathurai are much interested in employing padials anyway. (Average size of land holdings of scheduled castes: in Duli, 2·8 acres (cf. 3·1 acres among caste households); Meppathurai, 1·4 acres (cf. 3·5 acres). Only Vegamangalam (1·7 acres) and Sirungathur (1·5 acres) compare. The high average for Sirungathur is probably misleading, and is due to the large dry-land holdings of a very small number of households.)

Amudur and Vinayagapuram seem to be somewhat alike in having low wage rates, low proportions of landless households, some attached labourers, and meals supplied to labourers. Both appeared to be villages in which there are never labour shortages, and in Vinayagapuram there are records of scheduled caste labourers going outside to work, for example in sugar-cane harvesting in the northern part of the District. The fact that meals are offered (though not always or necessarily in Vinayagapuram) seems to be more of a reflection of the fact that these two villages approximate most closely to the model of the 'village republic'. Labourers and cultivators appeared to be rather tightly bound together in spite of indications of tension. In Amudur, for example, the village leaders even talked of the need to 'look after' the Harijans, but part of this involved the maintenance of the dependent status of the Harijans; and one of the big Reddiars had quite deliberately set about colonising some waste land, at considerable expense, in order to ensure that it would not be given to the Colony. The leaders said openly that if the Harijans had pattas issued to them they would become too 'independent'.

In order to account – even speculatively – for observed variations in labour relations, a variety of considerations come into play. These include the distribution of land ownership, and factors of a more ideological nature which hinge around caste as well as population saturation and the nature of the production process. There are serious problems arising from the quality of the data and from the very small size of the sample. Wage rates, however, do appear to be rather closely related to variations in the continuity of production. We can summarise the relationships as follows:

Quasi-industrial

Dusi Kalpattu Randam	indications of labour shortages, high wage rates, both sides have an interest in semi-permanent labour relations
Vegamangalam	the pattern disturbed by strength of scheduled castes
Vinayagapuram	the same level of demand for labour not evident; more equal distribution of landholding associated with modest demand for labour

Seasonal 'expansion' villages

Duli   ⎫   modest wage rates, no padials, no continuous
Meppathurai ⎬   labour shortages
            ⎭

Seasonal production process villages

Sirungathur   ⎫   indications of labour surplus strong; low
Veerasambanur ⎬   wage rates, few meals, little opportunity for
Vengodu   ⎭   semi-permanent employment

Vayalur   this pattern complicated by the fact that
                    scheduled castes have some 'independence'
                    and because of availability of higher paid
                    employment outside

Amudur   indications of labour surplus and low wage
                    rates but pattern rather distinctive because of
                    particular caste relations

The most significant finding is that, with the exception of Vinayagapuram (probably because of its particular pattern of 'involution'), the
highest wage rates are to be found in the quasi-industrial villages –
Kalpattu, Dusi, Randam and Vegamangalam – which are also believed to
provide the steadiest employment demand throughout the year (Table
20.5). This important conclusion may be compared with Ester Boserup's
suggestion that systems with the most continuous agricultural production
are likely to be associated with high population densities, high proportions
of landless households (as we have found), but low wage rates (Boserup,
1965).

PRODUCTION PROCESS AND OWNERSHIP OF THE MEANS OF PRODUCTION

The evidence that we have reviewed suggests a series of relationships
between demographic trends on the one hand and, on the other,
migration, cultivation practices, agricultural wages and some important
aspects of labour relations, all of which appear to be substantially
explained by the population – production process dynamic. There are
many other ways of comparing villages, and the particular dimensions on
which we have concentrated inevitably reflect our own values, expressed in
concern for rural livelihoods. It is important also to consider another
relative dimension of inter-village variation – ownership of the means of
production.

It seems possible that differences in the type of ownership of the means of
production and the form of appropriation of economic surplus are rather
closely related to variations in population density and in the continuity of
production. This is indeed part of Boserup's argument (Boserup, 1965).
For example, does a village made up by a peasant proprietors with 'family

Table 20.5 Daily wage rates for paddy cultivation operations, Samba 1973–4 (in rupees)

Village	Ploughing	Manuring	Plucking	Transplanting	Weeding	Harvesting	Threshing	Total
Dusi	3·50	2·50–4·00	2·00?	1·0–1·75	1·50–1·75	4 mm. +0·50	4 mm. +0·50	19·5–22
Vegamangalam	3·00	3·00	3·00	1·0	1·0	4 mm.	4 mm.	19
Randam	1·50	2·30	2·30	1·30	1·30	3 mm.	6 mm.	17·7
Kalpattu	3·50	1·00	1·00	1·00	1·00	3·5 mm.	3·5 mm.	17
Vinayagapuram	2·00	1·50	1·70	0·70	0·70	2·1 mm.	2·3 mm.	11
Duli	2·00	2·00	1·30	1·50	1·50	3·5 mm.	1 mm.	12·8
Meppathurai	2·80	2·30	1·80	1·30	1·30	3 mm.	4·5 mm.	17
Sirungathur	2·50	1·00–2·00	2·00	1·00	1·00	4 mm.	4 mm.	15·5–16·5
Vengodu	2·00	1·00–2·00	1·00	1·50	1·50	3·5 mm.	3 mm.	13·5–14·5
Amudur	2·00	2·30	1·80	1·30	1·30	2·5 mm.	3·5 mm.	14·7
Veerasambanur	0·75	1·50	2·00	1·25	1·25	3 mm.	6 mm.	15·75
Vayalur	2·50	2·30	2·00	1·00	1·00	2·5 mm.	5 mm.	16·3

Notes:

1 It is difficult to present data relating to all seasons and crops, and to show the range of variation in rates of pay for each operation, in one table; this table shows the modal values for the Samba paddy season (except for Kalpattu, the most important single crop). This is the period of maximum activity in agriculture.

2 Where two values are given, the distribution is bimodal. The values shown were summed to give the rough scaling shown in Table 28.4; but Kalpattu was rated equal first with Dusi because of the high wages paid in banana and turmeric cultivation – more important there than paddy cultivation. With the exception of Vinayagapuram, a special case because of its 'involuted' pattern, the 'industrial' and seasonal villages are well distinguished.

3 mm. = Madras measure (= 108 cu. in.).

farm'-sized units rather equally distributed among them respond differently to technological development and show particular demographic
trends as compared to a village dominated by a few big landowners? It has
been suggested that the way in which the Harijans of Randam have lost
control of land helps to account for its distinctive pattern of demographic
development, in which the numbers of scheduled caste people have
decreased by 20 per cent during a period in which the caste population has
increased by nearly 25 per cent (see above, pp. 232–4). It is possible to
imagine a situation in which the accumulation of property into a few hands
is associated with mechanisation of agricultural operations and consequent
loss of work for landless labourers, leading to emigration and consequent
fall in the rate of increase of the labourer population. Equally it could be
that the distribution of property in 'family farm'-sized units means
relatively more intensive use of family labour and less employment for
landless labourers, with similar results (as may indeed be the case in
Vinayagapuram).

There is, however, very little difference between our villages in these
terms: they are all predominantly villages of small owner-cultivators.
There is no clear relationships between inequality of landholding and
either end of the production process continuum. In the 'quasi-industrial'
villages the average land holdings of the top 10 per cent of households is 46
per cent of the cultivated area, and in the 'seasonal production' villages, 47
per cent. In the villages in which there has been 'room for
expansion' – Duli and Meppathurai – it is only 38 per cent. Differences in
terms of the ownership of the principal means of production are, then, not
marked in our sample, so that we cannot pick out strongly marked patterns
of variation based upon them. In another region, or in another sample of
villages, variations in the mode of production might have considerable
explanatory potential, and either complement or cut across the approach
that we have suggested.

CONCLUSIONS

Whether we have here the germ of a theory of village variation and
development may be a question for debate. To take matters further, more
detailed and rigorous analysis is needed – of other village studies as well as
our own, particularly in view of the important caveat entered in the
previous paragraph. In the meantime we must ask what practical
implications arise from our approach.

First, whether a village or zone of villages will develop and generate a
capacity to support a larger population appears to be much less dependent
upon its location in relation to urban services than on the continuity of
production through the year, which is in turn closely related to water
supplies. The growth of Kalpattu, like that of Wangala (Epstein, 1973),
and the support for in-migration depended on an expansion of reliable
irrigation more than on remoteness or otherwise. In supporting this

additional population, even if at a low level, they have fulfilled a vital function both directly in terms of human welfare and indirectly in terms of relieving the pressure on other rural and urban areas when 'the urban poor and especially the recent migrants from rural areas are probably those in the worst nutritional situation' (FAO, 1974, p. 6). Another striking conclusion is that villages in which production is 'quasi-industrial' not only support additional population, but pay them higher wages – which might not have been expected.

An implication of these main findings is that the siting of services might be considered at least as much in terms of irrigation growth zones as in terms of existing population patterns.

Then it is worth enquiring whether there are substantial rural areas which are saturated and stagnant. The striking examples of Vengodu and Amudur, neither of which has grown much during the past sixty years either in population or in resource exploitation, drive home the point that even in a district like North Arcot there may be substantial rural pockets which exist at a low level of livelihood and which continuously export people to the remainder of the economy. If this is so, such areas – once identified – might be examined to see whether special interventions could arrest this dependence (the export of surplus people being a liability to the country as a whole) and improve their levels of living.

But, quite apart from the needs of such pockets, the problem of supporting population in all rural areas is bound to become increasingly acute in view of the population projections for the immediate future: in this perspective the achievement of continuity of production is an objective which should perhaps be given as much priority as the search for higher yields – to stimulate the growth of more Kalpattus to attract and support more people for more of the year. Deshmukh's study of the sources of migration into Delhi found that all the three districts with negligible migration provided the average male labourer with over 300 days work a year, as against 216 days a year for the districts with high emigration (1956, quoted in Lipton, 1964). There is much other evidence that rural emigration is related to seasonality of labour demands (see for example, Connell, 1973, pp. 21–2), and the essence of a quasi-industrial agriculture such as that of Kalpattu is that it should provide a steady year-round demand for labour. In some villages such as Duli this is out of the question for physical reasons. In others, through new wells and pump-sets, it has been, and continues to be approached little by little. But given that groundwater supplies in villages other than Kalpattu are likely generally to have slower rates of recharge, and with the alarming experience of water mining and exhaustion in Randam and Vayalur, the issue, rather, is whether methods can be found for using less water and for substituting labour for water. Water might then go further and its use might be spread more evenly throughout the year. Moreover, the continuous labour shortage that rural India so badly needs might be created, and higher wages and better living follow in its wake.

These conclusions may not be startlingly novel, and an Indian administrator might with some justice object that they reinforce what is already being done and has been done for a long time. But the pump-set revolution in North Arcot District which has helped to buy time for a few years is running into diminishing returns. The great question now is whether other innovations can be introduced to buy more time and whether the experience of the village past can be used to help create a better future in spite of, or with the help of, the continuously growing population. A North Arcot District with a quasi-industrial agriculture, with a continuous demand for labour throughout most of the year, is a target worth bringing into closer focus.

REFERENCES

Adelman, Irma and Dalton, George (1971). 'A Factor Analysis of Modernisation in Village India' in Dalton, 1971.

Boserup, Ester (1965). *The Conditions of Agricultural Growth*, London, Allen and Unwin.

Connell, J. (1973). *Migration and the Rural Job Situation: The Evidence from Village Studies*, IDS Discussion Paper no. 26, University of Sussex, Institute of Development Studies.

Dalton, George (1971). *Economic Development and Social Change: The Modernisation of Village Communities*, New York, Natural History Press.

Deshmukh, M. B. (1956). 'A Study of Floating Migration' in *The Social Implications of Industrialisation and Urbanisation: Five Studies*, Calcutta, UNESCO; quoted in Lipton, 1964, 142.

Epstein, Scarlett (1973). *South India: Yesterday, Today and Tomorrow, Mysore Villages revisited*, London, Macmillan.

FAO (1974). 'Population, Food Supply and Agricultural Development', *Monthly Bull. of Agric. Econ. and Stats.*, 23, 9.

Lipton, M. (1964). 'Population, Land and Decreasing Returns to Agricultural Labour', *Bull. Oxford Univ. Inst. Econ. and Stats.*, 26, 2.

Lipton, M. and Moore, M. (1972) *The Methodology of Village Studies in Less Developed Countries*, IDS Discussion Paper no. 10, University of Sussex, Institute of Development Studies.

21 Hydrological Consequences of Agrarian Change

C. M. Madduma Bandara

The availability of water for irrigation has long been a severe constraint on the development of agriculture in the dry areas of South Asia. This is especially true for the dry, non-deltaic rice-growing areas of Tamil Nadu and Sri Lanka. As in many other areas of India the extraction of groundwater has played a prominent part in bringing the Green Revolution to the North Arcot District (see above, pp. 117–18 and 124–7), so that demands on groundwater resources represent an important effect of recent agrarian changes. In most research on the Green Revolution attention has been focused only on economic and social repercussions. Our project made an attempt also to assess some of the important hydrological consequences of recent developments: consequences which in turn have implications for the present and future potential for rice cultivation in North Arcot.

HISTORICAL BACKGROUND

Surface water has been used for irrigation in the North Arcot District since an early period of South Indian history. As in the dry zone of neighbouring Sri Lanka, strings of ancient irrigation tanks and anicuts bear ample testimony to this fact. But the large-scale use of sub-surface water appears to have become popular only during recent times, though there are references to ancient water-lifting equipment in early Tamilian literature. Increasing demands on irrigation water, due to increasing population pressure on land, must have compelled the ryots to turn towards sub-surface water. The exploitation of surface water probably reached a maximum during the British period with the construction of a large number of anicuts, irrigation channels and tanks (often upstream from older tanks so that these were increasingly robbed of water). Further, the clearing of the natural vegetative cover due to the increasing pressure of people and animals on land must have led to a gradual dwindling of available surface-water resources and to attendant hydrological consequences such as the silting of river beds. It is not unrealistic to speculate that a situation comparable to that of the present dry zone of Sri Lanka existed in North Arcot two to three centuries ago, although there are significant hydrometeorological differences between the two areas (see pp. 9–12).

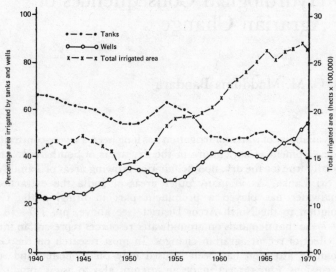

FIG. 21.1 *The expansion of the irrigated area in North Arcot*

The recent history of irrigation in the North Arcot District is well documented in the *Season and Crop Reports* of Madras and Tamil Nadu, although these are not totally dependable. According to these Reports, at the turn of the century the area irrigated by wells stood second to that irrigated by tanks. In 1905 the area under 'well irrigation' was 69,420 acres (28,090 hectares) which was about 20 per cent of all irrigated lands. The acreage irrigated by wells gradually rose while the acreage irrigated by tanks remained relatively static and the acreage irrigated by other sources rapidly declined. Thus by 1950 the area under the command of wells was 117,570 acres (47,530 hectares) and comprised about 30 per cent of total irrigated lands. By 1960 this rose to 186,190 acres (75,350 hectares) and accounted for nearly 50 per cent of lands irrigated by all sources. By 1971–2, well irrigation accounted for about 62 per cent of total net acreage of all irrigated lands (see Fig. 21.1). The area irrigated by wells has thus more than doubled within a period of twelve years. The crossing of 'well' and 'tank' curves around 1967–8 may indicate the demand on additional water resources directly or indirectly created by innovations associated with the Green Revolution (cf. above, pp. 182–203). The 'well rush' during this period was accentuated by the low rainfall conditions prevailing in 1968.

As the Reports indicate, there were more than 50,000 supplementary irrigation wells in North Arcot by 1905. By 1950 this had increased to 150,954. In 1971 there were some 229,394 wells (both masonry and non-masonry) in North Arcot. Thus the fastest growth was within the period 1950–1971, when more than 75,000 new wells were opened. The marked upward turn of the curve around 1967 in Fig. 21.2, further supports the contention that the 'well rush' was a concomitant of the Green Revolution. The current distribution of irrigation wells in North Arcot gives an average District density of more than 50 wells per square mile (20 per km²). In Randam the density of irrigation wells below the eri (tank) is around 200 per square mile (80 per km²) and about 145 per square mile (55 per km²) above the eri.

One of the formidable problems in utilising sub-surface water for

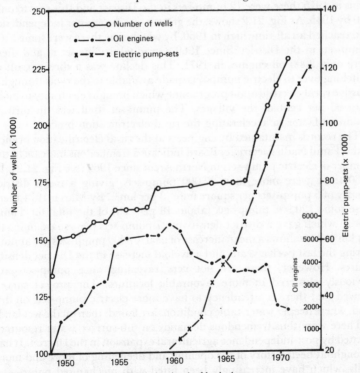

FIG. 21.2 *The development of lift irrigation in North Arcot*
    Sources: Season and Crop Reports *and Rural Electrification Branch of Tamil Nadu Electricity Board*

irrigation during the early periods was the lack of an efficient lifting mechanism. The ryots started lifting water with the aid of draught power which was the most accessible source of power then available to them. This marked the beginning of the use of the kavalai for lift irrigation. Although the kavalai is a highly inefficient method compared with the electric pump-set (cf. pp. 182–3), it had its own advantages. The equipment needed was simple, inexpensive and locally available. Moreover, during the critical periods of water shortage for crops, it was possible to use draught power and farm labour which otherwise remained relatively underutilised. The rate of lifting water was also not capable of creating any appreciable lowering of the water-table, given the number of wells then in use.

The gradual increase in the popularity of lift irrigation was mostly due to the increasing availability of mechanical pump-sets. First came the oil engines, then the electric pump-sets (cf. chapter 13). Although oil engines began to replace kavalais about the time of the First World War, up to the time of independence (1947) the growth in their numbers was very slow. Thus in 1915 there were 12 pump-sets in the District and this rose to only 150 by 1945. As Fig. 21.2 shows, the growth was faster after independence and reached an all-time high in 1960, by which time there were some 5500 pump-sets in the District. Since 1960 a gradual decline set in and there were only 2000 oil engines in 1971. This decline was a direct result of switching over to electric pump-sets made available to the ryots through a massive rural electrification programme which brought electricity to more than 90 per cent of the villages. The pump-set itself was, in turn, a dominant factor in accelerating the rural electrification process.

The records maintained by engineers at the rural electrification branch of the Tamil Nadu Electricity Board indicate a tremendous increase in the number of electric pump-sets in North Arcot since 1960 (see Fig. 21.2). In 1960 there were more than 20,000 pump-sets, giving a mean district density of 5 pump-sets per square mile (2 per km²). By March 1974 there were some 120,998 pump-sets (about 18 per cent of the total for Tamil Nadu) which gave a district density of 27 pump-sets per square mile (10 per km²). This shows a mean increase of nearly 8000 pump-sets per annum during the last twelve years, and a fivefold increase in the District density figures. However, these are not very revealing since pump-sets are obviously clustered in more favourable localities. The project survey showed that there is a tendency to have more electric pump-sets on dry land, where deeper water-table conditions are found, than on the wet land.

There were thus tremendous demands on sub-surface water resources created by post-independence agricultural expansion in the District. It has throughout been a story of the opening and deepening of more and more wells, which have increasingly been fitted with mechanised pump-sets. Thus, rapid changes in groundwater exploitation have taken place since Farmer (1956) wrote on this theme two decades ago. It is surprising that few systematic attempts appear to have been made, to study the hydrological and other ecological consequences of this massive lift irrigation process. For example, out of some 73 papers presented at the international symposium on the development of groundwater resources held in Madras in November 1973, only two presented a case for such studies (Burdon, 1973; Jagannadha Sarma and Subarao, 1973), though there were passing references to this subject in several others.

The main reason appears to be an inadequate official awareness and appreciation of the magnitude of the problems that are likely to be created by extracting sub-surface water on such a large scale. This, however, is understandable, since the study of a problem of this nature essentially requires an inter-disciplinary approach by which researchers from different branches of science such as climatology, hydrology, geology, geomorphology, groundwater engineering, water management and agriculture converge and co-ordinate their work. In highly compartmentalised government departments such co-operation is not always forthcoming.

In the following study an attempt is made to obtain an integrated understanding of some of the hydrological consequences of large-scale groundwater exploitation. However, the inadequacy of available data prevents the study from being as comprehensive as the author would wish.

THE GENERAL SETTING

Hydrometeorological conditions in North Arcot District have been outlined in chapter 2. Accordingly it is only necessary here to emphasise certain points, and to add detail where essential.

1 Geologically, almost the entire District is underlain by hard crystalline rocks, the exception being a small area in the north-east where small outcrops of sedimentary deposits are found. The crystalline rocks are poor aquifers, being by nature non-porous and virtually impervious: the occurrence of water in these rocks is determined by the existence of joints and fractures. However, these rocks are generally found under a thick overburden of weathered and alluviated material which permits the circulation of sub-surface water. A seasonally fluctuating water-table sensitive to recharge from rainfall and irrigation characterises the whole area and is tapped by shallow irrigation wells.

2 The river Palar and its tributaries (including the Cheyyar) drain almost the whole of North Arcot. All these streams are seasonal and carry water only during the three or four wet months from September to December. During the rest of the year their beds remain vast sandy stretches. In spite of their low-yield characteristics, most of these streams are fully used for irrigation. For example, there are seven anicuts across the Cheyyar, and a further anicut under construction.

3 In 1972 there were some 3189 tanks in North Arcot, giving an average

density of one tank for every 1·4 square miles (1 tank for every 2 km²). Most of these tanks are of 3–6 month capacity. Only a very few tanks such as Mamandur and Kauveripak have capacities exceeding 12 months. Thus the usefulness of the small tanks is necessarily dependent on the vagaries of the monsoons.

4 Climatically, North Arcot District is characterised by high temperatures and a marked seasonal rhythm of rainfall. The mean annual rainfall is about 850–1000 mm, of which nearly 60 per cent falls during the three or four wet months of the north-east monsoon.

5 Nearly the whole of the study area is devoid of a natural vegetation cover. This is the outcome of long and continuous human occupance and the increasing pressure of population on land.

NATURE OF AVAILABLE DATA

The hydrological data used in this study were collected from various governmental agencies during two field visits to Tamil Nadu in 1973. These included the following sets of statistical data:

1 Monthly rainfall data for 12 stations for the period 1921–74, obtained from the Department of Census and Statistics, the Groundwater Directorate of Madras and from various taluk offices.

2 Streamflow records for the river Cheyyar for the period 1950–72, obtained from the PWD office at Uthiramerur, the Thandarai project office at Cheyyar and the PWD offices in Madras.

3 Monthly groundwater level data for 36 observation wells in North Arcot for the period July 1971 to May 1974, obtained from the Groundwater Directorate, Madras.

4 Data on the history of irrigation in North Arcot, such as the number of wells, tanks and irrigated areas, extracted from the *Season and Crop Reports* of Madras and Tamil Nadu.

5 Data on electric pump-sets, extracted from the office records maintained by the rural electrification branch of the Tamil Nadu Electricity Board, Madras.

These data were supplemented by field investigations in the sample villages (see above, pp. 37–42); these included recording of water-levels in domestic wells and the analysis of water samples. Information on problems of water use were gathered from panel discussions with the ryots in sample villages. The official statistics – as is usual – contained gaps and, occasionally, dubious figures. However, in the absence of more reliable information, especially for time-series analysis for which long-term data are required, there was no alternative but to use them. Nevertheless, care was taken to examine their validity by cross-checking. Wherever there were gaps in the data or where the existing data were considered dubious and therefore rejected, estimates were interpolated using correlation

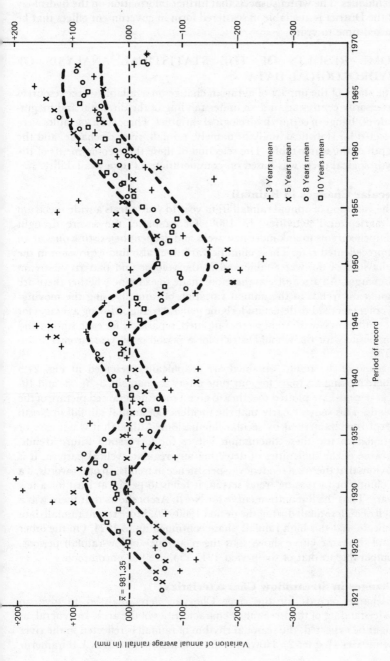

FIG. 21.3 *Rainfall fluctuations in North Arcot District*

techniques. The writer suspects that further information on the hydrology of the District is available in scattered form in government offices that he lacked time to visit.

SOME RESULTS OF THE STATISTICAL ANALYSIS OF HYDROLOGICAL DATA

The study of the impact of agrarian change on available water resources necessarily centres around an understanding of the direction and magnitude of change in certain hydrological variables. Three such variables were selected for statistical analysis: namely, rainfall, river discharge, and the depth of the water-table. The selection of these three components of the hydrological cycle was based on considerations of data availability.

Secular Changes in Rainfall

The variation of annual rainfall from year to year affects a wide spectrum of agricultural activities. In 1968, for example, the severe drought compelled ryots to sink more new wells and deepen the existing ones at an unprecedented rate. These climatic variations also find expression in the behaviour of the water-table and in the volume and pattern of stream discharges. An attempt was therefore made to examine whether there are significant trends in the annual variation of rainfall, using the moving-averages method to detect underlying general trends. Moving averages for 12 stations in North Arcot were computed, separately for each station and compositely for the whole District, for a period of 50 years from 1921 to 1970.

Some of the results obtained are graphically presented in Fig. 21.3 where moving averages for four time intervals (namely, 3-, 5-, 8- and 10-year periods) are plotted together to give a more generalised picture of the trends. This shows clearly that the incidence of annual rainfall in North Arcot is characterised by secular fluctuations. Although it is not easy or rational to use these fluctuation curves for forecasting future trends, because of the difficulties of detecting any regular cyclical pattern, it is obvious that there is a tendency to persistence in trends. In other words, if a declining or increasing trend sets in, it tends to persist at least for a few years. Thus the fluctuation curve for North Arcot shows that there was a spell of high rainfall during the period 1960–70. More recent rainfall data indicate that this high rainfall phase continued up to 1974. On the other hand the same curve shows that the recurrence of low-rainfall periods, comparable to that of the period 1945–55, are not uncommon.

Changes in Streamflow Characteristics

Discharge records for the river Cheyyar were analysed to give an understanding of the streamflow characteristics of the area. In general, as might be expected, the seasonal rhythm of rainfall is reflected in the river regime (see chapter 2). However, the flow measurements at Uthiramerur for the period 1958–70 suggest that despite the rainfall during May, June and July, it is only once in three or four years that the Cheyyar then carries some water (see Table 21.1). But there is generally some flow in the river in January, a dry month in most years. This is probably a reflection of the high infiltration rates during the rainy season and consequent outflow of groundwater into stream channels.

Table 21.1   *Number of years in which flow in river Cheyyar was observed to exceed a million cubic feet in given months (period of record 13 years, 1958–70)*

Month	Jan	Feb	Mar	Apr	May	June	July	Aug	Sept	Oct	Nov	Dec
No. of years	10	08	01	01	03	04	04	09	09	13	12	12

Data on streamflow do not cover sufficient years to permit a time-series analysis comparable to that made for rainfall. However, records of total annual yields for the river Cheyyar since 1950 were available at PWD offices. In order to examine secular trends in river flow, these data were analysed using 5-year moving averages. This reveals that the total annual yield of the river Cheyyar gradually increased during the period of record (see Fig. 21.4). Rainfall over the catchment for this period was then estimated using the Thiessen polygon method. A plot of these data shows that increased river flow is mainly due to an increase of rainfall during the same period. However, a much more important feature, which tends to be masked by the increase in rainfall, is the increasing gap between rainfall and discharge, particularly since 1963. This is brought out by the two curves and the corresponding regression lines in Fig. 21.4. The disparity has been more marked since 1966.

If this increasing gap between rainfall and stream discharge is non-random and real, it may indicate some instability in the hydrological system of the region. This may be explained mainly in two ways. First, this instability may result from an increased abstraction of water by farmers in the upper reaches of the river. However, the validity of such a hypothesis can be firmly established only by a comprehensive analysis of past water use data. Such data are hard to find, and likely to be non-existent in many areas. Secondly, the instability may be an indirect result of widespread exploitation of sub-surface water. Such a situation would occur if an increasing proportion of rainfall at the beginning of the rainy season goes to replenish a depleted water-table. It is also possible, indeed likely, that the observed gap between rainfall and streamflow is caused by the combined effect of both the above processes, which together reflect the impact of recent agricultural expansion.

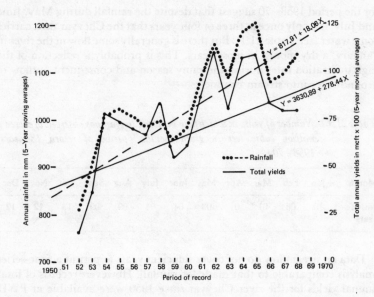

FIG. 21.4 *The changing relationship between rainfall and discharge of Cheyyar*

Fluctuations of the Water-table

An attempt was made to detect more directly any tendency to over-extraction, i.e. rates of extracting water greater than the rates of replenishment by recharge processes. In order to diagnose this tendency, records of water-table levels for at least a number of years are indispensable. In the North Arcot District such records have been maintained only since July 1971, and depend on measurements at monthly intervals from domestic wells. From these data, which cover only the short period of three years, it is no easy task to detect any secular trends in the behaviour of the water-table, unless the problem of overextraction has reached fairly serious proportions. With regard to recuperation rates and water quality, no data were available for an examination of any variations over the years.

In spite of these shortcomings an attempt is made to analyse the water-level records for 36 observation wells maintained by the Groundwater Directorate of Madras for the period July 1971 to May 1974. This analysis produced the following results (and see Table 21.2).

1 The average depth of the water-table in the District during the period of record is computed to be in the region of 6·38 m below surface. Table 21.2 shows that the mean water-table fluctuated between 4·85 m and 7·46 m in the first year of observation, between 3·86 m and 8·12 m in the second year and between 4·94 m and 8·35 m in the third year. Thus the

Table 21.2   Summary of statistics relating to monthly water-table depths (in metres below ground surface) of 36 observation wells

Year		Jan	Feb	Mar	Apr	May	June	July	Aug	Sept	Oct	Nov	Dec
1971	$\bar{x}$							6·97	6·34	6·09		5·37	4·85
	σ							2·98	2·89	2·90		2·80	3·26
	V							42·7	45·6	47·6		52·1	67·2
1972	$\bar{x}$	4·97	5·77	6·69	7·26	7·37	7·46	7·70	8·12	8·09	7·40	6·24	5·88
	σ	2·87	3·03	2·90	3·15	3·10	3·33	3·25	3·14	3·28	4·16	3·89	3·61
	V	57·7	52·5	43·3	43·4	42·1	44·6	42·2	38·7	40·5	56·2	62·3	61·4
1973	$\bar{x}$	3·86	4·42	5·10	5·94	6·70	6·93	7·42	7·38	7·40	5·91	4·94	5·39
	σ	3·20	2·97	3·09	3·03	3·04	3·19	3·26	3·32	3·27	3·47	3·36	3·15
	V	82·9	67·2	60·6	51·0	45·4	46·0	43·9	45·0	44·2	58·7	68·0	58·4
1974	$\bar{x}$	5·33	6·00	6·70	7·54	8·35							
	σ	3·14	3·09	3·07	3·14	3·15							
	V	58·9	51·5	45·8	41·6	37·7							

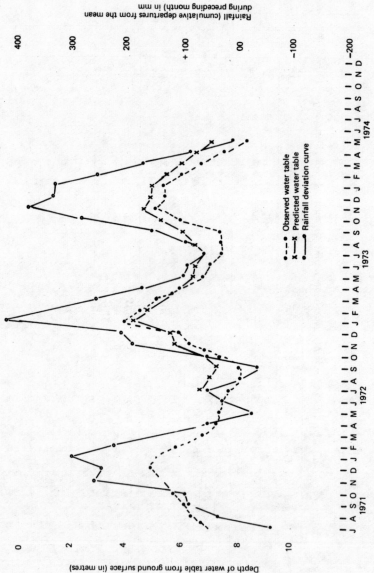

Fig. 21.5 *Seasonal regime of the water-table in North Arcot*

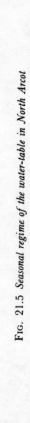

mean low water-levels continued to show a negative trend from 7·46 m to 8·35 m, indicating an average lowering of about 0·30 m per annum. However, the data for the months of lowest water-table conditions in 1974 (namely August and September) were not available at the time of writing, and it is likely that the annual rate of lowering will turn out to be greater than the figure quoted above. A similar conclusion was reached by Jagannadha Sarma and Subarao (1973, p. IIb, 37) who analysed the rainfall and recharge characteristics of the Chandrampalam basin in Andhra Pradesh.

2 The seasonal fluctuations of the water-table are shown in Fig. 21.5, along with the residual mass curve of monthly rainfall. This shows that the two curves follow each other closely, indicating the dependence of the water-table on the accumulated deviations of rainfall. However, the seasonal water-table curve alone is incapable of indicating any significant trends because random rainfall variations tend to mask them. A deeper analysis can be made in several ways. First, differences in water-table depth during comparable months in different years were analysed with the aid of the 't'-test. The results obtained are displayed in Table 21.3 where t-values for comparable months are given and significant t-values (at the 95 per cent level) are underlined. Out of the 32 monthly comparisons, there were seven significant t-values, and of these, six were negative – indicating a significant lowering of the water-table during the respective periods. The only positive value was obtained from the comparison of March 1972 water-levels with March 1973 water-levels. Apart from the high rainfall in December 1972, general power cuts around February and March 1973 which severely affected pumping operations may have given rise to this anomaly.

Table 21.3 Comparisons of mean water-levels for corresponding months in different years (t-values)

1971		July	Aug	Sept	Oct	Nov	Dec				
1972		−0·97	−2·26	−2·68		−1·06	−1·25				
1973		−0·59	−1·39	−1·77		0·57	−0·70				

1972	Jan	Feb	Mar	Apr	May	June	July	Aug	Sept	Oct	Nov	Dec
1973	1·52	1·88	2·21	1·78	0·90	0·68	0·36	0·95	0·87	1·62	1·48	0·60
1974	0·50	−0·30	−0·01	−0·37	−1·31							

1973	Jan	Feb	Mar	Apr	May
1974	−1·94	−2·17	−2·16	−2·17	−2·22

3   In order further to examine the changing relationships between
    rainfall and water-table depths another method has been adopted.
    During the first year of record (July 1971 to June 1972) the relationship
    between rainfall and the mean water-table depth was determined by
    simple regression analysis (see Fig. 21.6). Instead of using actual
    monthly rainfall and corresponding depths of the water-table, cumu-
    lative departures from the mean rainfall were plotted against the depth
    of water-table in the succeeding month, because the use of the latter
    parameter gave a better correlation. This yielded a regression equation
    of the form $Y = 7.00 - .0066\ X$. Similar equations for the two sub-
    sequent years give an indication of the changing relationships between
    rainfall and water-table depths in the District. This shows that in 1971
    an average rainfall (85.23 mm) brought the water-table to a depth of
    7.00 m from the surface, while in 1974 a similar rainfall could only
    bring the water-table to a depth of 8.10 m from the surface.

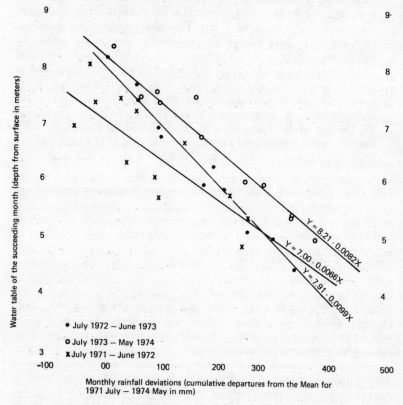

FIG. 21.6 *The changing relationship between seasonal rainfall and fluctuation of the water-
        table in North Arcot District*

The nature of the lowering in the water-table is further examined by extending this method. On the basis of the relationship that is found to have existed between rainfall and the depth of the water-table in 1971–2, water-table levels for the period July 1972 to May 1974 were predicted. The results obtained are graphically presented in Fig. 21.5 which shows the water-table curve that would have resulted if a relationship between rainfall and water-table depth similar to that which existed in 1971–2 prevailed during the subsequent period. It becomes clear from this diagram that the actual water-table remained lower than the predicted water-table from May 1973 to May 1974. This also shows that the discrepancy between the actual and predicted water-table depths has been greatest during the low water-table period from July to September.

Regional Distribution of Water-table Changes
In order to examine the regional patterns of water-table lowering, we considered the differences in water-table depth as between two periods during which significant lowering of the water-table took place. A study of the rate of lowering during September 1971 and September 1972, and during May 1973 and May 1974, revealed that the water-table lowering is high in the north-eastern and south-western sectors of the District. A reasonable explanation for this geographical pattern has yet to be found. However, it should be noted that the north-eastern sector is the driest area of the District, and it is likely that the difference between extraction of sub-surface water and recharge from rainfall is greater in that part of the District.

Summary of Results
On the basis of the foregoing analyses it is possible to diagnose that the hydro-ecological balance in North Arcot District is under strain, if not becoming rapidly upset. This is evidenced both by lowering water-table conditions, even within a period as short as three years, and by decreasing yields of natural streams in relation to the rainfall of the area. These results indicate such tendencies, in spite of several counterbalancing factors such as random rainfall events (as in December 1972) and occasional power cuts which tend to mitigate and mask the actual trends. It is argued that the overriding reason for these changes is the over-extraction of sub-surface water resources which in turn is a concomitant of the recent agrarian changes. Further, the analysis of rainfall fluctuations indicates that the above hydrological consequences have taken place during a phase of high rainfall. It is therefore possible that the hydrological conditions would be much worse if a phase of low rainfall comparable to that which existed during the period 1945–55 recurs in the future. In view of this situation, further expansion of lift irrigation may lead in the near future to unwelcome hydrological consequences such as lowering water-tables and dwindling of surface-water resources, unless suitable preventive measures

are introduced in time. If the present trend continues, extraction of sub-surface water may, before long, become a form of self-defeating 'agricultural mining'.

SOME PRESCRIPTIONS

As Burdon (1973, p. VI, 121) points out, the problem of over-extraction is essentially economic. In the long run a balance between available water and its use will somehow or other be reached. Meanwhile, however, a major investment in money, in effort and hope will have been lost. It is most important to recognise, in sufficient time, the existence and magnitude of the problem. Only such an awareness, not only among officials but also among farmers, will generate sufficient enthusiasm to take necessary corrective steps.

Planning to obtain maximum benefits without endangering future extraction is a complicated undertaking where competing interests have to be reconciled. In a country like India, where feeding the people is an urgent and continuing problem, over-extraction of water may be considered as a 'future-generation' problem and may thus be ignored, at least temporarily, by planners and statesmen. Further, if the preventive measures (including water management practices) are costly, this will be a further disincentive to the effective application of such measures, especially as returns for agriculture are traditionally less than those from industry.

It is clear, then, that there is a great need for careful appraisal of the available water resources in different areas, and for an organisation to keep constant vigil on water use in order to monitor any tendency to over-extract. If over-extraction is diagnosed, as in the present case, two lines of action – one negative, the other positive – are possible. The negative action should aim at discouraging the activities that lead to over-extraction. In this context, the investment policies of organisations such as the Agricultural Refinance Corporation and the Rural Electrification Corporation, in relation to yields and spacing requirements of wells, are undoubtedly far-sighted. Additional deterrents along similar lines leading to lower rates of extraction, especially during the low water-table periods, should be introduced by the State.

The positive line of action should aim at encouraging farmers to conserve and improve the management of water so as to maximise its utilisation for agricultural purposes. For example, the rate of night evaporation is significantly lower than that by day. This difference is more marked during the period from March to June and reaches nearly two and a half times in April and May. In view of this, it may be possible to induce seepage and save some water from evaporation by encouraging farmers to restrict pumping operations to the evenings. However, this has to be tried out before adopting it as a general policy. Further, the present practice of using tank water is wasteful and haphazard in many villages. There will be much scope for improving the management of water if a policy leading to a conjunctive use of water from rain, wells and tanks is efficiently pursued (Sabherwal and Potdar, 1973). As Warrier (1973, p. 291) emphatically points out, this requires an approach of 'totality' in planning regional development programmes.

Acknowledgements: The writer wishes to record his gratitude to the following for their kind co-operation: Thiru S. Panchanathan and his subordinates for making available the hydrological data collected by the Groundwater Directorate of Tamil Nadu; Mr G. A. P. Goonetilleke of the Faculty of Engineering, Peradeniya Campus, University of Sri Lanka, for computing assistance; Dr B. K. Basnayake of the Department of Geography, Peradeniya Campus for reading and commenting on some sections of the first draft of this chapter; Mr E. V. Christian for cartographical assistance; members of the survey team in Tamil Nadu – especially Thiru V. Rengarajan and Mrs B. Nanjamma Chinnappa – for their assistance in collecting data.

REFERENCES

Burdon, D. J. (1973). 'Challenge of Groundwater Development for Agriculture', *International Symposium on Development of Groundwater Resources*, Madras, 3, VI, 109–27.

Farmer, B. H. (1956). 'Land Use Lessons Learnt in Madras and Applicable to the Dry Zone of Ceylon', *Bull. Ceylon Geogr. Soc.*, 10, 9–19.

Jagannadha Sarma, V. V. and Subarao, C. (1973). 'Rainfall and Groundwater Recharge in Chandrampalam Basin', India, *International Symposium in Development of Groundwater Resources*, Madras, 1, IIb, 37–48.

Sabherwal, R. K. and Potdar, M. W. (1973). 'Planning for Conjunctive Use of Surface and Groundwater Resources', *International Symposium on Development of Groundwater Resources*, Madras, 3, VI, 97–107.

Season and Crop Reports of Madras and Tamil Nadu (1905–70).

Warrier, R. C. (1973). Comments on paper by L. E. Mack, *International Symposium on the Development of Groundwater Resources*, Madras, 4, 291.

22 Men and Water: the Organisation and Operation of Irrigation

Robert Chambers

To a remarkable degree, many writers on irrigation ignore and even appear unaware of the relationships between people and irrigation water. Attention is usually fixed on hydrological, engineering, agricultural and economic aspects. Especially in official documents it is rare to find described, let alone analysed, the human side of the organisation and operation of irrigation systems – the management of those who manage the water, the procedures for irrigation control, the processes of allocation of water to groups or individuals, the distribution of water within groups. There may be almost as many instances of these omissions as there are reports on irrigation.

Thus the report of the working group for the formulation of the Indian Fourth Five Year Plan proposals on soil and water management under irrigated conditions (ICAR, 1966) is entirely technically oriented, has no place for any social scientist on any research station, and proposes no research on organisational aspects of irrigation or on the management of the staff who manage the water. A report of an irrigation programme review in Sri Lanka (part of an IBRD/FAO co-operative programme: MPEA, 1968) is overwhelmingly oriented towards capital works and their planning and execution, and while recommending that there should be many more extension staff and stating the need for co-ordination at the field level, does not go into any detail about the procedures for achieving this. This was despite the terms of reference which included instructions to review and recommend institutional, organisational, managerial and technical measures to ensure successful execution *and operation* of existing and future projects (my italics). Nor were the operational and organisational aspects of water management and their economic and social implications a concern of an international seminar on economic and social aspects of agricultural development in irrigated areas, held in Berlin in

1967 (German Foundation for Developing Countries, 1967). Finally, a recent publication of the National Commission on Agriculture in India dealing with modernising irrigation systems and integrated development of commanded areas shows much the same blind spot: it embodies a top-down view of irrigation and omits operational detail (Government of India, 1973).

There are several reasons for this neglect (see also Chambers, 1975a, pp. 2–6): first, the common preoccupation with capital investment, construction and settlement processes at the cost of the vital operating processes which follow; second, cramped vision from within narrow disciplinary boundaries, including mutual ignorance between social scientists and technologists and a reluctance to explore a no-man's-land between disciplines; third, the intensity of research required to examine what happens at the lower levels of administration, and difficulties in generalising from one or a few cases, which are all that one researcher may hope to study; fourth, the maddening nature of water itself, with its tendency to flow, seep, evaporate, condense and transpire, and the problems it presents in measurement – problems which tie down natural and physical scientists to research–intensive tasks, denying them time, even if they had inclination, to branch out and examine wider aspects such as the people who manage the water and how they behave.

These tendencies have left several gaps in comparative knowledge. Where water is administered to communities, there is a gap geographically between the last point at which is officially controlled or measured and the point at which it enters a farmer's field. Organisationally there is a gap between what happens at the level of senior officials and what happens in the community which receives the water. Politically there is ignorance of the processes of decision-making and allocation which influence the timing and quantity of water which farmers receive. In terms of political economy there has been little analysis of who gets what, how, when and why, and with what costs and benefits. In terms of human management there is a widespread failure to perceive the problems and opportunities of managing those who manage the water, the men in organisations and communities.

This chapter uses the comparison of irrigation systems in the study areas in India and Sri Lanka as a basis for some preliminary steps among the minefields of inter-disciplinary no-man's-land which these gaps represent. Much of the evidence is used with misgiving, being based on one-off interviews on day visits to villages and cultivation committee areas (see pp. 51–2). For Sri Lanka, additional sources have been visits to, and studies of the records, of two major irrigation systems – Gal Oya and Uda Walawe. For India and elsewhere, some secondary sources have also been drawn upon. The purpose is to open up some comparative, analytical and practical aspects of the organisation, operation and political economy of irrigation.

A basic point is that water is usually a scarce resource for which men and groups of men compete and the benefits from which should be optimised in relation to other scarce resources. In the dry zone of Sri Lanka there is much evidence that water is more limiting than land (Chambers, 1975a, pp. 19 ff.), although scarcities of draught power and labour are also constraining (Harriss, 1976) and may at some times and places be more limiting than water. In parts of North Arcot the scarcity of water is even clearer and more acute. Surface irrigation water from tanks is often inadequate for a second crop and the groundwater level is undergoing a serious secular decline as numbers of wells grow, more pump-sets are installed, and groundwater extractions increase (Madduma Bandara, 1976 and pp. 324–7). As population presses more and more on the resources available for food production in these and other environments, so understanding the relations between people and water for irrigation becomes a more and more vital priority.

Table 22.1   Water source and storage categories

Cultivation committee	Minor/Major	Water source	Storage system
Kachchigala	minor	Small catchment run-off	Small tanks
Metigatwala	minor	Small catchment run-off (now supplemented by major irrigation)	Small tanks
Kataragama	minor	Small catchment run-off	Small tank
Tenagama	minor	Small catchment run-off and spills of higher tanks with small area sometimes supplemented by major irrigation	Small tanks in series, close together
Wellawaya	minor	Anicut and channel from permanent stream	Nil
Hanganwagura ⎫ Jansagama ⎬ Rotawala ⎭	major (WRB)	Anicut and long channel from Walawe river with perennial flow	Nil
Jayawickremayaya	major (KOLB)	Anicut and channel to tank from Kirindi river (water not always available)	Tank (Debarawewa)
Kachcherigama	major (KOLB)	Anicut and channel to tank from Kirindi river (water not always available)	Tank (Tissawewa)
Udasgama	major (KOLB)	Anicut and channel to tank from Kirindi river (water not always available)	Tank (Tissawewa)
Companniwatta	major (KORB)	Anicut and channel to tank from Kirindi river (water not always available)	Tank (Wirawila)

WRB=Walawe right bank, KOLB=Kirindi Oya left bank, KORB=Kirindi Oya right bank.

TYPOLOGIES OF IRRIGATION

A first step is to try to identify useful categories. The descriptive terms used by engineers and agriculturalists dominate discussion of irrigation systems. This is partly because they themselves have such key roles in irrigation, partly because their categories refer to physically observable phenomena such as structures, field layouts and methods of water application. These categories may not be the most useful ones for an analysis of the organisation and operation of irrigation. But classifying the irrigation systems encountered in Sri Lanka and India in terms of their more obvious physical characteristics does provide a starting point.

In the study area in Sri Lanka almost all irrigation is by surface gravity flow, most from storage tanks. Tank water is received from various combinations of catchment run-off and river diversion. Scarcely any wells are used for irrigation. The commonly used classification of gravity-flow irrigation into 'major' and 'minor' corresponds with differences in scale and organisation, not with differences in physical type of source, conveyance or storage of water. The management of water under major irrigation is the responsibility of the Territorial Civil Engineering Organisation (TCEO) which distributes it down to the field channel level. Water management on minor irrigation is the responsibility of village communities which organise their own distribution systems. Under a major irrigation project there are usually several cultivation committees, whereas under minor irrigation there is usually only one.

From the more obvious characteristics of scale and type of water source and storage, the cultivation committees in our sample can be classified as in Table 22.1. In all cases, distribution from the tank or from the main canal is by gravity through channels of diminishing size to farmers' fields. There is only one well and pump known under any of these systems (under Tissawewa tank) and that is not in one of the survey cultivation committee areas.

In the study area in India there is a greater variety and mixture of irrigation systems. The most common form of gravity irrigation consists of canals from anicuts from rivers which are dry for most of the year, and which supply chains of village tanks in series. In our sample, large tanks are represented only by Dusi, which is one of 18 villages served by the large Dusi–Mamandur tank. In addition, in all villages there are wells used for lift irrigation. Three forms of lift are used–etram (human power), kavalai (ox power) and pump-sets (oil, or much more commonly, electric power). These wells are usually found both on the dry land (land which is not under command for tank or channel irrigation) and on the wet land (under command for tank or channel irrigation). The villages in the sample can be classified as in Table 22.2.

The categories in the table follow the necessary but well-worn discipline-bound criteria of engineers and hydrologists. They are much concerned with the acquisition, transport and storage of water and less

Table 22.2   Village classification

Village	Non-well water source	Tank storage	Wells in wet land	Wells in dry land
Kalpattu	Nil	Nil	No wet land	Yes
Vegamangalam	Excavated springs near river, permanent flow	Nil	Nil	Yes
Dusi	Channels leading from large seasonal rivers	Large tank	Negligible	Few
Meppathurai, Vinayagapuram	Channel leading from seasonal large river direct to village tank	Village tank	Yes	Yes
Amudur, Duli, Randam, Sirungathur, Vayalur, Veerasambanur, Vengodu	Combinations of natural drainage lines and channels from seasonal rivers leading through chains of tanks to village tank	Village tank	Yes	Yes

Note: Some villages have additional small tanks which are fed by catchment run-off. All tanks receive some water from their catchments in addition to amounts received from the source named.

with its distribution. An engineer talks and thinks in terms of diversion channel, tank, dam, gravity, well, pump, major and minor irrigation, with type of structure and scale of operation as his main criteria. A hydrologist thinks and talks in terms of water cycles and sources of water – shallow or deep well, spring, surface run-off storage, and river diversion irrigation, for example. But other disciplines would classify irrigation systems quite differently: for an agriculturalist the field application of water is central and includes flood, border strip, check basin, furrow, underground, and sprinkler irrigation. In the social sciences the only large-scale attempt at comparative analysis of the organisation and operation of irrigation has apparently been Wittfogel's eccentric polemic on oriental despotism (1957), although a recent start in classification has been made by Thornton (1976). After considering the physical acquisition and transport of water, Thornton points out that it is with distribution that 'the largest number of organisational alternatives occur'. Distribution is also a potential focus for classification since it corresponds with much of the unexplored no-man's-land in irrigation.

Categories depend both on the subject-matter and on the orientation of the observer. Classifications of irrigation organisation can themselves be classified as top-down, bottom-up, or middle-outwards depending on the focus of concern and the stance of the typologist. Thornton's types derive from a top-down view, using formal organisation and the distribution of responsibilities within the organisation to separate out categories, with a major division into private and public organisations. A bottom-up view of irrigation, starting with the farmer and his preoccupations might differentiate between irrigation systems according to the cost, adequacy, convenience and reliability of the supply of irrigation water to the farm. A middle-outwards view of irrigation organisation would start geographically and organisationally in the middle of the distribution system. It might differentiate systems according to the decisions, communication and allocations which affect distribution, looking both upwards towards the source from which the water derives and downwards to the farmer. All three views – top-down, bottom-up and middle-outwards – deserve to be developed. Here we will start in the relatively unexplored middle ground and move outwards from there, paying particular attention to the organisation and operation of communities and bureaucracies in the distribution of water.

A central and universal issue in the distribution of irrigation water is who gets what, when and where. This is the very stuff of politics and it is surprising that political scientists, political anthropologists, and those who study political economy have not devoted more attention to it. Where water is scarce and often constraining and when individual farmers and communities of farmers compete for it, the focus is on the processes of allocation and acquisition which determine the access of users to water. These processes can be classified as:

Direct appropriation	The user acquires water directly from a natural source such as a private dam or well
Acquisition through contract	The user acquires water through agreement with a supplier in exchange for goods or services
Community allocation	A communal source of water is allocated among a community of users
Bureaucratic allocation	Water is allocated by bureaucratic organisation direct to individual users
Bureaucratic–communal allocation	Water is allocated by a bureaucratic organisation to one or more communities of users, each of which manages distribution to its members

These types are represented in the examples available as in Table 22.3. The categories adopted must be treated warily. They are designed for convenience without necessarily implying that they have great explanatory power. As with many other distinctions in the social sciences, the edges blur and overlap in practice. Thus Dusi is immediately a bad fit in bureaucratic–communal irrigation, since the size of the paddy tracts under the large Dusi–Mamandur tank would lead anyone familiar with irrigation in Sri Lanka to look for a bureaucracy which distributes the water; but in the strict sense of bureaucracy – an organisation with its own

Table 22.3   Water allocation

Type of allocation/ acquisition	Sri Lanka	India
Direct	Negligible	Very common (individual wells)
Contract	Negligible (except where tenancy carries water rights)	Negligible (except where tenancy carries water rights)
Community	All minor irrigation (Kataragama, Wellawaya, Tenagama, Metigat-wala, Kachchigala)	Amudur, Duli, Meppathurai, Randam, Sirungathur, Vayalur, Veerasambanur, Vegamangalam, Vengodu, Vinayagapuram.
Bureaucratic	Uda Walawe	Nil
Bureaucratic – communal	All major irrigation (Hangan-wagura, Jansagama, Rotawala, Jayawickremayaya, Kachcheri-gama, Udasgama, Compan-niwatta)	Dusi

norms, roles, terms of service, and so on – there is none. The PWD only controls issues from the tank sluices, leaving the rest to the traditional officers of the villages. Again, Amudur, though having a community system of allocation and acquisition, has something verging on its own 'bureaucracy' in the form of three Harijan thoddis who distribute the water to individual farmers. These two examples are cited not to undermine the classification, but to discourage any tendency to think that words refer to classes of entities which are more consistent and distinct than they really are.

Analysis will concentrate on those types of which there are numerous examples: direct acquisition, almost entirely through wells in India; community allocation, widely represented in both Sri Lanka and India; and bureaucratic–communal allocation, mainly in Sri Lanka. The focus will be further narrowed by concentrating on the levels at which decisions and actions affecting allocation and acquisition are taken; for these three irrigation types they are as shown in Table 22.4.

The main attention will be at the community and system levels. 'Community' here refers to users with an interest in a common source of supply, the water from which is distributed among themselves. This usually refers to what in Sri Lanka is called minor irrigation, to what in India is village tank irrigation, and in both countries to groups of users on larger irrigation projects who depend upon the same feeder. 'Systems' refers to whatever organisation or arrangement exists above the community level for the management and allocation of water.

Table 22.4   Levels of decisions actions

	Farmer level (within fields)	Community level (within community area)	System level (within irrigation system area)
Direct	Yes	No	No
Community	Yes	Yes	No
Bureaucratic – communal	Yes	Yes	Yes

The discussion which follows is in two sections: the first deals with the organisation and operation of community irrigation, examining allocation and appropriation of water, equity and productivity, enforcement and arbitration, and action by irrigation communities; the second deals with the organisation and operation of bureaucratic–communal irrigation.

COMMUNITY ORGANISATION AND OPERATION

The Allocation and Appropriation of Water

The allocation and appropriation of water can be described in terms of two stages: decisions about areas to be irrigated and about timing; and actual allocations and appropriations.

In the first stage a decision may have to be taken as to which areas under command to irrigate. Leach has described for Pul Eliya in Ceylon the nice decision which has to be taken with a village tank:

> The issue is a subtle problem of economic choice since, if the water resources of the irrigation system are over-extended, the outcome may be total crop failure. The village meeting makes its collective decision on the basis of the level of water in the tank and a gambling estimate of rain in the weeks to come. (Leach, 1961, p. 53)

This type of decision is not limited to village tanks. Wellawaya depends on diversion from a small perennial stream which is not always sufficient for all of its six blocks of asweddumised land: similar decisions have to be taken about which and how many of the blocks to cultivate in Yala. The only Indian village in the sample known to have a similar system is Duli where, when water is short, a decision is taken to allow the same fixed acreage to each holder of wet land and to supply water only for that. Under the other Indian villages with tanks there appears to be no formal decision about the acreage to be cultivated: the decision is left to individuals who must rely on their own judgement of the water likely to be available and their chances of obtaining enough of it, through whatever system of allocation and appropriation operates and subject to the physical layout of the irrigation system and of their fields. Where, as in Vegamangalam, there is a perennial supply of water adequate for more or less continuous cropping, the question of which land to irrigate or not to irrigate does not arise in the same form but depends on the timing and phasing of cultivation operations.

The second stage of decision is the allocation and appropriation of water within an irrigation community, affecting those areas which it has been decided to irrigate. There are at least four forms this can take:

1   A physical division of waterflows between channels. The karahankota described by Leach for Pul Eliya (1961, pp. 160–6) is an example. Water was divided by a wooden weir into which flat-bottomed grooves of various widths had been cut, the water allocations being the amounts of water which flowed through different grooves into different channels. The physical system (though not the proportional allocations) had fallen into disuse in Pul Eliya even in 1954 and no case of any similar system was found in our survey either in Sri Lanka or in India.

2   Rotational rationing on a roster basis. This is widespread throughout the world. The warabandi system in Haryana (Vander Velde, 1971, p. 132) and the waqt (sunrise to sunset or sunset to sunrise) system in Iraq (Fernea, 1970, pp. 124–5) are examples. In our survey we found that time had been estimated in various ways in the past including judging by the sun during the day and by the stars at night, measuring the lengthening shadow of a stick either in fingerbreadths or paces (Amudur), and taking the time a leaking pot took to empty (the murai palla system in Vengodu). These methods have, however, fallen into disuse and have been replaced by the wristwatch, sometimes in Sri Lanka combined with paper chits (tundu) as in Wellawaya and Companniwatta (where four-hour spells have been used in periods of scarcity). In several Indian villages in the sample there was a karai system in which a sequence of turns was taken by family groups, the duration of the turns being a matter of tradition. But given the dispersal of family lands and the complication of pump-sets, what happens in practice must be an open question. A principle often stated, however, was that the duration of water was related to the acreage owned or to the acreage actually cultivated in the season in question.

3   Allocation by restricted acreage. The rationing system at Duli is based on the principle that each cultivator should restrict his acreage to a fixed amount and then, in rotation, be supplied with the water needed. This has some similarities with the bethma system in some purāna villages in Sri Lanka (Farmer, 1957; Leach, 1961) in which, in a season when acreage had to be restricted, all holders of wet land were able to cultivate a portion of the irrigated field.

4   'Anarchy'. Water may be not so much allocated as appropriated, as described by John Harriss for part of Kirindi Oya right bank: 'I have found . . . the suggestion of a kind of anarchy in which in time of

scarcity water supplies depend upon the strength of a man's right arm' (1976, p. 16; see also pp. 370–5). The apparent disintegration of traditional allocation systems under Indian village tanks may also sometimes verge on this situation.

Equity and Productivity

These two sets of actions – deciding the location and timing of irrigation, and then the allocation and appropriation of water to those lands which are being cultivated – raise acute questions of equity. Rural inequity is often associated with differing sizes of land holdings. But this misleads when a man with a secure water supply is able to crop his land three times a year while a man who has to rely on only one irrigation takes but one crop. The physical position of fields relative to channels is critical. Those near the top of channels have an immense physical advantage of access which it can be very difficult for those further down to control. In the absence of countervailing custom, social sanction or physical force, the privileged top-enders satisfy their own needs first before allowing water to flow on down a channel to their less fortunate neighbours below. The tail-enders often receive less water, less reliably and in a less timely fashion than those near the top. There is a striking variation in the extent to which the communities studied in India and Sri Lanka moderate these inequities and in the methods they use.

In India the most common systems for distribution under tanks favour those at the top-end. In Meppathurai, Randam, Sirungathur, Vayalur and Veerasambanur top-enders are said to take water first. Moreover the karai system, and any other system of time-rationing, is liable to deliver less water to tail-enders because of seepage and evaporation losses *en route* (see Vander Velde, 1971, *passim*). However, informants from Vinayagapuram, Amudur and Vengodu all claimed to have systems which made special provision for tail-enders in time of water scarcity: in Vinayagapuram, the first issue was said to be from the top downwards with the second issue in reverse from the tail-end upwards back towards the top; in Amudur since about 1955 it was said that water had been issued to tail-enders first (this was part of a major reform in which the supervision of water allocation was also changed); and in Vengodu, where tail-enders had been suffering, a partially effective convention was said to discourage those with pump-sets in the wet land from using tank water so that it could be supplied to those less fortunate cultivators who did not have pump-sets. It is, however, Duli's system, allowing adequate water to equal plots of land which scores highest for equality. In Sri Lanka the systems also varied but information on them is incomplete. On major irrigation, however, the practices appeared to follow the principle of 'the devil take the hindmost'.

Questions of equity are linked with questions of productivity. With food production a major objective and water a critically scarce resource, measures which might be more equitable have to be weighed also in terms of productivity. The main issue is that the conveyance of water involves losses through percolation and evaporation. Duli scores highly for equity but the water losses in distributing water as in Navarai 1972 to small plots of 0·3 acres each scattered over the ayacut must have been substantial. Had it been possible to adopt an equivalent of the bethma system in which all cultivators participated but in which the water was applied to one block of land near the tank, then the productivity of water and the total output of the land should have been higher. Similarly the supply of water to tail-enders first is wasteful, not only in conveyance losses but also in the loss of opportunity to reuse drainage water and to raise the water-table: for when top-enders in an ayacut take water first, seepage in their fields may raise the water-table lower down and thereby reduce subsequent water duties there, and surface run-off into drains may be reused by cultivators nearer the tail-end, as at Kataragama and under Tissawewa in Sri Lanka.

The questions are complex and interlinked with the patterns of wealth and power in irrigation communities. Any government may hesitate to intervene in such a difficult policy area; but several of the Indian villages had themselves within living memory changed their water allocation systems, in one case at least (Amudur) in the direction of greater equity in distribution. The systems used are by no means a sacred part of the social fabric to be tampered with only at the risk of severe disruption. The evidence suggests that water distribution under tanks was usually both inequitable and inefficient in terms of productivity. A particular example is the tendency for those with water available from wells and pump-sets none the less to take tank water (since they do not have to pay for it), denying it to their less fortunate neighbours who may not have wells. The result may often be that a village cultivates a much smaller area than it could if the pump-set owners were to use only well water. Could those with pump-sets be persuaded or forced to forego tank water? The suggestion was greeted with laughter in Randam and Vayalur, but informants in Vengodu suggested that some such idea was at large there and might even be partially implemented. If, with the introduction of pump-sets in wet land and the progressive fragmentation and dispersal of family lands, the distribution systems under tanks in North Arcot are looser and less effective than in the past, this may be a time when an official initiative to increase both equity and productivity is feasible. Differential taxation to provide an incentive to pump-set owners in the wet land to abstain from using tank water might be considered.

Enforcement and Arbitration

An intriguing set of questions arises over infringements and disputes and their adjudication. There is a sharp contrast between Sri Lanka and India. John Harriss has described (pp. 366–70) the work of the Vel Vidanes who were appointed by government under the colonial regime in Sri Lanka, armed with authoritarian powers, and remunerated with a share of the crop; and the subsequent system of enforcement through the elected administrative secretaries (Govimandala Sewaka) of the cultivation committees, who received 40 per cent of an acreage tax. It seems to be widely accepted that the Vel Vidane system could be quick-acting and technically efficient, whereas the cultivation committee system has always been slow-acting and permissive. Cultivators canvassed in our survey gave responses which can be interpreted as preference for a system, whether Vel Vidane or other, which was authoritative, quick and effective (Chambers, 1976b, text and Appendix A). It would be easy, if no other system were known, to conclude from this that a more authoritative and more efficient system is needed at the irrigation community level; that a committee cannot perform this function; and that a man whose reward is unrelated to the value of the crop is unlikely to perform it well.

The contrast with the Indian villages is then striking. Under the South Indian tanks there is no equivalent of the Vel Vidane. There is no tradition of a government servant being concerned with allocations within the paddy tract under small tanks. The system is radically different. Whereas the Vel Vidane was usually an influential and prosperous local person, those responsible for the execution of water control in the South Indian villages are Harijans, the thoddis or neer thoddis. Their responsibilities vary considerably, as does their remuneration. In some villages they are responsible only for closing and opening the sluice. In Amudur, however, they have extensive responsibilities in executing the allocations in the paddy tract. One of the three Amudur thoddis said (1974) that he would never allow anyone else to move water and if they did there would be an ur panchayat meeting and the miscreant would be fined; but this had never happened. Evidently, if our informants were correct, rights and allocations in Amudur are clearly understood and the thoddis have clear guidelines to follow. One Amudur farmer went so far as to say that under the system practised before 1955 there were many disputes, but now he did not even bother to go to his fields when water was due as he had complete trust in the fair operation of the system by the thoddis.

The extent to which an arbitration role is demanded must depend on the extent to which there are infringements or, in the absence of clear rules, the extent to which there are acts which cause serious resentment. No doubt cultural differences and different developmental experiences profoundly influence attitudes towards different forms of arbitration. But appeals to outside authorities are common. On the basis of a comparison of fifteen irrigation systems in the Philippines, Ongkingco has written:

It is striking to note the satisfaction of farmers when somebody in authority, like a policeman or a major, attends to water distribution problems. Under these circumstances, farmers even seem to be satisfied with reduced water supplies. (Ongkingco, 1973, p. 242)

In Sri Lanka, one administrator has lamented the volume of cases and appeals presented to him over water matters, deflecting him from the main task of stimulating agricultural production (Weerakoon, 1973, p. 7). Performing these arbitration functions, whether the arbitrator is a government servant or a local person, is not easy. Administrative secretaries interviewed in Sri Lanka were generally unenthusiastic about their work, several of them complaining about the arduous duties involved. In the Philippines again, Ongkingco found one hereditary water master (whose duties were roughly similar to those of an administrative secretary) who wanted to relinquish his position because he got no benefit from it, but felt he could not do so because of community tradition (Ongkingco, 1973, p. 240).

One objective of government policy may be to improve equality and productivity while avoiding involvement in administrative costs. Once government intervenes, there is a danger of an endless series of cases and appeals, and of a need to provide more staff to deal with them. There is also a danger of inducing attitudes of dependence among communities. To secure a 'fair' distribution of water within irrigation communities may often be difficult (and in any case there are problems with the connotations and interpretations of 'fair'). But cultivators do appear generally to agree that they value quick action. And even where governments cannot institute 'fairer' distribution of water, there may be opportunities for them to enable crucial decisions and judgements to be made more promptly.

Action by Irrigation Communities

Governments benefit if they can rely on action by irrigation communities for the operation and maintenance of irrigation works. The survey villages are of interest because they present four cases in India where considerable communal labour is called for to maintain an irrigation system, one of which has collapsed; and one case in Sri Lanka of partial collapse.

The four cases in India all involve work required to acquire and transport a communal water supply. They are Dusi, Vegamangalam, Meppathurai and Vinayagapuram.

The Dusi case involved collaboration between the eighteen villages served by the Dusi–Mamandur tank. On 16 August 1971 the Dusi–Mamandur irrigation board, consisting of one representative of each of the villages, a secretary and a president, met to decide how to secure the flow in the channel from the anicut to the tank. This, they maintained, was the responsibility of the PWD, but as the PWD could not be relied on to act swiftly enough, the villages themselves had to take action. They decided that each village should send labour at the rate of one man to every 10 acres irrigated, in order to divert the Palar river into the channel. The work was apparently successful.

The Vegamangalam case is a continuing and customary activity. When the long channel bringing the spring water to the pangu lands of the village requires a cleaning-out, every family with a share provides labour at the rate of one man per anna of land (1·6 acres of wet plus 0·74 acres of dry). The system apparently works well.

The Meppathurai case is an example of a practice abandoned: of what it was there were several differing accounts. What was agreed is that the run-off flow into the Meppathurai tank had for many years been supplemented by a channel from the Cheyyar river. When the river flooded, villagers dug in the river and in the channel to divert water into the channel and along it to the tank. Much work was involved in removing silt from the channel. In about 1967 there was a heavy flood and the channel seriously silted up. According to some, the task of clearing was too great for the village and appeals for government assistance failed. Others state that there were political differences between the larger, older farmers (who were Congress supporters and stood to benefit more from clearing) and the smaller, younger farmers (who were DMK supporters and stood to benefit less). Yet another contributory factor may have been a high degree of absentee ownership of wet land. It is also possible that the larger farmers were not unduly concerned because they could anyway rely on their pump-sets in the wet land. But whatever the cause, Meppathurai failed either to obtain government assistance or to carry out the clearing itself. In 1974, some six years later, the situation was even less remediable; the two miles of channel were heavily overgrown with bush and the poorer people who used it as a source of firewood for sale were opposed to any clearing.

The Vinayagapuram case is an interesting contrast. The main water supply for the tank comes from a 5 mile channel taking off from the Cheyyar river. This requires extensive and heavy work to clear off sand during the period from the beginning of January until the end of April. All those cultivators who benefit from the channel have an obligation to clear 3 ft per day for every acre of wet land they hold. The work is closely administered and arduous, but the second (Navarai) crop depends on it. There is a long history of conflict with Konaiyur, a village which lies astride the channel above Vinayagapuram but which has no rights to the water. Twenty years ago when the channel silted very badly and Vinayagapuram was appealing for government help to clear it, Konaiyur people said they would clear it and take it over. However, Vinayagapuram obtained government assistance and managed to continue maintenance. More recently, theft of water by people from Konaiyur had led to violence and court cases. When the channel is running, Vinayagapuram posts night guards where it runs through Konaiyur. Since the main crisis twenty years ago the system of communal labour appears to have been continuously effective.

The final case, from Sri Lanka, raises the issue of the division of maintenance responsibilities between communities and bureaucracy. In one instance, a long canal was heavily silted and overgrown. Partly because of this, water only reached the tail-end four to six weeks after it began to flow at the top. It was in the interests of the tail-enders but not of the top-enders that the canal should be cleaned and maintained. The maintenance responsibility lay with the Territorial Civil Engineering Organisation which was unable to carry it out. The TCEO suggested that the communities themselves should clean the canal. The tail-enders, in whose interest it was that the canal should be cleaned, might have done the work, but by then the top-enders already wanted water. The result was no maintenance and continuing inefficiency and inequity in water distribution.

These examples support common-sense conclusions about communal labour. First, communal labour is most likely to be effective where the community will benefit directly and where labour obligations are proportional to expected benefits. Thus Dusi and the other seventeen villages could mobilise labour to divert the river into the tank, and Vegamangalam and Vinayagapuram maintained their channels. In all these cases the labour obligation was related to irrigated acreage. Conversely, where there is no direct link between the work done and the benefits gained, communal maintenance will be much more difficult. One of the reasons given for the abandonment of the Meppathurai channel was that the young men and small farmers felt that they were being required to do more than their share in relation to the benefits they might expect. Even more so, it is unrealistic to expect maintenance to be undertaken by people who will not benefit at all, as with clearing of silt at the top of channels by top-enders, which only helps those further down.

A second conclusion concerns the role of government. Intervention to help a community may be critical in sustaining a system of communal maintenance when it is under exceptional stress. Vinayagapuram's system survived after a successful appeal for government help; Meppathurai's collapsed after a similar appeal failed. The judgements involved are nice since too much help too easily given generates attitudes of dependence which in turn may lead to collapse. One error to avoid is uncertainty about the physical boundaries of responsibility for maintenance. Such uncertainty arose in Sri Lanka following an instruction to the TCEO (which was not well received by staff at the local level) that they should extend their maintenance work further down some channels. The outcome of such a situation is liable to be that neither government nor the community maintains the works. In general, government should unambiguously avoid doing what communities can do for themselves in their own interests, but should intervene when exceptional problems are beyond a community's power to overcome.

A third conclusion is that those who design irrigation systems in countries where labour is abundant, and government poor, should consider designs which encourage community action. These require that the maintenance work shall be within the capacity of the numbers of cultivators anticipated, and that *they* shall benefit from the work being done. The recurrent costs to government of the irrigation system should then be less than if government itself were obliged to provide maintenance. Higher capital costs, for example with more separate channels to communities which would then maintain them, might be justified by reducing the recurrent costs of maintenance by government.

BUREAUCRATIC–COMMUNAL ORGANISATION AND OPERATION

Perhaps the most interesting, important and difficult questions concern the organisation and operation of bureaucratic–communal irrigation – in which water is controlled first by a bureaucracy and then by a community or communities. The issues which arise within irrigation communities also arise now within the bureaucracy, between the bureaucracy and the communities, and between communities. The problems of water allocations between competitors, the questions of productivity and equity, and the difficulties over enforcement and adjudication which all occur within communities are now replicated but on a bigger, more visible and sometimes more dangerous scale on the larger irrigation system.

Although the variations are legion, a recurrent concern and source of inter-community conflict on bureaucratic–communal irrigation arises over the allocation and appropriation of water. With community irrigation, without a bureaucracy, we have already seen how the poaching of Vinayagapuram's water by farmers from Konaiyur, higher up the channel, led to violence and litigation. Similar incidents are common on bureaucratic–communal irrigation, with the difference that there is a mediating bureaucracy. Common practices include constructing illegal outlets, breaking padlocks, drawing off water at night, and bribing, threatening or otherwise in some way inducing officials to issue more water. Typically those at the top-end get their water first and get most of it, while those at the tail-end suffer. Many examples could be given. On Kirindi Oya right bank canal in Sri Lanka, there are several extra pipes off the main canal which were not part of the original irrigation design (personal communication, John Harriss) extracting water higher up, often to the detriment of those lower down. In North India the tension between villages may erupt into serious threats to law and order. Vander Velde reports an inter-village dispute in which ten cuts were made in an embankment in less than 24 hours and major violence between villages threatened (1971, p. 154). Both in the allocation of water and in the execution of the allocations the competition between communities is an inescapable problem.

Productivity and equity are involved here, as they are in intra-community distribution. Other things being equal, water is less productive after conveyance losses to the tail-end of a channel than if it can be applied at the top end. Moreover, when a canal is long, conveyance losses high, and delays in the arrival of water at the tail-end run into weeks or even months, as they do with the 17 miles of the Walawe right bank in Sri Lanka, then planting at the tail-end becomes untimely, either forcing cultivators to grow lower-yielding, shorter-duration varieties, or involving them in risks of inadequate water at critical periods in the growth of the crop, or condemning the crop to climatically sub-optimal conditions, or some combination of these. Excessive extractions higher up commonly contribute to these delays and inadequacies of supply to the tail-end. On much major irrigation in Sri Lanka it is notorious that top-end farmers flood their fields more than is necessary for the growth of paddy and substitute water for labour in weeding, with little or no regard for their neighbours waiting dry further down the channel. Their behaviour is rational, given their interests; but it is also antisocial, both in denying their less fortunate neighbours timely and adequate water, and in denying the country the additional paddy which their neighbours might be producing. The same is true with water issues on the two largest schemes in Sri Lanka – Gal Oya and Uda Walawe – where the acreage cultivated is much less than it might be because of permissive and excessive water issues. In the one Indian example of bureaucratic–communal irrigation (Dusi–Mamandur) the problem may be less acute, but even there tail-enders complained that they could grow fewer crops in the year than top-enders.

The challenge here is to be inventive in devising institutions and relationships which will moderate inter-community strife and be both equitable and productive in the allocation and application of irrigation water. There are four clusters of functions to be performed:

1 Strategic decisions about water use, including timing, amounts, allocations to communities, which lands to be irrigated, what crops to grow and the maintenance of channels.
2 The execution of those decisions.
3 Allocation of water and arbitration *within* communities.
4 Policing, and prosecution of infringements.

The question is how officials on the one hand and communities of users or their representatives on the other should be combined or separated in order best to perform these functions. A problem here is the word 'best'. The criteria for evaluating solutions already include the productivity of water and the equity of its distribution. To this some, democrats, would add maximising participation by the users, while others, technocrats, would add its antithesis, maximising the decision-making and control by technical staff.

In deciding the balance to strike between the democratic and technocratic views it is chastening to reflect on the side differences which can be observed. At one extreme is the system operated under the Dusi–Mamandur tank in India with its ayacut supporting eighteen villages.

Inter-community water allocation decisions are made by the president of the irrigation board elected by the villages. Villages send their traditional functionaries to him with requests for water which he then forwards, after whatever amendment he judges necessary, to the section officer of the PWD who instructs one of his staff to open or close the sluice from the dam accordingly. In Sri Lanka, on this size of irrigation system, the distribution from the channels below the tank would be the responsibility of government staff, but according to the evidence given, all water movement below the Dusi–Mamandur tank is the responsibility of an irrigation board of village representatives. Among the examples available, this is an extreme version of user participation in strategic decisions and their execution. At the other extreme are projects where the bureaucracy controls water issues right down to the level of the farmer (as on Uda Walawe in Sri Lanka) or even to his individual field (as on the Mwea irrigation settlement in Kenya (Chambers and Moris, 1973)).

Both extremes have disadvantages. The Dusi–Mamandur system is probably inefficient in water use: certainly there is an irrigation engineering opinion that water use would be much less wasteful if the bureaucracy controlled water issues from the main canals to the irrigation communities; certainly too, the tail-enders only manage one or at best two crops a year while those at the top end regularly have two or even three. With tighter management the distribution of water might be both more productive and more equitable. On the other hand the bureaucratic extreme, as on the Mwea irrigation settlement, is expensive in government staff and in the associated loss of community self-management and communal labour for maintenance. Government is liable to be doing for communities what they could and would otherwise do for themselves. Some middle course between these two extremes may combine greater productivity and equity without foregoing communal labour and without the need to maintain a large bureaucracy.

Taking this point of view, we can examine the four clusters of functions and see how they might be allocated.

First, there is a good case for strategic decisions being taken jointly by representatives of users and by government officials. Where representatives of users take decisions alone, they are likely to lack some of the technical knowledge needed, as probably on Dusi–Mamandur. Where administrators or technocrats take decisions on their own they are liable to ignore some needs of users, leading to later difficulties. Moreover, as the Assistant Government Agent, Hambantota, wrote in 1922 'the proprietors are more likely to adhere to dates which they have agreed to than to regulations imposed from without' (letter to Government Agent, Southern Province, 8 November 1922; Hambantota Kachcheri file E85). Better decisions are likely where they result from discussion which benefits from an engineer's knowledge of water availability, an agriculturalist's appreciation of the cropping position, farmers' knowledge of their resources and problems, and a presiding administrator's appreciation of all of these. This is very much the system practised in Water Meetings in Sri Lanka, presided over by Government Agents. In that form it has both strength and weakness in the openness of the meeting to all farmers affected and who may or may not fairly represent all the interests involved. Given the large attendances, it is not surprising that they decide on dates for operations (such as opening the sluices from a tank, starting cultivation and completing water issues) but do not decide the detail of rotational issues. Were there a more representative but smaller body, elected by 'irrigation constituencies' which would ensure that tail-enders were included, then it might be possible for such Meetings or a succession of them to decide in more detail what system of water issues to communities, with what volumes of water, should be adopted.

Second, with the execution of these decisions the question is how far the bureaucracy should extend down the irrigation system. On Dusi–Mamandur it is restricted to the sluice itself. On major irrigation in the dry zone of Sri Lanka it extends down the main channels to the points at which water is issued into field channels to communities. Communities are unlikely to agree among themselves that those higher up will take less in order that those lower down may benefit. More usually, an independent and impartial organisation is needed and this is mostly some form of bureaucracy. The need for such bureaucracy is underlined by the experience of the elected Thannimurrippu Paripalana Sabai, reported by Ellman and Ratnaweera, who state that while strategic decisions were satisfactorily taken, the problem was implementation and enforcement in which the elected body was not interested (Ellman and Ratnaweera, 1973, pp. 10, 15). There were difficulties over the blurred division of responsibilities between the elected body and the government officers and 'depersonalising the process of rule enforcement' was needed (ibid., pp. 8–9, 27). A crucial link is, it seems between the strategic decisions and those who implement them. A degree of impartial independence is required – with willingness and ability to carry out instructions earlier arrived at – without bowing to particularistic local pressures. For this, a bureaucracy loyal to the decisions, but with its discipline partly deriving from a larger national or regional department seems the most promising solution.

Third, allocation and arbitration within communities can usually be left to those communities, with perhaps some provision for appeal and for intervention by the bureaucracy in emergency. If water has to be rationed on a rotational basis, the difficulties of allocation within the community irrigation tract may be lessened if, as suggested by Levine *et al.* (1973, p. 11), the intermittent issues of water are large.

Fourth, there is a persistent need for policing and the prosecution of infringements above the community level. These are sometimes carried out by communities themselves. Vinayagapuram's night guards on its canal where it passes through Konaiyur, and the observation of the Dusi–Mamandur president (interview, May 1974) that, if government were to be responsible for distribution below the tank, it would be continuously necessary to call in the police, are reminders of the power of community organisation. But it is also noteworthy that under Dusi–Mamandur there was ten years of conflict between two villages, Pallavaram and Kanikillupai, over the height of a weir alleged to be diverting too much water to one village to the detriment of the other, a dispute which provoked intermittent damage and repair to the offending structure. Wherever water is scarce, communities resent extraction of water from higher up on their own supplies, whether apparently legal, as with a rubber company upstream from Wellawaya and with two pumps in the river above Vinayagapuram, or evidently illegal, as with the surreptitious raising of diversion weirs, the use of pumps at night to lift water from channels, the digging or breaching of canal banks, and the like. For these, if not a police force, then something like one is needed.

Police are anyway quite often called in to intervene both with allocation and enforcement. During the crisis of water shortage on Kirindi Oya right bank in Yala 1922, police helped with the allocation of water (letter, Divisional Engineer SD to the Director of Irrigation, 25 August 1922, Hambantota Kachcheri file E85). In the inter-village conflict in Haryana cited by Vander Velde: 'The resulting inter-village acrimony required the intervention of the police on a major scale to prevent serious violence' (Vander Velde, 1971, p. 154). In India the Irrigation Commission of 1972 drew attention to the need for efficient policing and prosecution and to 'the success which has been achieved in Haryana through extensive patrolling and inspection of canals and channels by flying-squads of officers, adequately armed. These flying squads carry out surprise night inspections and whenever offenders are caught, heavy penalties are imposed on them. The essence of the system is surprise, and prompt and condign punishment. A similar system of inspection by flying-squads could be adopted with advantage elsewhere' (MIP, 1972, p. 300). A widespread complaint in Sri Lanka was precisely the lack of 'prompt and condign punishment'. Within communities, administrative secretaries rarely bothered to file cases which they knew would be subject to long delays; and at a bureaucratic level many cases filed by government servants were not heard for months, or even years.

A careful mix of relationships may be best: with user participation in strategic decisions and with management by communities of their own water supplies once allocated, but with a disciplined organisation responsible for executing decisions, policing the system, and prosecuting delinquencies. It has to be made rational for the staff involved to deny resources to people who want them, in particular to issue less water to top-enders than they would like to receive. To achieve this the bureaucracy needs first, high-level political support, and second, an internal style and supervision and incentive system which supports and rewards such unpopular actions (Chambers, 1975b and 1976).

COMPARISONS, THEORY AND PRACTICE

These various comparisons help towards some theoretical and practical conclusions.

At the theoretical level, irrigation presents social scientists with tantalising invitations, too rarely taken up, to speculate. Expressions like 'irrigation society' and 'hydraulic organisation' hint that there may be strong causal links between irrigation systems and technology and social and economic relations. Irrigation organisation has an appearance of inevitability which lends itself to deterministic interpretations. Wittfogel (1957) succumbed to the temptations presented by the apparent imperatives of large-scale irrigation requiring, as he saw it, totalitarian organisation in order to muster the labour forces necessary for the maintenance of huge flood-control works and irrigation systems. This is not the place to discuss the validity of his thesis. The importance of Wittfogel here is that he illustrates the tendency to see the forms of irrigation organisation as unavoidable, as generated and required by imperatives of the physical system and its technology.

There are perhaps two main reasons for this tendency. First, on all irrigation systems which are larger than 'community' and in which water is controlled and allocated by a bureaucracy, that bureaucracy has to be fitted geographically to the permanent physical irrigation network. Certain tasks have to be carried out and staff are thought to be needed to perform them. Second, many statements about irrigation are based on detailed analysis of only one example from which generalisations are extrapolated. The rather superficial information gathered in South India and Sri Lanka has provided an opportunity to see what variations in organisation there may be over a wider range of examples than is usually available.

The outcome is surprising. It presents alternatives to the authoritarian, disciplinary and totalitarian organisations postulated by Wittfogel, and shows considerable variance in the discretion of the bureaucracy on major irrigation. It is sobering to think how much simpler the conclusions might have been had only Sri Lanka's irrigation been considered. As it is, with the corrective of the system of community management under Dusi – Mamandur tank in Tamil Nadu there seems nothing inevitable in the Sri Lanka pattern of a bureaucracy controlling issues down to the feeder level. The culture in which an irrigation system exists appears a major determinant of the form or organisation: thus in the Sri Lanka examples, where the society is more egalitarian and more anarchic, bureaucracy extends further down the physical system and the case for tighter bureaucratic controls seems clear; but in India where the controls already exist in the hierarchical structure of the society, it has not been necessary for bureaucracy to extend so far down the system and the need for stricter bureaucratic controls is less obvious.

The technologies used for water acquisition, storage and distribution, and for the maintenance of works, also underly the organisation and political economy of irrigation. Direct individual appropriation from wells is sensitive to technology and an innovation like pump-sets can radically differentiate access to water in a community and also deplete a communal resource (see pp. 332–9). When larger-scale technology is used, there arise multifarious problems of allocation and appropriation, some of which have been discussed above. As Wittfogel argued, the requirements of construction and maintenance are powerful influences on social organisation. Again, however, the technology used has a bearing. Wittfogel assumed that human labour was the main means used to build and maintain ancient irrigation works. It is at least possible that this was not the case with the ancient tanks of the dry zone of Sri Lanka, and that elephants were used as the bulldozers of that day. If so, then the form of organisation may well have been closer to a modern PWD or military engineering unit than to a totalitarian bureaucracy exacting forced labour from peasants. Moreover, with present-day irrigation it is only at the lower levels, as at Dusi, Meppathurai and Vinayagapuram (pp. 352–3), that communal labour and not machinery has to be mustered.

At a practical level, both organisation and technology are manipulable and subject to choice. The objectives of irrigation can be variously stated, but in the conditions of South Asia a list might include:

productivity (of water)
equity (in its distribution to users)
stability (in maintaining the water supply over the years) (see p. 393)
continuity (in water use throughout the year) (see p. 394)
carrying capacity (in sustaining population at acceptable levels of living) (see p. 394)

In achieving these objectives, and subject to trade-offs, the prescriptions vary by type of irrigation. For bureaucractic–communal and communal irrigation in the examples analysed, the key lies in the reform of organisation and operation – in short, in improved management of men. For direct-acquisition irrigation, the key lies in the design of appropriate technology for the acquisition process (see pp. 394–5). In both organisation and technology we are only at the beginning of appreciating the potential. In view of the rapidly increasing pressure of population on water supplies – especially in parts of India but elsewhere also – exploring and exploiting that potential is a high priority. On the organisational side it requires more and better research, especially by social scientists, combined with and supporting management consultancy and staff training. On the technological side it requires imaginative and vigorous research and development to create technologies appropriate for future rural life.

REFERENCES

Chambers, Robert (1975a). *Water Management and Paddy Production in the Dry Zone of Sri Lanka.* Occasional Series no. 8, Agrarian Research and Training Institute, Colombo.

Chambers, Robert (1975b). *Two Frontiers in Rural Management: Agricultural Extension and Managing the Exploitation of Communal Natural Resources,* Communication Series no. 113, Institute of Development Studies, University of Sussex.

Chambers, Robert (1976). 'On Substituting Political and Administrative Will for Foreign Exchange: the Potential of Water Management in the Dry Zone of Sri Lanka', in S. W. R. de A. Samarasinghe (ed.), *Agriculture in the Economic Development of Sri Lanka,* Peradeniya, Ceylon Studies Seminar.

Chambers, Robert and Moris, Jon (eds) (1973). *Mwea: an Irrigated Rice Settlement in Kenya,* Munich, Weltforum Verlag.

Ellman, A. O. and Ratnaweera, D. de S. (1973). *Thannimurrippu Paripalana Sabai: the Transfer of Administration of an Irrigated Settlement Scheme from Government Officials to a People's Organisation,* Occasional Series no. 1, Agrarian Research and Training Institute, Colombo.

Farmer, B. H. (1957). *Pioneer Peasant Colonization in Ceylon,* London, Oxford University Press.

Fernea, R. A. (1970). *Shaykh and Effendi: Changing Patterns of Authority Among the El Shabana of Southern Iraq,* Cambridge, Mass., Harvard University Press.

German Foundation For Developing Countries (1967). *Report on the Seminar on Economic and Social Aspects of Agricultural Development in Irrigated Areas,* Berlin, Reiher-Werder.

Government of India (1973). *Interim Report on Modernising Irrigation Systems and Integrated Development of Commanded Areas,* National Committee for Agriculture, New Delhi.

Harriss, J. C. (1976). *Aspects of Rural Society in the Dry Zone Relating to the Problem of Intensifying Paddy Production,* in S. W. R. de A. Samarasinghe (ed.), *Agriculture in the Peasant Sector of Sri Lanka,* Peradeniya, Ceylon Studies Seminar.

ICAR (1966). *Report of the Working Group for the Formulation of Fourth Five Year Plan Proposals on Soil and Water Management under Irrigated Conditions,* Indian Council for Agricultural Research, New Delhi.

IRRI (1973). *Water Management in Philippine Irrigation Systems: Research and Operations,* International Rice Research Institute, Los Banos.

Leach, E. R. (1961). *Pul Eliya, a Village in Ceylon,* Cambridge, Cambridge University Press.

Levine, G., Capener, H. and Gore, P. (1973). *The Management of Irrigation Systems for the Farm,* Research and Training Network reprint no. 2, Agricultural Development Council, New York.

Madduma Bandara, C. M. (1976). *The Prospects of Recycling Subsurface Water for Supplementary Irrigation in the Dry Zone*, in S. W. R. de A. Samarasinghe (ed.), *Agriculture in the Peasant Sector of Sri Lanka*, Peradeniya, Ceylon Studies Seminar.

MIP (1972). *Report of the Irrigation Commission 1972*, vols i–iii, Ministry of Irrigation and Power, New Delhi.

MPEA (1968). *Report of the Irrigation Program Review – Ceylon*, FAO/IBRD Co-operative Programme, Ministry of Planning and Economic Affairs, Colombo.

Ongkingco, P. S. (1973). *Organization and Operation of 15 Communal Irrigation Systems in the Philippines*, in IRRI (1973), pp. 235–42.

Thornton, D. S. (1976). 'The Organisation of Irrigated Areas', in Guy Hunter, A. H. Bunting and A. Bottrall (eds), *Policy and Practice in Rural Development*, London, Croom Helm.

Vander Velde, E. J. Jr (1971). 'The Distribution of Irrigation Benefits: A Study in Haryana, India', unpublished Ph.D thesis, University of Michigan.

Weerakoon, B. (1973). *Role of Administrators in the Context of a Changing Agrarian Situation – a District Point of View*, Seminar on Economic and Social Consequences of the Improved Seeds, Kandy, mimeo.

Wittfogel, K. A. (1957). *Oriental Despotism*, New Haven, Conn., Yale University Press.

23 Problems of Water Management in Hambantota District

John Harriss

The results of our survey of adoption of HYVs (pp. 57–73 and 117–18) point to the importance of adequate and reliable water supplies, and provide further support for the argument that water is more critically constraining than land in the improvement of agricultural production. Yet massive new irrigation projects are expensive, and the experience both of India and Sri Lanka suggests that all the benefits expected to accrue from them are generally not realised. According to Carruthers, 'The greatest potential source of large increases in the present levels of food supply in South Asia will come, in the next decade, from increasing efficiency of *existing* irrigation systems [my italics] and exploitation of known ground-water resources.' (Carruthers, 1974, p. 1) and Reidinger (1974), having shown the intertia of a system and style of irrigation management developed when irrigation water was expected to serve a function different from that now required of it, went on to suggest ways in which one large canal system in North India might be operated more efficiently without any changes in existing engineering structres. It seems likely that study of the management of water in irrigation systems – i.e. of the institutions and personnel concerned with making and implementing decisions regarding the allocation of water between farmers and its distribution to the fields – may lead to substatntial benefits (cf. Chambers, 1974).

The operation of all except an entirely individual irrigation system must bring a number of groups and individuals into a relationship with one another that requires of them some degree of co-operation, but also has considerable potential for antagonism; while in the allocation of irrigation water the potential for conflict between individual self-interest and social interest is brought into sharp focus. This potential is most likely to be realised when water supplies are uncertain and liable to be scarce, as they often are, even under major schemes in Sri Lanka, or in the Bhakra canals described by Reidinger. In these circumstances it is understandable if individual cultivators try to take as much water as possible, even exceeding the optimum requirements of their crops, but there is an evident clash between the interest of the individual paddy cultivator and the needs of a nation, struggling to achieve self-sufficiency in its basic food requirements, which could approach that goal more closely by more intensive use of its existing water resources (cf. ILO, 1971). There are also important conflicts of interest between individuals and other members of the communities in which they live.

It is because of this inherent potential for conflict, and of the evident need for individuals to forego taking all the water they might like, that many have thought that the management of irrigation water requires a high degree of discipline, and that that in turn implies central control and strong bureaucracy – as in Wittfogel's ideal type of 'hydraulic civilisation'. However, evidence from several case studies has failed to support Wittfogel's theory (Hunt and Hunt, 1974), while Reidinger's work suggests ways in which irrigation bureaucracy does not necessarily fit very well into the context of electoral democracies like those of India and Sri Lanka, where administration is subject to influence and control by elected politicians; nor is it consistent with other objectives of governments which are concerned to foster participatory democracy. Rigid enforcement may anyway prove more costly than control by the people themselves. In general the balance of enforcement and participation is a central concern in the management of irrigation, and it is likely to be closely related to the social organisation of the people whom the water supplies. In this chapter, I explore some general problems of water management with reference to the Kirindi Oya right bank scheme (KORB), and in the context of the social structure of Hambantota District.

THE KIRINDI OYA RIGHT BANK SCHEME

The specification for KORB was published as a Sessional Paper (no. xx) in 1907. The scheme was to use the same anicut across the river (that at Ellagala, restored in 1876) as the left bank scheme (KOLB) to divert water into a tank to be constructed by 'restoring the ancient bund known as Yodekandiya'. The specification stated that the storage in the new Wirawila tank, when filled from Ellagala during the Maha floods, would be sufficient to 'safely admit of the cultivation of about 5000 acres' which were to be supplied from a single main channel running about 10 miles down the right bank of Kirindi Oya.

In common with some other irrigation developments in South Asia under British rule, the scheme that finally emerged was much more restricted in scale. The most recent specification – drawn up for the purpose of collecting water rates – is dated 1954, and shows a total of 2421 acres. The reasons for the disparity between target and reality seem to have been that the planning and construction of works down to field level was

inadequate, partly because of uncertainties as to where the responsibility of
the Irrigation Department ended and that of the proprietors began; and
that some of the land which was sold as irrigable in 1920 when the storage
works and main channel had been completed was found not to be so. (For
sources on these points and for this chapter more generally, see pp. 246–7,
and particularly the AGA's diary entry for 16 June 1924.)

The lower sections of the main channel were never constructed. Today it
serves eleven yayas – not all clearly distinguished from one another – from
its eleven major outlets, though there are also a number of minor outlets,
some unofficial. None of the channels is lined, and the flow of water can be
controlled only by planking at the main outlet points.

There are management problems at several levels. At the highest level
are questions concerning allocation from Ellagala between KORB and
KOLB, which are not considered here; and then those concerning water
issues from Wirawila tank. Thereafter there are problems of allocation
between yayas; and, at the lowest level, between farmers within each yaya.

Management: 1920–58

KORB finally became operational during a period of dispute between the
Revenue and Irrigation Departments over the management of irrigation
schemes. A dual executive structure existed:

Cultivation matters	*Irrigation works*
Revenue Department: Assistant Government Agent (AGA)	Irrigation Department: Director of Irrigation Engineering, Southern Division, Tangalle
Cultivation Officer (CO)	Sub-divisional Officer (SDO), Tissamaharama
Vel Vidanes	'Guardian' (irrigation overseer) 'Watchers' (water issue labourers)

One salaried Cultivation Officer, seconded from the Irrigation Department and under the authority of the AGA, was responsible for both the
Right Bank and Left Bank schemes. There was one Vel Vidane for each of
four divisions on KORB. They had to request water issues through the
Cultivation Officer from the SDO, Tissa. Only the SDO had powers to
instruct the overseer, one of whom was responsible for Wirawila, others for
the Left Bank tanks, to release water from the tank. The overseers were
Irrigation Department men. The Vel Vidanes were the irrigation
headmen who had long been part and parcel of the whole administrative
system of headmen, all supposed to be local notables commanding respect
and authority, and originally appointed on that basis. In this period,
however, Vel Vidanes became subject to election every three years at
proprietors' meetings. They were paid huwandiram, a share of the yield,
by each cultivator and were able to apply punitive sanctions rapidly in case
of contravention of a code for water use ('cultivation rules') agreed at a
proprietors' meeting. The 'water issue labourers' (two for KORB) were

responsible for reporting on the condition of channels to the overseer, and for locking and unlocking 'gates' – in fact planks – under his authority.

In principle the Revenue Department through the AGA, Cultivation Officer and Vel Vidanes concerned itself with the allocation of water between and within yayas, while the officials of the Irrigation Department were concerned only with allocation of water to and from the tank and with the actual operation and maintenance of structures. In practice it was often difficult to define where responsibilities began and ended.

Decisions concerning the release of water from Ellagala were made by the Irrigation Officers though, in times of scarcity, proprietors attempted to influence allocations through the AGA, who might seek to alter the normal pattern in order to save the maximum possible acreage. Decisions concerning release from Wirawila tank were subject to rules agreed at a meeting of the proprietors of land on KORB, though in practice the gambārayas often substituted for them. The rules included dates of issue which were supposed to be invariable so as to guarantee two crops per annum with fixed maintenance periods – though the Irrigation Department at times tried to assert that the works were designed to supply Maha cultivation alone. The dates were the principal subject of the running battles between Irrigation and Revenue officials. The stress on fixed dates seems to have been related to a general view of British irrigation authorities that schemes should operate according to standard programmes so as to be subject to as little influence from events and personalities as possible. This inflexibility, while intended to guarantee smooth working and ensure adequate maintenance periods, may not have been desirable from the standpoint of making the most productive use of water (cf. Reidinger, 1974); it seems to have been simply impracticable in the conditions of Hambantota District (see below).

In times of scarcity the AGA, in consultation with the proprietors, set up rotations between yayas; and the rules by which the Vel Vidanes were to supervise the distribution within yayas were also agreed at these meetings. The practice of consultation and of administration through 'traditional' institutions had been of long standing in Ceylon under British rule. It was intended to make for flexibility and allow for a measure of 'self-rule' in accordance with local custom, and thus to minimise both administrative costs and the possibility of confrontation. But the population of the Kirindi area was almost entirely of recent settlement, so that there was no 'local custom'.

The records show that absolute water shortages occurred rather frequently (i.e. insufficient water for other than restricted Yala cultivation), and that there was always a problem of delayed cultivation. In every season from 1925 to 1931, for example, the AGAs requested extensions of water issues, which they always justified in terms of the inevitability of cultivation delays because of shortages of labour, credit and draught (most critically). The delays were cumulative, led to failure to complete maintenance, and meant that very often cultivators were unable to take advantage of rainfall or of the available water when supply was short, and that regularly an entire Yala crop would be lost. In order to cope with the delays the AGAs, in consultation with the proprietors, frequently attempted to impose cultivation of short-term 60-day paddy varieties on those who had not completed field preparation by a certain date; but few of them seem to have possessed the degree of ruthlessness apparently required to impose such a rule. Most of the AGAs seem to have been too susceptible to pleas to save 'standing crops'.

Revenue officers held that the Irrigation Department looked upon the maintenance of works as an end in itself, while Irrigation men always countered by pointing to the waste of water that went on in the schemes as a result of delayed cultivation and lax discipline, and by emphasising the costs of delayed or hastily completed maintenance. The Revenue Department believed in persuasion and participatory control, the Irrigation Department held that 'The effect of the . . . Irrigation Ordinance is to hand over to the proprietors of irrigable land under a Crown Irrigation Scheme the means for preventing the water supplied from it being used in the best and most economical manner possible. . . .' (Director of Irrigation to Colonial Secretary, 18 October 1922) Fears were often expressed regarding the dangers of setting up a system of dual control, but there is no doubt that there was in effect a duality, which left the AGAs to pursue the interests of the cultivators more keenly than would perhaps have been the case had theirs also been the responsibility for maintenance; while the rigid time-tabling that the Irrigation Department always wanted to impose threatened curtailment of some cultivation. The problems created by shortages of other agricultural resources were always exacerbated by the tendency to dual control.

In turn the tendency was easily exploited by the powerful proprietors, who were able to turn inter-departmental hostility to their own advantage, mainly by playing on the AGA's concern for cultivation and through the element of 'participation' guaranteed by the Irrigation Ordinance. The extent of 'participation' was of course limited because the majority of the land on KORB – as under the other major schemes in Hambantota – was held by a few large proprietors, some of whom were absentees like the Colombo businessmen or lawyers from Matara who operated their lands through the 'notorious gambārayas', while others were local officials and businessmen who sometimes managed the land themselves. The actual cultivators had no say at all in the allocation or distribution of water unless they were among the very few small owner-cultivators.

If we take equity of distribution as one of the criteria for evaluating irrigation organisation, the records leave us no doubt that the big landowners were often able to exercise manipulative power to obtain more water for themselves, though their activities also brought them into conflict with one another. And if we take productivity of water and stability of the system as criteria, then again it seems that the system described was ineffective because it never succeeded in securing timely cultivation.

The system could, however, be made to work by an energetic AGA who made cultivation his main priority, as did one of the Agents of the early 1920s. He was able to resist the pressures of the powerful landowners and to exercise his power ruthlessly with regard to late cultivation, but also to manipulate the Vel Vidane system to make optimum use of available water and offer positive inducements to timely cultivation. For the system did provide for a kind of monitoring organisation throughout the tract. The Vel Vidanes were responsible to the Cultivation Officer, with whom they had regular monthly meetings. Their reports to the CO, which they were sometimes asked to make weekly, enabled a close check on the progress of cultivation throughout the tract. Such regular reporting has not taken place since the end of the Vel Vidane system, yet it is hard to see how the system can be operated effectively without a rapid and regular flow of information up and down the line.

In theory the Vel Vidanes were the instrument of swift discipline, empowered to ensure water conservation by the application of a code which laid down automatic punishments for any practices which would waste water, such as poor levelling of fields. Robert Chambers found in a survey of cultivator opinion in Hambantota that a majority appeared to value the discipline that existed under the old system more than they value participation now. However, some historical evidence suggests that the Vel Vidanes were subject to influence by the big land controllers, so that performance of their duties was often slack and subject to bias. In May 1936, for example, the AGA noted in his diary: 'complaint of water shortage. The trouble lies in the villagers' incurable habit of pro-crastination . . . added to the proprietors' sketchy maintenance of field channels which elected Vel Vidanes will not correct (unless forced to) as they depend upon these same proprietors for re-election every three years. . . .' Far from being the 'dictators' of popular mythology the Vel Vidanes in Hambantota District seem often to have been pawns in the hands of the élite.

The system represented an ineffectual combination of bureaucratic control and of participation. The bureaucracy was divided and its powers were not sufficient to impose timely cultivation or the implementation of the formal rules regarding water conservation, largely because of the element of participation which effectively sanctioned the manipulative efforts of powerful men, who were also able to exploit conflicts within the bureaucracy. At that time there was no notion of popular participation, but the bureaucracy attempted in its paternalistic fashion to protect the interests of the weak. It was largely hindered from doing so because of the institutionalised pressure that élite members could exert through the proprietors' meetings and their ability to control the Vel Vidanes. It is possible that control of water through the system of headmen and 'traditional' committees worked in other areas where the big landowners were also local leaders with an interest in maintaining dependents, sharing power amongst themselves; but the system did not work in the case of the absentee élite of Hambantota, whose power was not similarly based on control of land.

MANAGEMENT UNDER THE PADDY LANDS ACT OF 1958, AND AFTER

The Paddy Lands Act was intended to undermine the traditional élite by providing guarantees for ordinary cultivators, and by encouraging participatory control on their part. Some general discussion of the results of the Act appear in an earlier chapter (pp. 250–1).

The major difference effected by the Act in so far as water management was concerned was that the Govimandala Sewaka, or administrative secretary of the cultivation committee replaced the Vel Vidanes, under the general supervision of the newly instituted Department of Agrarian Services. Also the proprietors' meetings became 'water meetings' which all registered cultivators were now allowed to attend, and it became regular practice to fix cultivation dates season by season rather than attempt to build them into published rules. Under this system all the registered paddy cultivators within a demarcated area took part in the election of a committee responsible for regulating all cultivation affairs. The administrative secretary was an officer of the committee and was made responsible for regulating water issues at the yaya level. He had more restricted punitive powers than the Vel Vidanes had had, for the system was considered to be one of 'self-management'; while the old huwandiram payments related to the level of the yield were replaced by a fixed cash payment levied per acre, whether or not cultivation was carried on.

Not surprisingly, in the absence of redistribution of agricultural resources, the chief offices in many of the cultivation committees came to be filled by local élites or their stooges – in Hambantota District by much the same class of people who had managed to exploit the Vel Vidane system to their advantage. In other cases, as in my fieldwork area, the cultivation committee was not even taken over by members of the élite, but rather ignored. It was an ineffectual body in which few people displayed sufficient interest even to seek election, as seems often to be the case in strongly individualistic societies (cf. below; and for comparison, Lison-Tolosana, 1966).

In terms of water management the system resulted in the loss of even the principle of institutionalised co-ordination up and down the tract, while there is abundant evidence of the continued abuse of the organisation by the big men. Homologous units – of the same size or function – such as cultivation committees, are rarely able to make decisions which concern one another, as should be the case with the allocation of water between two villages or cultivation committees served from the same channel (cf. Hunt and Hunt, 1974, p. 133). Such decisions usually have to be referred to a higher level of authority, in the absence of which the stronger of the two units generally grabs most of the scarce resource. In the case of an irrigation system this usually means the upstream units (cf. Glick, 1970, part I, chapter 6).

This has been so on KORB. The Water Meetings represented (and continue to represent) only a forum where homologus units came together, and while their different claims may be adjudicated and some pressure applied by the bureaucracy (or latterly by the MP), they have no authority to impose their advice. In practice the bureaucracy has attempted to operate rotations between yayas in periods of scarcity, but it has not had the organisational capacity to manage water issues in relation to plant needs of to impose discipline. Some changes in the administrative structure did take place after the Paddy Lands Act of 1958, and the kind of 'two-sided' organisation that existed in the earlier period has now been replaced by a more unified system under the Territorial Civil Engineering Organisation (TCEO), set up in February 1971. The whole management structure was as sketched out below, until establishment of the agricultural productivity committees under the Agriculture Productivity Law, no. 2 of 1972.

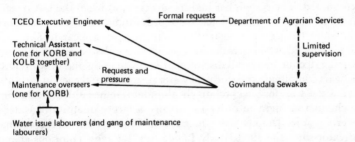

Under this system the old weaknesses due to division of responsibilities between departments were removed, but in its place was set a new disjuncture, for the TCEO command structure did not involve direct control of the activities of the Govimandala Sewakas while the co-ordinating organisation that existed in the days of the Vel Vidane system was not effectively replaced. A Technical Assistant is responsible for both KORB and KOLB, just as the Cultivation Officer was in the past, but the Govimandala Sewakas are not under his control.

Discussion with the present TA (19 June 1974) suggested to me that one man, primarily an engineer and helped by two maintenance overseers (one each for KORB and KOLB), who so far as I know do not have training in agriculture, cannot effectively manage the use of irrigation water throughout the several thousands of acres involved without strong support at local levels. And the support provided at present by the two water issue labourers on KORB and by the Govimandala Sewakas, who are mostly cultivators themselves and preoccupied with their own affairs, is inadequate. The Govimandala Sewakas do not have the same incentive to devote their energies to water distribution as had the Vel Vidanes, paid as they are a fixed rate per acre. The water issue labourers are not responsible for the quantities of water in the fields or in the drains, but are expected mainly to control the opening and locking of gates and to report damage. They are helpless anyway in the face of the opposition of a few farmers, and there is nobody throughout the management system whose job it is to judge – as a matter of routine at local level – how much water should be put where and when, in relation to the needs of paddy cultivation. Thus it is probably the case that, when the overseers are asked for more water, they will release water from the tank if they can, without checking on the extent of the need and without attempting to organise diversion within the system. Certainly there is nobody at the yaya level who is responsible for water conservation in terms like those of the 'Instructions to Vel Vidanes' of 1935, which lay down strict rules regarding such matters as the level of water in the fields.

The capacity of the system that has so far been operational for making and implementing decisions concerning the allocation of water between yayas, having in view both equity and productivity considerations, has been limited. The system has had its successes, as when the GA recently persuaded cultivators on the left bank of Kirindi to agree to rotations of Yala water from year to year. But such successes appear to have been heavily dependent on personalities, while there has been an apparently alarming decline in overall discipline. Everywhere up and down KORB, one hears complaints and stories of water poaching, and even in Yala 1974 when water was (for once) relatively abundant, some cultivators dammed the channel at night in order to procure a larger quantity of water at flowering time. Despite some increase in the freedom of the ordinary cultivator since the 1958 Paddy Lands Act, the most notorious channel blockage 'black spot' in times of water scarcity is at the gate of the largest and most powerful gambāraya on KORB.

Control of water piracy is now virtually non-existent. According to the Executive Engineer in Tissa (interview, 3 July 1974) there have been no prosecutions for water-poaching for a number of years, not a single case having been filed out of some 200 reports submitted. I know of one area of encroachment in which about 80 acres of paddy are irrigated by means of an unofficial channel which blatantly taps the main channel, and disrupts cultivation in the last yaya irrigated from Wirawila. This has been going on for about fifteen years, and while it illustrates the thesis that more land could be irrigated under Wirawila, given more stringent control of water, it is none the less a striking indication of the present lack of such control. The Executive Engineer also told me that the Govimandala Sewakas do not take punitive action. I confirmed this in interviews with three of them, all of whom said that they preferred to settle disputes 'on their own', although all three regularly file cases in the event of non-payment of the acreage taxes upon which they depend for their remuneration. The irrigation rates, however, have not been levied on KORB since about the time of the Paddy Lands Act of 1958. Other evidence has already been mentioned which further tends to support the Engineer's conclusion that 'there is no law now' even though clause 93 of the Irrigation Ordinance, regarding punishment for all acts of water piracy and all waste of water, is extant.

Of course, for any scheme to operate without some piracy is an ideal, and it is possible that a degree of permissiveness is essential both to avoid destructive conflict and (more significantly in our context), for the flexibility of the irrigation system, as Gray has suggested (1963, p. 141; cf. also Glick, 1970, p. 57). But the present state of affairs on KORB is not such as to make feasible the tighter control that has been advocated in order to facilitate more productive use of the water (ILO, 1971, e.g. paragraph 343; Chambers, 1974).

SOME GENERAL CONCLUSIONS AND SUGGESTIONS FOR THE FUTURE MANAGEMENT OF WATER IN HAMBANTOTA

In 1974 it was still uncertain how it was intended that water distribution should be managed under the Agricultural Productivity Law which modified the structure set up by the Paddy Lands Act of 1958. The Govimandala Sewakas were still functioning at the time the project was in the field; and although the agricultural productivity committees (APC) had begun to operate, the new cultivation committees had not. In principle the new organisation seems to hold out the possibility of overcoming at least one of the difficulties inherent in the former system – the problem of decision-making between homologous units. All of KORB comes under one APC and the authority of the APC will override that of the individual cultivation committees in charge of the yayas. However, for the decision-making to be impartial it is essential that the APC should not be dominated by the interests of one particular yaya, and, since the APC members are appointed by the political authority for the area, it is only he who can effect this. In theory, however, another part of the new legislation makes it possible for an independent set of standards to be applied, which might be used as a check on the abuse of power by APCs. This possibility is suggested by the clause in the Agricultural Productivity Law which states that farmers shall be penalised for inefficiency. A weakness of the Law is that nowhere does it say how efficiency will be judged, though it implies the establishment of technically based standards. Perhaps there is a need for an Irrigation Ombudsman, with a staff capable of evaluating the decisions of the APCs in terms of both equity and productivity, for these are often the two sides of the same coin. This general principle is rarely seen so clearly as in the case of water distribution. Most farmers try to use more water than is biologically necessary for productivity, which suggests that extractions by powerful individuals are likely to be harmful for productivity as well as for equity (cf. Alles, 1967).

Water management on KORB throughout its history shows the influence of the rural élite, and there can be little confidence in the efficacy of a participatory system so long as the distribution of resources leaves so much power concentrated in the hands of a few land controllers. And recent agrarian legislation in Sri Lanka has done little to affect the concentrated pattern of distribution of resources in the paddy sector (cf. pp. 250–1 above and also Sanderatne, 1972). The implicit suggestion here is that more efficient water management in terms of equity and productivity will be dependent to some extent on wider agrarian reforms or on the establishment of some check on the existing élite. This does not conflict with the conclusions of sociologists like the Hunts who think that 'power élites are crucial for conflict resolution over water' (Hunt and Hunt, 1974, p. 153). The points at issue are: 'Who shall constitute the élite? And to what sanctions shall they be subject?' For there can be no question of the need for some authority at the level of the whole system. If this is to be the authority of the people, then it is essential that some of the people should not have the capacity to coerce the others merely to their own advantage.

A particular feature of the agrarian social structure of Hambantota District has been that the élite is independent of local support, which has resulted in a dearth of 'social' control at yaya level. I was able to discover no consistent patterns of co-operation or conflict, and no structure of power or wealth in relation to access to water, at the yaya level. I have found instead the suggestion of a kind of anarchy, in which despite the frequency of quarrels over water there are no permanent feuds. Farmers from among the 85 households which I studied who benefit from blocks at the 'black spot' mentioned earlier are not subject to much censure by those of their residential neighbours who suffer. One reason is that it is difficult to assign blame to individuals, but more important, are that ties of neighbourhood, caste and kinship both interweave with, and cross-cut, potential groupings based on water, and that there is no truly local leadership because of the high degree of dependence of the cultivators upon an essentially 'external' élite. The fact that nearly all the cultivators are tenants who have always been dependent in some measure upon the landowners and gambārayas seems to have meant that so far relatively little systematic social and economic differentiation has developed amongst them. Among the ordinary cultivators a spirit of egalitarianism prevails, which is consistent with the facts of chena cultivation (cf. pp. 85–91 and 145 above, and also Yalman 1967, especially p. 237) and with the importance of the idea of 'jealousy' in daily life. I was given accounts, in a large number of households, of incidents which had caused my informants to suffer and which had been revealed to them by a specialist kattadia. Such a pattern of beliefs apparently quite often occurs in societies with a prevailingly egalitarian ideology (cf. Pocock, 1973). Certainly the hierarchical ideology of caste is not at all marked though that does not mean to say that caste feeling is not strong.

The society of KORB is altogether individualistic in tone. There seems to be something of a 'power vacuum' at yaya level, and conflicts are resolved in a rather haphazard way, often violently. While this might suggest the need for a kind of quasi-military force to police irrigation systems, as Chambers implies (1974), we must remember that an altogether different pattern would develop if the 'external dependence' of the cultivators could be replaced. There is at least a chance that the ethos of 'egalitarianism' might favour a system of self-management within yayas.

In general, then, the search for the best possible balance between enforcement and participation in order to achieve productivity and equity objectives in water management must be pursued with reference to the particular agrarian power structure and pattern of authority within local 'communities'. This is the case with regard to the making and implementation of decisions on allocations both between and within the smaller units of the system.

A good proxy for 'equity and productivity' might be 'reliability', for reduction of the uncertainties surrounding water supply would be beneficial to all, and likely to encourage more intensive cultivation. Thus it seems that the more independence that can be given to the smallest possible units of people within the design of a scheme the better – where 'independence' means 'independent control of water supply', and by extension, self-management within the units. Even then, one of the lessons of KORB is that small farmer units are generally more likely to be effective in managing their own affairs, especially in circumstances in which water is sometimes scarce, if they have other social relations in common as well as water supply.

General conclusions are (i) that the maximum possible control of water should be given to the smallest possible groups and that these groups should manage their own affairs, (ii) there must be some authority capable of adjudicating between the interest of the smaller units within the whole irrigation system, (iii) if the experience of KORB is a guide, this authority must be unitary and impartial, and capable of applying objective technical standards regarding the productivity of water use, certainly where water is scarce, (iv) there should probably be an effective authority with adequate personnel to ensure that the system is not disrupted by water piracy, especially from main channels, and (v) as these points imply, there must be efficient and rapid information flows between 'authority' and cultivators.

With particular reference to Hambantota District, the APC–CC organisational structure is most likely to work well if the control of agricultural resources can be further dispersed, so that the authority of the

APC is neither ignored nor abused. In any case it is important to back up the structure with sufficient technical personnel to apply objective criteria of efficiency and to guarantee the flows of information that will be necessary to co-ordinate the system.

REFERENCES

Primary Sources
Constraints of space prevented citation of all the detailed evidence necessary to substantiate various points. Much of it comes from files in the Records Room in Hambantota Kachcheri, Series E – Irrigation; and from the official diaries of the Assistant Government Agents from 1920 onwards, also lodged in the Kachcheri.

Secondary Sources
Alles, W. S. (1967). 'Soil and Water Conservation in the Dry Zone' in O. S. Peries (ed.), *The Development of Agriculture in the Dry Zone*, Colombo, Ceylon Association for the Advancement of Science.

Carruthers, I. D. (1974). 'Water Control, Irrigation and Hydrological Research', paper to Conference on Food Problems in S. Asia, 1975–90, IDS Conference 89, University of Sussex.

Chambers, Robert (1974). *Water Management and Paddy Production in the Dry Zone of Sri Lanka*, Occasional Series no. 8, Colombo, Agrarian Research Training Institute, mimeo.

Glick, T. F. (1970). *Irrigation and Society in Medieval Valencia*, Cambridge, Mass., Harvard University Press.

Gray, R. F. (1963). *The Sonjo of Tanganyika: An Anthropological Study of an Irrigation-based Society*, Oxford University Press.

Hunt, E. and Hunt, R. C. (1974). 'Irrigation, Conflict and Politics: A Mexican Case' in T. E. Downing and M. Gibson (eds), *Irrigation's Impact on Society*, Anthropological Papers of the University of Arizona, no. 25, Tucson, Arizona.

International Labour Office, ILO (1971). *Matching Employment Opportunities and Expectations: A Programme of Action for Ceylon*, vol i: *Report*, Geneva.

Lison-Tolosana, C. (1966). *Belmonte de Los Caballeros*, Oxford University Press.

Pocock, D. F. (1973). *Mind, Body and Wealth*, Oxford, Pavilion Press.

Reidinger, R. B. (1974). 'Institutional rationing of canal water in Northern India: conflict between traditional patterns and modern needs' in *Economic Development and Cultural Change*, 23, 79–104.

Sanderatne, N. (1972). 'Sri Lanka's New Land Reform', *S. Asian Rev.*, 6, 7–19.

Yalman, N. (1967). *Under the Bo Tree*, Berkeley, California University Press.

24 The Crisis and the Future

Robert Chambers, H. D. Dias, Barbara Harriss
and John Harriss

Our fieldwork was overtaken in its later stages by the crisis in energy and
fertiliser supply occasioned by OPEC's sudden increase in oil prices:
between March 1973 and August 1974 freight rates in North Arcot trebled,
while fertiliser prices in both India and Sri Lanka rocketed and the
problems of the supply of scarce chemical inputs, already introduced in
chapter 17, became even more severe. In this chapter some of us set out our
results and thinking (not necessarily in complete agreement) on the
consequences of fertiliser and other newly acute shortages, and on the
design of alternative technologies for the future – given both the likelihood
of continuing scarcity and expensiveness of energy and chemical inputs
and (so far as North Arcot at least is concerned) the projected growth of
rural population and the constraint exercised by limited water resources.

CONSEQUENCES OF FERTILISER SHORTAGE IN SRI LANKA (HDD)

When our work started in January 1973 fertiliser was freely available to
paddy cultivators, and a government subsidy covered 50 per cent of the
cost. By August 1974 the government, unable to bear the burden of a
subsidy on the vastly increased cost of fertiliser, withdrew it: the price to the
paddy cultivator went up several times over (Table 24.1).

The issue of fertiliser in Maha 1973–4 increased substantially, due
largely to the big government drive to increase food production. Even
cultivators who had defaulted on their loans were allowed to receive
fertiliser on credit. Between Maha 1972–3 and Maha 1973–4 the issue of
fertiliser nationally increased by 47 per cent: in Hambantota by 145 per
cent, in Moneragala by 77 per cent. The drastic price increase after Maha
1973–4 adversely affected the issue of fertiliser, and unsold fertiliser came
to be piled up in stores.

A small subsidy was reintroduced to defray the increased cost of
fertiliser – the guaranteed price of paddy was raised by Rs3 per bu. – but

Table 24.1   Price and quantity of fertiliser issued to paddy cultivators in Sri Lanka

Types of fertiliser	Price (Rs per ton)		
	Yala 1973	Maha 1973–4	Yala 1974
V₁ (basal)	378·00	522·60	2,184·00
TDM (mixture)	408·00	327·60	2,334·00
Urea	408·00	532·60	2,685·00
Fertiliser issued (in tons)	40,736	82,685	37,977

Source: Ceylon Fertiliser Corporation, Ministry of Agriculture and Lands and the Agrarian Research and Training Institute.

this was not adequate in most cases. The increased cost of fertiliser, if used as recommended, amounted to about Rs250 per acre. Only farmers who obtain a yield of 80 bu. or more could cover this: most of the farmers in our sample did not obtain such a high yield and will find it difficult to apply fertiliser as heretofore. They will either reduce the amount, or stop using it. A scheme of rationing which gave all paddy cultivators an equal share of the fertiliser available would have been wasteful, as the capacity to obtain a return from fertiliser varies among areas and among farmers (Table 24.2).

Table 24.2   Use of fertiliser in relation to yield

Fertiliser used per bu. of paddy produced (in lb)	Number of farmers in each cultivation committee*												Total	
	1	2	3	4	5	6	7	8	9	10	11	12	No.	Percentage
Under 2					1	1		1	3	4	5	6	21	13
2–5	3	6	6	8	4	4	2	3	4	9	4	8	61	39
5–10	8	2	4	3	3	3	5	1	6	3	4	4	46	30
10–15						2			18		2	4	26	16
Over 15									1				1	2

* 1 Jansagama, 2 Hanganwagura, 3 Rotawela, 4 Jayawickremayaya, 5 Companiwatta, 6 Udasgama, 7 Kachcheriyagama, 8 Kataragama, 9 Tenagama, 10 Wellawaya, 11 Kachchigala, 12 Metigatwala.

Table 24.2 shows a considerable variation in the amount of fertiliser used to produce a bushel of paddy (one lb of fertiliser per bu. of paddy may be taken as 2·13 kg per quintal; see also pp. 62–3). While most farmers use 2·0–5·0 lb per bushel and several use less, 30 per cent used 5·0–10·0 lb per bushel and 18 per cent, over 10·0 lb. The recommended amount of fertiliser for 4–4½ month new HYVs is 336 lb per acre, and for 4–4½ month early HYVs and traditional varieties 232 lb per acre. Under favourable conditions these recommended quantities should produce about 80–100

bu. per acre and 60 bu. per acre respectively, i.e. about 3·4−4·2 lb per
bushel and 3·9 lb per bushel. Of those who had used some fertiliser, only 39
per cent produced at such levels of efficiency. Most farmers, then, are using
fertiliser at levels of efficiency much lower than should be tolerated.
Several ecological and socio-economic factors account for this. We also
found evidence of the misuse of fertiliser due to ignorance of the
recommended application (cf. Agrarian Research and Training Institute,
1974). To the extent that the government subsidy had encouraged mis-use,
it had encouraged a waste of scarce resources. In the use of such resources,
the productivity potential of different areas should be taken into
consideration. The different cultivation committees showed varying levels
of fertiliser/paddy efficiency (Table 24.3) in terms of the amount of
fertiliser required to produce a given unit of paddy. (A more refined index
is the marginal productivity of fertiliser under different conditions.
Although some information is available about this in relation to fertiliser
trials carried out under controlled conditions, little is known under
farmers' field conditions. The cruder, fertiliser/paddy efficiency is, therefore, used here, despite its limitations: in the author's view, it provides some
valuable insights.)

Table 24.3   Level of fertiliser/paddy efficiency

Cultivation committee	Fertiliser used per bu. of paddy produced (in lb)
Kataragama	1·96
Jansagama	2·51
Wellawaya	2·87
Kachchigala	2·92
Hanganwagura	3·81
Kachcheriyagama	4·40
Companiwatta	4·53
Rotawela	4·72
Jayawickremayaya	4·98
Metigatwala	5·28
Udasgama	5·29
Tenagama	7·94

These figures show that areas such as Kachchigala and Kataragama,
where farmers used little fertiliser and obtained low yields (32·7 bu. per
acre), used fertiliser efficiently. Jayawickremayaya, on the other hand, had
used fertiliser much less efficiently, although the average yield for the area
was 74 bu. per acre. Tenagama, where farmers used a fair amount of
fertiliser but obtained a very low yield, (31·8 bu. per acre) had used
fertiliser most inefficiently. Within all these areas there were considerable
variations among farmers.

One beneficial result of fertiliser shortage and its increased cost may be its more efficient use. Farmers whose fertiliser/paddy efficiency level is low may decide to use less fertiliser. Only farmers whose paddy/fertiliser efficiency level is about 4·0 lb per bushel would find it possible to absorb the increase in cost of fertiliser. Farmers who need less than 4·0 lb per bushel would actually make more profit because the increased price of paddy would more than compensate for the increased cost of fertiliser.

Some of the consequences would be adverse. Even farmers who use fertiliser efficiently may find it beyond their means to buy fertiliser, or may not be able actually to get what they need even if they can pay for it: production and income would then decline. It is essential to guard against such consequences. Even in areas where there is an intermediate level of efficiency, there could be a decline in production if farmers stop using fertiliser. It could be rational for them to do so, as they could thereby increase their returns. Only farmers who obtain a yield of at least 80–90 bu. per acre and who do not need credit would be able to cover the increase in the cost of fertiliser from the increase in the price of paddy. Farmers dependent on credit would need Rs370 to Rs475 extra to cover the increased cost, equivalent to 125–160 bu. per acre. Hence a very large proportion of farmers will not be able to cover the increased cost of fertiliser and many, therefore, may give up using it or use less. There could be a consequent drop in production.

At this stage (September 1975) it is difficult to estimate the impact on production as a whole. If fertilisers are withdrawn or application reduced in areas with favourable conditions, there would be a drastic decline. If fertiliser is withdrawn in areas with unfavourable conditions, there would probably be very little impact on production: the limiting factor in these areas is not the level of fertiliser application, and cultivators should adopt a low productivity technology (see above, pp. 72–3). It is in the intermediate areas that the impact may be most severe. Because of lower yields it will be difficult to cover the increased fertiliser cost. Because of the less certain conditions, farmers will find it too risky to bear the additional costs especially if they need credit. If, consequently, they give up fertiliser, there would be a considerable decline in production. If, however, they respond by using an intermediate technology requiring less fertiliser, the decline may not be serious.

Fertiliser is, of course, not the only scarce input. Land suitable for paddy cultivation is also scarce in Sri Lanka, especially land with a good productivity potential. We cannot, therefore, compensate for production of paddy lost through the complete or partial withdrawal of fertiliser by substituting land for fertiliser. Maintaining and increasing production on the land available for cultivation is, therefore, necessary. This calls for more rational use of both fertiliser and land.

The consequences of the fertiliser crisis need not be disastrous if the response is positive. Cheap subsidised fertiliser has helped many farmers to reach yields obtainable through more intensive methods of cultivation, using labour which is relatively abundant. This is in the national interest. But farmers had preferred to substitute fertiliser because it had been made unrealistically cheap for them, although at high cost to the national economy. Seed-breeders also worked on the premise that fertiliser would continue to be cheap and abundant. Now that conditions have changed, the approach of farmers, seed-breeders and policy-makers should change. The extension services should make better use of the limited amount of fertiliser we can afford. Given such adjustments, we may make better use of fertiliser without suffering too much loss in production.

A NOTE ON THE COSTS OF PADDY PRODUCTION: MAHA 1973–4; WITH A SIMPLE PROJECTION FOR THE FUTURE (JH)

The objective of this section is to project likely costs of paddy production in Pahalagama, given the increased GPS price of Rs33 per bu. and increased fertiliser costs (both introduced in July 1974), and using as a base the actual costs of production in Maha 1973–4, of 32 cultivators.

The method follows that used by Izumi and Ranatunge (1973). It seemed desirable, however, to include as a cost 'interest payments' on loans purely for production purposes. 'Miscellaneous costs' include the four items: haulage costs, the cost of hire of spraying equipment and of threshing carpets, and acreage taxes. Throughout, the figures of Rs25 and Rs33 per bu. have been used for kind costs and in calculating incomes, although in a number of cases farmers obtained much more than the then GPS price of Rs25 by selling elsewhere. Rs25 is used for Maha 1973–4 because the majority of cultivators had sold their paddy before the price was increased to Rs30 in April 1974. In the case of tenants, rents are 'real' and entered as the cash equivalent of the actual payment to the landlord. Labour has been costed as follows. Family members treated as coolies were paid a daily rate but, whereas the cost of food and supplementaries are included in the costs of hired labour, they are not counted in the case of family labour. Labour employed for collecting paddy and transporting it to the threshing floor is usually paid in bundles of paddy. These have been neither counted as a cost nor included in output, so that real yields were rather higher than stated. No allowance has been made in labour or cost tabulations for the supervisory and managerial time of the cultivator or time spent in bird-scaring. The time of tractor drivers has been included, and is indeed one source of variation in the labour budgets, because more driver time is involved when 2-wheeled tractors are used.

In arriving at the projection for 1974–5 the new paddy and fertiliser prices have been substituted in the accounts for each of the farmers, with an allowance for a 20 per cent increase in labour costs and a 15 per cent increase in the cost of providing food. No allowance has been made for increased tractor costs. The fertiliser prices are those supplied by Co-operative Management Services on 16 July 1974. Fieldwork was still in

Table 24.4

Item	Tenants' costs (Rs)	(%)	Owners' costs (Rs)	(%)	Average costs for total population (Rs)	(%)
Cost of production per acre, Maha 1973–4						
Labour: hired	354·7	38·6	288	36·1	312·96	37·2
family	74·3	8·1	73·15	9·2	73·68	8·8
Buffaloes			18·7	2·3	11·69	1·4
Tractors	242·8	26·5	195·4	24·5	213·15	25·3
Materials used	151·1	16·5	140·2	17·6	144·28	17·1
of which fertiliser					55·2	
Miscellaneous	55·8	6·1	43	5·4	47·81	5·7
Interest	38·6	4·2	39·2	4·9	38·9	4·6
Total	917·3		797·65		842·5	
Projected cost per acre, Maha 1974–5						
Labour: hired	430·5	32·1	347·15	30	378·4	30·88
family	89·3	6·7	89·3	7·7	89·3	7·29
Buffaloes			24·65	2·1	15·4	1·26
Tractors	319·8	23·9	257·5	22·3	280·84	22·92
Materials	367·25	27·4	331·85	28·7	345·13	28·16
of which fertiliser					222·6	
Miscellaneous	67·8	5·1	51·5	4·5	57·63	4·7
Interest	64·9	4·9	55·2	4·8	58·84	4·8
Total	1,339·5		1,157·15		1,225·53	

progress at the time of the price increase so some impression was formed of the farmers' reactions. This impression has informed the interpretation offered here.

In Maha 1973–4 the greatest degree of variation was in expenditure on hired labour (from Rs130 to Rs521), for reasons that included differences (i) between labour requirements of sown and transplanted crops, (ii) between labour requirements on terraced fields as opposed to those on bigger fields on flatter ground, (iii) in the use of family labour (average 27·2 per cent of labour used, maxium 63 per cent, minimum nil), (iv) in the use of 2-wheel or 4-wheel tractors, or buffaloes; (v) in the use of a fan for winnowing rather than the wind, (vi) in yield and in the different characteristics of varieties in harvesting and threshing, and (vii) in the abilities of cultivators to get work done quickly and efficiently.

Variation is also shown in expenditure on materials used. This is in part accounted for by differences in the quantities of seed paddy used and in the use of agrochemicals (probably the most potent source of variation). Expenditure on fertilisers ranged between Rs106 and Rs16·50 per acre, excluding the two farmers who used no fertiliser at all (cf. pp. 148–9 above).

This analysis brings out the same characteristics of paddy production costs as that of Izumi and Ranatunge (1973). The major item is labour (46 per cent) followed by the costs of draught (25 per cent), reflecting the 'extensive' nature of paddy cultivation in the dry zone (see above, pp. 143–5). The cost of traction has been increasing both relatively and absolutely in Hambantota District because most owners are paid a fixed amount in kind, so that any increase in the GPS price automatically increases their gross cash income: the amount of paddy demanded has also increased recently.

Comparison of the actual figures for 1973 – 4 with the projected figures shows an increase in average total costs per acre of Rs383 or 45 per cent, half due to increased fertiliser costs. About Rs160 of the total increase comprises imputed kind costs, leaving Rs220 as increased cash demand. This gives some indication of the additional credit demand which will be felt by the co-operatives and rural banking institutions.

Table 24.5

Category	Value of paddy harvested	Total cost per acre	Profit margin per acre	Value of family labour per acre	Family farm earnings	Tenants after rent
Farm Earnings per acre, Maha 1973–4 (Rs)						
All	1,821·25	842·5	978·75	73·68	1,052·43	
Tenants	2,281·75	917·3	1,301·45	74·3	1,375·75	907·75
Owners	1,583·0	797·65	785·35	73·15	858·5	
Projected Farm Earnings per acre 1974–5 (Rs)						
All	2,404·05	1,225·53	1,178·52	89·28	1,287·8	
Tenants	2,928·75	1,339·5	1,589·25	89·3	1,678·55	1,061·55
Owners	2,089·56	1,157·15	932·41	89·3	1,021·71	

Note: A discussion of the differences between tenants and owners revealed by this table is found in chapter 10, pp. 150–2.

The most important conclusion that emerges from Table 24.5 is that, provided yields do not fall very much, farmers might increase their earnings over Maha 1973 – 4 despite increased costs. Separate analyses of the 32 sets of accounts shows that only one of the cultivators, who was ill, would earn less. However, the drop in yield for the group as a whole would only have to be about 6 bu. per acre for earnings to drop below the 1973–4 level. (It must be remembered that the 1973–4 Maha was exceptionally good, and that the locality studied is a favoured one.) If, as a minimum objective, we take the average costs per acre of Table 24.4 and the average acreage of 2·9 acres and assume that the farmer needs to cover costs and to leave himself with 35 bu. of paddy to feed his family for a season, then in the

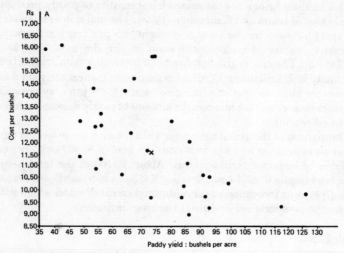

x : Average cost of average yield

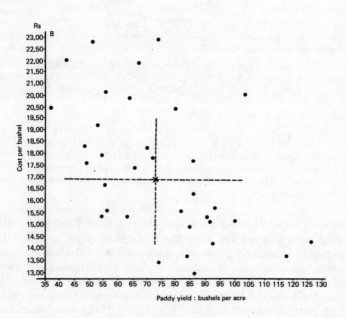

Fig. 24.1 *Relation between yield and cost per bushel*
A. *Before price increase*
B. *After increase of GPS price to Rs33*

old situation he needed to obtain only 45·8 bu. per acre, whereas with the new prices he needs to obtain 49·2 bu. per acre.

This gives some indication of increased financial risks in cultivation, with the new price levels, especially given that – on the whole – the lower the yield per acre the higher the cultivation costs per unit of output, and that cultivators who used quantities of fertiliser below the average for the sample are predominantly grouped in the high-cost/low-yields sub-set. The conclusion that a majority of farmers will earn less than in Maha 1973–4 seems unavoidable, in spite of the fact that Tables 24.4 and 24.5 appear to show that the increased GPS prices more or less cover the increased cost of fertiliser.

In the absence of data on the returns to different levels of fertiliser applications under different management practices and environmental conditions, it is difficult to give a precise statement of alternative strategies open to farmers. However, it seems safe to assume that in this area the farmers will lose more by reducing their usage of fertilisers drastically than they will by paying for fertiliser at the new prices. Certainly that is the view expressed by a majority of farmers. Farmers who had seemed previously to pooh-pooh the idea of using organic manures now began to talk of trying them, and to discuss ways and means of doing so.

None the less, given the additional cash requirements in the new situation, and the additional risk introduced by the new prices, it seems likely that more farmers will turn to the kind of low-cost/relatively low-yield strategy that a few farmers adopted even in the 1973–4 Maha season (Fig. 24.1). The accounts of these cultivators show that they all used relatively small quantities of fertiliser and more than average amounts of family labour.

Comparison of the cost/yield distributions at Maha 1973–4 rates and the new rates shows that those who used small amounts of fertiliser are likely to remain predominantly in that group which shows less than average yield at more than average costs. An important reason for this may be that they cultivate less fertile soils, while in general, cultivators who depart furthest from the trend line of inverse relationship between yield per acre and cost per bushel in the direction of high cost for moderate yield (Fig. 24.1) are those whose labour costs are exceptionally high for reasons which include illness and the unwillingness of family members to contribute to cultivation. The three cultivators of traditional varieties show high costs per bushel in both cost situations, which indicates that it will not be worthwhile to revert to the use of traditional varieties.

Finally, there can be little doubt that average yield levels will fall. If overall production is to be maintained and increased it seems that acreage must be augmented, for there are serious obstacles, certainly in the short and medium term, to the intensification of paddy production by such means as increased use of transplanting and hand-weeding (see above, pp. 149–50). There are some persuasive arguments for economising in the use of existing water resources with the objectives both of increasing yields and augmenting paddy acreage (see pp. 349–52 and 364–75). The trend towards lower yields, both because of the conscious adoption of low-cost/low-yield strategies and because of lower levels of fertiliser use, serves to strengthen the argument.

ALTERNATIVE TECHNOLOGIES (BH)

Seed-breeding strategy having been dominated till recently by the single objective of rapidly increasing yield, the involvement of large-scale modern technology was inevitable. Shortages of fertilisers, electric power and agrochemicals, together with the trebling of petroleum prices and quadrupling of freight rates, threaten the short-term viability of such technology. It is important, then, to look at the feasibility of alternative technologies. Discussion here will be confined to the two States studied and accepts two constraints: no decline in yield levels and no major change in political or social organisation. It will also be concerned with alternative technologies in non-mechanised agricultural inputs.

Pump-sets

In India pump-sets use five times as much energy and have needed 6·5 times as much capital as tractors (Majumdar, 1973). Tamil Nadu has 50 per cent of India's electric pump-sets. As long as the Tamil Nadu Electricity Board (TNEB) could provide power, no brake to their spread was necessary on any but ecological grounds. But demand for electricity is growing at over 15 per cent per annum while supply grows at under 10 per cent (TNEB, 1972, p. 5). If pressure on power supply is to be reduced, fewer pump-sets should be connected and rationing of current must continue.

Tamil Nadu has 30 per cent of India's diesel pump-sets which for equivalent hp have higher capital, fixed and variable costs. They become relatively attractive after 50–75 per cent electricity power cuts but less attractive after increases in oil prices. Loans for diesel pump-sets were suspended in April 1974.

According to The Hindu (9 March 1974) diesel pump-sets could run more cheaply on ethyl alcohol, a by-product of sugar-refining in which Tamil Nadu is self-sufficient. But diesel pump-sets are only 4 per cent of the total in the District. Unless atomic energy provides a palliative then other alternatives to the electric pump-set must be considered.

Wind- or solar-powered motors deserve experimentation (see below, pp. 394–5). In the absence of such alternatives farmers will have to revert to the kavalai but this brings increases in labour demand and in fodder costs. Capital costs of bullocks are also rising. The price of the older alternative technology is, in fact, rising at a faster rate than that of the modern technology.

To abandon well-irrigation outright would be a radical departure from tradition, would drastically reduce the multiple-cropped acreage; and might be very unreliable given the diminished attention now paid to the maintenance of tanks and anicuts. If less non-renewable energy were used for pump-sets, very high-yielding varieties would be needed for one season only: at other times the land would be under dry-land crops which (if leguminous) might help to replenish soil nutrients. But Table 24.6 shows that at current average yield levels a 25 per cent reduction in man-days of food would be the likely result of a water-sparing paddy–sorghum rotation. The substitution of water-sparing crops for paddy cannot be entertained given the present decennial population growth rate of 19·4 per cent.

Table 24.6 Population support potential of some simple crop combinations

Data		No. of man-days of calories produced per hectare	
1 Average yield of rice N.A. Dt kg per hectare	4,968	Single crop average, rice	7,281
Average yield of sorghum N.A. Dt kg per hectare	2,400	2 crops average, rice	14,562
2 Max. yield of IR.8 (Cuttack) kg per hectare	8,870	2 crops, rice/sorghum	10,692
Max. yield sorghum (Cuttack) kg per hectare	5,606	2 crops, sorghum	6,820
3 Average calories/kg milled rice	3,600	Single crop, sorghum	3,410
Average calories/kg sorghum	3,490	Single crop, max. rice	13,000
4 Average daily calorie requirements *per capita*	2,456	Single crop, max. sorghum	7,965

Sources:

1 Department of Agriculture Tamil Nadu, 1971 data
2 FAI, 1973
3 Ryan *et al.* (1974), p. 19

Tractors

It seems that the energy crisis has raised tractor job rates but had little effect on reducing demand either in Tamil Nadu or Sri Lanka. There is clearly a strong case for considering less energy-consumptive alternatives especially in Sri Lanka (see chapter 12). To revert to the buffalo would not be difficult. The present population is still 70 per cent of the maximum in the 1960s. The potential of bullocks and of improved implements for them should be reinvestigated. There is substantial information on efficient animal-drawn implements which would, in fact, improve the condition of many fields and therefore of paddy yields. The mammoti for field preparation has a similar type of labour-intensity and social stigma in Sri Lanka as the etram in Tamil Nadu, and would only be used in the final resort. Governments may have to discriminate actively against machines, through such policies as selective taxation, and breed seeds which do not require tractors for threshing.

Fertiliser and Manure

Very few farmers use the government fertiliser norms and many farmers appear to achieve creditable yields with over- under- or mis-use of chemical fertiliser (compare above pp. 62 and 378). This suggests that experiments which set out positively to vet the yield responses of a wide variety of crops to common sub-optimal conditions of fertiliser use ought to be made urgently. But the marginal productivity of output per unit of fertiliser is maximised at a fairly low level of fertiliser input, whereas maximising paddy production requires high levels of application.

Changes in Management Practices

A key and controversial issue is the extent to which chemical fertiliser, organic manure and management practices are substitutable and interact. It was estimated that in 1968, 30 per cent of dry zone farmers could achieve yields of over 100 bu. per acre, not by changing their existing low standards of husbandry nor by changing the varieties of paddy used, but simply with applications of NPK fertiliser in either 45:45:45 form or 45:35:28 form (Weerawickrema and Constable, 1968, p. 4). The 30 per cent increase in yield in Hambantota District in Maha 1973–4 could be due both to the quadrupling of fertiliser consumption and to timely application and other improved management practices (Williams, 1974, p. 41). The extent to which it is true that, with no change in fertiliser use – and independently of paddy variety – radically better management will raise yield levels, is now important. One well-known problem with HYVs is that, irrespective of fertiliser use, the higher the potential yield the better the level of management necessary to realise that yield. According to *The Hindu* (10 July 1974), if factors such as the age of seedlings at transplantation, the depth and spacing of transplanted paddy, careful field drainage before fertiliser application and reflooding 48 hours afterwards, and a 'high degree of control over water weeds and pest' (however achieved) were optimised, then average yields of 2–4 tonnes of paddy per hectare could be achieved without chemical fertiliser. This must be complicated by the fact that correct water management also affects both yields and the number of cropping seasons. Correct land preparation, combined with crop rotations, especially with leguminous plants, also acts to reduce the need for N fertiliser applications from 75 to 40 kg per acre without affecting yields. Besides needing to know to what extent this is true, and to what extent farmers already practise such levels of management, it is also necessary to predict their costs in terms of cash and types of labour, and their repercussions on other crops and land use.

Alternative Manures

Soil scientists and agronomists, from Joachim in 1931 (pp. 5–34) to Kalpage in 1967 (p. 86), draw attention to the false dichotomy between chemical fertiliser and organic manure and stress the value of using both, but urge caution in the use of organic manures under the potentially anaerobic conditions of paddy fields, where ammonia may turn to toxic nitrites. So far as nutrients are concerned, organic manures are 'low grade' and unbalanced; very large quantities are necessary to replace what paddy takes out of the soil. According to Kalpage at least 10 tons of manure per acre would be necessary to replace the total nutrients removed. But whereas in Navarai 1974 10 tons cost Rs200 in urban waste, lorry hire and labour, by Sornavari 1974 it cost Rs312·5, equivalent of three bags of urea and three times the official dose of N at current controlled prices. In India at least, the price structure of alternatives does not necessarily make them attractive. Let us, however, consider some of them: first, organic manure. Possible sources in Hambantota District are burnt husk (rich in potash, humus and silica), pangiri or citronella ash (expensive) and albecia leaves. In North Arcot District there is little such greenery: 'Takkai pundu', 'daincha', sunn hemp and wild indigo are recommended, also bagasse. Green manure provides humus and helps to conserve and aerate soil; it increases paddy yields by increasing the availability of N as ammonium and by supplying CO_2 to the film of algae in paddy fields, which in turn liberate oxygen to the paddy root (Lord, 1931, p. 154). Non-leguminous manure is counterproductive if grown in the area to be manured; plants have to be young and relatively low in lignin content; the cultivation of green manure diverts water from other uses, and the ploughing-in of green manure denies this source of fodder to animals. The early recommendations of 4–5 tons per acre (Joachim, 1931, pp. 5–22; Lord, 1931, pp. 154–5) assume that the paddy stalk is ploughed in, which no longer happens: the dose must therefore be doubled. As Panabokke says (1967, p. 128): 'there is a strong case for reviving these practices but very little advantages in organic or green manure applications to rice soils which are either poorly drained or boggy'. In Tamil Nadu the ratio of land for green manure to paddy land is 1:5 (from data in Rajagopalan, 1974) and the area manured has dropped by 30 per cent since 1970 whereas the All India area has increased by 40 per cent (FAI, 1973, pp. 1–438). The reasons for this deviant trend are not known.

Animal manures include cow-dung, urine (rich in N, P and K) and nightsoil (Table 24.7).

Clearly the most efficacious animal manure derives from poultry, goats and humans. None the less if we consider cattle manure alone and compare its nutrients with those in chemical fertiliser used by farmers in 1973 (Table 24.8) it is plain that the former greatly exceed the latter. 'In Sri Lanka animal manure is very poorly handled . . . and there appears to be no organised attempts to make the best of its potentialities' (Panabokke, 1967,

Table 24.7   Nutrient content of animal manure, green manure and composts

	Percentage		
	N	P	K
Cow	0·6	0·15	0·45
Horse	0·7	0·25	0·55
Goat	0·95	0·35	1·00
Pig	0·5	0·35	0·40
Poultry	1·6	1·75	0·90
Human	1·0	1·1	0·25
Urban compost	1·5	1·0	1·5
Rural compost	0·6	0·5	0·85
Green manure	0·6	0·15	1·2

Source: Panabokke, 1967, p. 110; FAI, 1973, pp. 1–299.

Table 24.8   Nutrient potential of manure and fertiliser in Tamil Nadu and Sri Lanka (1973)

Cattle population (m.)	Annual production manure (m. tonnes)	Annual use of fertiliser	Nutrient content		
			tonnes N	tonnes P	tonnes K
Sri Lanka					
1·5	7		42,700	10,700	32,000
		42,103	28,500	10,100	9,100
Manure as percentage of chemical fertiliser			144	100	350
Tamil Nadu					
14	63		378,000	94,500	283,500
		479,000	173,800	56,000	82,300
Manure as percentage of chemical fertiliser			217	168	344

Sources:

Sri Lanka: Agricultural Census; MOAL data for fertiliser, 1973.
Tamil Nadu: FAI 1973, Table 1.5.07 and Government of Tamil Nadu, 1973, p. 34.

p. 109). Its 'potentiality' being greater than the annual import of fertiliser, a great deal of organisation seems opportune. By contrast, in Tamil Nadu it is already extensively utilised for fuel as well as for agriculture.

A compost of animal and green manure and soil may be the most efficacious of all organic manures; but to Kalpage the procedure is 'time consuming and expensive' (1967, p. 89). In India, rural compost programmes are a feature of the Fifth Five Year Plan. At a conservative estimate, compost could be enough for 70m. acres of paddy land, 80 per cent of the All India extent, for one season. Because it may all be in use already, it is rash to attribute any great potential to these traditional technologies in India. Whether or not the presently underutilised potential in Sri Lanka's dry zone is used depends on the emergence of motivation.

Alternatives for Agrochemicals

Because of different factor endowments on either side of the Palk straits, quite different strategies are being adopted towards weedicides. Tamil Nadu is advocating the use of pre-emergent weedicides (at present little used) in order to reduce the N removed from soil by weeds. This practice is largely unadopted by farmers because of its cost compared with hand-weeding. In Sri Lanka's dry zone the use of weedicides is common. They constitute half the foreign exchange quota for agrochemicals and can be substituted by water (lavish use of which kills 75 per cent of weeds but has a social cost), hand-weeding (difficult because of lack of, and cost of labour relative to chemicals), and the Japanese weeder (a machine dependent on line transplanting, which raises labour costs).

Both countries recognise a continuing need for pesticides. HYVs have a greater susceptibility to pest attack especially where they are grown in monoculture. The pesticide controversy is a familiar one and will only be summarised here. *Pro*: Pesticides increase the average yields of traditional paddy varieties by 15 to 20 per cent and HYVs by 50 per cent (Mitra, 1974). In South Asia the ratio between money spent on them and money saved by them is very high. There is a dearth of alternatives: 'Feeding people is more important than polluting people'. *Con*: Dangers of concentration of persistent traces of organochlorine insecticides in living creatures. Pesticides may drift on to other land, crops and animals with toxic effects. Mutation may result in resistant pests. Pesticides may be indiscriminately toxic to wide ranges of organisms. There are also economic problems; pesticide manufacture is a highly energy-intensive process and foreign exchange costs are high.

In theory there are a number of alternatives: first, non-persistent pesticides. But these are no solution to the problems of widespread and indiscriminate toxicity or mutant resistance. Secondly, resistant plants may be grown: traditional paddy types are in any case more pest-resistant than HYVs. Thirdly, natural predators, parasites, bacteria and viruses may be introduced. This strategy faces many problems. Fourthly, food-attractant and/or sex-attractant chemicals which kill or repel insects might be used. Fifthly, organic pesticides could be developed which repel by taste or smell. Lastly, the males of pests might be sterilised.

The overriding practical problem is that, apart from non-persistent pesticides, none of these alternatives are available for paddy: all at present involve changes in the ecological structure of paddy cultivation. There would need to be more careful use of crop rotations; the favouring of a greater diversity of paddy varieties in any one wet-land area in any one season; breeding programmes emphasising pest resistance would substitute for scarcities in pesticides.

Conclusions

Traditional alternative technologies exist in both countries. Whether or not they are inter-digitated with HYV technology probably depends on population densities and on artificial distortions in the factor markets for modern technologies. New intermediate technologies for agricultural implements, for lift irrigation and for weedicides exist on the world market but have been transferred, if at all, only experimentally.

For the crucial inputs – fertiliser and pesticides – research needs to be done to determine conditions under which they cross-substitute with management and with traditional technologies for specific agrarian regions. If yields of paddy are to be maintained or increased there is no doubt that a complete innovation in reverse is out of the question. If intermediate technologies can coexist with, and compensate for deficiencies in supplies of modern input technology, then the gap between the sectors of a dual economy may begin to close.

However, historically, developments in technology are not brought about unless it is in the interests of a powerful social group to do so. There appear to be few cases of technology being used to determine social and economic change for the masses against the wishes of an élite, however paternalistic, and many cases of technology being used to bolster a social and political *status quo* (Dickson, 1974). Moreover, many recent appropriate technological models developed for field application 'are . . . ancillary types of industrial units which can only be established around large scale plant and are thus dependent on the very technology which they propose to replace' (Garg, 1974, p. 17). Also 'because of their training, planners and others find it difficult to conceive the role of science and technology in development' (Sussex Group, 1970, p. 20). If in future technology the developers, purveyors and users are to exist in a dialectical relationship, the developers and purveyors will have to be independent, 'enlightened and educated' (Gabor, 1963, p. 108) and the users articulate in a qualitatively different way from in the past. The problems involved in bringing this about are far more intractable than those involved in developing new alternative technology.

FUTURE-BASED PLANNING FOR TECHNOLOGY; LINKING POPULATION, WATER AND ENERGY IN AN INDIAN DISTRICT (RC)

There are already in South Asia many millions of rural poor who cannot adequately feed themselves. Yet, between 1970 and 2000, rural populations may well rise by 76 per cent (UN, 1971, chapter VI). Against this daunting background there are many who are resigned to a future of widespread poverty and starvation. But there is nothing inevitable about poverty and starvation: despair flows from a failure to recognise the potential of future-based planning, here to be illustrated from North Arcot. There are five steps: (i) estimating future populations, (ii) identifying critical resources, (iii) specifying criteria for a technology to combine those resources, (iv) describing an appropriate future technology and scenario, and (v) plotting paths for their development and introduction.

Population and Resources

The rural population of North Arcot District is expected to increase by 63 per cent from 1970 to 2000. At first sight it is exceedingly difficult to see how such an increase could be sustained: already most of the survey villages are labour-surplus for most of the year.

Two critical resources here are water and energy. Water is the more constraining on agricultural production. There is not much potential for increasing water-harvesting from catchments and there is now a secular decline in the water-table (see pp. 332—8). As the water-table drops, so more energy is demanded to raise water through greater heights. There is a shortage of electricity (p. 386 above). The most abundant energy endowment of Tamil Nadu is sunlight.

Criteria and Specifications

Five criteria can be suggested:

(i) *Productivity*.
The productivity of water is much more critical here than the productivity of land. But the pump-set has probably reduced the productivity of water in terms of calories of food produced per unit of water applied. It has supplied water in greater abundance and so encouraged practices and crops which are extravagant in water use: in particular, paddy, which has a high water/food calorie ratio. The future water-lift technology should encourage water-sparing practices and crops which have low water/calorie ratios.

(ii) *Equity*.
Pump-sets have enhanced inequalities. Those who have been able to obtain them have preferential access to groundwater; those with small holdings or shallower wells, or animal lift only, have suffered. The future water-lift technology should have economies of small scale and contribute to more equitable distribution of water and land.

(iii) *Stability*.
Pump-sets have made possible the mining of water and used non-renewable energy sources. The future water-lift technology should ration water extractions and not use non-renewable energy.

(iv)   *Continuity*.

Employment and food production should be more continuous. Sharp labour peaks leave labourers without support for much of the year and are associated with food abundant at harvest but scarce and costly when the landless find it hardest to gain employment. Here pump-sets have a mixed record; where groundwater is abundant, as in Kalpattu, they maintain continuous labour demand and production; where it is scarce, as in Vayalur, they have exhausted it, accentuated seasonal unemployment and reduced dry season cultivation. The future water-lift technology should encourage more continuous employment and food production.

(v)   *Livelihood-intensity*.

Pump-sets have probably generated additional livelihoods (pp. 227–8 and 312), but the ratio of livelihoods to water extracted has almost certainly declined. The future water-lift technology should promote a high livelihood-intensity of water use and so sustain a much larger rural population at an acceptable level of living.

It may appear that a future to meet these criteria could only be achieved through Utopian social engineering (Popper, 1945, Vol. I, pp. 138–43). An alternative is, however, provided by the choice of a technology, and a scenario centred upon it.

A Future Technology and Scenario

The technology is the solar pump, now being developed in several places including Harwell, UK (West, 1971; Hawkes 1974). A solar pump will probably lift much less water than a pump-set; but it should be possible to design one with an appropriate scale and capacity. Let us specify that the solar pump to be developed for North Arcot would, on a normal sunny day, lift through 10 ft enough water to irrigate half an acre growing a water-sparing crop such as groundnut.

With such a technology the future village has no pump-sets, and most wells have been filled in or made smaller. Many new smaller wells have been dug in wet land and dry land: each has its solar pump whose overhead receptor also reduces evaporation by shading the well. On the spoil from the well is a storage tank into which the pump lifts water during the hours of sunlight. The water is conveyed to the near-by land, through hosepipe, eliminating transmission losses and facilitating labour-intensive, water-sparing application. To reduce evaporation losses, water application takes place in the evening, each well and pump requiring one person at least.

Soils have been modified to make them more uniform, water-sparing and suitable for a wider range of crops. Tank-bed silt is spread on the sandier soils of the dry land to enrich them and reduce percolation losses. Seru paddy soils (see pp. 134–5) have been modified through the addition of sandy soils to grow more water-sparing crops. Groundwater has been stabilised through deliberate recharge bores in the tank bed, removal of whose silt also unseals it, and technological rationing (the fixed energy available to solar pumps provides a homoeostatic mechanism). Agricultural technology has become more productive, especially through varieties and practices substituting labour for water and using manures and fertilisers more efficiently and with higher labour-intensity.

The scenario can be measured against the five criteria:

1 The productivity of water has been vastly enhanced. Paddy has been abandoned because the new water supply is inadequate: water-sparing crops and irrigation techniques make the water/crop calorie ratios much lower.
2 Equity is greater because the pre-emption of communal groundwater by those with pump-sets has ended.
3 Stability has been improved through the homoeostatic mechanism and the elimination of power from hydro-electric and non-renewable energy sources.
4 Continuity of employment and food production has been much increased through a technology which pumps continuously, encouraging continuous agricultural activities.
5 A much larger population may be provided with livelihoods from the same land and water.

Paths to the Scenario
How could such a technology be developed and such a scenario be achieved? The development of suitable solar pumps from existing systems depends on the priority, resources and ingenuity devoted to the task. Even if solar pumps proved impracticable, alternative combinations of human, animal, renewable fuel, solar, hydro-electric, nuclear, tidal, wind and other sources of energy might well be designed to meet the same criteria.

The widespread adoption of the technology would depend partly upon its capital cost, but this might be subsidised with international assistance; partly upon the materials and skills needed for its production and installation. The phasing-out of pump-sets presents less difficulty. A politically resolute government might gradually make them illegal: an easier course would be gradually to raise the electricity tariff. Shifts would then take place, for example from paddy to more water-sparing crops; and so the water-table should stabilise at a higher level. The modification of soils would probably take place spontaneously; silt is already extracted from tank beds and transferred to upland soils, and (to a lesser extent) sandy soils on to seru soils. An agriculture in which labour increased the productivity of water, manures and fertilisers would be the outcome of research policies already initiated.

The path towards more equitable distribution opens up exciting possibilities. The implementation of land reforms now labours under the difficulties not only of a politically powerful rural élite but also of being unrelated to the water resources without which the land may be of low productive value. If solar pumps, small wells, and labour-intensive and water-sparing cultivation became economic sense, then we can imagine the following sequence for a man who now has 3 acres and a pump-set. As the pump-set became less economical he would dig a new small well and install a solar pump, perhaps with family labour, but his second solar pump might well require additional help. Gradually wells, solar pumps and labourers are added. Finally, the scene would be set for a redistributive land and water reform: a policy of land to the irrigator would be easier to implement, for what had been 3 acres with one pump-set and one family has become 6 half-acre plots intensively cultivated, each with its small well, and supporting several families. The outcome might be not unlike Vinayagapuram, with a very high proportion of the population as cultivators, with labour-intensive cultivation, spread round the year, and with a much higher population supported.

Conclusion
Future-based planning has here led to the specification of a technology which should be developed now to make possible a better future. The approach has been speculative and non-numerate. The next step is further to explore technological developments and to identify orders of magnitude for the parameters. Already, however, two suggestions are justified. First, future-based planning, using population projections, estimates of critical resources, and relevant criteria in order to specify desirable future technologies, may have a major potential for rural development. Secondly, the choice of technology to develop, and particularly whether large or small scale, may powerfully influence future income and asset distribution, and may even set the scene for a redistributive reform.

REFERENCES

Agrarian Research and Training Institute, ARTI (1974). *The Agrarian Situation in Relation to Paddy Cultivation in Five Selected Districts of Sri Lanka*, Colombo.

Dickson, D. (1974). *Alternative Technology and the Politics of Technical Change*, London, Fontana.

Fertiliser Association of India, FAI (1973). *Fertiliser Statistics, 1972–73*, New Delhi.

Gabor, D. (1963). *Inventing the Future*, Harmondsworth, Penguin.

Garg, M. K. (1974). Problems of Developing Appropriate Technologies in India, *Appropriate Technology*, 1, 16–18.

Hawkes, N. (1974). 'The Amazing Solar Engine', *Observer*, 21 July.

Izumi, K. and Ranatunge, S. (1973). *Cost of Paddy Production Yala 1972*, ARTI Research Study Series no. 1, Colombo.

Joachim, A. W. R. (ed.) (1931). *A Manual of Green Manuring*, Colombo, Department of Agriculture.

Kalpage, F. S. C. P. (1967). *Soils and Fertilisers*, Colombo, Department of Agriculture.

Lord, L. (1931). 'Green Manuring of Paddy' in Joachim (ed.) (1931), pp. 149–56.

Majumdar, P. S. (1973). 'Farm Mechanisation in India', paper to IDS/ARTI Seminar on Economic and Social Consequences of the Improved Seeds, Colombo.

Mitra, R. B. (1974). 'Bid for Self Reliance in Pesticide Know How', *The Hindu Survey of Indian Industry*, Madras.

Panabokke, C. R. (1967). *Soils of Ceylon and Fertiliser Use*, Colombo, Ceylon Association for the Advancement of Science.

Popper, K. (1945). *The Open Society and Its Enemies*, London, Routledge.

Rajagopalan, V. (1974). *Fertiliser Crisis and Rice Production – Implications to Research and Development*, paper to the Annual Rice Conference, IRRI, Los Banos, p. 11, mimeo.

Ryan, J. G., Sheldrake, R. and Yadav, S. P. (1974). *Human Nutritional Needs and Crop Breeding Objectives in the Semi-arid Tropics*, Economic Statistical Unit, ICRISAT Occasional Paper no. 4, Hyderabad.

Sussex Group (1970). *Science and Technology to Developing Countries during the Second Development Decade*, IDS reprint no. 101, Brighton.

Tamil Nadu Electricity Board, TNEB (1973). *15th Ann. Admin. Report, 1971–72*, Madras.

UN (1971). *The World Population Situation in 1970*, United Nations Department of Economic and Social Affairs, Population Studies no. 49, New York.

Weerawickrema, S. K. A. and Constable, D. H. (1968). *Ceylon Fertiliser Project: 8th (last) Field Report to the Government of Ceylon*, Colombo, mimeo.

West, C. (1971). *The Fluidyne Heat Engine*, UK Atomic Energy Authority, Research Group Report, Harwell.

Williams, L. B. (1974). *The Hambantota Story*, Colombo, Co-operative Management Services Centre.

25 Challenges for Rural Research and Development

Robert Chambers

This chapter sets out some of the challenges for research and development for rural South Asia that emerge from the experiences of this project. It is written against the frightening background of the world food and economic crisis, at a time when many of the people in South Asia cannot afford to buy or otherwise obtain the food they need, and when the early promise of the Green Revolution has faded. But despite disappointments there have been considerable technical advances in agriculture and in scientific organisation: a visitor to the higher-level research and plant-breeding stations – such as AICRIP and ICRISAT in Hyderabad, the Tamil Nadu Agricultural University at Coimbatore, or Maha Illup-pallama and Batalagoda in Sri Lanka – cannot fail to be impressed by the achievements of the past and excited by the possibilities for the future. Those who decry the Green Revolution and the imagination and skill that have made possible such as it has achieved fail to realise what conditions would be if nothing had been done. The fact is that very large quantities of additional food have been produced in hungry and food-importing poorer countries. It is too easy and safe for privileged observers who have never themselves been hungry to lament that big farmers have gained more than small, that the main beneficiaries have been the multinational corporations and their investors, that the effects have, in fact, been bad. The burden on us is not only to criticise but also to construct, not only to analyse what has gone wrong but also to learn from it how to create something better.

In trying to do this, it is not difficult to suggest fields of research which have been relatively neglected by social scientists. These have dimensions both of subject – for example, case studies of landless families and studies of intra-rural migration appear as two needs and opportunities – and of geographical area, some more favoured areas being surveyed and resurveyed, and others neglected (see pp. 30–4). But the main thrust of this chapter is not directed towards subjects which social scientists might on their own open up, but on the linkages and complementarities between the work of social scientists and natural scientists.

Now, less than ever, can we afford to allow social and natural scientists to proceed independently. In the past they have contributed to understanding and to rural development working largely in isolation. Seedbreeders, for example, faced with the potential from HYVs, were probably (notwithstanding social scientist critics) right to proceed with their development. A plethora of consultations, conferences and criticisms might have paralysed the programme. Similarly, social anthropologists have been right to do their thing in villages and write up their monographs, because not enough has been understood about village life and we need to describe before we can prescribe. This stage is now passing. The easy things have been done. Genetic yield-potential ceilings have been approached. The better work of social scientists has revealed and recorded some of the anatomy of rural life. But the next steps, for social scientists and natural scientists alike, ought to be much harder. There is always the option of 'more of the same' and 'in the same places'; these are easy to accept and so likely to be accepted.

Social scientists have seriously failed their natural scientist colleagues, indeed the community as a whole. There is no adequate theory of rural development; no analytical framework for categorising rural situations which can be used prescriptively; no theory of stages in rural development which can identify what should be done in any particular situation (see, however, Hunter, 1970). Moreover, with the exception of confident and sometimes arrogant economists, social scientists have tended to be bold only in criticism, and feeble or misguided in advice. Sociologists in particular tend to be either banal or wrong: banal in writing wordy reports which say, 'if the people like it, they will accept it, but if they don't, they won't'; and wrong in that they are not trained to make the sort of judgements at which administrators and politicians are more expert, and in being liable to make sweeping generalisations for policy which are not justified by the evidence (see Moynihan, 1969 for an example). Social scientists have to break out of the ruts in which they are stuck and to strike out in two directions: first, in search of practical theory, and second, in search of the types of experience which enable them to give more practical advice.

For their part, natural scientists engaged on agricultural, irrigation and seed-breeding research have been reluctant to learn from social scientists. Partly this has been based on their appraisal of lack of competence and versatility among social scientists. Partly, too, they have seen economists and others as threats to their decision-making autonomy. It is true that good social scientists will raise questions about the social effects of decisions taken in the seed-breeding process and about the criteria used for choices of characteristics (see for example Palmer 1972, pp. 84–6), but such questions should be welcomed by natural scientists since they affect the ultimate social benefits to be derived from their work.

There is a strong case for mutual service and education between social and natural scientists. Rural situations are not intelligible in terms of any one discipline or group of disciplines. Often on this project we found ourselves thrown up against questions with a technical scientific side: farmers in Sri Lanka rejected the basal application of fertiliser – who was right, they or their advisers? Farmers in North Arcot would not grow IR.8 in Samba – who was right, they or the extension staff? It is at the farm level, where farmers themselves make no distinctions between natural and social sciences, that such questions arise – technical scientific questions for us as social scientists, but equally, social, economic and political questions for natural scientists. Understanding the farm level and prescribing for it cannot be done well from within the narrow confines of any one discipline. Rather the major disciplines complement one another.

The conventional wisdom is that such complementarity is best achieved through multi-disciplinary teamwork. But multi-disciplinary teams are notoriously difficult to manage. Often much greater benefits may be gained if research workers learn to take a more holistic view of rural situations, combine different ways of thinking and analysis, and themselves adopt the modes of thought and points of view of other disciplines. Much of the best inter-disciplinary teamwork takes place in the same brain.

This is not, then, a prescription for an additive approach to rural research and development; it is not an injunction that every discipline should be represented on every project, or that a way forward can only be found after studying every detail. That would be nonsense. Every discipline added to a research team is liable to add to the costs in communication within the team (Lipton, 1970). We are concerned with optimising, not maximising; with costs and benefits, with returns to scarce research effort. The span of concern of those who work on rural development should be broader rather than narrower; there should be little respect for disciplinary boundaries, and social and natural scientists should take pains to learn from one another.

Two modes of thought and analysis of potential benefit to social scientists concerned with rural development are systems thinking (Emery, 1969) and ecological energetics (Phillipson, 1966). Systems thinking helps to ensure that all major stages of a process are listed and considered. Ecological energetics helps to reveal human ecology as the management of energy, focusing attention on the efficiency of energy transfers.

Two modes of thought from which natural scientists can benefit are, first, an economist's view of relative resource endowments, substitutions, trade-offs and marginal productivities, and second, a value system which includes a practical concern for human life and welfare and the equitable distribution of resources and services. Natural scientists should never dismiss as 'people's problems' or 'social constraints' whatever happens to the technology they have developed or the advice they have given, once it is released to actual people. The purpose of the scientific effort is to benefit people; and this has crucially to determine the form that the scientific effort takes and the criteria by which it is judged.

If we apply these modes of thought to the survey areas in India and Sri Lanka, and set the experience there against current government research priorities and programmes, four challenges stand out as likely to have high returns in terms of human welfare both in the areas concerned and more widely in South Asia and elsewhere. They concern research and development for future human ecosystems, seed-breeding, water management, and the social and psychological technology of research.

RESEARCH AND DEVELOPMENT FOR FUTURE HUMAN ECOSYSTEMS

It may seem inappropriate for a person from a country profligate in its wastage of non-renewable energy sources to observe the need in South Asia to develop rural ecosystems which are both stable and adaptable to change. In the world perspective the SALT negotiations, on which future energy consumption and technological investment in the West and Russia so largely depend, have an overarching importance, greater in the longer term than the population-food problems of the next few years. It is also quite correct, as Mrs Gandhi has pointed out (1974), that the West bears heavy responsibility for the world economic crisis. Many of the solutions must be sought and found in more sparing use of resources in the developed countries. But this must not divert attention from the problems and the opportunities for designing and creating ecosystems in rural South Asia which might sustain at a tolerable standard of living the much larger populations which can be expected.

There are two complementary types of approaches, the first subject-specific, the second environment-specific. An example of subject-specific research and development (R and D) where many ideas are being followed up is presented by plant nutrients. In 1969, in contrast with the US, Australia, the UK and even Ethiopia, India had a negative nitrogen balance (Nutman, 1974, Table 9). To meet the need reflected in this fact and to provide the additional nutrients for the very much higher food production needed in the future is a formidable task. Many natural and organic forms of manure are used including dung, ash, green manure, nightsoil, urban and other composts, and tank mud. Research is being conducted on seeding paddy fields with nitrogen-fixing blue-green algae (which might also perhaps be grown and harvested on tanks), on improving nitrogen-fixing micro-organisms in the rhizosphere of paddy plants, and on combining biological nitrogen-fixation (by blue-green algae and micro-organisms) with applications of chemical nitrogen (which inhibits biological fixation) late in the life of the plant. Innumerable

experiments are being conducted with labour-intensive fertiliser place-
ment in the soil, with careful timing of nitrogen applications in the life of
the plant, with the introduction of legumes into cropping patterns, with
closer spacing of crops to increase nitrogen fixation and uptake, with slow-
release nitrogenous fertiliser. Nutrients are indeed an obvious high priority
and a manageable area in which to develop new technologies.

Other less obvious subject-specific issues for R and D can be thrown up
from analyses of systems and efficiencies in resource use and in energy
transfers. Following water, energy and other resources right through the
processes of combination and use identifies striking gaps in knowledge and
research, errors in thinking, inefficient transfers and neglected wastages.
Five quite disparate examples are:

1   To think of water (where appropriate) as a scarcer resource than land,
    leading to an examination of water use efficiencies (pp. 393 and
    408–10).
2   The pre-harvest losses of grains to rodents (Roy, 1974, found losses of
    7·1 per cent on a research station and regarded this as an under-
    estimate).
3   The efficiency of the human gut in absorbing carbohydrates. Little
    research appears to have been done on this (but see Ramana Murthy
    and Belavady, 1966) but efficiencies are believed to be about 90 per
    cent. How this varies, under what circumstances, and what scope there
    may be for improvement through adjustments in diet or other
    measures, is apparently a vast area of ignorance. Yet in India an
    improvement of only 1 per cent would be worth over 1 million tons of
    foodgrains.
4   Calorie losses to intestinal parasites.
5   To think in terms of calorie yields of grains instead of yields by weight.
    The proportions of digestible calories vary considerably, yet crude
    yields by weight are still used by agricultural scientists.

Different though they are in many respects, these five examples have in
common that they present problems in measurement or calculation.
Returns to water are much harder to record than returns to land; pre-
harvest losses of grain, as Roy points out, are exceedingly difficult to
estimate; measuring the efficiency of the human gut in digesting carbohydrates requires metabolic wards, total systems of control of experimental
subjects, and intensive and exacting supervision and measurement; calorie
losses to intestinal parasites are by no means easy to estimate; and although
grain weight to calorie conversions are in principle simple to carry out, it is
easier to think in terms of grain weights. All researchers tend to do what
can be done safely and written up in nice little papers for journals. Risk-
aversion and respectable conventionality have high costs in breakthroughs
foregone. We need a change of values within research communities, to
encourage daring exploration even when it fails, to reward those who work

in new and difficult fields, and to be much more ready to accept imprecise results when the alternative is no results at all.

The second, environment-specific approach, examines particular types of human environment. Steps in this direction have been taken in the Drought-prone Areas Programme and in the Command Areas Development Programme for major irrigation systems, both in India. Similar initiatives could be taken for other environments such as semi-desert pasture lands and mountain zones. The approach should go beyond conventional research and include future-based planning (pp. 392–6). In this form of planning, estimates are made of population and critical resources at some future date and an attempt is made to write a scenario for an acceptable future. It is then necessary to think backwards from that future to specify the technologies and other means necessary to achieve it, and the possible paths that might be followed.

The specifications for such futures will vary. But in South Asia, widely applicable criteria may be productivity of the more limiting resources, equity in their distribution, stability in their exploitation, continuity in the demand for labour and the production of food throughout the year, and livelihood-intensity of the technologies devised (p. 393). Technologies with economies of very small scale may be desirable almost everywhere. It may well emerge that the choice of technologies to develop and their subsequent introduction has almost revolutionary implications for future resource and income distribution. In the case of North Arcot, the development of small-scale solar pumps might set the scene for a redistributive land reform (pp. 395–6). The potential of technology for creating the preconditions for agrarian reform is largely unexplored but it might in some environments provide the crucial element in a break-through to redistribution which has almost always in South Asia been prevented by lack of effective political will. (There have, of course, been partial exceptions such as the land reforms in Kerala and Sri Lanka.)

It is questionable whether natural and social scientists are ready for the types of interaction and leaps of imagination required by this future-based approach. This is partly because it would affect their work and ways of thinking. To take one example, labour demand profiles in farming systems might be a prime focus. To design future farming systems with this in mind would give a new twist to the work of agricultural economists and might revolutionise the work of a seed-breeder or agricultural research scientist. In West Africa a long and bitter argument ensued before agricultural scientists were finally persuaded to conduct research based on sub-optimal times of planting, for the cotton crop, because there was no prospect that sensible farmers, who gave priority to food crops as soon as the rains came, would ever plant cotton at the optimal time. Similarly, elsewhere research could and should be carried out with a view to fitting into that system which is rational by the farmer's own criteria, as well as into those which appear desirable to the planner. This requires a very open-minded approach on the part of the scientist, open both to the insights of other disciplines and to the realities of the farmer's world.

Finally, future-based environment-specific planning and R and D involve a sort of thinking different from that involved in the normal project and programme approach. In the past, development has been promoted through projects and programmes such as road-building, installing irrigation potential, providing access to family planning and the like, which are securely rooted in the present and move forward from it. In contrast, one part of future-based planning requires an imaginative leap to a future or to alternative futures, and then working back from them in order to specify the technologies to be developed now to make those futures possible. In the extremities of food shortage in South Asia, the temptation will be to concentrate on the former, short-term common-sense approach, which has much to commend it. The argument here is that for any long-term solution the second, future-based approach is essential; that the cost of not adopting it with vigour and imagination may be unspeakable, but avoidable, suffering.

SEED-BREEDING

The most dramatised R and D in recent rural development has been that carried out by seed-breeders. They have also been subject to attacks from the Jeremiahs who denigrate what the Green Revolution has achieved. Breeders should feel complimented at this attention. It follows from the importance of their work and the priority (and jealousy perhaps) with which others regard it. It is precisely because their decisions (often hidden away and protected from sight in technical corners or preliminaries) are so important that they should be opened up to much more public view and careful appraisal. Seed-breeding is too important to be left to the seed-breeders.

A crucial aspect lies in the trade-offs between alternative target characteristics. Some are easier and quicker to obtain; others more difficult and take longer. Some may be mutually compatible; others mutually incompatible. An estimate of costs (breeders' time, benefits foregone through longer lead-times, opportunity costs of various sorts) and of benefits (increased production, distribution of benefits within the society, adaptability of the seed to a range of conditions) ought to be made before and during the process of developing a new seed or family of seeds. This is eminently a task for a good agricultural economist who should be able to serve breeders both through calculations of trade-offs and through estimates of benefits by diffusion.

Breeders may claim they can do these things themselves. Certainly the tendency for them to spend time out in farmers' fields listening to farmers is likely within reason to be time well spent; but with the high returns in terms of benefits and production to the expenditure of their time on their highly skilled breeding activities, it would be wasteful for them to devote substantial periods to work for which agricultural economists are more qualified.

Questions of priorities for target characteristics are, moreover, complicated and difficult. There are many alternative or complementary characteristics towards which breeding may be directed. To genetic yield potential and nitrogen response can be added non-lodging, dormancy, drought tolerance, parboiling and milling quality, palatability, grain colour, grain shape, resistance to various pests and diseases, the content of various amino acids, photoperiodic insensitivity, duration, adaptability to particular environmental circumstances (salinity, high flooding, high, medium or low altitude, etc.) and nitrogen-fixing capability in the rhizosphere. A further complication is the manner in which perceived priorities change. In Coimbatore, grain colour was abandoned about ten years ago, since breeding for it was holding up the release of new strains. Protein content has come in as a priority and then gradually fallen from favour. Pest and disease resistance has become a priority with which no one would wish to argue, with its potential for reducing risk for farmers and also for saving the foreign exchange otherwise required for pesticides.

The injection of agricultural economists into the decision process might make it a little more lengthy, but it is not that that matters but whether the anticipated improvement in the decisions which emerge is worth the costs. There are five most obvious areas of potential benefit:

1 The choice of crops to which to devote seed-breeding expertise.
2 Prediction of characteristics of the receiving environment.
3 The improved specification of desired characteristics in the crop.
4 The anticipated yield effects from the receiving environment.
5 The distribution, income and nutrition effects.

In order to illustrate the general point, only the last item will be taken. The disillusion with political and administrative measures for reaching the poorer rural people is deep. But technology is not neutral. It too has considerable distribution effects. And the choices made about seed-breeding priorities are surprisingly wide-ranging. If reaching and helping the smaller, poorer farmers and the poorer rural people is an objective, then the following apply:

1 Preference for stable over unstable seed. Smaller, poorer farmers have difficulty in obtaining inputs such as seeds. If they once obtain a stable seed, they can replant from their own resources year by year without loss of yield.
2 Higher-yielding varieties of the food crops grown and eaten by the poorer sections of the community can be expected to benefit them disproportionately; this applies also to the crops grown in the less well-endowed areas (e.g. millets).

3   Preference for varieties with high yields of calories under conditions of
    low fertility, and with high slopes in the early stages of their nitrogen-
    response curves, will favour the smaller, poorer farmers who have more
    difficulty in obtaining fertiliser.
4   Water-stress tolerance will benefit those less well-endowed farmers
    whose fields are more likely to be short of water. A stress-tolerant
    variety may make the difference between a crop or no crop, or between
    two crops and one crop for a farmer who lacks a really reliable water
    supply.
5   Short-duration varieties may disproportionately benefit those farmers
    who are unable to plant in a timely fashion, whether for difficulty in
    obtaining inputs (labour, tractors, buffaloes or oxen; seeds, fertiliser) or
    water at the tail-end of major irrigation systems. They may (as BG.34-6
    and BG.34-8 have done in Sri Lanka) have a beneficial effect for those
    who otherwise would suffer.
6   Photoperiodic insensitivity has a similar effect.
7   Varieties with a high return to labour-intensity may tend to favour the
    very small farmers who can rely on their family labour with a negligible
    opportunity cost.
8   Varieties which will fit into existing farming systems and existing or
    anticipated farm labour demand profiles will tend to benefit the poorer
    smaller men who are unable or less able than their better-off
    neighbours to attract or pay casual labour.
9   Varieties which can be inter-planted with other crops to reduce risk
    and increase calorie yields (and perhaps nitrogen fixation) may benefit
    those with very small plots of land.
10 Varieties which are independent of mechanical requirements will
    reduce dependence on those who monopolise tractors or other
    machines. H.4 in Sri Lanka, for all its other excellence, is difficult to
    husk without a tractor, and this requirement increased the dependence
    of smaller farmers on their richer patrons.

An example of the benefits from a multi-disciplinary approach is provided
by Ryan, Sheldrake and Yadav (1974). Sorghum-breeding has been
dominated by the United States and has been prominently pursued in
Purdue University which serves the needs of livestock producers in the
Midwest. The main criteria of successful breeding there are protein
content and yield for beef fodder. As has been amply demonstrated it is
wasteful and largely futile to supplement calorie-deficient human diets
with protein since this is used by the body not as protein but as energy.
Moreover, most Indian diets are not protein-deficient; it is calorie
deficiency that is widespread. The priority for people in India therefore, in
contrast with steers of the Midwest, is for sorghums with high usable
carbohydrate content. Ryan, Sheldrake and Yadav (1974, pp. 26–7)
explain that the position is not simple:

The major component of both the cereal and pulse grains is carbo-hydrate. But by no means all of this carbohydrate provides dietary calories. A small proportion of it is made up of soluble sugars, some of it starch, which is digestible, and the remainder consists of cellulose and other cell wall materials which are not digestible.

In Sorghum the amount of starch in the grains varies considerably from variety to variety. It may be as low as 42 per cent or as high as 68 per cent. The starch content of the grains varies independently of the protein content. The large varietal differences in starch content mean that varieties which may have the same protein content and grain yield per hectare may differ by more than 50 per cent in their calorific food value. Such differences cannot be known nor selected for unless the grains are analysed for starch.

In the Indian context effective protein absorption by the body is more likely to be achieved by concentrating on improving the starch content, not the protein content, of sorghums. Sorghum-breeding for the semi-arid tropics might have produced sorghums with higher protein but with lower calorie yields, and in the absence of critical appraisal by economists and others this might not have been identified.

A further important aspect of seed-breeding in which seed-breeders must surely welcome insight and advice is the reasons for low or high levels of adoption. Some of these have been analysed elsewhere (pp. 57—65 and 103—22). In terms of total food production resulting from innovation it is alarming, and must surely repay further investigation, that over-adoption should be identified in Sri Lanka. But in India, the survey findings that adoptions of new HYVs are much lower than those appearing in official statistics suggest a need to look much more closely at the specifications for successful varieties. More environment-specific and season-specific var-ieties need to be developed. An HYV for the seru soils in North Arcot for the Samba season is, for example, needed. But in order to arrive at sound priorities, a continuous appraisal of need, of the scale of possible adoption, and of the degree of benefits accruing, is required. This is something which no seed-breeder can be expected to do for himself.

In the new situation following the energy crisis the shifts in priority have been sensible. There has been much heart-searching. Among other questions it seems right to ask about the physical conditions in which breeding takes place. The gibes about specially favoured conditions on research stations, with their reliable water, their fertile soil, their access to inputs, and their unlimited supplies of (unmeasured, uncosted) labour ought to have passed into history, but they appear almost as justified now as ever. There may be a lesson from the experience of Hector Weeraratne at Batalagoda in Sri Lanka. He modestly attributes the wide adaptability of H.4 (which he developed) partly to the unfavourable drainage conditions on the Batalagoda plant-breeding station. Any variety which did well in those conditions had to be robust. One wonders whether a similarly automatic (but adverse) form of selection may not have taken place over the past ten or fifteen years through the heavy doses of nitrogen (reportedly 80–160 kg per hectare) given to paddy plants while being grown for selection through the crucial F2–F4 generations. Is it possible that varieties which would have been more adaptable have not been selected? That we have been left with varieties which do well under ideal conditions, but which were not designed for the rough-and-tumble of the poor man's fields? Could it be that more varieties like H.4 could have led to higher field calorie yields than some of the more spectacular varieties that have been produced, and the adoption of which has been rather limited? For the benefits from a lower-yielding variety which is widely grown may be much greater (in terms of distribution of benefits among farmers, in terms of gross food production, in terms of lowered foodgrain prices) than those of a higher-yielding variety which is only adopted by a few who can afford and obtain expensive inputs.

Finally, one may ask whether the status and reward systems of seed-breeders provide the right incentives. 'Super-gene competitions' (as I have heard biannual conferences of breeders described) may not be the best means of encouraging pursuit of the best objectives. The field adoption of a lower-yielding variety on a wider scale should be a bigger feather in the cap of a breeder than the achievement of a yet higher genetic yield potential in a variety which does not become widespread. This is perhaps largely the case; and if so, should be reinforced.

WATER MANAGEMENT

Water has been a strangely neglected component of the agricultural system. To be sure, there have been huge investments in irrigation, in tube-wells, in pump-sets. But there have been bizarre gaps in perception and in research. One example must suffice. The Mahaweli Ganga irrigation and hydropower project in Sri Lanka is the single largest project in the country and has as part of its object to irrigate new land and to provide supplementary irrigation. The UNDP/FAO multi-disciplinary multi-member mission of experts in its final report stated that out of 1·5m. acres potentially under command only 0·9m. acres could be irrigated because of the limited water available (UNDP/FAO 1969a, pp. 55–6). It might have been supposed that, with water more constraining than land, careful attention would have been paid to the arrangements for managing the distribution of the water. But the volume of the final report on organisational and management requirements apparently considers improved seed, fertiliser, other agrochemicals, tractors and equipment as inputs; but not water – 8 pages are devoted to the supply of these inputs, 7½ to marketing, a further 7½ to agricultural credit and co-operatives and 8½ to agricultural research, extension and education. Apart from tangential references, the main presentation on managing water distribution is less than a page and this mentions structural but not operating arrangements (UNDP/FAO 1969b, pp. 72–3). And this neglect was the more reprehensible given the well-known difficulties in water management which have beset other large-scale projects in Sri Lanka and which have been constraining on the acreages cultivated.

An explanation of what appears culpable negligence seems to be that the management of people who manage water is not a recognised subject. The water management specialist on the UNDP/FAO team was an irrigation engineer concerned with quantities and flows and structures. The agricultural economist sensibly did analyses in terms of returns to water with different cropping patterns. The sociologist carried out surveys and noted that the distribution of irrigation water appeared to be a concern of both staff and settlers elsewhere, but did not take it any further. Blinkered, it seems, by their narrow disciplinary views, all the experts (and there were many others as well) missed the most important point of all.

There are compelling reasons, not just past neglect, why water and water management should be moved into the centre of the stage in South Asia. First, a very recent opinion is that 'The greatest potential source of large increases in the present levels of food supply will come, in the next decade, from increasing efficiency in existing irrigation systems and exploitation of known groundwater resources' (Carruthers, 1974, p.1). This point can be substantiated from the low rates of utilisation of many existing surface gravity irrigation systems, the improvement of which in India is actively in hand with the Command Areas Development Programme. Second, water is a peculiarly crucial input. Nitrogenous fertiliser has been something of a *prima donna* during the past ten years or so. But, if there is water, crops can usually be grown whether there is chemical fertiliser or not; if there is no water, chemical fertiliser is useless. Third, water is land-augmenting. More water more sparingly used can increase the cropped acreage, the cropping index and the food produced. Fourth, water has strong implications for adoption of HYVs. The evidence of the survey confirms that adoption of HYVs in paddy is strongly associated with reliable water supplies in North Arcot (pp. 117–18). Fifth, reliable water supplies have equity implications; in particular, one of the less expected findings of the North Arcot survey was that it was precisely in those villages which had the more reliable water supplies (Vegamangalam, Dusi, Vinayagapuram and Randam) that very small cultivators had adopted HYVs. Sixth, it is a reliable year-round water supply more than any other factor which appears to be responsible for the higher wages and greater employment demand of North Arcot villages like Kalpattu. If as is argued elsewhere (pp. 301–22) a quasi-industrial rural economy is a desirable target in order to provide more continuous employment, the careful husbanding of water and its utilisation throughout the year are critical.

The implications for research are considerable (see also p. 361). The first priority is that holistic systems thinking should be applied to water, rural environment by rural environment, relating surface water to groundwater, considering alternative storage and delivery systems, and considering above all the human and organisational aspects of water allocation and appropriation. Research on the management of water management needs urgently to be initiated and pressed ahead. The returns to such research in terms of additional food produced might be very high indeed, comparable with the very high returns from seed-breeding; there would also be major equity and distribution aspects. A second priority is that all the implications of treating water as more critically scarce than land should be followed through. To be sure there are very substantial areas – most of the wet zone of Sri Lanka, the Kaveri delta, the Godavari delta, much of Bangladesh – where for part of the year at least water is not only not scarce but sometimes too abundant. But these areas have dominated thinking to the neglect of areas like the dry zone in Sri Lanka and North Arcot District, where water is much more constraining. In research for areas such as these latter, benefits should be measured as returns of water. Research stations in such areas should be more concerned with water-sparing crops and methods of water application, and as a rule, present tables of yields in terms of units of water used as well as land.

Water management is *par excellence* a field in which natural scientists and social scientists must learn from one another, and must individually move out from the narrow boundaries of the disciplines in which they have been trained. It is a field calling for research of a new sort, requiring a high degree of innovation. The outcome in extra food produced might be of the same order of magnitude as that achieved by the revolution in seed-breeding and fertiliser use.

THE SOCIAL AND PSYCHOLOGICAL TECHNOLOGY OF RESEARCH

The argument has been weighted towards the need of natural scientists to learn from social scientists. But social scientists are at least as badly in need of being drawn out of their routines and cramped perceptions and exposed to the larger world of a holistic and ecological view of the environments which they study. For each group to learn the ways of work and thought of the other can be exciting and mind-stretching. More important, it appears essential to improve the quality and usefulness of the research done in these three fields of future-oriented R and D for rural environments, seed-breeding and the management of water. The question is, how to bring it about.

It is here that we appear peculiarly barren and ritual-bound. We seem unable or unwilling to invest time and imagination outside the status systems of our own disciplines. Why has no social scientist written a text on social sciences and the rural environment with seed-breeders and agricultural scientists as the intended audience? Why has no seed-breeder written a text for social scientists explaining the methods of his art or science, the nature of the choices he makes, and the constraints and opportunities with which he is faced? Why is it, with sublime irony, that only on a farmer's fields do all the disciplines meet, in a world which the farmer, in his genuinely superior wisdom, does not divide up into mutually exclusive categories?

We need to be much more creative and daring in the social and psychological techniques used for thinking and communication. Total immersion think-tanks, new techniques of prediction, communication networks involving several disciplines but with the same non- or inter-disciplinary focus, approaches rather like group therapy – these are among ideas which might be tried. We have to break away from being too careful, to become vulnerable in order to become inventive. New truth often appears absurd and one of the most important qualities to be fostered is a willingness to risk looking an ass. We worship intelligence, but far too often intelligence is thought of as the quality of avoiding being demonstrably wrong about anything. The generation of original ideas about the problems and opportunities of South Asia (as indeed of other parts of the world) can be deliberately nurtured by bringing about particular social and psychological situations. The vast majority of new ideas may be rejected. But those which survive the necessary tests of stringent criticism may transform a situation of ominous foreboding of doom into one of buoyant hope for better lives for rural people. Let it not be for lack of daring that we, the collective human we, fail. The challenge is open and crucial.

REFERENCES

Carruthers, I. (1974). 'Water Control, Irrigation and Hydrological Research', paper to IDS Conference 89, The Food Problem in South Asia: 1975–1990.

Emery, F. E. (ed.) (1969). *Systems Thinking*, Harmondsworth, Penguin.

Gandhi, Mrs Indira (1974). Speech inaugurating a national conference on population, New Delhi, reported in *The Times* (London), 7 December 1974.

Hunter, G. (1970). 'Agricultural Change and Social Development' in H. Bunting, *Change in Agriculture*, London, Duckworth.

Lipton, M. (1970). 'Interdisciplinary Studies in Less Developed Countries', *J. Develt. Studies*, 7, 5–18.

Moynihan, D. P. (1969). *Maximum Feasible Misunderstanding: Community Action in the War on Poverty*, New York, The Free Press; London, Collier-Macmillan.

Nutman, P. S. (1974). 'Biological Nitrogen Fixation', paper to IDS Conference 89, The Food Problem in South Asia: 1975–1990.

Palmer, Ingrid (1972). *Science and Agricultural Production*, Geneva, United Nations Research Institute for Social Development.

Phillipson, J. (1966). *Ecological Energetics*, London, Arnold.

Rajagopalan, V. (1974). 'Fertilizer Crisis and Rice Production – Implications to Research and Development', paper to the Annual Rice Conference of the International Rice Research Institute, Los Banos.

Ramana Murthy, P. S. V. and Belavady, B. (1966). 'Faecal Loss of Calories on Indian Diets', *Indian J. Medical Research*, 54, 1087–90.

Roy, S. K. (1974). 'Pre-harvest loss of rice due to field rodents', *Econ. Pol. Weekly*, 9, Rev. of Agric., A.66–7.

Ryan, J. G., Sheldrake, R. and Yadav, S. P. (1974). *Human Nutritional Needs and Crop Breeding Objectives in the Semi-arid Tropics*, Occasional Paper 4, Economic and Statistics Unit, ICRISAT, Hyderabad.

UNDP/FAO (1969a). *Mahaweli Ganga Irrigation and Hydropower Survey, Ceylon, Final Report*, vol. i: *General*, Rome.

UNDP/FAO (1969b). *Mahaweli Ganga Irrigation and Hydropower Survey, Ceylon, Final Report*, vol. iii: *Organizational and Management Requirements*, Rome.

26 Perceptions, Technology and the Future

Robert Chambers and B. H. Farmer

Each chapter in this book stands on its own. It would be superfluous to repeat conclusions already stated, even those of direct practical consequence. Earlier chapters also make clear the conclusions we were able to reach on our initial questions and hypotheses. There are, however, some further conclusions about perceptions, technology and future policy which incorporate and build on some of those already presented by the contributors, and which will be outlined in this final chapter.

Conclusions derive from perceptions. In the course of the project, the problems of perception, of seeing things as they are and seeing them whole, became a central preoccupation. As we learnt more about the survey areas we became increasingly doubtful about some of our early findings, some of which we rejected and many of which we modified. We have tried to present briefly in chapter 5 a critical appraisal of our methods. The reader will draw his own conclusions and we ourselves retain sceptical reservations. We have tried, however, through cross-checks and through a battery of approaches, to reduce the dangers of serious error. We have also tried to allow for a number of different interpretations of what has been observed.

The main outcome of this laborious and often painful process has been to throw doubt on some of the ideas and impressions which researchers, writers and governments have acquired and continue to retain about the Green Revolution. John Harriss has shown in chapter 4 how orthodox dogma is often based on a selective and distorted view of events. Delta bias and IADP bias in agrarian research in India have focused attention on areas which are atypical in their endowments, being favourably provided with water, and which have been subject to special programmes and staffing. The prejudices, perceptions and misperceptions of observers and analysts have been mutually reinforcing. The Kilvenmani incident in Thanjavur in 1968 (p. 35) is a striking example of how one event in one part of India can be quoted again and again to provide evidence of the 'green revolution' turning 'red': one is hard-pressed to find any major writing by a Western scholar on the Green Revolution which does not cite it.

More generally, official statistics and much of the data from surveys appear to be seriously misleading. Barbara Harriss's analysis of paddy and rice statistics in Sri Lanka (chapter 3) shows up the wide margins which are open to interpretation even when official figures can be cross-checked. In the case of agricultural extension, survey methodology itself may generate a spurious finding of widespread direct contact between extension staff and individual farmers, as appears to have happened in both India and Sri Lanka (see chapter 11). Most seriously, Nanjamma Chinnappa's meticulous work on the North Arcot survey (chapter 8) indicates beyond any reasonable doubt that official statistics for the adoption of HYVs in North Arcot District are grossly inflated, those for the areas under HYVs by a factor of at least 3. Deep scepticism is justified about some of the conventional impressions of what has been happening. All too often there have been distortions in statistics and a consistent superficiality in selective perceptions which together have presented a false picture of progress and success.

Table 26.1   Percentage of adoption of improved varieties

		Hambantota	North Arcot	
		Maha 1972–3	1972–3	1973–4
Percentage of cultivators growing paddy	Cultivators growing HYV plus IV	97	39	26
	Cultivators growing HYV	58	29	17
Percentages of total paddy area under improved varieties	Paddy area under HYV plus IV	95	18	13
	Paddy area under HYV	47	13	10

The closest approximation to a true picture we have been able to obtain presents patterns which defy simple or unicausal explanations. For example, the two surveys (Table 26.1) show that HYVs and IVs have been very much more widely adopted in SE. Sri Lanka than in North Arcot (chapters 6 and 8).

The impression is given that cultivators in SE. Sri Lanka must be much more progressive and the implication is that they are more productive than those in North Arcot: 95 per cent of the former paddy area was under HYVs and IVs in Maha 1972–3 compared with only 13 per cent in North Arcot in 1973–4. But the yield figures for the same season were lower in Sri Lanka (2971 kg per hectare) than in North Arcot (3555 kg per hectare). We are confronted with lower yields with higher adoption and higher yields with lower adoption. Several explanations for this contrast can be put forward, one of the most powerful being the greater reliability of water control in North Arcot. Another explanation, not unrelated, is the long-continued pressure of population and consequently higher general intensity of cultivation in North Arcot as compared with SE. Sri Lanka.

The point, however, is not that the differences can be explained but that detailed comparison of this sort continually throws up anomalies which, like this one, challenge simple assumptions.

The sharp contrast in levels of adoption of HYVs in the two areas studied is much greater than we initially believed on the basis of the inflated official figures for North Arcot (the corresponding figures for Hambantota–Moneragala do not seem to be seriously distorted). Many factors appear responsible and have been outlined in chapters 6 and 8. Some reasons for not growing HYVs in North Arcot at the time of the survey were the higher prices commanded by traditional varieties, the lower risks entailed by their shorter durations and lower water duties than most HYVs, the dietary preferences of farmers growing for their own family consumption, and difficulties experienced by many farmers in obtaining the complementary inputs, notably of fertiliser, for HYVs. For North Arcot, too, seed-breeders had yet to produce an HYV which would do well in the main Samba season. In contrast, in Sri Lanka H.4 and the new HYVs which followed it appeared much more profitable to cultivators than were traditional varieties, having higher yields and not being subject to markedly lower prices, (though there is still need for an HYV suited to the full length of the Maha season).

A further factor which helps to explain the higher levels of adoption in SE. Sri Lanka than in North Arcot is the amount of choice actually open to cultivators. The great majority of farmers in North Arcot had a high degree of choice: not only were many types of seed easily available but also most farmers were largely independent as decision-makers, relying on their own wells for water. In contrast, in SE. Sri Lanka, seeds of traditional varieties were not in easy supply, and decisions about what varieties should be grown – and especially their duration – were usually taken collectively for each yaya. Moreover, because of the irrigation system, cultural activities were more synchronised than in North Arcot, and there was a long tradition of disciplined timing of operations (this in spite of near anarchy in the tapping of channels at field level: see above, pp. 372–3). In such circumstances the cultivator may not be the true 'adopter' or 'innovator' at all. In one instance (see p. 148) the Government Agent was the real adopter or innovator since it was he who persuaded farmers to grow BG.34-6 and 34-8 on one major irrigation system and then ensured that seed was available. Thus farmers in North Arcot, often with independent wells, tended to make independent decisions; farmers in SE. Sri Lanka, relying on communal irrigation water, were subject to collective pressures and physical limitations on their freedom of choice. Early questions in any study of adoption have, then, to be: Who decides? And how much effective choice do they have? Further, does the Sri Lanka form of decision-making lead to the over-adoption of HYVs and fertilisers as postulated by H. D. Dias (see pp. 65–73), so that cultivators do not develop the full potential of the new HYVs? And is the Sri Lanka government culpable for losing sight of the law of diminishing returns in the chase after self-sufficiency?

Our findings that in North Arcot HYVs covered less than one-third of the area reported in official statistics, and that, despite high adoption rates in SE. Sri Lanka, yields there were relatively low, together reduce the force of another question. One can only ask whether a 'green revolution' is turning 'red', and if it is green and a revolution in the first place. Our conclusion is that in paddy-growing in the areas studied, in the limited sense of adopting new varieties and packages of practices, and of achieving dramatic increases in yields, the changes which have occurred have been less green than supposed and rather less than revolutionary in their effects. Rarely, indeed, is the whole package adopted in the prescribed manner; though equally such revolution as there has been in both our study areas has not been a single-factor revolution, whether in terms of seeds or fertilisers. Nor have small farmers completely failed to be 'adopters'.

Social and economic changes have, in fact, been more closely related to energy-using technologies than to cultural practices. Pump-sets in North Arcot and tractors in SE. Sri Lanka have had more marked effects on social and economic relationships than have HYVs. In both cases they have tended to widen the gap between the richer and the poorer cultivators.

In North Arcot, where lack of water is the most important single constraint, pump-sets have had a greater effect on paddy production than have HYVs. They have enabled those farmers who have been able to install them on good wells to appropriate communal groundwater, to cultivate larger acreages and to increase multiple cropping. Their reliable and often abundant water supply makes adoption of HYVs and the use of other inputs less risky and more profitable for them. But, as the water-table drops in consequence, their less fortunate neighbours without pump-sets find that the old lift technology of the kavalai becomes gradually more marginal, or that they cannot afford to deepen their wells. The land of some of the poorer and smaller cultivators thus goes out of irrigated cultivation while multiple cropping is extended on the land of the richer and larger cultivators.

Turning to SE. Sri Lanka, there tractors have concentrated power even further in the hands of the rich and influential traders and gambārayas who own them. Tractors are critical for timely cultivation. Those who lack them are often deeply dependent on owners. Those at the end of queues for tractors lose yields from untimely cultivation besides having, like others, to pay grossly exploitative fees for their hire.

With both pump-sets and tractors, whatever the national benefits in increased food production, the poorer and weaker cultivators have tended to lose out relative to their richer and more powerful neighbours, and sometimes in absolute terms as well. As so often in accounts of agrarian change, the introduction of an alien technology means 'Unto every one that hath shall be given, and he shall have abundance; but from him that hath not shall be taken away even that which he hath'. At the same time, the new technologies and practices, as has been shown (p. 252) reinforce the need of smaller farmers for the patronage of larger farmers in order to gain access to machinery or inputs. The 'feudalism of technology', in Jayaweera's phrase (quoted p. 197) can be exaggerated; changes are sensitive to the characteristics of the technology which influences them. But wherever a new technology heightens competition for access to scarce resources such as water, fertiliser, pesticides, seeds or traction power, poorer cultivators are liable to be forced into greater dependence on their richer neighbours or on traders. This applies with particular cogency to those small cultivators who adopt HYVs and fertilisers, to a greater extent than those with slightly larger holdings: perhaps they cannot afford *not* to adopt.

Effects on the very poor, especially the landless labourers, appear to vary more than effects on the smaller, poorer cultivators and are especially sensitive to the balance of population and exploitable resources. In crude terms and with current technologies, SE. Sri Lanka is seasonally much more labour-deficit than North Arcot, and also has slack resources accessible to those willing and able to exploit them. Chena cultivation presents a frontier, an extensive margin for cultivation, an alternative to labouring in paddyfields (chapter 7 and p. 249). Here then the choice of technology in paddy cultivation is unlikely yet to have catastrophic effects on a labouring class since there are alternative sources of food and livelihood, albeit risky ones, in the chena. In North Arcot, in contrast, the very small cultivators and the agricultural labourers (not mutually exclusive categories) are trapped. If a new technology or mounting population pressure displaces them they have no chance of becoming small cultivators elsewhere. The effects of any new technology in such a labour-surplus environment are thus very much more critical than in labour-deficit SE. Sri Lanka. As John Harriss has shown (pp. 226–32), pump-sets in North Arcot have tended to reduce the demand for attached male labourers (who formerly operated the more labour-intensive kavalai) and to increase the demand for female labour for activities such as weeding. The situation varies between villages (pp. 311–18). In villages with

abundant underground water resources subject to rapid recharge, like
Kalpattu, pump-sets may increase labour demand around the year and
attract in-migration of labourers. In the many villages which are saturated
with population, pump-sets may do little to alleviate the plight of the
landles and there is reason to believe that, after the initial impact, the
position of landless males is liable to deteriorate disproportionately. The
prospect for many of the landless in North Arcot scarcely bears con-
templation. Extruded from the bottom of the pile, forced in desperation to
leave their villages, these 'least enviable of men', in Charles Elliott's phrase
(1975, p. 129), will swell the numbers of urban migrants and of rural
transients whose lot will be more terrible for being so often unseen and so
easy to avoid seeing.

Population control provides an obvious long-term line of attack on these
problems. In India at least, the fewer the people who need livelihoods,
services and food, the less desperate their conditions are likely to be. But it
is notorious that the adoption of voluntary family limitation has in the past
followed rather than preceded rises in living standards. Short of coercion or
a social-psychological breakthrough, it seems unlikely that the next few
decades will see the application by family planning of a massive brake on
India's population growth unless there is also a rise in living standards. The
trap is cruel. The growth of population impedes a rise in living standards;
and static or declining living standards impede the control of population
growth. While campaigns for family planning deserve support (see Blaikie,
1975), the more critical fronts to attack are the creation of livelihoods, the
more equitable distribution of incomes and the raising of levels of living
generally, in order to achieve the preconditions for the success of these
campaigns.

Faced with such acute problems as the exploitation of tenants and small
farmers by the gambārayas in Hambantota, the poverty and misery of
landless labourers in North Arcot, and the need to raise levels of living in
order to limit population growth, the observer turns naturally to
governments and to political solutions. The record here is not encouraging.
It is true that the rice ration in Sri Lanka, issued to all but the most
prosperous, and the Fair Price Shops in India which sell food at low prices
to the poorest (or at least the urban poorest), do contribute to income
redistribution and mitigate some of the worst inequities. But in the field of
agrarian relations neither the Paddy Lands Acts in Sri Lanka nor the land
reform legislation in Tamil Nadu have been effective in securing rights,
improving conditions or redistributing assets. In the absence of a change of
political power at the local level, government intervention all too often
merely reinforces existing patterns of inequity. There seems much
justification for the view that redistribution of productive resources can
only follow radical changes in power at the local level involving political
organisation and action by the disadvantaged groups. Short of outright
revolution, the question is whether constitutional laws and reformist

political movements can be enough to effect such changes.

Such questions are especially difficult for foreign observers. If they pronounce upon them, they are accused of interference in matters which are none of their business. If they ignore them, they are accused – with equal force – of evading some of the most important issues. Among the observers themselves, a wide spectrum of attitudes is found. At one extreme is the confident paternalism of the far Left preaching the simple clean sweep of revolution; and at the other the timid reticence of academic analysis which shrinks from any prescription whatsoever. Perhaps the most useful contribution we can make from the studies carried out by this project is to suggest that in addition to political action, indispensable though that may be, governments have a supplementary tool which can reinforce and support political initiatives designed to make rural life better and fairer.

For if the technologies we have studied have a powerful influence on contemporary social and economic relationships, then technologies not yet devised or not yet introduced provide a means for influencing the future nature of society. Research and development (R and D) for some of the technologies which have already been introduced into SE. Sri Lanka and North Arcot must have been completely blind to the effects they would have. The tractor and the pump-set were invented in other continents and for other needs. Even the HYVs developed in Sri Lanka and India were often selected according to criteria which did not take into account many of the likely effects in rural society. Any approach to R and D which takes account of such effects and of the sort of rural society desired can be based upon specified criteria. Five possible criteria, deriving partly from our research, have been suggested (pp. 393–4). They are: productivity in terms of whatever resources are scarce; equity in the distribution of benefits; stability in the human ecosystem; continuity (non-seasonality) in employment and the flow of benefits; and livelihood-intensity. Measured against these criteria the technologies analysed have often been disappointing and harmful. The productivity of water in North Arcot may well have been diminished by pump-sets, encouraging as they do the profligate use of groundwater and the cultivation of paddy – a water-intensive crop. Equity has suffered through the concentration of power in the hands of tractor owners in Hambantota. Stability of the human ecosystem has suffered through the secular decline in the water-table in North Arcot associated with the spread of electric pump-sets. Continuity in employment and the flow of benefits have, however, sometimes improved, for example through multiple cropping. Finally, the livelihood-intensity of technologies has varied. At its worst, in the form of the Modern Rice Mill in North Arcot, a new technology has an appalling potential for displacing from work large numbers of precisely the most vulnerable class, the landless labourers, aggravating their poverty and that of others with whom they then compete for scarce livelihoods and scant means of survival.

The need here is often seen in terms of choice of technology. Thus Schumacher has suggested that 'the biggest single collective decision that any country in the position of India has to take is the choice of technology' (1973, p. 196). For Schumacher this choice is sought mainly among existing technologies and modifications of them designed to make them more appropriate. This is sound and important, but does not go nearly far enough (cf. above, pp. 392–6). In recent years the rate of technological development has accelerated and we can expect that in the next few decades a new generation of technologies, based on new principles emerging from basic and applied research, will flood into rural South Asia. The danger is that, as with tractors, pump-sets, IR.8 and the Modern Rice Mill, these technologies will be devised to meet criteria which may be irrelevant or harmful to many people there. Tractors were devised for rich-country agriculture, to reduce labour requirements, precisely the opposite of what is required in many Asian environments; pump-sets were devised to lift large quantities of water, not to ration it; IR.8 was bred to be responsive to heavy doses of chemical nitrogen which tend to be available only to the wealthier and more influential farmers and anyway suits only a limited range of natural conditions; and the Modern Rice Mill was designed for conditions in which labour is scarcer and capital more abundant than in India or Sri Lanka. The pressures of population on resources, and the painful inequities in many parts of South Asia, cannot permit the blind development of cruel technologies which strike des-titution into rural lives. This means that criteria specific to rural conditions have to determine both the choices of basic research to pursue, and the decisions taken during the R and D process. In the words of the UN report on the social and economic effects of the new varieties of foodgrain, 'A social policy should be built into the new technology beginning with the basic research itself' (UNRISD, 1974, pp. 52–3).

If then, relevant R and D in rich and poor countries alike can be consciously planned, geared to poor country needs and given high priority, a huge potential may be realised. From the marked difference between and within North Arcot and SE. Sri Lanka, it will be clear that many of the R and D priorities need to be derived from specific environments; and such R and D may best be carried out in the countries concerned or in neighbouring countries with similar conditions. But much R and D has a much wider applicability and it may be here that the richer countries have a special contribution to make. Two fields in which there might be a general breakthrough are, first, energy sources and use of energy in agriculture and second, natural nitrogen-fixation. Both have been men-tioned in the preceding chapter. All that need be added here concerns the second field. Suppose that on-going research into nitrogen-fixing in the rhizosphere of paddy produced a new combination of micro-organism and paddy variety which fixed large amounts of nitrogen around the roots of the growing plant. Paddy variations and micro-organisms should be far more 'rascal-proof' than other inputs such as fertilisers, especially if once obtained they become a permanent, self-reproducing asset to the farmer. At one stroke then, the cultivator, however small he might be, would – once he had obtained the variety and micro-organism – possess a source of nitrogenous fertiliser independent of patron, gambāraya or trader, and be a participant in a Green Revolution that was indeed scale-neutral.

To achieve the dramatic priority needed for poverty-orientated R and D such as this, related both to the poorer countries and to the poorer sectors within them, requires a breakthrough in perceptions and in international communication, involving social and natural scientists and those engaged on relevant R and D. It also requires that governments, commercial organisations, and bodies which fund research be influenced and impelled to give to such work the orientation, priority and resources it so urgently deserves.

In such a course there are daunting difficulties. Vested interests, narrow-mindedness, lack of vision, and the notorious problems of the transfer of technology are all likely obstacles. To overcome these a central need is accurately to perceive the physical and human environment for which a technology is to be developed and correctly to anticipate the effects which it will have. Here experience already gained and analysed should be of use. As many others have shown, and as the research reported in this book has confirmed for two areas in South Asia, the technologies which have been described as the Green Revolution have had mixed social and economic effects, both creating and destroying livelihoods, both reinforcing and weakening exploitative relationships, both helping and depriving those whose lives are most precarious. Those who develop the next generation of technologies have an awesome responsibility to learn from experiences such as these. By a great effort of imagination and will, they may be able to design and devise those technologies to meet new criteria – to create livelihoods, to reduce exploitative forms of dependence, to distribute benefits more fairly to those who are worst off. If this imagination and this will can be mustered there is at least a chance that the spectre of unspeakable suffering that hovers over South Asia may be dispelled and that a prospect may open up of better lives for those who are most deprived and most at risk. The alternative is unthinkable. The effort surely has to be made.

REFERENCES

Blaikie, Piers M. (1975). *Family Planning in India: Diffusion and Policy*, London, Arnold.
Elliott, C. (1975). *Patterns of Poverty in the Third World*, London, Praeger.
Schumacher, E. F. (1973). *Small is Beautiful*, London, Blond and Briggs.
UNRISD, (1974). *The Social and Economic Implications of Large-scale Introduction of New Varieties of Foodgrain*, Geneva.

Index

No attempt has been made to include all place names mentioned in the text. The only sample village (Tamil Nadu) and Cultivation Committee(Sri Lanka) listed (see pp. 37–40, 44–5 and 73–6) are those called Randam and Pahalagama (to facilitate cross-reference between passages dealing with the sample surveys and those dealing with study in depth); and Dusi, because of its inclusion in earlier researches (see p. 40).

Abeyratne, E. F. L., 85, 91
Adelman, I., 301, 304, 322
Administration, see Bureaucracy
Adoption of new seeds and practices, see Technology, adoption of new
Age (of cultivators), 115, 123
Agricultural extension, see Extension and support services
Agricultural Officers (District, etc.), 155–8, 162–4, 260
Agricultural Productivity Committees, Law (Sri Lanka), 169, 176, 250–1, 371, 373, 375
Agro-chemicals, see Pesticides, Weedicides
Ahmed, I., 70, 83, 168, 169, 170, 174, 180
Aiyasami, U., xii, 32, 36
All India Co-ordinated Rice Improvement Project (AICRIP), 2, 398
Alles, W. S., 145, 154, 168, 180, 374, 376
Amerasinghe, N., 149, 154, 217, 224
Amunugama, S., 178, 180
Arni, 124, 127, 192, 234, 239, 304–5
Arya, H. P. S., 156, 166
Assistant Government Agent (Sri Lanka), see Government Agent

Bananas, 102, 122, 145, 314
Bangladesh, 1, 2, 70, 410
Belavady, B., 402, 412
Belshaw, D., 165, 166
Béteille, A., 33, 36, 205, 224, 235, 236, 239, 242, 245
Bethma, xiv, 348, 350
Black market, 137, 141, 262–7, 274

Blaikie, P. M., 32, 33, 36, 187, 197, 202, 418, 421
Block Development Officer (BDO), 136, 156, 158, 164
Boserup, E., 4, 6, 153, 154, 318, 322
Breman, J., 237, 245
Broehl, W. G., 261, 267
Brown, D. D., 31, 36, 276, 287, 299
Brown, I. A., 185, 197, 202
Brown, L. R., 1, 6, 70, 84
Buffaloes, 144, 168–9, 179–80, 247–8, 367, 382–3, 387
Burdon, D. J., 327, 338, 339
Bureaucracy, 136–7, 163–6, 234–5, 327, 340–7, 350–61, 364–76
Byres, T. J., 2, 3, 6, 30, 36, 225, 245

Canals, irrigation, 93, 102, 117; see also Tank irrigation
Cantor, Atac, 286, 299
Capener, H., 358, 362
Carr, M., 168, 176, 180
Carruthers, I. D., 364, 376, 409, 411
Caste, 5, 116, 193, 226, 232, 235–42, 248–9, 305, 317–18, 374–5
Cattle, 127, 143–4, 387
Chakravarty, T. K., 156, 166
Chambers, Robert, 165, 166, 341, 342, 351, 357, 360, 362, 364, 373, 375, 376
Chena cultivation, xiv, 4, 85–91, 145, 221–3, 249, 374, 417
Chillies, 14, 85, 90, 145
Chockalingam, K., 156, 166
Cholam, xiv, 14, 122, 128

Class structure, conflict, 5, 34–5, 136, 225, 235–44
Climate, 7–13, 99, 288–9, 328; *see also* Rainfall
Collonnege, I., 71, 84
Communal action, 161, 341, 345–61, 415
Connell, J., 321, 322
Constable, D. H., 388, 397
Co-operatives, 18, 47, 114–15, 169, 177–9, 191, 250, 256–66, 275, 277–9, 287, 293
Corea, G., 2, 6
Corruption, 163–5, 265–7, 273
Cox, A. F., 127, 136, 142
Credit, 17, 66, 71, 105, 114–15, 121–2, 123, 140, 148, 149–50, 152–5, 163, 169–70, 174, 176–9, 191–2, 197, 247–50, 252–3, 260–1, 263–5, 275, 304–5, 367, 377, 380–1, 383, 386; *see also* Finance
Crop insurance, 18
Cultivation Committees (Sri Lanka), 17, 146, 148, 343–4, 370–4

Dalton, G., 301, 304, 322
Danda, A. K. and D. G., 136, 142
Dandekar, V. M., 162, 166
Data, *see* Research methods
David, P., 196, 202
De Alwis, K. A., 12, 18
Dealers, *see* Traders
Deepak Lal, 3, 6
Deshmukh, M. B., 321, 322
Dias, H. D., 4, 20, 29, 46, 53, 57, 75, 84, 174, 180
Dickson, D., 392, 396
Differentiation of the peasantry, 242–3, 249, 253
Diffusion of innovations, 182–202
Diseases, *see* Pests
Drainage, 81, 102
Draught animals, *see* Buffaloes, Cattle
Dry land (as a class of land), xiv, 117, 124–5, 129, 141, 226–7, 308–10, 326, 394
Dumont, L., 34, 35, 36, 239, 245
Duncan, A., 168, 176, 180
Dusi village, 30, 40, 159, 161, 164, 302, 307–14, 344–6, 352, 354, 356–61

Economic consequences of technical change, 4–5, 176, 204–44, 416–17; *see also* Employment; Incomes; Livelihoods
Ecosystems, future, 401–4
Education, 60
Electric pumps, *see* Pump-sets
Elliott, C., 418, 421

Ellman, A. O., 358, 362
Emery, F. E., 400, 411
Employment, 16, 208–10, 216–34, 293–5, 298, 310, 312, 314–18, 394–5, 409, 419
Encroachers (on land), 143, 145, 150, 249, 372
Energy crisis and consequences, 256–67, 377–86, 393–6, 401, 420
Environment – specific research and planning, 401, 403–4, 407, 420–1
Epstein, S., 235, 236, 243, 245, 320, 322
Étienne, G., 3, 6
Etram, xiii, 182, 227
Extension and support services, 4, 18, 32, 50–1, 60–1, 71, 121, 128, 133, 136–7, 140, 148, 153, 155–66, 197, 340, 414
External relations (of village), 234–5, 242, 247–8, 253–4, 302, 304–5, 308, 310, 312, 380–1

Family planning, 418
Farmer, B. H., 10, 18, 44, 53, 85, 89, 91, 326, 339, 348, 362
Faulkner, M. D., 276, 287, 299
Fernea, R. A., 348, 362
Fertiliser Corporation (Sri Lanka), xii
Fertilisers, 3, 4, 14, 16, 17, 58, 59, 61–2, 66–72, 87, 90, 99, 102, 105, 120–3, 127–8, 132, 137, 138, 140–1, 145, 148–9, 152, 160–1, 163–5, 209–10, 218, 229, 234, 256–67, 304, 377–86, 388, 395, 400–2, 409, 420–1
Finance for agricultural operations, 90, 132, 137–8, 196, 198, 233, 263–4; *see also* Credit
Fliegel, F. C., 155, 157, 161, 166
Flour, *see* Wheat
Ford Foundation, 136, 276, 299
Foster-Carter, A., 242, 245
Found, W. C., 197, 202
Frankel, Francine, 34–6

Gabor, D., 392, 396
Gambāra, gambāraya, xiv, 75, 148, 151–2, 154, 176, 178, 246–53, 367–74, 417–18, 421
Gandhi, Indira, 401, 411
Garden land, gardens, xiv, 117, 124–5, 135, 145
Garg, M. K., 392, 396
Glick, T. F., 371, 373, 376
Gopalswamy, T. P., 295, 299
Gore, P., 358, 362
Gough, K., 35, 239, 245
Gould, P., 185, 197, 202

INDEX

425

Government administration, *see* Bureau-
cracy
Government, Agent (Sri Lanka), xiv, 148,
161, 246, 260, 358, 366–9, 372, 415–16
Grain, *see* Pulses
Gram(a) Sevak, xiv, 97, 136–7, 156, 158–9,
162–4
Gray, R. F., 373, 376
Griffin, K., 3, 6, 204, 224
Griliches, Z., 196–8, 202
Groundnut, 4, 14, 114, 119, 123, 125, 127–9,
132–3, 216, 237, 243, 305, 394
Ground water, *see* Water-table
Guaranteed Price Scheme (GPS) (Sri
Lanka), 17, 21, 377
Gunawardena, Kusuma A., xii, 57, 84
Gupta, V. K., 288, 295, 299

Hagerstrand, T., 185, 188, 202
Hambantota and Moneragala Districts (Sri
Lanka), 3, 4, 7–12, 18, 21, 44–50,
54–83, 85–91, 143–54, 156–62,
169–80, 204–5, 217–23, 256–67, 276,
341–61, 365–76, 377–86, 389,
414–21; society in, 46–54
Harijans, xiv, 116–17, 127, 132, 142, 226–7,
232–4, 236–42, 302, 310–12, 314–18,
351
Harriss, Barbara, xii, 299
Harriss, John., 2, 348, 362
Haryana, 32, 348, 359
Haswell, M. R., 40, 53
Hawkes, N., 394, 396
Hawkey, R., 299, 300
Heginbotham, S. J., 155, 162, 166
Hena, xiv; *see also* Chena cultivation
Herring, R., 154, 174, 180, 239, 247, 250,
254
High land (Sri Lanka), xiv, 145, 159, 223; *see
also* Chena cultivation
Holdings, agricultural, 4, 20, 43, 76, 86, 93,
109–19, 123, 129–32, 137–8, 145–7,
201
Households, characteristics of, 205–6,
218–21
Hunt, E., 365, 371, 374, 376
Hunt, R. C., 365, 371, 374, 376
Hunter, G., 155, 162, 166, 399, 411
Hydrometeorology, 10–12, 327–8, 330–1,
335–9
HYV (high-yielding varieties), HVP,
HYVP, xv; *see also* Rice, varieties

IADP (Intensive Agricultural District Programme), xv, 13, 30–6, 156, 413

Implements, agricultural, 118–19, 144–5,
168–9
Incomes, 14, 16, 85, 90, 141, 145, 151, 176,
208, 210–12, 216, 223–4, 243, 383,
393, 396, 409, 416–18
Indebtedness, *see* Credit
India, general, 30–3, 401–3, 406–7, 409,
420; rice production, 1–2, 12–17,
93–6, 390; *see also* Karnataka; Maha-
rashtra; N. Arcot District; Punjab;
Tamil Nadu; Thanjavur District
Information, sources of, 60–1, 71, 136–7,
148–9, 155–66, 197, 260–2; *see also*
Diffusion of innovations; Extension of
support services
Inputs, *see* Fertilisers; Labour; Manure;
Pesticides; Rice cultivation, costs of;
Seed, supply of; Water; Weedicides
International Rice Research Institute
(IRRI), 2, 3, 6, 13; IRRI (IR) variet-
ies, *see* Rice, varieties
Inter-regional variation, 73–9, 337; *see also*
Inter-village variation
Inter-village variation, 100–3, 301–22, 379;
see also Inter-regional variation
Irrigation, 4, 9–12, 58–9, 71, 77–82, 92,
100, 117–19, 124–5, 129–32, 143–5,
147–9, 152, 161, 182–202, 209, 212,
227–32, 247, 308, 310–11, 321, 323–7,
340–61, 364–76, 394–6, 399, 408–10;
see also Tank irrigation; Water; Wells
Izumi, K., 381, 383, 396

Jagannadha Sarma, V. V., 327, 335, 339
Jajmani, xv, 235
Jayaweera, N., 18, 177, 181, 417
Joachim, A. W. R., 389, 397
Jones, G. W., 54, 84

Kuttali, *see* Labourers, attached
Kalpage, F. S. C. P., 389, 390, 397
Karkal, G. L., 178, 181
Karnataka, 32
Kavalai, xv, 117–19, 202, 225, 308, 326,
386, 416, 417
Kilvenmani incident, 35, 413
Kivlin, J. E., 155, 157, 161, 166
Klatt, W., 2, 3, 6
Krishnamurti, S., 84
Kurakkan, xv, 14, 85, 93, 145
KVS (Krushikarma Vyāpthi Sevak), xv,
149, 156–9

Labour, 4, 16, 87, 89, 105–6, 121–2, 127,
141–2, 144–5, 149–50, 152–3, 168–9,

426

INDEX

208–9, 212–17, 227–32, 237–8,
243–4, 265, 302, 311–12, 314–18,
321–2, 326, 352, 354, 367, 381–5,
394–5, 403, 406, 417–18; see also
Labourers
Labourers, agricultural, 5, 15, 35, 93, 132,
141–2, 145, 153, 204–6, 210–12, 216,
218–24, 227–32, 250, 305, 314–18,
394, 396, 398, 417–19; attached, 237,
240, 314–18, 417; relations with farmers, 235–43
Lal, D., 197, 198, 202
Land reform, 250, 251, 396, 403, 418
Land tenure, 4, 17, 35, 77–8, 88, 100,
115–16, 123, 129–30, 143, 145–6,
150–2, 176, 233, 245, 249, 303, 310,
315, 317–20, 393; see also Holdings,
agricultural
Landless labourers, see Labourers
Landlords, 143, 151–2, 154, 164, 178, 235,
246–54, 273, 368–71, 374, 381
Leach, E. R., 347–8, 362
Leaders, leadership, 136, 234–5, 249–50,
304, 374
Lele, U. J., 204, 224, 281, 299
Levine, G., 358, 362
Lipton, M., 301, 321–2, 400, 411
Lison-Tolosana, C., 370, 376
Literacy, 60, 115, 305
Livelihoods, 141–2, 394, 418, 419; see also
Employment; Incomes
Locational considerations, for rice mills,
289–93; for villages, 304–5, 320–1
Lord, L., 389, 397

Madduma Bandara, C. M., 10, 81, 84, 342,
362
Madhya Pradesh 32, 287
Madras, University of, xiv, 3
Mahalanobis, B., 43, 53
Maharastra, 32
Majumdar, P. S. 386, 397
Manure, organic and natural, 105, 120, 122,
124–7, 143, 209, 218, 228, 233, 266,
385, 388–91, 395, 401–2
Marketing, markets, 4, 21–4, 47–50,
256–67, 268–75
Marx, Karl, 34
Mathur, D. P., 295, 299
Mechanisation, 3, 16, 221; see also Pump-
sets; Tractors
Meillassoux, C., 236, 240, 245
Mellor, J. W., 204, 224
Mencher, Joan, 32, 35–6, 133, 142
Mendras, H., 137, 142

Methodology, see Research methods
Migration, 308, 311–12, 320–1, 398
Millets, 405; see also Cholam; Kurakkan;
Sorghum
Milling, see Modern Rice Mill; Rice, milling
Misra, R. P., 197, 202
Mitra, R. B., 391, 397
Modern Rice Mill (MRM), 3, 274–5,
277–99, 419
Moneragala District (Sri Lanka), see Ham-
bantota and Moneragala District
Moneylenders, see Credit
Mook, B., 155, 162, 167
Moore, E., 185, 197, 202
Moore, M., 301, 322
Moris, J., 357, 362
Morrill, R., 185, 203
Moynihan, D. P., 399, 411
Multiple cropping, 212–13, 227, 416, 419;
see also Rice, seasons

Nagarajah, S., 58, 84
Natural and social scientists, linkages between, 399–411, 421
Nitrogen fixation, 402, 420–1
North Arcot District, Tamil Nadu (India),
3–6, 7–13, 30–3, 37–44, 47–50,
52–3, 92–123, 124–42, 155–66,
175–6, 182–202, 204–16, 219,
225–44, 256–67, 268, 299, 301–22,
323–7, 342–61, 389, 392–6, 403, 404,
407, 409, 410, 413–21
Nutman, P. S., 401, 411
Nutrition, 402, 406, 407

Occupational structure, 15, 60, 93
Ongkingco, P. S., 351, 363
Orissa, 32
Over-adoption, 72–3, 407, 416

Paddy, xv; see also Rice
Paddy Lands Acts (Sri Lanka), 17–18, 146,
169, 246, 250, 370–3, 418
Paddy Marketing Board (Sri Lanka), 17, 21,
170, 277, 296–9
Padial, see Labourers, attached
Pahalagama village, xi, 3, 143–54, 219,
246–54, 381–6
Palmer, Ingrid, 36
Panabokke, C. R., 12, 18, 168, 181, 389, 390,
397
Panchayat, xvi, 37, 234–5, 240, 266
Panse, V. G., 43, 53
Parboiling (of rice), xv, 21–4
Parthasarathy, G., 204, 224

Participation, popular, 369–75
Patel, K. V., 187, 197, 203
Patel, S. M., 187, 197, 203
Patron–client relationships, 5, 234–43, 267, 417, 421
Peiris, J. W. C., 57, 65, 67, 70, 84
Perception (of cultivators), 121–2, 132–8, 148–9, 152–3, 160–1, 207, 209–10
Peries, O. S., 154
Pesticides, pests, 3, 4, 16, 58–9, 61–2, 70, 81, 87–90, 99–100, 104–5, 120–2, 128, 133, 160–1, 210, 218, 221, 234, 256–67, 382, 388, 391–2, 405
Phillipson, J., 400, 412
Plant-breeding, 404–8; see also Rice, breeding
Plantains, see Bananas
Pocock, D. F., 374, 376
Politics, political considerations, 234, 242, 246, 250–2, 365, 371, 403, 419
Popper, K., 394, 397
Population, population changes, 232–4, 246–7, 305–14, 321–2, 392–3, 417–18
Population pressure, 4, 12, 153–4, 302, 305–11, 323, 348, 361, 392–3, 415, 417, 420
Poromboke, xv, 125, 233
Potdar, M. W., 339
Poverty, 6, 393, 398, 405, 416–21; see also Incomes
Pulses, 15, 85, 123, 128–9
Pump-sets, 4, 9–10, 100–2, 112, 117–19, 122–3, 124, 130–1, 139–42, 161, 182–202, 212, 227, 232–3, 289, 303, 310–13, 321–2, 326–8, 349–50, 353, 361, 386–7, 393–6, 416–20
Punjab (India), 32, 136, 238

Radhakrishnan, K. C., 40, 53
Ragi, see Kurakkan
Rainfall, 7–13, 77, 87–8, 92–3, 99, 123, 129, 139, 327–8, 330–1, 335–8
Raj, K. N., 168, 181
Rajagopalan, V., 2, 389, 397, 412
Ramachandran, R., 10, 19
Ramana Murthy P. S. V., 402, 412
Ranatunga, S., 381, 383, 396
Randam village, xi, 3, 43, 124–42, 161, 165, 225–44, 266, 304–5, 308, 312–14, 316, 325, 350, 409
Ratnaweera, D. de S., 358, 362
Reed, G. W., 276, 287, 299
Reidinger, R. B., 364, 367, 376
Religion, 238–40

Research and development (R and D), 392, 398–411, 419–21; see also Rice, research
Research methods, xi–xiii, 2–4, 30–6, 37–53, 86, 122, 155–8, 170, 185–6, 205, 217–18, 302–3, 327–32, 399–411, 413
Rice
adoption of new technology, see Technology
breeding, 12–13, 32, 34, 98, 123, 135, 386–7, 398–400, 404–8, 419
competition of other crops, 4, 129, 133, 145
consumption and nutritional need, 22–8, 54–5, 71
cultivation, costs of, 104–5, 138, 149, 172–6, 198, 210–11, 317–18, 381–6
cultivation, relation with chena, 85–91, 128–9, 145, 153, 221–2
harvesting, 209–10, 212, 216, 218, 221–4, 228–9, 317–18
levy, 268–75
lodging of, 63–4
marketing, 21–4, 106–8, 139, 268–75
milling, 3, 20, 144–5, 274–5, 276–99, 420
pests, see Pesticides, pests
ploughing and land preparation, 169–76, 208, 212, 216, 218, 221–4, 228–9, 317–18
prices, 14, 16–18, 99–100, 106, 122, 124, 133, 138–42, 147, 160, 268–75, 415
production in India, 1–2, 13–17, 92
production in Sri Lanka, 2, 17–18, 20–9, 54–83
profitability, 104–6, 121–2
research, 2–3, 13, 30–6, 97–8, 135, 138, 392, 399
seasons, 12–13, 86–7, 95–100, 106, 117, 132–4, 212–13, 394, 407, 415
technology, see Technology
threshing, etc., 127, 173–4, 209–10, 212, 216, 219, 221, 224, 228–9
transplanting, 58–9, 62–4, 120–1, 127, 134, 137, 143–4, 149–50, 209, 216, 218–24, 227–9, 238, 310, 317–18, 385, 388
varieties, 1, 3, 13–14, 32–3, 56–9, 61–2, 70, 95–100, 104, 122, 128, 132–6, 139–41, 146–8, 150, 152, 160, 208–10, 269–71, 274, 286, 288, 298, 406–8, 415–16, 420
world production, 15–16
yields, 18, 20–1, 55–8, 66–9, 72, 73, 77–82, 92, 103–4, 122, 128, 149,

150, 153, 212, 296, 378, 385–8, 405, 406, 415
see also Fertilisers; Manure; Irrigation; Pesticides; Weedicides
Risk, 88–9, 104, 133, 143, 198, 415, 417
Roberts, M., 153, 154, 247, 254
Roy, P., 155, 157, 167
Roy, S. K., 402, 412
Rudra, Ashok, 30
Rural development, 398–411; theories of, 301, 303–4, 320–2, 399
Ryan, J. G., 24, 29, 387, 397, 406, 412

Sabherwal, R. K., 339
Sagar, Vidya, 21, 27, 29
Samarasinghe, S. W. R. de A., 362
Samuelson, P., 192, 203
Sanderatne, N., 18, 19, 251, 254, 374, 376
Scheduled castes, *see* Harijans
Schumacher, E. F., 420, 421
Scott, J. C., 236, 245, 248, 255
Seed, supply of, 3, 14, 72, 104–5, 147, 161, 247, 405, 415; *see also* Rice, varieties
S.E. Sri Lanka, *see* Hambantota and Moneragala Districts
Selvaratnam, S., 84
Sen, B., 2, 6
Sen, L. K., 155, 157, 167
Sen, S. R., 92, 123
Settlement types, 302; *see also* Inter-village variation
Sharma, S. D., 13, 16
Shastry, S. V. S., 13, 16
Shaw, R. D.'A., 217, 224
Sheldrake, R., 24, 29, 387, 397, 406, 412
Shifting cultivation, *see* Chena cultivation
Silva, W. P. T., 57, 84
Sinha, P. R. R., 155, 167
Slater, G., 40, 53
Snodgrass, D. H., 17, 19
Social and natural scientists, linkages between, 398–411, 421
Social consequences of technical change, 5, 34–5, 212, 225–44, 246–54, 416–17, 419–20; *see also* Caste; Class structure; External relations; Labourers; Land tenure; Patron–client relationships; Politics
Soils, soil conditions, 3, 12, 58, 78, 82, 98, 102, 121–2, 134–5, 138, 140, 147, 152–3, 168, 176, 305–8, 383, 394–5
Solar power, pumps, 286, 393–6, 403
Somasundaram, T., 286, 300
Sorghum (*Sorghum vulgare*), xiv, 406–7
Soya-beans, 85

Sri Lanka, 256, 323–4, 341, 403, 408–10, 418; rice milling, 277, 296–8; rice production, 2, 17–18, 54–83; University of, xii, 3; *see also* Hambantota and Moneragala Districts
Statistics, official, 5, 13, 20–9, 93–7, 328–30; unreliability of, 5, 20–9, 46–7, 93–7, 162, 291, 328, 414–15
Stokes, Eric, 34, 36
Study areas, choice of, 7–12, 30
Subarao, C., 327, 335, 339
Swaminathan, M. S., 70, 89

Tainsh, J. A. R., 299, 300
Tamil Nadu, 32–6, 256–60, 268–75, 277, 386–7, 389; rice production in, 13–17, 92–3, 97, 124–39, 418; *see also* North Arcot District
Tank irrigation, 9–10, 93, 100, 117, 124, 129, 143, 147, 161, 227, 246–7, 308–11, 323–5, 327–8, 338, 342–61, 364–76
Technology
  adoption of new, 3–5, 54–83, 92–123, 130–42, 146–54, 155–6, 159–66, 193–5, 198–9, 204, 206, 217, 289–91, 310–11, 313–14, 407–9, 414–16
  alternative (for future), 380–1, 386–96, 403–4, 414–16, 419–21
  choice of, 276–99, 386–96, 419–21
  intermediate, 298–9, 380, 392
  over-adoption, 72–3, 153, 201
  package of practices, 3–4, 58, 63, 66, 72, 92, 119, 139
  selective adoption, case for, 79–83
  see also Diffusion of innovations; Pumpsets; Research and development; Rice; Milling; Tractors
Tenants, 35, 88, 115–16, 123, 130–2, 145–6, 150–4, 176, 205, 246–54, 381, 418
Thanjavur (Tanjore) District, Tamil Nadu, 33, 35, 217, 239, 242, 263, 277, 286, 288–9, 297, 413
Thomas, P. J., 40, 53
Thompson, E. P., 236, 240, 245
Thornton, D. S., 344, 363
Timmer, C. P., 299, 300
Tractors, 4, 88, 119, 121, 122, 127, 141, 144, 145, 150, 152, 153, 168–80, 217, 227, 238, 247, 381–3, 387, 388, 406, 416, 419, 420; profitability, 170–6, 227–32, 233
Trade, traders, 14–16, 25–8, 47–50, 139,

178, 185–93, 205, 223, 232–4, 247, 260–6, 268–75, 279, 304–5, 417, 420

Untouchables, see Harijans
Ur Panchayat, xvi, 235

Vander Velde, E. J., 348, 349, 355, 359, 363
Vel Vidanes, xvi, 350, 366–67, 369–72
Villages, typology of, 303–4, 308–13; see also External relations; Inter-village variation; Settlement types
VLW (village-level worker), see Gram(a) Sevak

Warrier, R. C., 339
Water, control of, supply of, 4, 51, 52, 58, 81, 99, 102, 103, 106, 117, 118, 121–3, 130–4, 138, 143–5, 147, 148, 149, 152, 161, 233, 323–7, 350, 351, 360–1, 364–76, 393–6; waste of, 169, 350, 355, 357, 368, 369, 373, 385, 386, 393, 402, 408–10, 415, 416; see also Irrigation
Water-table, 4, 7–12, 81, 82, 123, 125, 138–40, 143, 199, 241, 323–37, 364, 393–6, 409, 416, 419; lowering of, 199, 308, 321, 322, 326–37, 342, 416, 418–20
Weedicides, weeding, 3, 58–9, 62, 70, 81, 87, 90, 120, 128, 143–4, 149, 208–9, 216, 218, 221, 228–9, 238, 256–67,

317–18, 382, 385, 388, 391–2
Weerakoon, B., 352, 363
Weeraratne, H., 58, 64, 70, 84, 407
Weerawardena, I. K., 71, 84
Weerawickrema, S. K. A., 388, 397
Wells, well irrigation, 4, 9–10, 16, 93, 100, 112, 117–18, 122–3, 124–5, 130–1, 139–42, 161, 182–202, 212, 227, 232, 234, 289, 303, 308–13, 321–39, 342, 346–7, 349–50, 353, 361, 386–7, 393–6, 415–20
West, C., 394, 397
Wet land (as a class of land), xvi, 117, 124–5, 127, 129, 227, 308, 326, 348–9, 352–3, 394
Wharton, C. R., Jr., 35, 36
Wheat, 1, 14–16, 25, 27–8
Wickremanayake, B. W. E., 46, 53, 75, 84, 174, 180
Williams, L. B., 388, 397
Wind power, 386
Wittfogel, K. A., 363, 365
Wolf, E., 234, 245
Wood, G., 240, 241, 245

Yadav, S. P., 24, 29, 387, 397
Yalman, N., 248, 249, 255, 374, 376
Yields, to land, see Rice, yields; to water, 402, 410